W9-BMN-463

EDITION 6

Self-Directed Behavior

Self-Modification for Personal Adjustment

David L. Watson

University of Hawaii

Roland G. Tharp

University of Hawaii

Brooks/Cole Publishing Company
Pacific Grove, California

For our parents,
Faye and Manly Watson
Berma and Oswald Tharp

Brooks/Cole Publishing Company
A Division of Wadsworth, Inc.

Printed in the United States of America
10 9 8 7 6 5 4 3 2 1

Library of Congress Cataloging in Publication Data
Watson, David L., [date]
Self-directed behavior : self-modification for personal adjustment
David L. Watson, Roland G. Tharp. — 6th ed.
p. cm.
Includes bibliographical references and index.
ISBN 0-534-18978-4
1. Behavior modification. 2. Self-management (Psychology)
3. Adjustment (Psychology) 4. Success—Psychological aspects.
I. Tharp, Roland G., [date] II. Title.
BF637.B4W38 1992
158′.1—dc20 92-27472
CIP

Sponsoring Editor: *Claire Verduin*
Editorial Associate: *Gay C. Bond*
Production Editor: *Marjorie Z. Sanders*
Manuscript Editor: *Laurie Vaughn*
Permissions Editor: *Marie DuBois*
Interior and Cover Design: *Katherine Minerva*
Art Coordinator: *Susan Haberkorn*
Interior Illustration: *Andrew Myer*
Photo Editor: *Larry Molmud*
Typesetting: *Weimer Incorporated*
Printing and Binding: *R. R. Donnelley & Sons Company/Crawfordsville*

Preface

This book is designed to acquaint you with a general theory of behavior, to guide you through exercises for developing skills in self-analysis, and to provide you with concrete information on how to achieve the goals you hold for yourself. The most important purpose of this volume is to help you, the reader, achieve more self-determination, more "willpower," more control over your own life.

The book can serve as a textbook in psychology courses but does not depend on a formal course structure. Any reader can use it for self-instruction; no "prerequisites" are necessary. Clients of therapists or counselors can use it as an adjunct in planning their own self-change.

You should be warned about one possible side effect: you may become interested in the science of behavior. A number of people delve deeper into the subject as a result of studying this material and in response to the experiential learning that can result from the self-change process.

The vehicle for learning will be your own self-analysis, your own program for implementing your values. Throughout, you are urged to accompany your reading with your own self-improvement project. In a sense, your daily life will become the laboratory in which you will study and develop your own behavior.

Foreword to the Professional

This book's sixth edition maintains the authors' original intentions: to provide scientifically based instruction in the principles and practices of self-applied psychology. In the proliferation of self-help manuals, we have defined our niche as the one that offers an opportunity for students to learn principles of scientific psychology in the laboratory that is most important to them—the laboratory of their own life problems. Simultaneously, they will learn verified coping skills for personal problem solving.

To achieve these goals, we have set certain standards: to maintain an up-to-date review of all important literature, including both empirical and theoretical publications relevant to self-managed behavior; to maintain accuracy of summary and interpretation so that instructors can be confident in assigning this text; to be conservative in making recommendations that arise only from a secure data base; and, finally, to advance integrative interpretations that offer some coherence to a vigorous and expanding field. We have also striven to maintain the readability that has characterized our previous editions.

The field of self-directed behavior began as self-behavior modification, but it has expanded in a vortex that has swept in vicarious and observational learning, cognitive behaviorism and verbal self-control, imagery, and information science. It now includes theoretical and empirical concepts of skills analysis, delay of gratification, learned resourcefulness, control theory, relapse prevention, neo-Vygotskian developmental theory, self-efficacy, commitment theory, decision making, attribution theory, and rule-governed behavior. This enrichment has provided key conceptual links that have made self-direction more coherent, more understandable, and more integrated.

Since the fifth edition, new developments in the field of self-directed behavior have taken place mainly in the intense study of self-regulation as applied to specific difficulties: depression; anxiety; the management of general stress and the hassles of daily life; lifestyle issues of better diet, exercise, balanced interests, relaxation, and the like; and especially the behavioral problems associated with maintaining good health and wellness—exercise, diet, and stress reduction. While maintaining our conservative stance toward recommending procedures, we have incorporated most of these new developments through a considerably expanded series of "Tips for Typical Topics."

Empirical field testing of this book has been uniformly positive: students using this text in courses have achieved their goals for self-change in percentages varying from 66% to 84% (Brigham, Moseley, Speed, & Fisher, in press; Clements & Beidleman, 1981; deBortali-Tregerthan, 1984; Deffenbacher & Shepard, 1989; Dodd, 1986; Hamilton, 1980; Rakos & Grodek, 1984) and have reported a general improvement in lifestyle (Castro, 1987).

The organization of the book is designed to make it as useful as possible for students. Reading can be guided by the learning objectives at the beginning of each chapter. Key terms are highlighted in boldface, and a special rule identifies the successive steps of the self-direction project throughout the book. The "Tips for Typical Topics," included in most chapters, facilitate rapid formulation of self-modification plans, and a topic index allows the student to retrieve all information relevant to a particular behavior.

Acknowledgments

For this edition, we are particularly indebted for the excellent critical analyses provided by William Coe, California State University–Fresno; Richard A. Coleman, Oakland City College; Douglas P. Jowdy, Virginia Commonwealth University; Richard Rakos, Cleveland State University; and Edward P. Sarafino, Trenton State University. Special thanks go to Richard Suinn, Jerry Deffenbacher, Jack Kirschenbaum, Richard Rakos, Owen Aldis, and Freida Deresh for their useful advice and correspondence.

Our greatest debt of gratitude is to all our students at the University of Hawaii at Manoa. Their self-change projects have taught us much and have made this edition, like the previous ones, possible. The list of all these student names has grown too long to cite. We have always disguised their identities in the case reports that illustrate the book; we hope that in this anonymity each of them will accept a tribute to the Unknown Student.

David L. Watson
Roland G. Tharp

Contents

1 *Adjustment and the Skills of Self-Direction* 1

Outline 2
Learning Objectives 2
Adjustment and Self-Direction 3
Alternative Ways of Thinking about Self-Direction 5
The Skills of Adjustment and the Purpose of This Book 9
Behavior and the Environment 11
The Process of Self-Modification 14
Does Self-Modification Really Work? 19
Chapter Summary 25
Your Own Self-Direction Project: Step One 26

2 ***Specifying the Goal, Overcoming Obstacles, and Building Commitment*** **29**

Outline 30
Learning Objectives 30
Specifying the Targets for Change 30
Overcoming Obstacles: Why You Might Self-Sabotage 40
Building Commitment 51
Tips for Typical Topics 59
Chapter Summary 59
Your Own Self-Direction Project: Step Two 61

3 *Self-Knowledge: Observation and Recording* 63

Outline 64
Learning Objectives 64
Structured Diaries 65
Recording Frequency and Duration 72
Recording the Intensity of Emotions 78
Practicalities of Record Keeping 81
Planning for Change 92
Tips for Typical Topics 96
Chapter Summary 100
Your Own Self-Direction Project: Step Three 102

4 *The Principles of Self-Regulation* 103

Outline 104
Learning Objectives 104
Regulation Theory 105
Regulation by Others and Regulation by Self 107
Language Regulation 108
Consequences 110
Antecedents 116
Respondent Behavior and Conditioning 119
Modeling 122
Chapter Summary 125
Your Own Self-Direction Project: Step Four 128

5 *Antecedents* 131

Outline 132
Learning Objectives 132
Identifying Antecedents 133
Modifying Old Antecedents 137
Arranging New Antecedents 145
Tips for Typical Topics 154

Chapter Summary 160
Your Own Self-Direction Project: Step Five 161

6 *Behaviors: Actions, Thoughts, and Feelings* 163

Outline 164
Learning Objectives 164
Substituting New Thoughts and Behaviors 165
Substitutions for Anxiety and Stress Reactions 169
Relaxation 174
Developing New Behaviors 183
Shaping: The Method of Successive Approximations 190
Tips for Typical Topics 197
Chapter Summary 204
Your Own Self-Direction Project: Step Six 206

7 *Consequences* 207

Outline 208
Learning Objectives 208
Discovering and Selecting Reinforcers 209
Using Others to Dispense Reinforcers 214
Self-Administered Consequences 220
Techniques of Self-Reinforcement 222
Self-Punishment and Extinction 234
Reinforcement in Plans for Self-Modification 238
Tips for Typical Topics 242
Chapter Summary 248
Your Own Self-Direction Project: Step Seven 250

8 *Putting It All Together* 251

Outline 252
Learning Objectives 252

Combining A, B, and C Elements 253
The Features of a Good Plan 258
Is It Working? Evaluating Your Plan for Change 266
Changing Targets 272
Tips for Typical Topics 274
Chapter Summary 274
Your Own Self-Direction Project: Step Eight 275

9 *Problem Solving and Relapse Prevention* 277

Outline 278
Learning Objectives 278
Problem Solving 279
Relapse Prevention 291
Chapter Summary 301
Your Own Self-Direction Project: Step Nine 302

10 *Termination and Beyond* 305

Outline 306
Learning Objectives 306
Formal Termination: Planning to Maintain Gains 307
Beyond the Ending 314
Chapter Summary 317
Your Own Self-Direction Project: Step Ten 318

Bibliography 319
Name Index 343
Subject Index 350
Topic Index 355

1

Adjustment and the Skills of Self-Direction

Outline

- Adjustment and Self-Direction
- Alternative Ways of Thinking about Problems in Adjustment
- The Skills of Adjustment and the Purpose of This Book
- Behavior and the Environment
- The Process of Self-Modification
- Does Self-Modification Really Work?
- *Chapter Summary*
- *Your Own Self-Direction Project: Step One*

Learning Objectives

Each chapter contains a set of learning objectives, phrased as questions, in which all the major points in the chapter are listed. When you can answer all the questions, you will have mastered the material in the chapter. The learning objectives are divided into sections that correspond to the sections in the chapter. Just before you read each section, read the learning objectives for that section.

Adjustment and Self-Direction

1. How is adjustment defined?
2. What is the best way to study this book?

The Skills of Self-Direction

3. What are the implications of thinking of self-direction as a skill?

Alternative Ways of Thinking about Self-Direction

4. What are the various approaches one can take to adjustment, and what are their implications for self-direction?

Willpower

5. What are the problems with the idea of willpower?

Inner Problems and Outer Symptoms

6. What is the medical model? What are its advantages and disadvantages?

The Skills of Adjustment and the Purpose of This Book

7. What are the two elements of skill? What are the stages in the development of a skill?
8. Explain the purpose of this book.

Behavior and the Environment

9. What are antecedents, behaviors, and consequences? How does learning affect them and their relationships to one another?

The Process of Self-Modification

10. What are the steps in most self-change programs?

Does Self-Modification Really Work?

11. Are people able to change themselves when they have a relatively serious problem with their behavior?
12. What does the research show about the success of students who use this book?
13. When a self-modification plan doesn't work, what are the likely causes?

Adjustment and Self-Direction

To arrange, to harmonize, to come to terms; to arrange the parts suitably among themselves and in relationship to something else—that is the definition of *adjustment.* Adjustment can mean harmony among parts of the self—harmony of thoughts, actions, and feelings. The person who is torn by internal contradictions, the person who wants love but hates people, is not balanced or happy. We might say that such a person is badly adjusted, or disturbed. Significantly, we say that a person who is mentally ill is "unbalanced."

Adjustment can also mean harmony between the self and the environment. When people are out of phase with the world around them, we say they are "out of touch," "gone," "way out"—words implying that these people are not in harmony with the environment. We are more likely to be well adjusted if there is a good fit between ourselves—or our abilities—and our environment (Lerner, Baker, & Lerner, 1985).

When we say someone is "badly adjusted," we are making a value judgment. To the total conformist, any individualist seems badly adjusted, out of line with the group. To the individualist, total conformity seems bad adjustment, lack of harmony with oneself. It is sometimes difficult to know whether one should conform or rebel.

We make value judgments about our own behavior, too. You may feel that you eat too much and weigh too much, and you'd like to be slimmer. You believe your life would improve if you weighed less. You'd be more attractive, feel more energetic. You might make new friends or be more captivating to old ones. If that is your own value judgment about your weight, you would probably like to change your eating habits.

But can you? Do you have the skills to change? If you don't, people who can make a decision to change themselves and then do so probably seem a marvel to you. A slim friend says, "I decided I was about five pounds overweight, so I just took it off." You listen with mouth agape—you have been trying unsuccessfully for years to do the same thing.

All of us have certain goals we cannot reach "just like that." Most of us have skills for some situations, but not for others. For example, you might easily increase your studying, whereas your slim friend needs to do the same thing but lacks the skill. When we have the ability to change ourselves, we have the skills that make up good adjustment. Box 1-1, "How to Study This Book," will assist in learning those skills.

BOX 1-1
How to Study This Book

At the beginning of each chapter is a set of learning objectives that are phrased as questions. The learning objectives cover all the major points in the chapter. If you can answer them, you have mastered the text material. Your task while studying is to find the answers to those questions and then learn them well.

Here are the steps we suggest you follow in learning the material in each chapter. These are not just based on our opinion, incidentally. Research shows that students who follow a procedure something like this get better grades (Kirschenbaum & Perri, 1982; Mayer, 1988; Robinson, 1970).

1. You will find a chapter outline at the beginning of each chapter. Break up your reading so that you do just one or two sections of the chapter at a time. The learning objectives and chapter summary are divided into sections that correspond to the sections of the chapter.
2. Read the outline for the whole chapter. Then read the learning objectives and the part of the chapter summary that correspond to the section you are working on.
3. Read the section itself.
4. Reread the summary material.
5. Close the book and try to answer the learning objective questions for that section.
6. Repeat this process for each section.

When you are studying for a course exam, give yourself a pretest by answering the learning objectives. Check your answers against the text. Reread the chapter summary and those parts of the chapter you need to review to answer the learning objective questions. This method may sound cumbersome compared with your present way of studying, but research has shown that it is the best way to learn the material in a textbook (Kirschenbaum & Perri, 1982; McKeachie, 1978; Robinson, 1970). As you practice the method, it will become increasingly easy for you. Our advice is this: *Try it, then evaluate it.* You can always go back to your old way of studying if this doesn't work better for you.

Adjustment is better understood as a skill than as a condition. Self-direction means that your behavior is under your control—that when it is necessary to change, you can. Our environments change, and as we devise new goals, we need to change our responses. We want to be able to control our behavior so that we change in the desired way—to increase study time, to develop better social skills, to stop overindulging in food or television.

Self-direction means recognizing the changes you want and being able to actualize your own values. The skills of self-direction include choosing goals and designing strategies to meet them, evaluating outcomes, changing tactics when needed, and solidifying new gains. Self-direction is the combination of skills by which goals are achieved.

The Skills of Self-Direction

What is a skill? A skill is the ability to do something well. It is developed through knowledge and practice. If one person practices certain behaviors while another does not, we expect that the person who practices will become more skilled at those behaviors. (We may have an aptitude for certain skills—that is, we may be able to learn them easily—but in all cases we acknowledge that skills have to be learned.) It does not surprise us to learn that our friend who has been practicing the piano six hours a day has become a skilled musician. Nor are we surprised to learn that many great musicians come from families in which music is an important part of daily life. The example set in the family and the opportunity to develop skill are important precursors of the development of musical skill.

The idea of skill implies behavior that is adapted to a particular situation. We do not necessarily expect a skilled pianist to be skilled at languages. The idea of skill, then, implies *specific* skills. We do not learn general skills that apply across a wide range of situations, but rather specific ones that apply to specific tasks. The same thing is true of the skills of adjustment: You might be skilled at controlling your weight but not at avoiding procrastination.

Skill implies the ability to deal with variations in the task. Being skilled at something means that action is adapted to the event (Fischer, 1980). Every time an action is carried out, it is done a little differently. Exactly how the pianist plays G-sharp depends on just where her hands were on the previous chord, how rapidly she is playing, the condition of the piano, any distractions from her surroundings, and so on. Being skilled implies that one can perform a specific action despite variations in the task. A soccer player who could kick a goal only from one precise spot on the field would not be considered skilled. It is the ability to kick from any position, through opposing players, having received the ball from various other positions on the field and at different speeds, that makes a player skilled.

If self-direction is a skill, we must think about both the behavior we need to perform and the situations in which we will perform it. Our goals for self-direction are defined in terms of particular behaviors in particular situations. For example, if you can only kick a goal from one spot on the field but your position on the field keeps changing, then you need to practice kicking from a variety of spots.

Alternative Ways of Thinking about Self-Direction

What should you do to change yourself when you want to, to direct yourself toward your goals? The answer depends upon your view of what has been keeping you from reaching those goals.

How should we think about problems in adjustment, that is, self-direction? Consider our student, Calvin, who can't hold a job for more than a few weeks, even though he is 21 and needs the money. Calvin feels something is wrong.

But what? How Calvin thinks about the problem has a strong impact on what he thinks should be done about it. There are different ways to think about a problem in self-direction, and each has a different implication for

Calvin's response. It will improve your **critical thinking** skills (Zechmeister & Johnson, 1992) to examine various ways of thinking about problems in self-direction.

We could say that Calvin has a bad astrological sign, is unlucky in his stars. This explanation has certain implications: There is nothing to be done but wait to see what happens. Fate will unfold, and the stars will determine if Calvin is to be a perpetual failure or not. Some people like to talk about astrology, crystals, or pyramids as party chatter, but should we take these ideas seriously when faced with important life problems? Not if we really want to do something about our lives. As Shakespeare says in *Julius Caesar,* "The fault . . . is not in our stars, but in ourselves. . . . "

Willpower

People often speak of problems of adjustment such as Calvin's in terms of willpower. Calvin can't make himself get up to go to work in the morning. He can't resist taking too long for lunch. This is a common way of thinking about our problems in self-direction. "I want to quit smoking, but I don't seem to have any willpower."

What do we gain by thinking about problems of self-direction in terms of willpower? The word *willpower* implies some entity, something in your psychological makeup, something that allows you to do hard jobs, overcome temptations, stick to your goals. But what is it—an electric current, some form of energy? It's just a word, a label we use when we want to describe how people deal with problems in self-direction. "She could do it because she has lots of willpower. He couldn't do it because he doesn't have much willpower." As a label, the word has certain problems.

It overlooks the fact that you may be able to stick to your goals in some situations, but not in others. Calvin, for example, is able to get along with his girlfriend, and they've been together for nearly a year. Also, he quit drinking a few years ago. Most of us find that in certain situations we have plenty of "willpower," but in others, not enough. If you observe yourself, you may find there are certain things you can do—for example, resist smoking although you used to smoke, or get your assignments done on time—and certain things you can't do—for example, relax on a date or quit biting your fingernails. You might say, "Well, I have *some* willpower, but I could use *more.*"

A better way of thinking about these strengths and weaknesses is to realize that they are tied to certain *situations.* When faced with the situation I-have-to-do-my-assignment, you are able to do what has to be done, but when in the situation I-should-relax-on-this-date, you don't do what has to be done. In the situation With-girlfriend, Calvin does OK, but not so well in the situation Need-to-go-to-work. The simple concept of willpower overlooks important variations in our behavior from one situation to another.

A second problem with the idea of willpower is that it is not clear what you can do to get more of it. What do people do who seem to have lots of willpower? How can we be more like them? If Calvin decides that he lacks willpower, what does he do next?

Some people say, "I can't give up my old habits. I have no willpower." They speak as though willpower involved standing in the face of temptation, fists clenched, jaws tight, refusing to do what one shouldn't do even though one wants to do it. After several decades of practicing chastity, for example, Mahatma Gandhi sometimes slept beside attractive young followers to demonstrate his ability to abstain from sex. Most people with effective willpower avoid that kind of situation in the first place. It is far easier to remain chaste while sleeping alone. People use foresight, self-analysis, and planning to avoid temptation. This point can be found in many ethical and religious systems. St. Paul, St. Augustine, and St. Thomas Aquinas, for example, taught that to avoid sin one should avoid the occasion for sin.

For each of us there are powerful temptations. That is, there are situations in which we make the choice for immediate pleasure even though it goes against our long-range goals. If you, like Gandhi, can resist temptation, then you don't need the techniques in this book. But for most of us there are situations in which we choose for the short run over the long run, even though we regret it later.

How can we make ourselves do things we find so difficult? This has been a topic of concern from time immemorial. Western mythology shows, for example, how one wily man scored a victory over temptation. In Homer's *Odyssey,* written about 800 B.C., Odysseus and his crew sailed through straits where the Sirens sang a song so alluring that it drew sailors to their death on the rocks. Odysseus wanted to hear the Sirens' wonderful music, but he wanted to avoid sailing too close to the rocks. He used a clever strategy to achieve both goals. He ordered his men to lash him to the mast and—no matter how much he begged to be set free—to keep him there until they had passed through the straits. Then he plugged their ears with wax so they could carry out his orders and row safely through without hearing the music (Ainslee, 1975).

The same strategy—acting in advance to prevent a behavior we do not want—is used by many of us every night when we set an alarm clock. The crucial element is to make the desired choice when we are most likely to choose correctly. We choose to set the alarm before we are sleepy, not in the drowsy morning hours (Rachlin, 1974). We might even place the clock across the room, to make sure we get up. Self-direction is not just lots of willpower. It is "a skill involving anticipation and cleverness, so that immediate and tempting rewards do not impede progress toward a long-range goal" (Fisher, Levenkron, Lowe, Loro, & Green, 1982, p. 174). Odysseus made sure that the temptations of the Sirens did not lead him away from his long-range goal.

Inner Problems and Outer Symptoms

What about Calvin? He has a long-range goal of developing some sort of career, but currently he cannot keep a job. How does Calvin differ from people who are able to keep their job? Is Calvin psychologically "sick"?

Sigmund Freud, the father of psychoanalysis, viewed behavior problems as symptoms of inner sexual or hostile conflicts and frustrations. Later theorists agreed with Freud that the inner problem was conflict, but they denied that it was necessarily sexual; it might be low self-esteem or an unresolved conflict about power. These theorists argued that any unresolved inner problem can lead to outer problems in behavior. Perhaps Calvin self-destructs on the job as the result of some unknown inner conflict.

This point of view is called the **medical model** of adjustment. The basic idea is that outer behaviors are caused by inner conditions. If there is something wrong with your outer behavior—you can't keep a job, you can't speak up for your rights—it is a sign that something is wrong with your inner psychological condition. The basic characteristics of the medical model are the ideas of inner cause and outer symptom. Inner problems cause outer symptoms, and the proper course of treatment is to eliminate the inner problems.

Suppose you have a fever of 102 degrees. The doctor sees that fever as a symptom, or signal, that something is wrong inside you. Eliminating the fever would only take care of the symptom, leaving the inner illness untreated. Therefore, the doctor tries to discover and eliminate the inner problem. If the inner problem can be eliminated, the outer symptom—the fever—will disappear. (Of course, doctors also give treatment that provides symptomatic relief, but whenever possible they seek to eliminate the basic problem.)

What are the implications of this model for Calvin? He is unable to keep a job for more than a few weeks. From the viewpoint of the medical model, Calvin's inability to hold jobs is a symptom of some inner tension or conflict. The implication is that he must discover and cure that inner problem.

There are advantages to adopting this point of view. Human beings are both biological and psychological, and we err if we focus on only one aspect (Temoshok, 1990). Physicians have in fact discovered medical reasons for certain psychological problems—for example, some forms of mental retardation and diseases of the nervous system. Further, physicians have discovered symptomatic treatments, such as drugs to reduce hallucinations, that are effective in alleviating the suffering that so often accompanies major psychological disturbance.

But the approach has not borne fruit for less serious problems, problems in adjustment or in self-direction. No one has found a drug that would help Calvin keep a job. The medical model has its limitations. The approach doesn't help you understand your own striving toward goals. For example, if you are making no progress in selecting a career, does that mean that you have some psychological disease? No, probably not. Is Calvin sick, or does he lack crucial skills? Is Calvin a passive victim of his illness, or can he actively learn new and effective ways of coping?

If he is sick, then he should seek expert treatment. But if he needs to learn new skills, he can acquire them by knowledge and practice. That, of course, is what we offer here.

The Skills of Adjustment and the Purpose of This Book

We are back to the idea of skill. Skill differs from ability in that skills are learned and are improved with practice. Mental skills, such as knowing how to change yourself, function the same way as other kinds of skills, such as knowing how to serve in tennis. What are the characteristics of skills (Adams, 1987)?

Skills are based in *knowledge*—someone has to teach you what to do—and developed through *practice*—you then have to rehearse doing it. For example, if you want to be a good tennis player, a coach shows you how to do things such as serve or hit a backhand, and then you practice over and over, trying to get them right. Sometimes the coach shows you again what to do and points out what you are doing wrong. That is exactly what we offer in this book: knowledge and practice in self-direction.

Purpose of This Book

The purpose of our book is to present self-direction skills for personal adjustment. The same principles can be employed whether you want to become less shy, to give up smoking, to lose weight, or to increase your studying. The same principles are involved in improving your tennis game, taking examinations, or reducing anxiety. We will deal with specific topics, but our goal is to teach you the basic skills for maintaining good adjustment.

Why teach basic skills instead of simply telling you specific things to do for specific problems? "If you want to lose weight, cut down your calories to 1200 per day," or "To increase your studying, gradually work up to eight hours per week." First, you may not be aware of some elements of your current problem. Also, as you change yourself, new problems will appear. You need general skills to deal with these unanticipated problems. If you learn only very specific tactics for specific problems, you will have learned nothing to help you deal with different issues in the future. The age-old axiom has it right: *Give a hungry man a fish, and you have fed him for one day. Teach him to fish, and you have fed him for life.*

As you progress though life you can develop control over more and more of the situations with which you have to cope (Rodin, Schooler, & Schaie, 1990). Our goal is to teach you general skills for coping with problems of self-direction, so here you will learn more than specific recipes: You'll learn coping skills that you can use in a variety of situations (Goldfried, 1986).

As in all teaching, our success depends on you, the learner. Understanding requires effort and study; perfection requires practice. In fact, we typically go through stages when developing a skill, and this is true whether it's a coping skill for life or a skill at some sport like tennis (Adams, 1987). At first, you have to acquire knowledge—what is a good backhand? What is a good way to relax? Second, you must practice the skill over and over. Finally, the skill becomes so well practiced that it becomes automatic.

Specific exercises are suggested at the end of each chapter. It is important that you carry out these practice assignments. Like someone learning to ride a bicycle, you must actually ride, be willing to wobble a bit, even take a fall. The only way you can learn to ride "just like that" is through practice.

In specific situations, some people are more skilled at self-regulation than others. For example, when a person is in a stressful situation, it is not simply how much stress the person experiences but how the person copes with stress that makes the difference (Schafer, 1992). Learning an active skill to use when faced with anxiety-provoking tasks actually prevents the anxiety (Barrios & Shigetomi, 1980). Students may begin to feel nervous while taking a test, realize that the anxiety will make their performance worse, and deliberately take a couple of minutes out to calm down. They can tell themselves to be calm, think calming thoughts, avoid thoughts that lead to the anxiety, and consciously relax. The person who does not do this lacks the skill that calmer students have (Rosenbaum, 1983).

Walter Mischel (1981) has shown how children learn self-control by increasing the skill with which they deal with tempting situations. Very young children have greater difficulty in coping with temptations than do older children. What do older children do that younger ones don't do? Children who successfully resist temptation tend to think about the tempting object—for example, a marshmallow—using "cool" thoughts. "The marshmallows are puffy like clouds." Children who are less successful tend to think about the tempting object with "hot" thoughts. "The marshmallows taste yummy and chewy." *"Hot" thoughts make it harder to resist temptation.* Children who successfully resist temptation also distract themselves from "hot" thoughts. They avoid thinking about the tempting object altogether, and think about other, irrelevant objects not currently present.

Thus, the ability to resist temptation appears to be a learned skill. Indeed, research has shown that self-control can be learned (Eisenberger & Adornetto, 1986) and that it is tied to specific situations (Barrios, 1985). Many people learn these skills without being aware of it. This suggests that we can study what skills are necessary to resist certain temptations—for example, what should the chronic overeater learn to do and think?—and then set out to learn these skills.

Task/Skill Mismatches

There are times when one's skills at self-direction are not up to the task at hand (McFall & Dodge, 1982). Whatever skills one has, there are always tasks that call for more than one can muster, whether it be the fairly good tennis player matched against the state champion or the person unskilled in resisting good food faced with a table full of tempting morsels. If self-control and self-direction are skills, then one would expect that some tasks would call for more skill than a person possesses. Since people differ in their level of skill, what is easy for one person may be impossible for another. Our slim friend takes off five pounds "just like that," while we cannot. Some tasks call for skills we have not yet learned.

There are times for all of us when our usual self-control skills fail us. Our usual behavior won't let us reach our goals. In this situation, we begin to self-regulate more self-consciously (Kirschenbaum & Flanery, 1984; Rosenbaum, 1988). A planned, continuing effort to change behavior to cope with a task we cannot presently master is called **self-modification.**

Our goal in this book is to teach ways to improve your skills in situations where the task has been difficult for you. This requires a planned effort at self-modification. We will do this by teaching new actions, coping skills, problem-solving skills, and knowledge to use in generating adequate matches between your skills and the tasks you face. Box 1-2 shows how one of our students learned new coping skills using the ideas in this book.

Is it really possible to learn self-direction? The answer is *yes.* You can increase the control you exercise over your own behavior and your own life. Obviously, you can't control all the events in your life. We are all limited by lack of talent, energy, or plain bad luck. But within these broad limits, you can direct yourself toward your chosen goals and can change when you want to.

To start, you need knowledge, just as the tennis player needs to be shown how to serve. The first piece of knowledge you need is a point of view, a way of understanding your own behavior. Here's the start.

Behavior and the Environment

If you are shy, just seeing a roomful of strangers at a party is enough to make you feel uncomfortable. Nothing bad has actually happened, but you feel nervous. You think, "I don't know anybody here!" Feelings and thoughts of discomfort have been triggered by the sight of a roomful of strangers. This party isn't for you, you think. Suppose you flee. Immediately your nervousness begins to fade. You feel relaxed, and your thoughts turn to where you will go next. Fleeing has consequences: you feel better. Having learned the benefits of flight, you are more likely to do something similar the next time you are in that situation.

You have begun to learn a way of dealing with that kind of situation—fleeing—but you can see that in the long run this will create other problems. Often we learn things that work in the present but create other problems later. For example, A. S., whose narrative appears in Box 1-2, learned to fear being in enclosed, dark places and learned that he could avoid the fear by avoiding such places. But later this created other problems for him.

Your behavior, thoughts, and feelings are always embedded in a context—the situation. Situations can be divided arbitrarily into two elements: the events that come before a behavior and those that follow it. In psychology

BOX 1-2

Freeing the Captured Mind: Overcoming a Fear of Elevators

A. S. was a small, but athletic, middle-aged man who took our course in self-change in night school. Here is a summary of his report at the end of the term.

When I was seven my Dad, the wild pig man, used to scare us to death at bedtime. Snorting loudly, he'd come grunting down the hall to eat us. I used to run into the closet to hide, but once a stick fell onto the tracks of the sliding door and I couldn't get out. The wild pig man kept coming and coming, and I was trapped in the dark with no place to run. The louder I screamed in fright, the closer he came.

My brothers learned that I was afraid of the dark and of being in an enclosed place. Once to tease me they locked me in a dark storage room. I felt I was about to die. The more I begged to be let out, the more they laughed. It was like being trapped in a dark coffin in the center of the earth. I began to kick and punch the door, and after a few minutes it began to break. With a burst the door flew open and I fell on the driveway. From then on I had a strong fear of being in a closed, dark place. By the time I was grown I would never enter an elevator, fearing the closing doors and the chance that the lights would go out. I quit a good job as a telephone repairman when they asked me to work on the phones in elevators.

Flying in an enclosed plane also became a problem. Once on a trip to Disneyland I had to take four sleeping pills and drink a pint of vodka just to get the nerve to get on the 747. I woke up three days later at Knott's Berry Farm, with my family very angry at me. They had to wait ten minutes each time we went up to our room on the 16th floor, so I could walk up. My kids thought I was crazy.

So I set out to get over this fear of being in elevators. First, I started keeping records of how often I had bad thoughts about elevators and how often I climbed steps to avoid them. I began working on getting rid of bad elevator thoughts and practiced this every night. I also practiced being relaxed while thinking about elevators.

Second, I began gradually approaching elevators. I worked out a detailed schedule to gradually deal with real-life elevators. In step one I would walk into an elevator, keep one hand on the door, press a button, and then walk out. In step two I would put one hand on the "Door Open" button, let the doors close, then push the button and exit. I made sure to practice being relaxed while doing these steps. In step three I rode up one floor while practicing relaxing and doing the multiplication tables in my head to distract myself from fearful thoughts.

I also carried out each practice step in my imagination at least three times each day. I went through 24 steps and rewarded myself each day if I had done the step for that day.

At the end of my project I was riding all the elevators I came into contact with. I'm still not totally comfortable being in one, but I'm not avoiding them, either, and I'm no longer embarrassing my family.

these are called **antecedents** and **consequences.** Antecedents are the setting events for your behavior. They cue you or stimulate you to act in certain ways. They can be physical events, thoughts, emotions, or inner speech. Consequences affect whether you repeat certain acts or not. They reinforce behavior or fail to do so. And they affect how you feel. Like antecedents, consequences can be physical events, thoughts, emotions, or inner speech.

The antecedent for the behavior of the shy person is seeing the roomful of strangers and thinking "Get out of here!" The behavior is turning around and walking out of the room. The consequence of fleeing is feeling better, and that is reinforcing. A simple way to remember this idea is to remember A-B-C: Antecedents-Behavior-Consequences.

The effects of situation—antecedents, behavior, consequences—are influenced by the learning experiences a person has had in similar situations. Entering a roomful of strangers, one person, who has learned to be nervous in this situation, flees. Another, who has no experience of fear in a roomful of strangers, thinks, "Terrific! A party!"

Different learning experiences produce different behaviors even when we are dealing with the same antecedent or consequence. When you enter an elevator, you just think about what floor you want to go to, but A. S., in Box 1-2, used to think, "I'm going to die!" And it's pretty clear where he learned to fear elevators: locked in closets and storage bins when he was a child.

One of our students, John, was the night manager of a small grocery store. He had many male friends, found time for some weekend basketball, and played the piano. But he had one goal that remained unachieved: he was lonely for female companionship and felt pessimistic about his future love life. John analyzed his behavior in terms of situations. When he talked to women in class or at the store, he felt relaxed and spoke fairly easily, but when the talking occurred in a social context, such as a party or a date, he became ill at ease and acted very awkward. In these situations he would initiate a series of abstract conversations, looking away from the woman and speaking in a vaguely philosophical way that he himself admitted was impossible for anyone to understand. He gave the impression of being aloof, although he was actually nervous and shy. At the beginning of a conversation, a woman might be interested in John, but after several minutes of what appeared to her to be uninterested, aloof, unintelligible talk from John, she was no longer interested. John's behavior in the social situation changed the nature of the situation, and as the woman became uninterested in him, John acted more aloof. His behavior produced a new situation, one that made him unhappy, but one that he seemed unable to remedy.

John later undertook a self-modification project. He told us that he profited from observing the behavior of a friend who was not at all nervous or aloof when dealing with women in social situations. John was struck by the great difference between his own behavior and that of his friend, and he began to try to imitate his friend's behavior. John's learning history had been very different from that of his friend. Consequently each young man felt and behaved differently, even though the situation was outwardly the same.

Although much of our behavior is learned, we don't just keep on doing the same things we learned in childhood. We change, grow, and develop throughout the life span. New or changed situations may produce new behaviors. For example, a young woman who has become a mother finds herself in a novel situation. She has a real, breathing baby to cope with, and she will learn ways of behaving as she deals with the novel situation. Some of her behavior, however, will have been learned in the past. She didn't come to motherhood completely naive about caring for a baby. She has learned certain attitudes, ideas, and specific ways of dealing with babies. For example, she may have had practice in caring for someone else's baby, she may have observed others caring for babies, or she may have taken classes or read books about child care. The environment, then, has two types of effects: evoking behaviors already learned *and* teaching new behaviors.

The implication is that adjustment reflects behaviors learned for specific situations. You deal with your problems in adjustment by dealing with what you have learned—or not learned—to do in a particular situation. Thus, in the process of self-modification, you set out to produce new learning for yourself in specific situations. To modify your own behavior—to bring it under control or determine its course—you will have to learn new skills for particular situations (see Figure 1-1).

The Process of Self-Modification

Successful self-modification always includes certain essential elements: self-knowledge, planning, information gathering, and modification of plans in light of new information. There is a definite sequence in deliberate self-modification. Most self-change programs involve these steps:

1. Select a goal, and develop a commitment to change in order to reach that goal. Specify the behaviors to be changed. These behaviors are called **target behaviors.**

(A) Antecedents	*(B) Behavior*	*(C) Consequences*
You can change the triggering events for a behavior by building in antecedents that lead to wanted behavior and by removing antecedents that lead to unwanted behavior.	You can change actions, thoughts, feelings, or behaviors themselves by practicing desirable acts or substituting desirable alternatives for unwanted acts.	You can change the events that follow your behavior by reinforcing desired actions and not reinforcing unwanted behavior.

Figure 1-1 The A-B-Cs of self-change

2. Make observations about the target behaviors. You may keep a kind of diary describing those behaviors or count how often you engage in them. Try to discover the antecedents that stimulate your acts and the consequences that reward them.
3. Work out a plan for change. Your plan might call for changing a pattern of thought that leads to unwanted behavior, gradually replacing an unwanted behavior with a desirable one, and rewarding yourself for desired behavior.
4. Readjust your plans as you learn more about yourself. As you practice analyzing your behavior, you will be able to make more sophisticated, effective plans for change.
5. Take steps to ensure that you will maintain the gains you make.

A Sample Self-Change Project

Here is the report of one of our students who carried out a self-change project in our class. Her name is Mary, and she is 21 years old. Mary's experience with her self-modification plan is presented largely in her own words, along with our comments (in italics).

> I gossip too much. I do it when I'm bored, with friends or family, just about anywhere. I thought this was a terrible habit, and at first I wanted to rid my life of gossip entirely. However, after discussing this idea with several people, I realized that it's really one particular kind of gossip that upsets me—saying negative things, or putdowns, about other people. My goal was to decrease these putdowns. *Mary has taken the first step in self-modification: she has translated a vague sense of dissatisfaction into a concrete goal.*
>
> I began collecting my data on a 3″ × 5″ card, which I kept with me at all times. On the card I wrote the date, the name of the person I was talking to, and the number of times I said something negative about another person. Sometimes I would forget to mark my card, and I'm sure I missed a few, but I was very shocked and surprised at the outcome. I said something negative about another person approximately 98 times per week—about 14 times each day! I noticed that keeping a record of the number of putdowns cut down on these numbers, so the real figures would have been even higher.

Mary has taken the second step in self-modification: making observations. She was wise to make this record before attempting to change. To begin an improvement program before carefully gathering information often results in failure. Mary wouldn't have known enough to change successfully unless she had first observed herself. Also, her counting record made it possible to measure the success or failure of her self-modification program.

> I noticed that these putdowns of other people occurred in particular situations—when I was with my sister or my cousin, and when I was feeling down and out, or depressed. I think I put down others because

it made me look better than them. If I saw a pretty girl, for example, I might say, "Oh, she's pretty, but her nose is too big." Or if I saw a handsome guy, I'd say, "He's cute, but he's too short and stubby." It seemed I always found fault with everyone. This somehow made me feel better than the other person. But I realized I was telling myself, "I really shouldn't be saying this. Well, I'll quit doing it soon." But I never did quit.

Often self-observation results in the realization that the target behavior occurs, or fails to occur, because of specific circumstances. This makes changing easier because you can change the circumstances. And that is what Mary did, as we will see in a moment. Notice that you have to make self-observations in order to discover the circumstances.

Mary now took the third step in self-modification: she made a plan for change.

My plan for changing:

First, I decided to decrease putdowns of other people and to increase saying positive things about them. I kept a record of how often I did each of these. I started out at a very low level of saying nice things, about one per day, and gradually increased the number of positive things I said each day.

Second, I gave myself instructions. When I was in one of the tempting situations, I would tell myself, "I don't need to put down other people in order to look good. In fact, this turns people away from me, and it lowers my self-respect. So don't do it."

Third, I used thought stopping. In my mind, I'd tell myself "Stop!" if I started saying something negative and would tell myself something positive to say about the person instead.

Fourth, I used imaginary practice to imagine myself in a situation in which I performed the desired behavior flawlessly. This sounds corny, but it worked beautifully!

Last, I rewarded myself with extra spending money for each day that I did all these steps in my plan.

Mary's plan is a good one, for several reasons:

1. She uses several techniques for change.
2. She deals with the antecedents, the behavior itself, and the consequences.
3. She changes the behavior gradually.
4. She gives herself extra practice, rewards, and instructions to increase the chances that she will be able to change.

All these aspects of her plan are good simply because they increase her chances of success.

Mary adds,

The plan really worked! I cut down negative statements from an average of 14 per day to nearly zero, and increased saying nice things from an average of once per day to 7. I can say I have an inner sense of self-worth now. I feel good about myself and others around me. Now that

I know a lot more about myself, I feel I can control my thoughts and behaviors. I can say that I really like myself better today!

Applying Principles

What makes a self-modification plan such as Mary's different from any New Year's resolution? Is self-modification nothing more than a resolution to do better? Sometimes we just make up our minds to change and then do it. "I turned over a new leaf!" or "It was time to get my act together." But it is not always so easy. Mary, for example, had been intending to stop her bad habit for years, but had not. Often something more than just good intentions is needed. That something more is a correct, conscious application of the principles of behavior change.

Self-modification is a set of techniques that must be learned. To see if you already know some of the major points, evaluate the following report, which is a first effort at a self-modification plan by one of our students. Is it a good plan? Does it make sense to you?

Bryan, a 21-year-old college junior, writes:

I'm a nail biter, but I wish I weren't. It's embarrassing, sometimes it's painful, and it seems childish to me—something that is OK when you are a kid, but not now.

Target behavior: Reduce nail biting to zero

Count:

I counted for three weeks. The frequency of nail biting ranged from one to eight times a day, with the average about four or five at first. During this last week it's down to two times per day. I think counting the biting makes me more aware of it, and sometimes I stop myself from doing it before I begin.

The situations that seem to produce more biting are (1) watching TV; (2) being bored, almost anywhere; and (3) listening to lectures. I don't see any way I can change these situations, since I don't want to give up TV, I have to go to lectures, and how can anybody completely avoid being bored?

Plan for changing:

I have signed the following contract and put it up on the mirror where I see it every morning. "I promise not to bite my nails at all each day. If I don't bite my nails all day, then (1) I get to eat dinner, and (2) I get to see my girlfriend that night. If I refrain from biting my nails all week, I get to go out Saturday night, which I usually do. Otherwise, I must stay home. Signed, Bryan W."

This plan has some good points and several bad ones. The good points are that Bryan has an accurate count of how often he bites his nails and that he knows the situations in which he is likely to bite them. Having a self-contract is also a good idea. One of the bad points—bad because it decreases Bryan's chances of success—is that if he bites his nails, he intends to do away with a major pleasure, being with his girlfriend. This is self-punishment. We recommend *against* the use of self-punishment because, as you will see, it usually doesn't work. We suspect Bryan won't stick to his intention. Is he really going to give up eating dinner every night and never see his girlfriend if he continues to bite his nails? Another weak point is that Bryan has no plan for developing a behavior to replace nail biting. Compare that with Mary's plan not just to decrease saying negative things about others, but to increase saying positive things.

Think critically about the many cases that are included in this book. What about them will increase the chances of success, and what will decrease the chances?

Adjusting and Changing Plans

If Bryan is going to succeed in changing his nail-biting habit, he will have to change his plan as he learns more about the skill of self-modification. Often people start with what they think is a sound plan, but as they try it, they find that it needs adjusting. Plans must be changed as one finds parts that are not working. Sometimes an entire plan must be redesigned, as our next case illustrates.

> Kate felt that she was not studying enough.
>
> Like a lot of students, I only study just before a test or when some deadline is coming up. I decided to reward myself with some favorite activity—going out for pizza, watching TV, playing with my parakeet—if I completed at least two full hours of studying each day. I planned to increase this later to three or four hours per day, since actually I think I would like to go to graduate school. If I didn't do the studying, I would get to play with the bird anyway—he needs the attention—but wouldn't go out for pizza or watch a TV program.
>
> My plan quickly ground to a halt. I didn't do any studying; I just didn't go out for pizza or watch TV. After about a week of that, I quit keeping records. So I was pretty much back where I started.
>
> Then you announced in class that we would have to make progress reports on our projects, so I got serious again about keeping records. I realized that my thoughts at the time I was supposed to study were probably keeping me from studying. I was thinking things like "I don't want to do this now . . . I really don't have to do it now. . . . It's so boring"—things like that. So I have decided to begin a new plan. I will schedule study times for myself and will figure out some rewards that are actually worth working for. But more important, I will watch myself for those kinds of thoughts that lead me to avoid studying. I really do want to study more, as I feel I'm not living up to my potential, and—let's face it—I won't have a chance to get into graduate school with my present grades. So when those thoughts occur, I will try to spot them and change them.

It often happens that once you begin a plan, you realize that you need to change some of the details, as Bryan did, or even that you have to reorient the goal of your plan entirely, as did Kate. Start with a simple plan that seems to meet your needs. Then *find out what interferes with success.* That was Kate's approach: she found that her thoughts at the moment she sat down to study were interfering with her studying. Whatever interferes with your success will tell you what the new, changed plan should be. Thus, Kate worked on changing the thoughts that discouraged studying.

But will any plan work? Can you change yourself?

Does Self-Modification Really Work?

When people have a moderately serious problem with their own behavior, are they able to change themselves? Of course. An estimated 29 million Americans quit smoking between 1965 and 1975, following the first Surgeon General's report that indicated that smoking causes cancer (Prochaska, 1983). Ninety-five percent of the people who quit smoking do it without any professional help (Cohen et al., 1989). About the same percentage of overweight people are able to change themselves without professional help (Orme & Binik, 1987).

The success rate for such relatively serious problems may be higher than is usually thought. It has been noted, for example, that a surprisingly large number of veterans who returned from the Vietnam War as heroin addicts were able to stop their habit (Horn, 1972). Research estimates of the number of obese people who have returned to normal weight vary from 29% to 55% (Jeffery & Wing, 1983; Schachter, 1982). Whatever the frequency, a substantial number of people who have been overweight no longer are.

Thus, people do change problem behaviors by themselves—they engage in successful self-modification. But why are some successful, while others are not? Studies of people who are competent at self-modification—who can quit smoking or lose excess weight—teach us principles we can all use to deal with our problem behaviors. That's exactly what Mary did in her successful approach to stopping putdowns: she used a set of principles that has helped in coping with difficult-to-change behaviors.

Published Cases of Successful Self-Modification

Several successful cases of self-modification have been reported in the professional psychological research literature. They illustrate the wide range of applicability of the techniques. People have been successful at

- increasing their creative productivity (Herren, 1989);
- controlling bulimia (Posobiec & Renfrew, 1988);
- improving their study habits (Richards, 1976);
- controlling their weight (Mahoney, Moura, & Wade, 1973);
- handling anxiety in social situations (Rehm & Marston, 1968);

- controlling nervous habits such as scratching, nail biting, and hair pulling (Perkins & Perkins, 1976; Watson, Tharp, & Krisberg, 1972);
- overcoming depression (see Box 1-3) (Hamilton & Waldman, 1983; Tharp, Watson, & Kaya, 1974);
- eliminating teeth grinding (Pawlicki & Galotti, 1978);
- speaking up in class (Barrera & Glasgow, 1976);
- exercising (Kau & Fischer, 1974; Sherman, Turner, Levine, & Walk, 1975); and
- reducing conflicts with co-workers (Maher, 1985).

Certainly not every problem will yield to self-modification, and not every reader will master self-control. Our purpose is to detail the procedures that make mastery more likely. What is the likelihood of your own personal success? To answer this, more than case histories is needed. After all, case histories are good illustrations of an idea, but case histories cannot prove an idea because they are too unique. We can't be sure the results will generalize to whole groups of people. For example, when entire college classes are examined, what is the success rate of the students in the class?

Research in Self-Modification Courses

The kind of self-help book you buy in the drugstore almost never has been evaluated to see if its ideas really work or not (Rosen, 1990). Even books in which the author has a Ph.D. or an M.D. are sold by hype, not by their scientific status. *Ten Days to a Better You, Be Happy by Thinking Happy, Lose Weight while Watching TV*—all these kinds of books may or may not work. No one knows because no one has ever tested the books scientifically. Many of them make the process of self-change seem too easy and too simple, and if the methods in these books were tested scientifically, they probably wouldn't work. Changing yourself is possible, but it's complicated and requires effort.

On the other hand, our book and the ideas in it have actually been tested. People have conducted experiments to see what percentage of people improve after reading this book and then compared their improvement rate with that of people who didn't read the book. In each edition of this book we have reviewed the research on its use in teaching self-modification to students. Each year new studies show that students can change in a course like this one.

For six years Jerry Deffenbacher and Jeffrey Shepard (1989) taught a course in stress management at Colorado State University; the course was based heavily on the ideas in this book. After the course the students reported that they felt significantly less anxious generally, became angry less often, and showed fewer physical symptoms related to stress.

Thomas Brigham and his associates (in press) taught a course in academic skills designed to help minority students succeed at a large state university. The researchers adapted the ideas in this book to help the minority students self-modify their class attendance, studying, speaking to professors outside

BOX 1-3

Successful Self-Modification of Depression during a Course in Self-Modification

In the journal *Cognitive Therapy and Research,* Scott Hamilton and David Waldman (1983) report the case of Al, who successfully reduced his moderately severe depression. The case illustrates the process of self-modification.

Al was a 20-year-old student taking a course similar to the one you are taking, in which he was asked to carry out a self-modification project. He chose to attack his depression, which had lasted for four years. It was associated with severe family stress, the divorce of his parents, and continued criticism from his mother. Al often engaged in self-criticism—"I'm stupid and a total failure because my grades are bad"—and often had negative thoughts about his insufficient studying, poor grades, inadequate time scheduling, and lack of career goals. These negative thoughts sometimes lasted as long as four hours, leading to intense depression.

Al began by counting the number of negative thoughts he had each day—ignoring whether they were long or short—and also rated how depressed he felt each day on a scale from 0 for no depression to 6 for extreme depression. He made this count for 18 days. During this time he averaged 3.2 negative thoughts per day, and his average depression rating stayed at about 3 on his scale.

For the next 14 days Al tried to lift his depression by doing something about the topics that depressed him. He attempted to reward himself for gathering information about various careers, meeting daily study goals, and following through with his appointments and deadlines. He continued to count his negative thoughts and to rate his moods.

During this period his average number of negative thoughts dropped to 2.8, a slight improvement over his earlier average, but his rated mood actually worsened—to an average of 4 on his scale.

Al now started a second attack, a new self-modification plan in which he worked directly on his negative thoughts. As soon as he began a negative thought, he required himself to record what had set it off, how depressed it made him feel, and a rational reevaluation of the situation. He also required himself to review written positive statements about himself every day while engaging in pleasant activities and to imagine himself in a stressful situation but coolly working out the best possible solution to it. This period of working on his thoughts lasted 70 days.

Throughout the 70 days Al's number of negative thoughts per day dropped, and in the last 10 days of the period he had only 1. His rated mood also improved, and in the last 10 days he felt no instances of depression. When asked to comment, Al's roommate rated him as much less depressed. Six months later Al again recorded negative thoughts for two weeks, during which time he had an average of less than 1 per day, and his mood stayed undepressed during that period. He had successfully changed himself.

class, note taking, and other academic activities. A second group of minority students—the control group—was not trained in applying self-modification to the students' academic problems. The experiment was repeated for several school terms. The results: In one term the students who learned to self-modify their academic skills had a grade point average of 2.10, whereas those who did not had a grade point average of 1.27.

For several years Felipe Castro (1987) at UCLA has conducted a course in health promotion in which he teaches procedures adapted from this book. Students who learned the procedures, compared with those who did not, increased their amount of exercise and decreased their consumption of high-calorie foods. In addition, students who learned the procedures showed other, nonprogrammed changes in lifestyle, such as eating more salads, vegetables, or fruits. Learning the techniques in a class clearly benefited a majority of the students.

David Dodd (1986) at Eastern Illinois University taught a course in self-modification for several years and found that on the average about 70% of his students were able to reach their own goals for change by the end of the semester. Scott Hamilton (1980) used this text to teach self-change techniques to 72 students. He reported that 83% of the students met their goals for behavior change. He also found that having a successful experience with self-modification increased students' expectations of success in later projects.

In New Zealand, Gail deBortali-Tregerthan (1984) taught self-modification to 100 high school students who had *not* volunteered to learn self-modification but were required to do so as part of a psychology class. She found that 66% of those who learned self-modification were able to change their target behaviors, while only 26% of those who selected a behavior to change but did not learn the techniques were able to change.

Richard Rakos and Mark Grodek (1984) at Cleveland State University used an earlier edition of this text in a course in self-modification. Comparing this class with another that did not use the text, they concluded:

> Participants in the class demonstrated improvement in their target behaviors and reported significant positive changes in dysfunctional attitudes, fear of negative evaluation, and general self-control skills. The absence of self-reported change . . . in controls suggests that the gains were a function of the specific class (p. 160).

Other systematic reports have been presented, with similar results (Barrera & Glasgow, 1976; Clements & Beidleman, 1981; Menges & Dobroski, 1977; Payne & Woudenberg, 1978). Typically two-thirds or more of students who use self-modification techniques are able to change successfully. The question "Can one teach self-modification to students?" has been answered with a resounding *yes.*

Of course, self-modification does not always work (see Box 1-4). When does it and when does it not? Michael Perri and Steve Richards (1977) studied the differences between people who succeeded at self-change and those who did not. They found that successful self-modifiers used *more* techniques for a *longer period of time.* For smokers, using several techniques also helps in quitting (Kamarck & Lichtenstein, 1987). Similar results have been found for

BOX 1-4

Unsuccessful Self-Modification of a Case of "Writer's Block "[1]

Not everyone who tries self-modification is successful. There are, however, very few published examples of unsuccessful cases. Here is one, in its entirety:

The Unsuccessful Self-Treatment of a Case of "Writer's Block "

DENNIS UPPER
Veteran's Administration Hospital, Brockton, Massachusetts

REFERENCES

[1]Portions of this paper were not presented at the 81st Annual American Psychological Association Convention, Montreal, Canada, August 30, 1973.

SOURCE: From "Unsuccessful Self-Treatment of a Case of 'Writer's Block,'" by Dennis Upper, 1974, *Journal of Applied Behavior Analysis, 7*. Copyright 1974, Pergamon Press, Ltd. Reprinted by permission.

college women taught good dental hygiene—brushing twice and flossing once each day—by the use of self-modification techniques. Three months later they were interviewed. The ones who were still following good dental hygiene reported using *several self-modification techniques* to control their own behavior, but the women who had given up the rigorous schedule of brushing and flossing were not using any techniques (O'Neill, Sandgren, McCaul, & Glasgow, 1987).

In general, people do not fail at self-modification because the techniques don't work; they fail because they don't use the techniques. For example, in one study a manual was developed for people who have a strong fear of open places—agoraphobia (Holden, O'Brien, Barlow, Stetson, & Infantino, 1983). The manual described the techniques that subjects could use to lessen their agoraphobia. The subjects in one group were simply given the manual and invited to change themselves. The manual was not effective because the subjects did not use the techniques suggested. Similarly, when therapists gave depressed patients homework assignments that involved self-modification, the only patients who improved were those who actually did the homework (Neimeyer & Feixas, 1990). It has also been shown that when schoolchildren are taught to use self-modification techniques to improve things such as the amount of time they focus on their work, the more techniques they are taught and use, the greater the effect on their schoolwork (Fantuzzo, Rohrbeck, & Azar, 1987).

This book is not a magic bullet: you have to do the work, and you have to use the techniques. The particular techniques you use will depend on the things you want to change, but the message is clear: to increase your chances of success,

use the techniques,
use as *many* as you can, and
use them *long enough* to have an effect.

The Uses of Self-Modification

In the past, medical doctors have typically treated their patients in offices, clinics, or hospitals. And because early theories of psychotherapy were based on a medical model (Freud was a medical doctor), psychotherapists, too, relied almost exclusively on treatment administered in the office. Changes in medicine and psychotherapy, however, have led in the past few years to an increased emphasis on treatment in the natural environment. In medicine, for example, the treatment of long-term, chronic diseases such as diabetes—in which the patient requires an injection each day and has to carefully monitor his or her food intake—means that the doctor cannot have the patient come into the office each time treatment is needed. Indeed, the treatment needed may not be medication at all, but some change in lifestyle, such as increased exercise for diabetics or reduced cholesterol in the diet of heart-disease patients. Similarly, behavior-change specialists have turned to treatments that occur in the setting in which the problem behaviors occur; for example, treating hyperactive children at school. In such a setting, the doctor or behavior-change specialist is not even present when treatment is needed.

For these situations, self-modification of behavior is the treatment of choice: people can learn to change their own behavior in the settings in which it needs changing. The diabetic can increase her exercise at home; a person with mental retardation can learn to control his anger in the special school. Self-modification techniques have been used in a variety of medical and psychological settings in the past few years.

In the medical area, self-modification has been used to treat

- insomnia (Morawetz, 1989; Turner, 1986)
- Type-A (heart-attack–prone) behavior (Nakano, 1990)
- diabetes self-care (Karoly & Bay, 1990; Wing, Epstein, Nowalk, & Scott, 1988)
- irritable bowel syndrome (Blanchard, Schwarz, Neff, & Gerardi, 1988)
- chronic pain (Turk, Holzman, & Kerns, 1986)
- chronic headache (Radnitz, Applebaum, Blanchard, Elliott, & Andrasik, 1988; Tobin, Holroyd, Baker, Reynolds, & Holm, 1988)
- menopausal hot flashes (Stevenson & Delprato, 1983)
- smoking during pregnancy (Aaronson, Ershoff, & Danaher, 1985)
- severe physical disabilities (Broder & Shapiro, 1985)
- insufficient aerobic exercise (von Schlumperger, 1985)

In psychological settings, self-modification is now a major component of treatment in these situations:

- teaching teenagers to control their discipline problems (Brigham, 1989)
- lack of self-control in individuals with mental retardation (Agran & Martin, 1987)

- teaching children to resist pressures to take up smoking (Gilchrist, Schinke, Bobo, & Snow, 1986)
- encouraging underachieving children to do better in school (Loper & Murphy, 1985; Stevenson & Fantuzzo, 1986)
- helping depressed children (Stark, Reynolds, & Kaslow, 1987)
- helping the hard-core unemployed find work (Kanfer, 1984)
- helping students with mental retardation perform at a higher level (Bloomquist, Heshmat-Farzaneh-Kia, Swanson, & Braswell, 1987; Sowers, Verdi, Bourbeau, & Sheehan, 1985)

Chapter Summary

Adjustment and Self-Direction

Adjustment is better understood as a skill than as a condition.

Alternative Ways of Thinking about Self-Direction

One can think of problems in adjustment from several points of view:

- as a lack of willpower
- as symptoms of inner malfunctions
- as a lack of the skills necessary to cope with certain situations.

The Skills of Adjustment and the Purpose of This Book

Two important elements of skill are knowledge and practice; these can be learned even for the skills of self-direction.

Behavior and the Environment

One's behavior, thoughts, and feelings are embedded in contexts—the things that go before them (antecedents) and the things that come after them (consequences). A shorthand way of expressing this is A-B-C: Antecedents-Behavior-Consequences.

The effects of situations (As and Cs) upon our behavior (Bs) are influenced by learning experiences that continue throughout our lives.

The Process of Self-Modification

In the process of self-modification, you produce new learning for yourself in specific situations. You

select a target behavior,
make observations,
work out a plan for change using psychological principles, and
readjust your plans as you learn more about yourself.

Does Self-Modification Really Work?

Millions of people have successfully changed their behavior to stop unwanted acts such as smoking or overeating, and there are many published case histories of successful self-modification. Self-modification is increasingly used in problems of chronic ill health.

Research has shown that students using this book can learn the principles of self-change and carry out successful projects. You are more likely to be successful if you use a variety of techniques for a long period of time and if you follow the exercises at the end of each chapter.

YOUR OWN SELF-DIRECTION PROJECT: STEP ONE

There's a big difference between knowing ideas well enough to pass a test on them and knowing them well enough to use them in your daily life. To reach this more advanced stage, you must *practice* self-change.

Your first task is to select a goal to work on for your practice in self-modification. Make a list of three to five personal goals. These might be expressed as things you want to do—to study more, to date more, to exercise more, to save money—or things you want to stop—drinking too much, swearing, watching TV, being nervous.

Think over your list for a day or two, perhaps adding goals or changing some goals. Then select one goal for a learning project. How do you know what goal to select for your practice? Here are some things to consider.

The goal can be a major, long-term one, such as overcoming shyness, or a minor, short-term one, but it should be important to you. You won't learn much by trying to change something trivial.

If you are involved in a complex problem—one that will require changing several aspects of your life—reaching your final goal and maintaining it may take longer than one semester. If you are overweight, for example, you will have to change several different things about your pattern of overeating and underexercising. Working on only a few aspects of the problem can be a major project in itself. If you choose a less ambitious project, you may achieve complete success, but of course it's success at a lesser project (see Box 1-5).

It is important to tackle a project on which you feel you have some chance of success (Kanfer & Schefft, 1987). Failure is discouraging, and you might give up efforts at self-change prematurely. If you really don't think you can change some aspect of your behavior now, don't tackle that project. As you learn the ideas in this book, your skill level will increase, and you may realize that in fact you do have a chance to make those changes.

Thus, the ideal choice is a project that (1) is interesting enough to be a challenge, but (2) has some chance of success.

Here's one last thing to keep in mind if you're thinking of attacking a big problem. It comes in the form of an anecdote: A woman in her 40s had gone back to school to become a doctor. After a year she ran into a friend who asked how her new career plans were shaping up. She said she was considering dropping out. The friend asked why, and she replied, "It will take me six more years before I will be in practice. By that time I'll be 50!"

"Oh," the friend asked, "and if you drop out, how old will you be in six years?"

BOX 1-5

Criteria for a Good Project

Your instructor will probably tell you that success or failure in your self-change project is *less* important—even to your course grade—than your sophistication in carrying out the project. Sophistication (or complexity) refers to the number of different techniques you try and to the relationship between the techniques and your self-observation.

Consider the difficulty of the problem you have undertaken and the adequacy of your solution to it. If you observe yourself carefully, you will see ways to use more techniques. Sheer effort also makes a difference. If you want to take on a difficult project, be sure your instructor realizes that the project is a difficult one *for you* and agrees to grade you on sophistication and effort, not just on success.

Here are some tips that we give our students. Your instructor may have additional ones that will influence your grade.

Make careful observations. Learn about the actual A-B-C relationships in your behavior. Identify the conditions that facilitate or compete with the target behavior. Keep good records throughout the project, even if you change plans.

Use a variety of techniques. These techniques for change are grouped under the A-B-C headings in the book. Try to use some techniques from each category.

Change your plans as you find out what works and what doesn't. Tinker with your system. Be creative in your use of the techniques. Experiment with them.

Be persistent. Keep trying to change, and redo your plans as you learn more about yourself and your A-B-C relationships.

Be well organized in your final report. Here is a possible outline for the report:

- The goal you selected (Chapters 1 and 2).
- Your observations about your behavior (Chapter 3).
- Your first plan for change. Use several techniques (Chapters 5, 6, and 7).
- Your results (Chapter 8). Your second plan for change.
- If the first plan is not successful, readjust. Draw on ideas from Chapters 5, 6, and 7; tinker with the system; or draw up a new system altogether (Chapter 8).
- Your plans for the future—what will you do to maintain your gains (Chapters 9 and 10).
- Conclusions.

2

Specifying the Goal, Overcoming Obstacles, and Building Commitment

Outline

- Specifying the Targets for Change
- Overcoming Obstacles: Why You Might Self-Sabotage
- Building Commitment
- *Tips for Typical Topics*
- *Chapter Summary*
- *Your Own Self-Direction Project: Step Two*

Learning Objectives

Specifying the Targets for Change

1. What are three basic tactics for specifying behaviors-in-situations?
2. What tactic should you use when your goal is to eliminate some undesirable behavior?
3. What three tactics should you use if you are not sure how to specify a behavior-in-situation? Explain *brainstorming.*
4. What tactic should you use even if your goal is not related to a specific behavior?

Overcoming Obstacles: Why You Might Self-Sabotage

5. List the nine common reasons that people fail in self-change efforts. Explain each reason.
6. What are self-efficacy beliefs? What steps can you take to increase your self-efficacy beliefs regarding the behaviors you want to change?
7. Why is it a good idea to make a list of the long- and short-term advantages of changing? How do you make such a list?

Building Commitment

8. What eight steps can you take to avoid being tempted to stop your self-change project? Explain each.
9. Explain the use of subgoals in working toward a long-term goal.
10. Explain how many problems in self-change are due to conflicts between long- and short-term goals. What can you do about this kind of conflict?
11. What is a self-contract?

Specifying the Targets for Change

All of us use abstract words—*aggressive, dependent, strong, ambitious*—to describe personality traits or motives. Thinking in terms of personality is typical in our society, and it works fine so long as we are only speculating in the abstract about psychology. But if we want to think critically enough to be able to change our own behavior, we have to beware of thinking in terms of personality traits; they tend to oversimplify and to mislead as to the *causes* of our behaviors.

"Personality" terms pose two problems: (1) they don't specify the situations in which the behaviors occur, and (2) they don't specify particular behaviors. To think clearly enough to change your own behavior, you have to consider both the specific behaviors to be changed and the specific situations in which they occur.

You might think "I'm an independent person." But this term can be misleading because you may act independently in one situation but not in another. For example, Derek might be emotionally dependent on his girlfriend but more independent in his schoolwork and in relationships with his professors. Also, what exactly does Derek do when he is "emotionally dependent"?

Think of your behavior in conjunction with the situation in which the behavior occurs. Even if your problem relates to feelings, you should think of it as a reaction in a particular situation. You might think, "I'm nervous and depressed. I'm becoming neurotic." But a better formulation—one that can help you change—would be, "At work, after I finish a big task, I get depressed," or "At night, in the dorm, I feel nervous." You must be specific, because you can change only specific things in specific situations.

Stop a moment and think about the list of goals for change you made at the end of Chapter 1. Do your goals specify particular behaviors, or are the goals overly general? Do they specify the situations in which the behaviors occur, or do they ignore the situation? One of the major goals of this chapter is to translate your goals into statements that stipulate particular behaviors to be changed and the particular situations in which they occur. You're going to move from "I want to be less nervous" to "I want to stop telling myself I'm going to fail when I'm taking tests." This is exactly what a psychotherapist would do if you consulted one.

Regardless of the type of problem or goal you are dealing with, you must have well-defined objectives that are specified in terms of particular behaviors in particular situations. Here are several tactics that will help you specify your goals clearly.

Specifying Behaviors-in-Situations

Tactic 1: *Make a list of concrete examples.* Suppose you're dissatisfied with yourself. You think "I'm too self-centered." This self-statement doesn't tell you what to change because it is too vague. Give a concrete example of the problem: "I talk about myself too much when I'm with my friends." This specifies both the behavior and the situation in which the behavior occurs.

"I eat too much" is also too vague. Do you eat too many carrots? Do you eat too much at every meal? A better statement might be "I eat reasonably enough at breakfast and lunch, but tend to overeat at supper"; or "Whenever I go on a picnic, I eat too much"; or "I eat too much on special occasions, such as Thanksgiving and Christmas."

Sometimes thinking of examples of the problem in question will make you more aware of the kinds of situations in which the behavior occurs. Sally started with the vague statement "I'm not assertive enough." But when she gave specific examples, she turned a vague idea into a clear statement about her behavior and the specific kinds of situations in which her problem occurred.

> It's not that I am always unassertive. I can deal with people who try to push ahead in line or with friends who ask too much of me. But when men my age ask me to do things related to dating, going out, or being together, then I am not as assertive as I want to be.

Now she has labeled the kind of situation in which her problem occurs and can begin to change the way she reacts in those situations.

Tactic 2: *List the details of your problem.* To solve problems, you must attend to the details (D'Zurilla & Nezu, 1989). Make a list of these details; then select those that seem critical to the solution of the problem. Often our thinking about a problem is unfocused, and listing the details helps us to see precisely what our goal should be. Research in problem solving suggests that people who list details improve their problem-solving ability compared with those who do not list them (Nezu & D'Zurilla, 1981).

The use of such details is illustrated by a woman who originally entered psychotherapy seeking treatment for severe anxiety while taking tests. She had two university degrees, but lately she was becoming so nervous during tests that her performance was in jeopardy. The first detail she listed concerning her problem was that she did not have enough time to study. Listing other details revealed that because of her newborn baby, she sometimes had difficulty getting to class and sometimes couldn't even get to exams on time. Instead of treating her test anxiety directly, her therapist suggested she focus on coping with the problems that were interfering with her schoolwork. After learning ways to cope with the *details* of her problem, she found that her test anxiety was reduced (Mayo & Norton, 1980). Her focus had shifted from the problem of test anxiety to the specific details that were leading to the test anxiety. When she dealt with those problems, the anxiety diminished.

Tactic 3: *Become an observer of yourself.* A critical step in specifying a problem is to stop speculating about your behavior and start observing it. Your thoughts about your problem will probably remain unfocused until you begin to actually watch yourself behaving in various situations.

Besides observing your behavior, you should keep notes of your observations. You might keep a narrative account of your daily life, or simply note instances of behavior that seem related to the problem. For example, a father who felt he wasn't dealing with his children very well began to notice how he actually dealt with them, and he made notes to himself about how he acted.

After you have recorded observations of your behavior in various situations, read your notes and see if a pattern emerges. The best way to make these observations is to write down your behaviors and the situations in which they occur as soon as you think you have found an instance of the problem.

In the case of Sally, mentioned earlier, she began to observe her own behavior. When a man she didn't like asked her out on a date and she said yes, she asked herself, "Was that an example of my being unassertive?" She decided that it was. Thus, she realized that her lack of assertion occurred when a man asked her for a date. Later, a man who lived in her rooming house barged into her room, and she didn't say anything. Again she asked herself, "Was that an instance of my being unassertive?" Eventually she saw that her problem was very specific. It occurred only in certain personal situations, and it almost always involved men.

When You're Not Doing What You Want to Be Doing

Sometimes your goal is to start doing something that at present you're not doing. For example, you may realize that you are failing in college because you're *not* studying. What can you do? You should specify the situation in which you *want* the behavior to occur:

My goal is ______________ when ______________.
(what you want to do) (the situation)

Paul wanted to increase his studying. He kept a journal to record situations in which he might study. It contained entries like this:

> *Wednesday:* Roommate went out. Room quiet. Got out my history text and turned to the assignment. Remembered a baseball game was on TV and started watching it. Tried to study between innings but gave up. Studied about five minutes the whole afternoon. *Thursday:* Went to the library to study. Saw Karen. Didn't study.

These notes specify two situations in which studying would have been desirable. The journal contains other valuable information: It tells Paul what he did *instead of studying.* Paul was not simply "not studying." He was actively performing behaviors that made studying impossible. In other words, as far as studying was concerned, he was performing the *wrong* behaviors. Thus, his task of problem specification was the same as those we have already discussed: specifying the situation in question—"room quiet"—and then specifying the behavior he wants to develop—"studying instead of watching TV."

Remember to specify not only the situation and the fact that the desirable behavior is *not* occurring, but also the behaviors that *do* occur *instead* of the ones you want. Thus, Paul should first specify the situation in which he wants the behavior to occur—when he is alone is his room or when he is at the library—and then observe what occurs instead of the desired behavior.

When the Problem Concerns Eliminating Some Undesirable Behavior

Paul might express his goal in one of two ways: (1) "I want to quit goofing off and study more," or (2) "I want to increase studying in those situations in which I should study." The second way is better because it expresses the goal in terms of behaviors that need to be increased.

Tactic 4: *Your strategy should always be to increase some desirable behavior.* Even if the problem is that you are doing something you want to stop, you should specify your problem in terms of an alternative behavior. You can't just get rid of a behavior; something always pops up in its place. There's no such thing as a behavioral vacuum. Therefore, you have to develop an alternative behavior to replace one you want to get rid of.

Suppose your problem is that you procrastinate too much. You might say, "I have to stop procrastinating." But what do you actually have to *do?* You need to increase certain behaviors: planning work ahead of time; working out goals and subgoals, along with plans for meeting them; taking small steps to get yourself started; keeping records of your progress; assigning priorities to your work and then doing it in priority order; planning to cope with diversions; dealing with the negative elements of the work to be done; and so on (Tec, 1980). Those are the behaviors you want to increase. As you do so, you will automatically decrease procrastination.

Laura complained about depression. As she began searching for possible causes, she found that many situations seemed to produce depression. A friend's mild criticism, her cat's disappearance, spilling coffee on her new dress—many relatively minor occurrences set off hours of deep sadness. When asked to specify a desirable alternative, she replied that feeling good was an alternative. We suggested she search for events that made her feel good and keep in mind the goal of attempting to *increase* them. She found, for example, that exercising each day made her feel good, so she set out to increase her exercising, and in the process, decreased her depression.

Earl's original statement of his problem was, "I think I am morbidly shy, and I want to get rid of my shyness." After observing himself and analyzing his problem, he decided, "Actually, I need to relax and learn how to make a good impression." Thus, he replaced his goal of "getting rid of shyness" with "increasing relaxation" and "making a good impression." Later he was able to become even more specific: "I want to relax when I'm with women. I want to make eye contact, smile, use good body language, and be able to express an interest in the person." These goals are easier to achieve because they are more specific than "getting rid of shyness" and because they involve developing new behaviors.

Denise began by saying that she wanted to be more assertive. But what exactly did that mean? What would she do when she was more assertive? She recorded instances in which she had not been assertive and later thought about what she could have done in each situation that would have been properly assertive. This gave her ideas for the kinds of behavior she wanted to increase. Here is a portion of her records:

> *Situation:* 10:00 P.M. Buddy called me for a date.
>
> *What I did:* I started to lie. "I have to work. I'm so busy. . . ." He wanted me to come over to his apartment. I didn't know what to say. Finally I told him I would see him. (Damn!)
>
> *What I should have done:* I wish I had said, "No, Buddy, I don't feel comfortable around you. We just don't get along. So no, thanks."

Situation: 3:00 P.M. A guy sat next to me on the bus and put his bag right in my lap. I was in a state of shock.
What I did: I didn't know what to say. I pretended not to notice, looked out the window, but I was thinking "You SOB." He started a conversation, and I irritably gave one-word answers.
What I should have done: I should have said, "Excuse me, can you get your bag off my lap?"

When You Aren't Sure How to Reach a Goal

Suppose you're not reaching some goal and aren't sure how to do so. Joanne wanted to be a poet but complained that she never seemed to get around to writing poetry. We pointed out that writers usually set aside some time at which they sit at the typewriter whether they feel inspired or not, and we suggested that she choose a specific hour, every other day, to do nothing but write poetry. She agreed, but as she was leaving, she turned back to say, "Actually, I tried something like that last week, but I couldn't keep the schedule." She went on to explain that she had begun to worry about how her poem would sound to other people before she had even written it. This fear prevented her from writing and made the act of trying to write very unpleasant.

Joanne was able to state precisely the full chain of actions that would produce her goal: Keep a firm schedule for writing, develop a feeling of confidence, and concentrate on the poem itself rather than on future readers' reactions. She chose the last link of the chain as her self-modification project, and in time she developed good concentration and became more productive.

If you aren't sure what to do to reach a goal, additional tactics are available. You've just read an illustration of the first one.

Tactic 5: *Specify the chain of events that will lead to your goal.* The things that happen to you are the result of a series of events. There is a chain of behaviors (your own and other people's) that, once set in motion, leads inexorably to a conclusion. The case of Joanne and her poetry illustrates such a chain. Your task in designing a plan for self-modification often involves specifying not only the simple, targeted behavior, but also the chain of behaviors that will produce it.

Suppose that your goal is to avoid eating ice cream before you go to bed at night. What chain of events might enable you to reach this goal? One is simple: Don't buy the ice cream; then it won't be there at bedtime, calling your name. This tactic is often used by successful dieters. Some compulsive overeaters break their unwanted chains by shopping only from a list, thus avoiding the items that would later place them in a tempting situation.

These examples illustrate the power of a careful chain-of-events analysis. Once you know what events need to take place in order for a desired behavior to occur, you can set them in motion. At the same time, you can avoid chains of events that lead to undesired behaviors.

Tactic 6: *Observe people who do well what you are trying to do, and then try it yourself.* Sometimes you just don't know what chain of events would lead to your goal. Ken wanted to "be a nicer person socially, have more friends." What should he do to reach that goal? What chain of events should he try to set in motion? He decided to observe a friend of his, Mary, whom Ken considered a really nice person. "You know what she does?" he asked us. "She listens to other people when they talk. She is the world's champion listener. When you're talking to her, she concentrates on you fully. She doesn't look around the room or interrupt or talk to other people or anything. She listens, hard. And that makes her seem terribly interested, very nice." Now he knows one event—listening—that will lead to his goal of being better liked, and he can build that into his social behavior.

We can't emphasize enough how important it is to observe others who do well what you want to learn to do. Tennis players know this, for example, and carefully watch what the champions do. If you grew up with people who did certain things, you probably know how to do them now, as you follow their example, but if you didn't grow up with a chance to learn those things, you can learn now by watching people who do them well.

Often it is better to observe other people performing the behavior you want to perform than to ask for advice. Most people are not expert at behavioral analysis and may give you bad or worthless advice. "Just quit eating so much" is not much help. Observing a slim person might be a lot more helpful. One of our overweight students told about watching his slim wife when she ate. "She never takes seconds. Not even at Thanksgiving. Not even when the food is fantastic. Never."

However, if you can't observe people performing the desired behavior, you may need to ask their advice. "Jan, you always get A's on your term papers. How do you go about researching and writing them?" Remember that you are asking for descriptions of particular behaviors and chains of events that lead to the goal. "I just try hard" is a useless response. "I schedule two library sessions, consult with the reference librarian about what materials are available, then write a draft and ask the professor to look it over and make comments" is extremely helpful because it describes the chain of events that leads to producing a good term paper.

Tactic 7: *Think of alternative solutions.* D'Zurilla and Nezu (1989) suggest that you think of several alternative solutions to the problem and then select one or more to implement. Your first thoughts may not be the most creative, so try for several and then choose the best. It's helpful here to use a technique called *brainstorming.* This technique has four simple rules:

1. Try for quantity; quality will follow.
2. Don't be critical, greeting every idea with a "Yes, but. . . ." Criticism can come later; for now, let the ideas flow.
3. Be freewheeling. Some ideas may be unrealistic or even weird, but that's OK.
4. Try to improve ideas by combining them. The case described in Box 2-1 illustrates this approach.

BOX 2-1

The Case of the Worn-Out Student

Ruth is 26, married, working, and also going to college. She first majored in elementary education, then added a second major—general science—to increase her chances of getting a teaching job. Her first attempt to state the problem was vague: "I'm losing my motivation for school. I've become too emotional. I argue with my husband too much. I can't really get into my science projects, even though I love the field." We asked Ruth to list all the details of her problem and search for a specific goal. She wrote:

I feel that the arguments with my husband are due to my being upset about my schoolwork.
My generally bad moods are also reactions to school.
I haven't been going to classes regularly.
I feel under a lot of pressure from the buildup of assignments.
My study habits are deteriorating.
Classes just don't seem as important to me as they used to.
I am spending more time playing tennis.
The pressure is strongest in the two graduate courses in education.
I am having trouble with these two courses. I'm actually getting frightened. The most difficult is history of education.

Ruth then brainstormed several possible solutions to her problem:

I could drop out of school.
I could change my major, go back to elementary ed.
I could drop the education courses and forget about graduate school.
I could find someone to help me with my studies.
I could sell my car, so I couldn't get to the tennis courts.
I could go to a hypnotist.

After thinking about various solutions, Ruth decided to drop the difficult history of education course, a plan she had not even considered in the beginning. She reasoned that the time she gained would enable her to catch up and do well in her other courses. At the beginning she had difficulty specifying her problem, but by listing details and brainstorming several solutions, she was able to formulate a reasonable plan.

When Your Goal Is Not a Behavioral One

There are times when your goal is not related to a particular behavior but rather to a result you want to achieve—being up on your homework, being less overweight, gaining weight, holding your weight stable, having a stack of your own completed poems.

To achieve some of these results, the behavior you have to change is obvious. For example, the stack of finished poems will grow if you increase the time you spend writing them. But for other results, what you need to change may not be so obvious. If you want to lose weight, what behavior should you change? Of course you need to change what you eat, but unless you change the behaviors that led to your being overweight—that is, *how* you eat—you will not achieve permanent weight loss.

Tactic 8: *Even if your goal is not related to a specific behavior, reaching the goal will require changing certain behaviors.* To lose weight, you need to control snacking, cut out empty-calorie foods, stay way from leftovers, eat smaller meals, eat more slowly, avoid reading or watching TV while eating. To keep the weight off, you have to change other behaviors—for example, you have to exercise regularly. Here's a sample of behaviors engaged in by many overweight people: They keep a ready supply of fattening foods in the house; they eat to avoid waste; they pile too much food on their plates; they eat rapidly and while reading or watching TV; they eat when they are emotionally upset (instead of making some other, nonfattening, response); and they eat many times each day (LeBow, 1989; Stuart & Davis, 1972). They rarely weigh themselves and don't exercise enough. Also, they often skip breakfast. They starve themselves and then overeat (Mayer, 1968). In the long run, these behaviors will have to be changed (Brownell & Foreyt, 1986).

Suppose an overweight person asks, "How would I be acting if I were slim?" The answer is implicit in the preceding paragraph: as a slim person, he or she would engage in behaviors opposite to those that contribute to the problem of overweight—eating smaller meals, exercising regularly, and so on. The goal of slimness is not related to a specific behavior, but to reach it the necessary behaviors must be developed.

To reach a nonbehavioral goal, you still must change certain behaviors. You need to eliminate old behaviors that contribute to the problem and develop new ones that help you reach the goal.

Start observing yourself, and continue doing so over a relatively long period of time. You will begin to see relationships between what you do (or don't do) and the goal you want to reach. You'll notice patterns. For example, you may observe that each time you feel down in the dumps, you respond by eating. If you keep records of your behavior in social situations, you'll see things you do that put others off—such as not listening or interrupting—and discover things that you can do that will make you more attractive. You become a scientist of yourself, seeking aspects of your behavior that prevent you from reaching your goal and finding new behaviors that will help you reach it. Self-analysis will enable you to answer two essential questions: (1) "What acts do I perform, what thoughts do I have, that keep me from reaching my goal?" and (2) "What behaviors do I need to develop in order to reach my goal?"

The Evolution of Goals

As you learn more about how your own thoughts or actions interfere with the goal you want to reach, you may go through a series of self-discoveries. A night-school student of ours named Michael was often depressed. He began a self-change project with only a vague idea of how to get rid of his depression. His first step was to record the situations that made him feel depressed. From his record, he learned that daily frustrations were a major cause of his depression. Michael then observed his reactions and realized that once he was frustrated, any additional disappointment made him depressed. He continued to observe himself, now asking "Why do frustrations make me feel so bad?" The answer was that he brooded over the frustrations. For example, if his child misbehaved, he'd spend hours thinking that he was a terrible father and that he was responsible for raising a spoiled child. He decided that brooding was self-defeating and unnecessary.

After several weeks of self-observation, recording, and analyzing his records, Michael made a breakthrough. "All along I've suspected that not *all* frustrations have the same effect on me. My kid isn't really at the root of the problem. It's my own self-esteem. Frustrations that call my self-esteem into question are the ones that I magnify." Michael analyzed what "frustrated self-esteem" meant in terms of behavior and realized that he often compared himself with people at the top. In his sales job, he knew what the top people were achieving, and he felt bad because he couldn't do as well. He concluded that his standards were too high and that always comparing himself to the leaders made him unhappy. "I seem to think that if I'm not the very best, I'm no good at all." So he set out to change his reference group. He would learn to compare himself to people who were at his own level.

People who are successful at self-change go through a series of successive approximations, often changing the target of their self-change efforts several times. For example, people seeking permanent weight control might start with the goals of learning the nutritional value of foods, exercising a little, and trying to eat less. As these people learn more about their personal eating habits, they set new targets for themselves—for example, eating more slowing, eating only low-calorie foods, or not saying "I'm starving!" to themselves when they are merely a little hungry. Later, the target of not eating when depressed might be added, and so on. As you learn more about yourself and about the actions that support or hamper your progress, you add new target behaviors.

As your understanding of yourself deepens with self-observation, so will your understanding of the appropriate techniques for change. The two questions you need to ask and reevaluate throughout the process of self-change are "What is the target I should be working on?" and "What techniques should I use to reach that target?"

For complex goals, where do you begin? Which of several possible behaviors should be your first target? The basic rule is to start by making self-observations. *First, gather data about yourself.* Second, work on specifying your goal clearly.

If developing more friends is your goal, start by observing yourself in situations in which you might work on that goal, and try to specify what behaviors you want to develop in order to reach the goal. How do you act when you are with other people? What behaviors might you develop? If weight control is your goal, your first steps are to observe your eating behavior and start specifying the behaviors and chains of events you want to change.

Overcoming Obstacles: Why You Might Self-Sabotage

There are several reasons why you might not carry out any self-modification plan at all:

- You don't anticipate reasons for failure and cope with them.
- You don't believe you can change.
- You are ambivalent about changing.

Dealing with these issues *now* will increase your chances of success.

Common Reasons for Failure at Self-Modification

A tennis player has just lost an important match and is dejectedly talking to his coach. The coach says, "What happened?"

"He beat me. I lost."

"Yeah, I know he beat you. But why?" The coach is thinking ahead to what needs to be done next.

"Well, for one thing, his backhand was better than mine."

"True," says the coach. "Specifically, what was it about your backhand that was weak?"

"Uh, well, I held it too high at the beginning of the swing, I turned toward the net too soon so I didn't follow through correctly, and I hit the ball too close to my body."

"Right," says the coach. "Now let's get to work to be sure that doesn't happen again."

Can you see what the coach has done? Instead of just thinking "I lost and don't know what to do about it," the player can now think of specific things he has to do to improve his backhand so that he won't lose next time. In this section you will read about some specific things that might go wrong in your attempts at self-change so that you can anticipate them and cope with them.

Psychologists have been studying people's attempts to change their own behavior for many years, and it's possible to make a list of the common reasons people fail in their efforts (see Box 2-2). If you know this list, you can anticipate the problems and do something about them *before* they occur.

Stress

Carol said to us,

> Three years ago, when I was getting divorced, I started eating to comfort myself and began putting on weight. I tried to go on a diet but couldn't stick to it. Life was just too hectic—what with the pain of the divorce, working, and taking care of the kids—and I couldn't cope with the added stress of dieting. Now I'm calmed down, life is smoother, and I think I can cope with weight loss.

She's right. When people are already under stress, it may be harder for them to engage in serious self-change projects, and they are more likely to

BOX 2-2

Nine Common Reasons for Failure in Self-Modification

Stress
Social pressures to repeat the old habit
Not expecting mistakes
Thinking that making mistakes means you can't cope
Blaming problems in self-modification on your personality
Lack of effort
Not believing you can change
Not taking steps to increase your confidence about changing
Ambivalence about changing

fail (Goodall & Halford, 1991; Kirschenbaum, 1987). Self-change can be stressful, particularly if you're trying to cope with something that is very challenging for you.

In these cases the best approach is to start a self-modification project to cope with the stress. Carol, for example, began an exercise program. (Actually, that was also a good way to begin a weight control plan.) Once your stress level is lowered, you can begin work on your other goals for change.

Much has been written about stress, so you may recognize this list of symptoms. Symptoms of stress include feeling emotionally drained, tense, or depressed; having a hair-trigger reaction to little things; not getting over frustration rapidly enough; or experiencing physical symptoms such as muscle tension, stomachache, headache, and so on (Schafer, 1992). If this list describes you, your first self-modification plan should be to cope with the stress.

Social Pressures to Keep Up Your Old Habits

The other people in our life strongly affect us. If you are trying to give up smoking but a friend says, "Oh, come on, have one with me. One won't hurt anything," you will feel a lot more pressure to smoke. If you're trying to lose weight and Grandma says, "I baked this especially for you," you will feel the pressure to eat. Other people can put pressure on you to keep your old habits, or they may not support your new behaviors; this will make it harder to change (Goodall & Halford, 1991; Kirschenbaum, 1987). We will discuss tactics to cope with such problems later. The basic strategies will be to teach others not to pressure you and to ask your friends to support your plans for change. You can temporarily avoid the people who can't seem to resist tempting you.

You Should Expect to Make Mistakes

Will you run into problems? Will you make mistakes? Absolutely. Guaranteed.

When old, unwanted behaviors have been automatic for a long time, one slips back into them at unguarded moments. This happens to everyone. Particularly in times of stress, habitual behaviors that helped you get through the difficulty will recur.

A typical reaction is to become totally discouraged, think, "There's nothing I can do. I'm never going to be able to control it," and give up. This phenomenon happens so frequently that it has been given a name: the **abstinence violation effect** (Marlatt & Gordon, 1985). We'll cover the abstinence violation effect in detail in Chapter 9.

For now, the point is this: Every good plan for change includes what to do when you slip—when you fall off the wagon. A man who had been trying for nearly a year to quit drinking too much told us,

> I was working very hard and had a difficult time sticking to my prescribed number of drinks. I really expected to get high because some days that seemed about the only reward I got. But I also knew that I wanted to stop drinking so much. So I made a plan: I would continue to keep a record of my drinking even when I was drinking too much. That got me through. I felt I was still somewhat in control and figured that when I got time I would deal with my problem.

Such persistence pays.

And you can learn from your mistakes. The tennis player who lost because of a weak backhand wanted to learn from his mistakes, to raise his level of skill, and you should have the very same attitude. You are going to lose a few games on the way to better self-management. Each loss is just information about skills that still need work.

Blaming Problems in Self-Modification on Your Personality

When you make mistakes, give in to temptation, or backslide, you should think of this as due either to *pressures from the environment* or to *your own current lack of skills.* If you blame problems on your personality—"I just don't have enough self-control"—you are more likely to give up. When dieters fail to stick to their diet and tell themselves it's because they don't have enough self-control, they are more likely to stop the diet (Jeffery, French, & Schmid, 1990). If you blame problems on the environment or on your own lack of skills, on the other hand, the implication is that there is something you can do—change the environment, develop your skills—so you are more likely to persist.

Watch yourself for any self-talk that says the problem is due to something wrong with your personality. For example, as you once again see that you are procrastinating on your schoolwork, are you saying to yourself, "I really don't have any self-control. I can't plan ahead"? Those kinds of thoughts lead to failure. Better to tell yourself, "Well, I don't have enough skill yet to deal with this kind of situation. Let's see, what can I do to either change the situation or develop the skill?"

Lack of Effort

One kind of error some people make is not trying hard enough. Remember, this book is not called *Change Yourself without Thinking.* You will have to do the work of self-change (Forsterling, 1985; Kirschenbaum, 1987). More often than is commonly understood, people fail at all sorts of things—school, marriage, self-control—due to lack of effort. We've found in teaching introductory psychology, for example, that most of the students who fail study only about one third as much as the students who make A's or B's (Watson, 1992). The failing students *think* they are studying as much as the ones who do well, but actually they are not.

Your Beliefs about Changing

The heavyweight Russian weight lifter Leonid Taranenko, a huge, immensely strong man, for several years held the world record for free-lifting 499½ pounds. He had tried on several occasions to lift 500 pounds above his head but had failed. In the Olympics he was once again at the top of the class in lifting, and some hoped he would break his own record. His trainer knew that Taranenko did not believe he could lift 500 pounds. At the end of the trials, when all the other strong men had been eliminated, Taranenko was allowed one more lift. "No point in failing now," he told his trainer, "I've already won. Put on 499½ pounds. I can tie my record."

"Sure," said the trainer. But he put on 500½ pounds. Taranenko looked fierce, turned red, strained—and lifted the weight above his head. It was a new world record, one not soon to be broken, and it was achieved primarily because Taranenko thought he was lifting 499½ pounds—a weight he believed he could lift.

A *self-efficacy belief* is your own estimate of your skill in dealing with some task (Bandura, 1986). It's not a general belief about yourself, but a specific belief that is tied to a particular task. It is not a yes/no belief, but a yes/maybe/no continuum.

What we believe about our ability to change affects how hard we try to change, and that in turn affects our success. Taranenko believed he could lift 499½ pounds if he tried hard enough, so he tried very hard. Many research studies have shown that if people believe they can change difficult target behaviors, they are more likely to be successful (Bandura, 1989, 1991).

When people encounter challenging situations, if they think of the situation as a challenge to their level of skill, *they are more likely to learn the skills necessary to deal with the situation.* In one study, for example, people had to manage a challenging work situation. Those who thought of the task as a set of managerial skills they needed to learn performed well and learned the new skills, whereas those who thought of the task as something not quite possible did not learn the new skills and did not perform well (Bandura & Wood, 1989).

The same principle applies to your self-modification efforts, which also involve learning a new set of managerial skills. Some people do control their studying, or eating, or moods. That means they are using skills you have not yet learned. For example, in one study, which involved people who were extremely afraid of snakes, a 6-foot Burmese python was used. The subjects were given a detailed series of training experiences—such as watching a person who was not afraid of the snake approach and handle it—and used the same kinds of skill-building techniques we will teach you in this book. The subjects were gradually taught first to approach and finally to fondle the snake (Bandura, Reese, & Adams, 1982). Their self-efficacy beliefs about performing the various steps increased, and so did their actual ability to perform the steps leading to touching the python. Thus, it is possible to increase one's self-efficacy beliefs.

Three hundred years ago the philosopher Spinoza said, "So long as a man imagines he cannot do something, so long as he is determined not to do it, then it is impossible for him to do it." The belief that you can cope does not in itself eliminate all difficulties. But the self-confidence makes for greater effort in attempting to overcome difficulties and allows you to tackle problems with less emotionality. It also allows you to think of the specific skills you need to develop.

Do you believe you can do the things you have to do in order to change yourself? You can become aware of some specific beliefs that will affect your behavior by answering these questions:

1. Will you be able to read carefully to the end of the book? This means thinking about what you read and applying the ideas to yourself, figuring out how to use the ideas so you can change.
   Yes ☐ No ☐ Maybe ☐
2. Sometimes we evaluate an idea and reject it without really trying it out. In order to change, you will have to try out the ideas in this book. Will you be able to try the ideas in the book before you evaluate them?
   Yes ☐ No ☐ Maybe ☐
3. Will you be able to do the exercise at the end of each chapter, in which you apply the ideas from that chapter to your own self-modification project?
   Yes ☐ No ☐ Maybe ☐
4. Do you really *intend* to change (Ajzen & Fishbein, 1980; Ford, 1989), or are you just hoping for a "magic bullet"?
   Yes ☐ No ☐ Maybe ☐

How to Increase Your Self-Efficacy Beliefs

You should take the following steps in order to increase your confidence that you can make the changes you need to make.

First, pick a project for which you can say "yes" or a strong "maybe" to the preceding questions. Don't start with something you expect to fail at. As you develop skill at self-modification, you can undertake projects that previously would not have been possible.

Second, discriminate between your past performance and your present project (Goldfried & Robins, 1982). That was then, this is now. You may have learned from past failures that you cannot do certain things. But past failures are not necessarily a portent of future failure. You can gradually develop skills you never had before. All the people who successfully learned to handle the Burmese python had previously been extremely afraid of snakes. The researchers used techniques such as gradual approximations to a goal—see Chapter 6—to teach the subjects to approach the snake, and the subjects learned to perform the new behavior.

Third, pay close attention to your successes, no matter how small they are. Some people have a tendency to remember their failures but not their successes. If you expect failure, you are likely to look for signs of failure. If you force yourself to look for signs of success, it affects your beliefs and your behavior. George, who wanted to improve his social relations with women, said,

> I think I always expected not to make a nice impression, so I was looking for that. If there was a pause in the conversation, I'd think "Oh, she's bored," or "I'm not making a good impression." I taught myself to look for positive signs instead. Now if there's a pause in the conversation, I think, "She feels relaxed—good."

Focusing on your successes means that you should keep good records about your project (see Chapter 3) so that you can see if you are making some progress. A person who sticks to a study schedule for four days and then fails to do so on the fifth should not think, "It's no use. I can't do it." This ignores the four days of success.

Fourth, list the specific kinds of situations in which you expect to have the greatest difficulty. For example, Rosa, who wanted to become more assertive, made a list of "situations in which I have a hard time doing what I need to do."

> Easiest: dealing with strangers—for example, clerks
> Fairly easy: students at school
> Moderate: my two brothers, my mom
> Getting difficult: my boss
> The most difficult: my dad

Once she had made this list, her strategy was clear: begin with the easier tasks and tackle the harder ones after she had experienced success—and built some skill—with the easier ones.

Rank-ordering the situations in which you anticipate difficulty allows you to put off dealing with the harder ones until you are better prepared and helps you avoid discouraging failures early in your self-change plan. It also allows you to discount mistakes you make early in the plan. If Rosa finds herself in a situation in which she fails to be assertive with her father, she can say to herself, "Well, I knew I was going to have a lot of trouble being assertive with my dad." Then she can remind herself of successes in other, easier situations. This way she is less likely to abandon a potentially successful plan.

Some projects—such as weight loss—require several separate subprojects; for example, you have to increase exercise, cut out fatty foods, eat more slowly, and so on. Improving your study habits might require subprojects on managing time, changing how you study, and changing what you think about studying. To begin, pick a subproject that seems relatively easy for you.

Use a scale like the one Rosa used to evaluate the different kinds of situations you will face in terms of how difficult they will be for you.

	Situation
easiest	____________________
fairly easy	____________________
moderate	____________________
getting difficult	____________________
most difficult	____________________

For example, Andrew intends to give up smoking. Here's how he filled out this scale.

	Situation
easiest	mid-afternoon smokes
fairly easy	late-night smokes
moderate	smoking alone
getting difficult	with coffee or alcohol
most difficult	after meals

This kind of analysis allows you to realize that you have greater control in some situations than in others and to begin with the situations in which you have greatest control (see Box 2-3).

Ambivalence about Goals: The Pros and Cons of Changing

Teruko was bothered by her poor performance at college. She had been valedictorian of her high school class and was considered brilliant by everyone, but now she was making mostly C's. She started a self-change plan to increase her studying, but after a few days it fizzled. "You know," she said, "it's really comfortable this way. I don't have to work at all to make C's. And I don't have to find out what my upper limits are, something my dad is always urging me to do. I can just coast. For now, that's all I want." Teruko found her present behavior rewarding and really didn't want to change.

As the American humorist Dorothy Parker wrote:

I shall stay the way I am
Because I do not give a damn.

BOX 2-3

The Eating Self-Efficacy Scale

Drs. Shirley Glynn and Audrey Ruderman (1986) developed a questionnaire to measure a person's perceived self-efficacy in coping with a variety of tempting eating situations. This gives you a fine-grained analysis of the different situations in which a person has to learn to control his or her eating. Use of the scale allows a person who wants to develop greater self-control over eating to see that there are a number of causes of overeating and to realize which situations are easiest or most difficult to deal with.

Instructions: For each item, rate the likelihood that you would have difficulty controlling your overeating in that situation. Use this scale:

1	2	3	4	5	6	7
no difficulty controlling eating			moderate difficulty		most difficulty controlling eating	

How difficult is it to control your overeating . . .

1. after work or school
2. when you feel restless
3. around holiday time
4. when you feel upset
5. when you feel tense
6. with friends
7. when you are preparing food
8. when you feel irritable
9. as part of a social occasion dealing with food (at a restaurant or dinner party)
10. with family members
11. when you feel annoyed
12. when you feel angry
13. when you are angry at yourself
14. when you feel depressed
15. when you feel impatient
16. when you want to sit back and enjoy some food
17. after an argument
18. when you feel frustrated
19. when tempting food is in front of you
20. when you want to cheer up
21. when there is a lot of food available to you (refrigerator is full)
22. when you feel overly sensitive
23. when you feel nervous
24. when you feel hungry
25. when you feel anxious or worried

A student told us, "It wasn't until I tried to stop drinking that I realized how I use a beer to cheer myself up. Then I saw that I really get a lift from it."

When you cannot change some problem behavior or reach a desired goal, it may be because the payoff of the behavior is greater than you suspected. Any behavior that you have continued for a long time offers some advantages. People who bite their nails find comfort in their habit. People who don't exercise enjoy the pleasure of inactivity. People who accomplish little like the freedom of not working on a schedule. Ask yourself, *"What will I lose by changing?"*

Changing can also lead to new situations that we are not prepared to deal with. Faith had been about 50 pounds overweight, and in the previous year she had lost almost 40 pounds. She explained,

> I didn't lose it equally all over, though, and I was, to be candid, pretty busty. Men liked this, but I didn't like it at all. I hated all the attention they paid to my body. So I just let myself go and regained 30 pounds. Now I'm fat and unbothered once more.

Lizette Peterson (1983) has reported similar cases. She mentions a young man who improved his study skills and saw his grades go up, only to find that his parents expected more of him than they had before. Sometimes changing ourselves leads to other issues that we have to cope with.

There are long- and short-term advantages and disadvantages to any self-change plan. You are more likely to succeed if you examine these at the beginning of your self-modification project. Using Box 2-4 as a guide, make a list of the long- and short-term pros and cons of changing your behavior. List your hopes and your fears about changing. For example, you might hope to look good and feel as though you're in control if you lose weight—advantages—but also fear that you will be hungry all the time or will suddenly start binge eating—disadvantages (Fanning, 1990). Your fear of trying to change is normal, and your fear that you may not be able to change is normal (Flanagan, 1990). But things are new now because you are going to move at your own pace, under your own control—a real advantage of self-modification. At this point, you want to face the real advantages of not changing and think about them.

People who make this kind of list are more likely to be successful in their plans for change (Janis, 1982; Kirschenbaum & Flanery, 1984). As another example, Box 2-5 suggests the advantages and disadvantages a heavy drinker might have to face in the decision to stop getting drunk.

Once you've made your list, keep it. Take it out now and then to remind yourself of the reasons that you want to change. Once your project is under way, you will forget some of the reasons, or they may no longer seem as important as they did when you were really suffering with your problem. If you begin to falter in carrying out your project, rereading your list can help you see the reasons to keep going (Curry & Marlatt, 1987).

Why does making this kind of list help? *First,* it helps you anticipate obstacles to changing so you can take steps to overcome them. For example, if you know your spouse is going to be made uncomfortable by the new you, you can make the changes gradually or try to build protection into your plan. *Second,* making the list encourages you to be realistic—to face what you

BOX 2-4

Advantages and Disadvantages of My Self-Change Project

Instructions: Consider the short-term and long-term advantages and disadvantages of changing. Take into account the effects both on you and on others, both tangible and intangible. Consider how you will feel about yourself and how others will feel.

Short-term advantages of changing:

____

____

____

Long-term advantages of changing:

____

____

____

Short-term disadvantages of changing (advantages of staying the same):

____

____

____

Long-term disadvantages of changing:

____

____

____

want and don't want, and what you are willing to do to get what you want. If you know you hate to sweat and feel tired but think you ought to increase your exercising, realizing this now may enable you to work out a plan to deal with these obstacles. You could try swimming, for example; swimmers don't get hot. *Third,* making the list allows you to plan ahead. You can be more realistic in your plans and goals, which makes it more likely you will succeed. Lani, a 19-year-old sophomore living off campus, wrote:

> It helped a lot when I listed the pros and cons of changing and then did something to minimize the disadvantages. My goal was to increase my studying. I modeled myself on Linda, who did all her studying at school, while I seemed to spend a lot of time socializing during the day. I thought I'd be more efficient if I did my work during the day, too. But when I listed the disadvantages of changing, I realized I was going to lose all that time with my friends at school. Linda wasn't a good model for me. She is married, and when she goes home at night she's with her husband all evening. I live by myself, so my socializing comes during the day, and I really wouldn't have wanted to give it up. I revised my plan to increase my studying, but during the evening. That worked great!

BOX 2-5

The Pros and Cons of Stopping Drinking

Here are some issues a heavy drinker might consider in making the decision to drink less (Curry & Marlatt, 1987):

1. Why should I moderate my drinking?

Short-term considerations	
Pros	*Cons*
Feeling that my drinking is under my control Avoiding illness from overdrinking Reducing tension Saving money Social approval from light drinkers	It's work to break old habits Social pressure from heavy drinkers Initial awkwardness with new habits
Long-term considerations	
Pros	*Cons*
Increased self-control and self-confidence Improved health No hangovers Weight loss New friends and hobbies	Loss of friendships with heavy drinkers Loss of the joy of being blasted

There are also things to consider in the decision to continue or resume an old habit. Think about the short- and long-term advantages of continuing your old "problem" behavior.

2. Why should I continue or resume heavy drinking?

Short-term considerations	
Pros	*Cons*
Immediate gratification Consistency with past self-image Approval from heavy drinkers Excuse for irresponsibility Faster sleep onset Perceptions of increased personal power	Illness from overdrinking Financial loss Social embarrassment Disapproval from light drinkers Impaired coordination Possibility of personal injury
Long-term considerations	
Pros	*Cons*
Consistency with old self-image Friendships with heavy drinkers	Decreased self-esteem Financial loss Added health problems Interpersonal conflicts Occupational disruptions Physical dependency on alcohol

Building Commitment

Even with the most detailed, specific plan, certain problems are bound to arise during the process of self-modification. You will be tempted to go astray, and you may grow weary of the work involved in changing. An effective plan takes these future problems into consideration. This section discusses how you can build commitment to change and how you can anticipate and neutralize the inevitable temptations. *Commitment to change is not something you have; it is something you do* (Coates & Thoresen, 1977). Commitment itself is a set of behaviors.

Commitment means making plans on how you will reach your goal in spite of the obstacles you will encounter. It's not just an inner feeling of determination; it is a set of specific things you can do to reach your goals. Box 2-6 tells the story of one person's efforts to build and maintain the commitment to stop smoking

Prepare for Temptations

Temptations to stop your self-change project are almost certainly going to occur. There will be times when studying more seems like a really dumb idea, or when exercising seems ridiculous, or when a cigarette is calling you to come. If you have a plan for dealing with temptation, you are more likely to be successful in your self-modification project (Shiffman, 1982). (See Box 2-7.) You make these plans long before the temptation occurs, not immediately before. You should actually make a list of the times when you expect temptation to occur and devise ways to cope with those situations.

Avoid situations you know will be tempting. Don't go to places where you might be tempted. Don't do things that will tempt you too much (Kelley, 1983). Later, when your newly developed behavior has become more or less automatic—"I'll have a ginger ale, please"—you can go back to parties where beer drinking is heavy. Some people think the only way to show "real" self-control is by meeting temptation head on and staring it down, as Gandhi did when he slept beside female members of his entourage. But it is wise to pick your own time and place to do battle with your demons. Begin by choosing situations where you will win.

Minimize the tempting quality of the situation. For those who want to reduce alcohol or food consumption, it is useful to drink water before going out so as not to arrive thirsty. The effect is to reduce the tempting quality of the food and drinks that are offered. The woman who drank a glass of skim milk whenever she began to feel too hungry was minimizing the temptation to overeat. A man who found many women attractive but wanted to remain faithful to his new wife told us, "Whenever I meet someone who is very attractive, I immediately find something about her I don't like and think about that a little bit so I won't be tempted to flirt or even think she might be as desirable as my wife."

When you are in the tempting situation, distract yourself. Small children are able to deliberately distract themselves to get through tempting periods (Pat-

BOX 2-6

Borrowing Self-Confidence, Coping with Temptation, and Building Commitment: A Well-Planned Attack on Smoking

Ron, a 30-year-old student in an introductory psychology class at a California college, decided to do a self-modification project for extra credit. He wanted to give up smoking by using the techniques of self-modification, and he drew up a very careful plan. He had successfully given up overdrinking earlier, and that had built up his confidence that he could now give up smoking—psychologists call this "self-efficacy."

First, Ron spent a week keeping a diary of every cigarette he smoked, noting when, where, and how he felt, plus any consequence of smoking. He was smoking one and a half to two packs each day.

Ron decided to cut down by one cigarette per day so that he would be completely off smoking in 35 days. He hoped that by cutting down by only one per day, he would minimize the withdrawal symptoms. He decided to set aside the money he saved (which was considerable!) toward buying a motorcycle he had wanted for a long time. He figured that the money he saved by not smoking would pay for the cycle on the installment plan.

Ron knew that if he carried lots of cigarettes he might smoke them, so he coped with that temptation in advance by carrying only the number of cigarettes he was allowed each day. He stopped carrying his pack in his breast pocket—with a backup pack nearby—and instead carried only a few cigarettes at a time in a plastic bag. He stored the rest of the daily allotment with his friends or in his car.

Ron committed himself publicly to his plan by talking about it with his instructor and his friends. He discussed it at length in his weekly AA meeting. He had talked with his instructor and believed that the would only receive credit for his project if he succeeded. (His instructor wasn't sure about this but thought it best not to disabuse Ron at this point.)

Ron also substituted some new behaviors. He found himself hitting his breast pocket with his right hand whenever he would normally go for a cigarette. The empty pocket served as a reminder that he was now "clean" in yet another area of his life, and that made him feel good about not smoking.

Ron was able to buy his motorcycle and after a year and a half has not gone back to smoking.

Note that Ron specifically felt he could stop smoking—he had high self-efficacy—because he had been able to stop drinking. He knew it would require a thoughtful plan, however. He set realistic goals and had many subgoals (such as cutting down each day), so he could see frequent progress. He kept records so he knew he was progressing. He knew there would be many temptations, however, and he planned in advance to cope with them. For example, he didn't carry more cigarettes than he was allowed each day, and he used his friends to help him stay straight. He substituted hitting his breast pocket for pulling out a cigarette, and that reminded him that he was moving toward his final goal. He also arranged to be rewarded for quitting, both by his friends' encouragement and by the instructor's grade in the class. Finally, he built his commitment by involving his friends, his AA group, and his instructor.

SOURCE: Suellen Rubin, Cabrillo College.

BOX 2-7

Tactics to Cope with Temptation

1. Avoid tempting situations.
2. Minimize the tempting quality.
3. If you are in a tempting situation, distract yourself.
4. Invest a lot in your project early.
5. When tempted, remind yourself of your goal.
6. Remind yourself of any long-term, delayed punishments for some unwanted behavior.
7. Be explicit in your escape clauses.
8. Ask other people to remind you of your goals.

terson & Mischel, 1975). We adults can do the same. Faced with a luscious but fattening sundae, think about the person sitting across from you at the dinner table, the chair you're sitting on, the topic of conversation—anything. but don't think about the dessert. A man who lost a lot of weight told us, "I realized that I would eat my meal and then sit looking at the rest of the food on the table. Just staring at it. And sooner or later, I'd start eating it. So I consciously tell myself, 'Don't look at it, look away.' " If you cannot resist looking at the food, use "cool" perceptions: it is pink; it is made of milk products; it looks like plastic.

Invest a lot in the project as early as possible (Cooper & Axsom, 1982; Kelley, 1983). Put as much effort into it as you can. Do all the exercises suggested in this chapter, and keep very careful records, beginning with Chapter 3. When you are tempted, the more you have invested, the less likely you will be to give in. The exerciser coming home after a hard day thinks, "I could skip today's run. I'm not in the mood. But I've put a lot of effort into this exercise program, and that's worth more than loafing today." Tie your most rational thinking to the project. "It would be a real mistake not to make this self-modification a success, because it's something I really want."

Another way to increase your investment in the project is to make a public commitment that you are going to change (Meichenbaum & Turk, 1987; Shelton & Levy, 1981). Ron, in Box 2-6, told all his friends that he was going to quit smoking. If you tell people you intend to change, the threat of a public failure may keep you working on your project. Unwillingness to tell people may be a sign that you don't really intend to change or that you don't believe you can change.

When you are tempted—when you hear the Sirens singing—*remind yourself of your goal* (Graziano, 1975; Lazarus, 1971). Grace took up jogging to lose weight and be healthier. But she realized that she jogged along thinking, "This is stupid—and so boring—I'm going to quit." These thoughts were self-defeating, so instead she reminded herself, "I really want to look better and be healthier, and the best way is to jog. It's worth it. I won't quit." John wanted to improve his grade point average so he could have a better chance of getting a good job after college. But at times the temptation to do some other activity was great—for example, when his friends asked him to play basketball in the afternoon. When that happened, he reminded himself, "No, I really do want to improve my grades, and that means I have to study now."

Making statements about your long-term goals can help you resist momentary temptations. "As much as I would like to just go to sleep, I am going to practice my relaxation exercises; in the long run I'll get more rest!" "It would be a relief to tell him to go to hell, but I really do want to learn to deal with people in a friendlier way." "I'd like to give in and watch TV, but I watch too much TV, and I do want to cut down." "I'm tired, and it would be easy to say 'No, I don't want to make love tonight,' but I really do want to be more loving."

When tempted, remind yourself that it was *your free choice* that got you started on the self-modification project (Meichenbaum & Turk, 1987). Sometimes we lose sight of that and come to treat the self-change plan as though it were imposed on us by someone else. A woman we know began smoking but not recording the cigarettes she smoked, as if she were hiding the fact that she was smoking from someone. "But wait," she thought. "Who am I hiding this from? Myself!" Whenever you are tempted to stop the self-change project, remind yourself that you started it out of free choice: Don't you want to continue?

Remind yourself of the long-term but delayed punishments for unwanted behaviors. "Yeah, I want to smoke a cigarette right now, but in the long term it could kill me." "Telling him off would feel good right now, but in the long run he'd stop being my friend, and I don't want to lose any friends." "Not studying might feel neat right now, but in the long run I'd really pay for it."

Prepare a written list of self-reminders you can use when temptation strikes. Include in your self-reminders all the advantages of reaching your goal: "I'll feel so great when I have caught up with my homework—free as a bird!" "I'm going to look terrific when I've lost ten pounds—slim and sexy!" "I'm going to enjoy having new friends, so it's worth overcoming my shyness and going to the party."

Sometimes you will be tempted to think, "Well, just this one time . . ." But life can become a string of just-this-one-times, and before you know it, years have gone by without your being a step closer to your goal. Lots of smokers go to their (early) graves thinking, "Someday I'm going to give up cigarettes." Prepare a special reminder for the just-this-one-time situation: "I'm always telling myself 'Just this one time.' But I really do want to (reach that goal)."

Be explicit about the situations in which you do not intend to change. As you develop your plan for self-change, you should specify occasions when you will intentionally allow yourself to engage in the old, unwanted behavior—these parts of your self-change plan are called **escape clauses.** Escape clauses account for times when you know you're going to overeat, or drink too much, or goof off even though there are things to do.

Make these escape clauses explicit, and set limits for the behaviors you want to control. A plan should clearly state all intended escapes, whether or not they are wise. If you really intend to overeat every Sunday when you are with your parents, say so. If this escape clause wreaks havoc with your diet, you can then make an intelligent choice as to which is more important—Mom's cake or weight loss. An unexamined escape clause may ultimately destroy your plan altogether. But if you are explicit about the situations in which you intend to continue your old behavior, you are actually bringing that behavior more under your own control, and that's good. The important thing is to choose when you will or will not perform the old behavior; don't just let the situations control you.

Ask other people to remind you. Darrell has been trying to cut down on his drinking. Tonight he and his wife, Tina, are going to a party. Darrell says to Tina, "Do me a favor. I'm going to be tempted to drink too much tonight, and you know I want to stop that. So if you see me taking a second drink, would you please remind me that I really want to cut down?" Research by Richard Passman (1977) suggests that you can increase your chances of success if you prearrange with another person to remind you when you are faced with temptation. Groups such as Weight Watchers and Alcoholics Anonymous use this technique (Stuart, 1977).

You are *not* asking the other person to punish you. Darrell doesn't want Tina to tell him he's a lush and a bum because he has taken a second drink. He wants her to remind him of his *own* resolve not to drink too much. If others misinterpret the task and begin to inflict punishment on you, remind them that you're asking for a *reminder of your own goal,* nothing more. At the same time, you need to beware of the tendency to punish the person who does the reminding: "I know it's my second drink! I'm not stupid!" Sometimes people work out a code in order to avoid an embarrassing interaction. One of our students reported that she and her husband had agreed that he tended to put her down in conversations with others, and he agreed to stop. He still occasionally did it out of habit, though, and both agreed she should remind him when she felt he was doing it. But they soon discovered she couldn't say, "You're putting me down," in front of others, as the couple found that embarrassing. Now when she feels he's putting her down, she touches the corner of her mouth. He gets the message, but others do not.

Set Goals and Make Plans to Reach Them

You can increase commitment by setting goals and planning how to reach them. *Are your current actions getting you what you want?* If you have goals you are not reaching, make a specific statement of the goal, and then break the goal into subgoals (Locke & Latham, 1990). What are you doing that keeps you from reaching your goal, or what are you not doing?

Long-term goals can be broken into subgoals, which can be worked on one at a time. Patricia's long-term goal was to place her relationship with her lover, Rick, on a more egalitarian basis. This issue included such themes as who did chores, who made decisions, who would be responsible for child care, and so on. But she started with one subgoal, that of being more assertive in issues relating to their love life. She gave herself instructions about how to act in a particular situation: "When Rick touches my body when I'm not expecting it, I'll say to him, 'Rick, please don't do that when I don't know it's coming. It's not sexy, it just startles me, and I don't enjoy it at all.'"

Goals should be moderately specific (Cervone, Jiwani, & Wood, 1991; Kirschenbaum, 1985). Most people realize that specific goals—"I'm going to study at least 15 hours per week"—are better than vague goals—"I'm going to study more." Short-range goals are more motivating than long-range goals. "I am going to study from 6:30 to 8:30 tonight" is more motivating than "I'm going to study on Tuesday of next week."

However, *how you phrase your goal is very important.* Be specific, but be sure to leave room for flexibility. Do not tie your goal to a particular time or place; it's the final result that matters, not precisely where or when you do the work. It is better to say, "I'm going to study 15 hours per week," than to say, "I'm going to study Friday night from 6:30 to 8:20." If you do not meet that particular goal, you might assume that you are not capable of self-control and stop trying. On the other hand, if your goal is to study a certain number of hours per week, then if circumstances prevent it on Friday night, there's always Saturday afternoon for catching up.

Whenever you don't meet a subgoal, it just means that you have some more learning to do, a greater degree of skill to develop. What kept you from studying on Friday night? You should not expect to show mastery from the beginning (Elliott & Dweck, 1988).

Conflicts between Short-Term and Long-Term Goals

One element that often keeps people from mastering their own behavior is the simple fact that *they are caught in a conflict between their long-term goals and their short-term goals.* In fact, this is one of the major problems in many self-modification efforts. For example, in the long run Judy wants to be an assertive, self-possessed woman. In the short run, on the other hand, she may worry that if she speaks up she will hurt her boyfriend's feelings or not seem to be a "nice" person. In order to change, Judy has to realize this conflict in goals exists and to cope with it.

Many problems in self-control can be seen as a conflict between your short-term goals and your long-term goals (Malott, 1989). A person who wants to quit smoking, for example, has the long-term goal of being healthier, but when the addiction calls she has the short-term goal of gratifying the urge to smoke. A person who wants to lose weight faces the same kind of conflict: in the long run, he wants to be slimmer, but in the short run he may very strongly want to eat. The rewards for giving in to temptation are immediate, whereas the punishments for the behavior are delayed (Epstein, 1984).

If you can anticipate these moments, you can be on guard against them, prepared to remind yourself of your long-term goals. Part of your planning

has to involve dealing with conflicts between your short-term goals, which may in the long run make you unhappy, and your long-term goals, which in the long run may make you happy, but in the short run can make you unhappy.

This kind of problem comes up not only for people who are trying to rid themselves of some unwanted behavior like smoking or overeating, but also for people who are trying to develop some behavior, such as studying, that will help them reach their long-term goal. Procrastination is often a conflict between your short-term goal of goofing off and your long-term goal of accomplishing something. In the short run not studying, doing something else, is appealing, but in the long run that defeats your goal of getting through college. In this case, too, you need to cope with the conflict between your short-term desire to goof off and your long-term desire to get through college. Box 2-8 outlines these kinds of situations. The techniques for coping with temptation (listed in Box 2-7) also apply to coping with this kind of goal conflict; use them all.

Sometimes, even if your goal is happiness, the wisest course of action is to give up some immediate happiness in order to get more happiness later (Baumeister & Scher, 1988). Sometimes you need short-term pain for long-term gain. When you are faced with the temptation to give in and act for short-term gratification, even though in the long run doing so will make you

BOX 2-8

Conflicts between Short-Term and Long-Term Goals

	Short-Term	*Long-Term*
Behavior excesses (undesired acts that bring some pleasure but that you want to eliminate)	wanted	unwanted
Behavior deficits (desired acts that bring some displeasure but that you want to increase)	unwanted	wanted

SOURCE: From R. F. Rakos, personal communication with the authors, 1992.

unhappy, tell yourself, "Well, I've got to give up that little happiness right now in order to get a lot more happiness in the future" (Lydon & Zanna, 1990). As one of our students told us,

> I always gave in to slight pangs of hunger and ate, which meant that I never lost any weight. I felt like I couldn't cope with hunger, that I just had to eat when I was hungry. In fact, at that moment it really didn't make any short-term sense to cope: I was hungry, that made me unhappy, so I ate. Then I realized I don't have to be happy every short-term minute, particularly if that is making me unhappy in the long run. I just told myself, "I'm not going to worry about being happy right now. I will be a lot happier in the long run if I don't worry about it right now." That thought has allowed me to stick to my weight-loss plan for several weeks.

People who successfully lose weight have been found to talk to themselves about long-term goals (Schwartz & Inbar-Saban, 1988).

The Self-Contract

As you build commitment to your goal for change, write out each element of your plan as a *self-contract.* The first paragraph of the contract is a statement of your intention. You will be able to add more details to your self-contract by the end of each chapter, from Chapters 3 through 8. For now, write your goal and intentions as clearly as possible. Then add:

> I am willing to change my behavior as necessary to reach the goal I have chosen and will carry out the steps suggested in the text. Specifically, I am willing to do the work suggested in Step Two at the end of this chapter, even though it will take an hour or so to do.

Then—if you are willing to do the work—sign your name.

Does this really help? Yes. In several different experiments, some people who were undertaking a self-change project were asked to write a self-contract and others were not; among all the participants, the people who signed the contract increased their chances of success (Griffin & Watson, 1978; Seidner, 1973, cited in Kanfer, 1977). By itself, a self-contract won't keep you from all temptation, but it is one more effective technique to use in building your commitment to work at self-change.

Tips for Typical Topics

Most chapters in this book contain a section called "Tips for Typical Topics," in which we point out how you can apply the ideas discussed in the chapter to the most common types of self-modification projects. Specific pieces of information that are helpful for each kind of project are included in the "Tips" sections. Here is a list of topics commonly addressed in our classes in self-directed behavior:

- Anxiety and stress
- Assertion
- Depression and low self-esteem
- Exercise and athletics
- Relations with others: social anxieties, social skills, and dating
- Smoking, drinking, and drugs
- Studying and time management
- Weight loss and overeating

For each topic, the Tips section suggests specific ideas, but these cannot be substituted for reading and thinking about the principles offered in the whole chapter. The specific ideas should be integrated into your overall plan for self-change.

At the end of the book is a topic index, which lists all discussions of each topic throughout the book. For example, everything said about assertion is listed together for ready reference. Thus, you can check the topic index and read all the information about your particular topic for self-modification now, if you like.

Chapter Summary

Specifying the Targets for Change

You need well-defined objectives that are specified in terms of particular behaviors in particular situations. The aim is to be able to complete this sentence:

My goal is to change ______________ when ______________.
(thought, action, feeling) (situation)

To specify behaviors-in-situations, try these tactics:

1. Make a list of concrete examples.
2. List the details of your problem.
3. Become an observer of yourself.

Even if your goal is to eliminate some unwanted action,

4. Always try to increase some desirable behavior.

If you aren't sure what to do to reach your goal,

5. Specify the chain of events that will lead to your goal.
6. Observe other people who do well what you are trying to learn to do.
7. Think of alternative solutions.

And even if your goal is not related to some behavior,

8. Reaching it will require changing certain behaviors.

With complex problems, you are likely to move through a series of approximations to your goal as your self-understanding deepens. Start by making self-observations and specifying your goal clearly.

Overcoming Obstacles: Why You Might Self-Sabotage

You may not anticipate reasons for failure and cope with them. These are the most common reasons for failure at self-modification:

1. Stress
2. Social pressures to repeat the old habit
3. Not expecting mistakes
4. Thinking that making mistakes means you can't cope
5. Blaming problems in self-modification on your personality
6. Lack of effort
7. Not believing you can change
8. Not taking steps to increase your confidence about changing
9. Ambivalence about changing

How to Increase Your Self-Efficacy Beliefs

To increase self-efficacy beliefs, pick a project that will allow you to say "yes" to the questions on page 44. Discriminate between your past performance and your present project. Keep good records. Pay attention to your successes. Identify subgoals that you have a good chance of attaining. List the specific kinds of situations in which you expect to have difficulty carrying out the necessary behaviors, and use this list to guide your early experiences.

Ambivalence about goals: the pros and cons of changing. Make a list of the advantages and disadvantages of changing so that you can rationally evaluate whether you really want to change.

Building Commitment

Commitment is not something you *have,* it is something you *do.* Plan for temptation—for times when it will seem better not to change than to do so. What can you do to be prepared?

1. Avoid tempting situations.
2. Minimize the tempting quality.
3. If you are in a tempting situation, distract yourself.
4. Invest a lot in your project early.
5. When tempted, remind yourself of your goal.
6. Remind yourself of any long-term, delayed punishments for the unwanted behavior.
7. Be explicit in your escape clauses.
8. Ask other people to remind you of your goals.

Set goals and make plans to reach them. Work out subgoals and make plans for how to reach them. Relatively specific plans on how to reach a goal are better than vague plans. However, your subgoals should not be too short-range, and your plans should not be overly specific. Intermediate goals with moderate degrees of specificity of behavior to be performed may be best because such goals allow some flexibility and you will not feel discouraged if you fail on just one occasion.

Conflicts between short-term and long-term goals. Many problems in self-control can be seen as conflicts between your short-term goals and your long-term goals. Your "undesirable" behaviors may be appealing in the short run but detrimental in the long run. On the other hand, certain "desirable" behaviors may not appeal to you now, but you know that performing them now will help you in the long run. To deal with this conflict, you can use all the tactics you learned for dealing with temptation. You can also tell yourself that you may have to be a bit unhappy in the short run in order to be happier in the long run.

The self-contract. Write a self-contract detailing the work you have to do to achieve self-change, and sign it if you intend to do the work.

YOUR OWN SELF-DIRECTION PROJECT: STEP TWO

Before going on to Chapter 3, do the exercises suggested here for specifying the problem and building commitment. A few students have said to us, "Gee, this is a big assignment." They're right. You have to do a bit of thinking in order to overcome the bad habits of the past. The good part is that if you do the exercises, you will succeed.

Part One: Specifying the Goal

Specify your goal as some behavior-in-a-situation that you wish to either decrease or increase. Even if you want to decrease some undesirable behavior, you should be able to state as your goal an *increase* of some other behavior that is incompatible with the undesired one. If at this point you cannot state your problem as a behavior-in-a-situation, go through each of the procedures in this chapter, step by step, for your chosen goal.

Part Two: Overcoming Obstacles
Make plans for what to do when you slip back into your old, unwanted behaviors. What will you do to be sure you don't quit your self-modification efforts?

Answer the questions on page 44 about your self-efficacy beliefs. List the situations in which you expect to have difficulty performing the desired actions, and rank the situations according to their degree of difficulty.

List the pros and cons of changing. What will you gain? What will you lose? What are the short-range and the long-range pros and cons of changing?

Part Three: Building Commitment
Make plans for dealing with tempting situations. Answer these questions: How can I avoid tempting situations? How can I invest as much as possible in the project as early as possible? How can I minimize temptation or distract myself from it? To whom will I make the public commitment that I am going to change? List these people.

Make a list of reminders to give yourself when you are tempted. What are the delayed punishments for your unwanted behavior? Write down your escape clauses. Also make a list of the people you are going to ask to remind you to stay on track.

Establish subgoals leading to your final goal, and make plans for reaching them. Make a list of the subgoals.

Now write a self-contract. First specify your goal, then include this statement: "I am willing to change my behaviors as necessary to reach the goal I have chosen and will carry out the steps suggested in the text." Sign the contract.

This series of acts doesn't mean that you are permanently committed to your first goal. You may decide to change it as you progress. The point of this self-promise is that you start with a goal that is important enough for you to actually perform the steps in self-modification.

When you have completed all three parts of Step Two, go on to Chapter 3.

3

Self-Knowledge: Observation and Recording

Outline

- Structured Diaries
- Recording Frequency and Duration
- Recording the Intensity of Emotions
- Practicalities of Record Keeping
- Planning for Change
- *Tips for Typical Topics*
- *Chapter Summary*
- *Your Own Self-Direction Project: Step Three*

Learning Objectives

Structured Diaries

1. What do you record in a structured diary?
   a. What can you record under "Antecedents"?
   b. What can you record under "Behaviors"?
   c. What can you record under "Consequences"?
2. What is the purpose of a structured diary?

Recording Frequency and Duration

3. Give an example of recording the amount of time you spend doing something and the number of times you do it.
4. Why is it important to record positive events as well as negative ones?
5. What are the advantages of computing your percentage of success?

Recording the Intensity of Emotions

6. Give an example of a rating scale. In what situations are these scales most useful?
7. How can you combine various systems for keeping records?

Practicalities of Record Keeping

8. What are the reasons for recording your target behavior as soon as it occurs?
9. What can you do to make recording easier?
10. How does one use written storage records?
11. What are the four rules of self-observation?
12. What does it mean to say that self-observation is reactive?
13. How can you use this reactivity to your advantage?
14. What is negative practice, and in what kind of situation is it most useful?
15. How do you record behaviors you perform absentmindedly?
16. How do you record behaviors that occur while many other things are going on?

Planning for Change

17. What is the "baseline period"?
18. For how long should you record in the baseline period?
19. What is reliability? What can you do to increase it?
20. Should you ever omit the baseline period?

Self-knowledge is the key to successful self-modification. Your behaviors—actions, thoughts, and feelings—are embedded in situations, and each of these elements must be carefully observed. Most of us assume that we understand ourselves, and we place great faith in our memories of our own behaviors. We rarely feel that we need to employ any systematic self-observation techniques. But real surprises and genuine discoveries may be in store for the person who begins careful self-observation.

Have you ever had a childhood memory and asked your parents about it, only to discover they do not remember things the same way at all? People do not necessarily remember their own past accurately (Johnson, 1985; Ross & Conway, 1986). Casual assessments of ourselves are often inaccurate (Nisbett & Ross, 1980). People often do not remember accurately how much food they eat, for example. In one study, a group of people who wanted to lose weight were asked by an experimenter how much they ate. Many assured themselves and the researcher that they "really didn't eat very much." Then they were asked to remember and write down everything they had eaten in the preceding two days. Their lists were checked, and it appeared that the people were *not* overeating. The researcher then put them all on a diet consisting of the foods they had reported eating. Every one of them began to lose weight (Stunkard, 1958).

In order to change yourself, you have to know what you're doing. The purpose of this chapter is to present a set of techniques for gaining knowledge about your behaviors, thoughts, and feelings and about their relationships to specific situations. In order to select and design the best possible plan for change, you need careful records of your behavior and the specific situations in which it occurs. In Chapters 5 through 8, you will learn to use this information to design a plan for self-directed change.

Structured Diaries

A **structured diary** is a record you keep of your target for change and of its antecedents and consequences. Keeping this record will allow you to see what kinds of situations have an effect on your target. This is not the kind of diary in which you write random thoughts or musings about the day. In fact, you don't wait until the end of the day to write your entries.

The target of your change will be some form of behavior—whether thoughts, feelings, or actions. Each of these behaviors is embedded in a situation, with antecedents before it and consequences after. As soon as you notice that a relevant behavior—thought, feeling, or action—has occurred, note it, along with the events that preceded and followed it.

Antecedents (A)	*Behaviors—Actions, Thoughts, or Emotions (B)*	*Consequences (C)*
When did it happen? Whom were you with?	What were you saying to yourself?	What happened as a result?

(continued)

What were you doing? Where were you? What were you saying to yourself? What thoughts were you having? What feelings were you having?	What thoughts did you have? What feelings were you having? What actions were you performing?	Was it pleasant or unpleasant?

Under "Behavior" (B), list the action, thought, or feeling that is your special focus—because it is your current problem or because it is an example of the eventual goal. Then enter the antecedents that preceded it and the consequences that followed. *Your thoughts, feelings, and actions can be monitored this way.*

We'll start with Les, whose straightforward goal was to eliminate nail biting. Les kept a record of the antecedents and consequences of biting his nails. Here are some entries from his diary:

Antecedents (A)	*Behaviors (B)*	*Consequences (C)*
Waiting for the bus	Nail biting	Embarrassed that others might see
Sitting in class listening	Nail biting	Same
Lying in bed thinking	Nail biting	Just wish I would quit
Reading	Nail biting	Same
Stressed	Nail biting	Gives me something to do

He wrote, "I knew I bit my nails when I was stressed, but I was surprised to find that I did it in other situations, too. It happens when my mind is occupied but my fingers are not." Knowing this, Les is in a position to make a plan to eliminate nail biting in those specific situations.

Here is a selection from the structured diary of Mike, a father whose goal was to stop spanking his children and start using nonphysical punishment. As soon as he had disciplined the children, he made an entry in his diary:

Antecedents (A)	*Behaviors (B)*	*Consequences (C)*
April 3. Sat. morning at breakfast. Kids bickered a lot.	I spanked both of them.	Made them even more cross.
April 6. Came home from work feeling tired. My boy talked back to me.	Started to spank him but stopped. Grounded him for an hour instead.	Felt pretty good about that. Was glad I didn't hit him. He calmed down while he was grounded.

(continued)

April 10. Had an argument with Dora [his wife]. Then in the car the kids started quarreling.	Spanked them—actually, slapped them.	It spoiled our whole outing. I felt guilty. They felt rotten.

Mike sees from his diary that he feels better when he doesn't spank. He may also note that it's not simply the children's behavior that determines whether he spanks them or not. An argument with his wife or feeling "down" after a hard day at work influences his behavior, too. By noting both his feelings and his behaviors, Mike can see what leads to the spanking that he wants to stop. As you can see, Mike noted not only the times he spanked his children, but—just as important—the times he used a nonviolent discipline technique.

Evelyn, a young college student, felt that she needed to be more assertive, but she wasn't sure when and in what situations. She recorded in her diary the times when she thought she *could* have been assertive but was not, as well as the times when she *was* assertive.

Antecedents (A)	*Behaviors (B)*	*Consequences (C)*
11:30 p.m. I am about to fall asleep. Ed telephones. He starts to ramble.	I'm angry, it's late, and he is boring, but I don't say anything.	He talks about 20 minutes.
Noon the next day. Walking to work, I see Ed, try to avoid talking to him. He calls me. I keep on going. He grabs my arm. He asks me to lunch.	I look away, say "I don't know . . . (pause) OK."	We have lunch. He asks me out again.
Polly wants me to see a movie I swore I would not see. She complains that I haven't been to a movie with her in a long time.	I say, "I really shouldn't. I need to get some rest." But I give in and go.	The movie was gross.
1:00 p.m. Went to meet Jill. We were supposed to go jogging, but she wants to do it later in the day.	I tell her I can't go later. I have to work.	
6:00 p.m. My sister comes over to ask me to baby-sit.	I tell her I can't. I have other plans. A bunch of us are going out.	

Several days of this kind of observation revealed a pattern: When other people asked Evelyn to go places with them and she had nothing else specifically scheduled, she usually went, even if she didn't want to. If they asked but she had something specifically scheduled, she didn't go with them. "But," she wrote, "why should I have to have something scheduled before I feel I can say no? Isn't the need to go to sleep enough? I need to be able to refuse even when I have no specific activity planned but just don't want to do it." Once we've pointed it out to you, Evelyn's goal seems obvious, but it was not apparent to her until she began keeping a structured diary.

The Mechanics of Diary Making

As soon as you realize that you have performed some undesired target behavior or failed to perform some desired one, make an entry in your structured diary. Describe the physical setting, the social situation, your thoughts, and the behavior of other people. Journalism students learn that to write a good story they must answer five questions: *Who? What? Where? When? Why?* To keep a good structured diary, you must answer these same questions.

Be sure to make the diary entries as soon as the target problem occurs. Don't wait. It's easy to overlook important details when you're reconstructing a past event. For example, if Mike had waited until the next day to record the events just before spanking his children, he might never have realized that coming home tired from work or having an argument with his wife was affecting how he disciplined his kids.

Recording Thoughts and Feelings

Thoughts, feelings, and your actions can be either the antecedents to your problem or the target problem itself. Therefore, they are listed under both columns A and B in the chart. Thoughts can lead to behaviors, behaviors can lead to thoughts, feelings can lead to both, and both can lead to feelings—there are no one-way signs in the streets of the mind. Causation can go either way. All three elements may be considered both as antecedents and as the target problem itself.

You can record all three: feelings, thoughts, and actions. For example, Steve is trying to learn more about his shyness. He notes that when he enters a room full of people he (1) feels nervous, (2) thinks "Oh, boy, I don't know anyone in here," and (3) begins to act stiff and aloof.

Here is a more detailed example of the relationships among thoughts, feelings, and actions. Martina was an older woman who had returned to college to finish her degree. Although doing quite well, she was bothered by feelings of insecurity, which she called "my stupid lack of self-esteem." Sometimes this problem would appear as a bad feeling, sometimes as an unwanted behavior. The records in her diary looked like this:

A	B	C
Classmate made a very good comment in a class discussion.	I thought, "He's so smart. I can't express myself like that." So I said nothing, even though I had a comment.	I felt stupid.
Woke up thinking, "There is so much work to do! How will I ever be able to keep up this pace?"	Then thought, "And this is only undergraduate school. I'll never be able to cope with graduate school." Had a fantasy of being exhausted in graduate school.	Felt depressed. Thought about changing my plans, not going to graduate school.
Typing my notes into the computer. I had to type something I had studied last semester, but couldn't remember correctly.	Thought, "God, there's too much to learn. I'll never be able to remember all of it." Had a fantasy of being in an important test in graduate school and not being able to remember all I needed to know.	Felt discouraged.
In class. The instructor was rattling off information like a computer.	Thought, "I'll never be able to remember things like that. I can't even remember things I learned last semester. I'll never be able to be a Ph.D." Actually went to my adviser to talk about changing my plans for graduate school.	Was depressed; felt really bad for several hours.

After a week and a half of this pattern, it became clear to Martina that her overgeneralized self-criticisms and unflattering comparisons of herself to others were discouraging her. "I saw three kinds of negative thoughts I was having, which would sometimes lead me to feel bad, and sometimes lead to self-defeating behavior, such as not asking a question in class or thinking about dropping my plans." Now she could begin a plan to rid herself of these negative thoughts. Notice that sometimes her thoughts led to bad feelings she wanted to be rid of and sometimes to behaviors she wanted to change.

Thoughts can be visual as well as verbal. Sometimes Martina's thoughts came in the form of things she said to herself in her mind—"He's so smart. I can't express myself like that"—and sometimes in the form of fantasies, like little film clips she ran in her mind, as when she fantasized being exhausted in graduate school.

Record your thoughts or fantasies as soon as they occur. If you delay in making entries in your structured diary, it will be difficult to remember all the important details—and you will need to have those details in order to see what effect the thoughts and fantasies have on your actions and feelings.

What the Diary Tells You

People working on indulgent behaviors—such as overeating, drinking, or smoking—find that situations they expect to be unrelated to the problem can be closely connected to it. For example, a man who had been dieting successfully for several weeks kept a diary of the times he began to binge. He found that the only two times he had binged—such as eating most of a package of Girl Scout cookies—occurred in the evening of days when the stress at work had been severe. This surprised him, as he had been unaware of any connection between the day's stresses and his overeating problem.

A smoker who kept a structured diary centered around the question "Why do I light a cigarette?" found that all the following situations stimulated him to smoke: any social gathering; a cup of coffee; being bored, angry, depressed, or excited; certain times of day; and after every meal. If you don't believe that a situation can control your behavior, watch people who are trying to stop smoking when they are in certain settings—for example, during a morning coffee break when others are smoking.

The purpose of keeping a structured diary is to find out which situations are affecting your behavior. Discovering the pattern of your behavior may take time and patience, and you may need to make many entries. For some people, this may become a long-term project. We suggest that overeaters keep track of all the food they eat over a period of several weeks. In this way, they can learn the various situations that cue their eating. Often they find that they eat in response to particular situations rather than in response to an internal feeling of hunger. Here are excerpts from the eating records of Hal.

A	*B*	*C*
Invited to Bill's for supper. Thought "Great, all that free food."	Had second helpings of everything.	Tasted so good! But I was stuffed.

(continued)

Three weeks later: Thanksgiving at the family's. I was thinking, "Time for stuffing."	Ate immense amounts of turkey, dressing, cranberry sauce, potatoes, pie, coffee.	Literally got sick, I ate so much.
Office party at Christmas.	Ate all afternoon.	Stuffed again.

Most of the time Hal did not eat too much, but at certain times—when invited out, on festive occasions—he grossly overate, and each time he put on weight that he never lost. Record keeping over several weeks revealed this pattern of antecedents, behavior, and consequences.

The process of long-term diary keeping like this can be helpful in showing you what you need to change. The analysis may shift your focus of interest from the original behavior of concern to some feature that seems to influence it. For example, Hal does not actually need to change his day-to-day eating habits, but he does need to change his overeating on certain occasions.

Here is another example of this process. An elementary school teacher, Jill, observed her patterns of depressed feelings. She wrote,

> I was in my yard gardening, which usually makes me feel very happy. But I began to feel uncomfortable and stopped to think why. It felt like depression, but there was nothing to be depressed about. So I wondered about what I had been thinking just before I felt depressed. And then I remembered that, a minute before, I had imagined this scene: I'm in my classroom, at the beginning of next year, and I'm teaching fifth grade (just as I will be) instead of my usual third. The class is a shambles. The kids aren't understanding anything, they are misbehaving, and I can hear the principal coming down the hallway. She comes in the door, stands, and glowers at me. . . .
>
> I imagine things like this often. I even have a name for them—my incompetence fantasies. And I believe they do depress me. So I'm going to record instances of fantasies about incompetence, find out what sets them off, and try to get rid of them.

She then moved "incompetence fantasies" to the center column of her diary and recorded antecedents and consequences of her fantasies.

The general technique here is to get yourself to notice events that lead to your unwanted actions, feelings, or thoughts. Simply tell yourself, "Notice what happens just before my target appears." Jill had set herself to notice what she was thinking just before feeling depressed. A man who wanted to lose weight was trying to hold himself to 1800 calories each day. He realized that he went over the limit every day. So he told himself to notice what he was doing, feeling, or thinking when he made the decision to go over the limit for the day. In this way, he noticed a pattern of thinking, "Well, just this once; a couple of hundred extra calories won't matter." But of course it did. Keeping records enabled him to discover the pattern.

Keeping records also encourages you to think about *why* you are doing certain things. Martina, the woman who overgeneralized her weaknesses and too often compared herself unfavorably to others, said,

> I felt I was being realistic in my self-evaluations, but I wasn't. I'm still an undergraduate, but I was comparing myself to graduate students and my professors. It's because I'm their age that I made the comparison, but it isn't realistic, because they have had lots more training. Someday, maybe, I'll be as good as they are.

You learn to make this kind of differentiation by keeping records of your thoughts and behaviors and thinking about the patterns that emerge.

Recording Frequency and Duration

Some psychologists suggest that self-direction is a process of "personal science" (Mahoney, 1974). Keeping that definition in mind, you can see that the structured diary is a way of seeing what may cause your thoughts, feelings, or actions. But another aspect of science is measurement. You may need to know *how often* you do something or for *how long* you do it. You will have to decide if it makes more sense to count how often or how long you engage in a given behavior.

Simple Counting

The easiest kind of record keeping is a simple count of how often you do something. Allan wanted to know how often he practiced his music, so he kept a chart in the same drawer where he kept his recorder and music sheet. The sheet looked like this:

	Recorder Playing			
	Week 1	*Week 2*	*Week 3*	*Week 4*
Monday	✓	✓	✓	
Tuesday				
Wednesday	✓		✓	
Thursday		✓	✓	
Friday	✓	✓	✓	
Saturday				
Sunday				

Whenever Allan took out his recorder to practice, he made a mark on the sheet. He could quickly see how many times a week he practiced and ask himself whether it was enough. Also, if he later decided that he wanted to increase his practicing, he knew exactly the level he was starting from. But the chart yields even more information. Just by glancing at it, Allan noticed that he never seemed to practice on Tuesdays, Saturdays, or Sundays. This observation led him to ask, "Why don't I practice on those three days?" Then he could determine what it was that interfered with his practicing on those days.

Hal wanted to get himself to walk up three flights of stairs to his office instead of taking the elevator. He put up a piece of paper just inside his office door, and for each day, he made a check mark whenever he climbed the stairs:

Climbing Stairs	
Monday	√√√
Tuesday	√√√√
Wednesday	√√√
Thursday	√√√√
Friday	√√

Debbie wanted to increase her vocabulary. When she encountered a word she didn't know, she wrote it down in her notebook. Later she looked up its meaning in the dictionary. Inside the dictionary she kept a chart like this:

Number of Words Looked Up					
Mon	√	Mon	√	Mon	√√
Tues	√√	Tues		Tues	√
Wed	√	Wed		Wed	
Thurs	√√√	Thurs	√√	Thurs	√
Fri	√	Fri	√	Fri	√√√

Maureen decided to record the number of minutes she actually spent studying and the number of minutes she was "ready to study." The latter category included long sessions deciding which course she should study for, as well as sitting at her desk talking to her roommate, thinking about other things, or reading a novel that was not assigned. Her chart looked like this:

	Mon	*Tues*	*Wed*	*Thurs*	*Fri*
Ready to study	45	30	35	50	0
Actually studying	15	10	20	30	0

Maintaining a strict count like this helps you understand the difference between engaging in the actual target behavior and engaging in other, related behaviors. You may come to realize, as in this example, that you spend a large amount of time doing things that are not your target behavior. Being "ready to study" is not studying. By keeping a strict count of the amount of time you actually engage in the target behavior, you can learn what you are doing instead of the desired behavior and how that interferes with the desired behavior.

Maureen recorded the *duration* of her behavior. This is desirable whenever length of time is an issue. People who want to increase their study time may keep records of how long they spend studying their easy courses versus their hard courses (Richards, 1985) or of how much time they spend looking ahead to see what is yet to be done rather than actually doing it. Allan might have recorded not only how many times a week he practiced the recorder and when, but also how long he practiced each time. People who eat too rapidly can keep track of how long they take to eat each meal (Britt & Singh, 1985).

There are many behaviors, of course, for which a simple count of *frequency* is appropriate—for example, number of cigarettes smoked, number of times fingernails are bitten, or number of swear words uttered per day.

People undertaking self-change projects have counted many different behaviors. For example:

- A man records if he has paid each of his regular bills each month.
- A student records each day if he goes to class or not.
- A young man records what he spends his money on, particularly concentrating on impulse buying.
- An office worker records the number of self-critical thoughts she has when dealing with rejection by others.
- A father counts how much time he spends with his children.
- A writer makes a note of the exact time she begins her daily writing, carefully notes each time she takes a break, and at the end of her scheduled writing period marks down the total time spent writing.
- A jogger keeps track of how many miles he runs each week.
- A walker keeps track of the number of hours she walks per week.
- An overweight man counts daily instances of "eating errors," when he eats something he knows he shouldn't.
- A dieter records all the food eaten each day.
- Another dieter keeps track of junk food eaten, between-meal snacks, and bedtime snacks.
- A skin scratcher records the number of hours she goes without scratching.
- A student keeps track of the number of times per week that he says something nice to his parents.

If you keep a record of the number of instances of a certain behavior in each of various situations, use code marks for the situations. For example, Nancy, who wanted to quit smoking, counted the cigarettes she smoked each day. She also noted the situations in which her smoking occurred, using this coding system:

E
(for eating) during or after a meal
S
when nervous in a social situation
D
when driving her car
O
other times

On the first day Nancy's 3″ × 5″ card looked like this:

Smoking Record—Monday, December 7		
Morning E E D O S S S E	*Afternoon* O S S D S E E E	*Evening* E O

Her records for several days were very consistent, and she was able to plan a realistic antismoking program that concentrated on eating and social situations.

Avoiding Discouragement

Don't record only negative information. Self-recording can be discouraging if you record only the negative or unwanted things you do. A lengthy record of all the times you are depressed or have negative thoughts about yourself may lead you to think even more negatively about yourself. Keeping records of your successes, even if they are small compared to your final goal, will increase your confidence that you are making progress and enhance your feelings of self-efficacy—the belief that you are indeed capable of reaching your final goal.

Whenever possible, record positive behaviors as well as negative ones (Johnston-O'Connor & Kirschenbaum, 1986). This allows you to see progress as well as problems. For example, dieters should keep records of the times they *avoid* the temptation to eat too much, as well as of the times they give in to temptation. A mother should record the times she avoids spanking her kids and thinks of some more positive response, as well as the times she hits them. If you stick to your diet for six days and then overeat, you should feel good about the six days even if you regret the seventh. Too often, dieters notice only the times when they fail to stick to their diet (Ferguson, 1975). Depressed people suffer a similar distortion of perception, failing to notice the pleasant events of life. As a result, they see their whole lives as disappointing. Recording positive events will help in this situation, too (Rehm, 1982). One current treatment for low self-esteem and depression is to teach clients to notice the good things that happen to them and not to focus on the bad things (Layden, 1982).

If you only record a series of failures, you are likely to stop self-observation (Kirschenbaum & Tomarken, 1982), and that will lead to the collapse of your self-modification plan. Don't keep a record just of the cigarettes you smoked; keep a record of the urges to smoke that you resisted, too. Don't just record the days you didn't exercise; note the days on which you *did* exercise. Don't just record the times you were depressed; note the times you felt good, too. Don't just record the times you failed to be assertive; note the times you were successfully assertive.

Your successes may be small at first, but this is all the more reason to record them. "Well, it's true that I only studied for the scheduled amount of time one day last week, but I *did do well* on Tuesday. Now I've got to build on that. I'll make better grades if I do."

Dieters who weigh themselves too often can experience discouragement (Mahoney, 1977). In the first two or three days of a diet, a person's weight may drop several pounds. But after those first few days (when much of the weight loss is only water loss that will be replaced as soon as the dieter resumes normal eating), the amount of weight lost daily is small. Dieters who weigh themselves every morning soon begin to feel that such a small weight loss is hardly worth the sacrifice the diet requires. The solution is to

BOX 3-1
Poor Richard's Records

North Wind Picture Archives

Benjamin Franklin—statesman, scientist, inventor, and author—knew the value of record keeping in changing one's behavior. He had in mind writing a book called *The Art of Virtue* on how to achieve goals such as not overeating or overdrinking ("temperance," to use his word), letting others talk, keeping things in order, meeting goals, avoiding waste, being clean, staying calm, and being industrious (Knapp & Shodahl, 1974). Franklin never did write *The Art of Virtue,* but he left records in his personal journal of his attempts at self-modification, using techniques of self-observation much like those in this book.

North Wind Picture Archives

weigh themselves less frequently, perhaps once a week, so that a real weight loss can be seen. On a daily basis, dieters need to record not their weight but whether they actually follow the diet.

Keeping track of successes as well as failures allows you to compute the percentage of successes you have. At first the percentage may be low—"I am being successfully assertive in 12% of the situations in which I could be assertive"—but 12% is better than nothing and gives you something to build on. By knowing that at least you're successful 12% of the time, you avoid total discouragement.

Our students have computed the percentage of success for targets such as the number of times they asked a question in class compared with the number of times they thought of a question, the number of urges to smoke they resisted versus the number of times they gave in, the number of urges to eat junk food versus the number of times they substituted some healthy food, and the percentage of time they were "on target" for studying versus the amount of time they were in place but not actually studying.

Box 3-1 contains an example of how Benjamin Franklin, a productive and accomplished leader, used records to keep track of his goal-related successes and failures.

Franklin first made a list of the target behaviors, which he called *virtues.* He then kept records of his successes and failures for each target. Here is a sample of one of his record sheets:

	Sun	Mon	Tues	Wed	Thurs	Fri	Sat
Temperance							
Letting others talk	x	x		x		x	
Keeping things in order	xx	x	x		x	x	x
Meeting goals			x			x	
Avoiding waste		x			x		
Being clean							
Staying calm							
Being industrious							

He worked on one set of behaviors at a time, adding an *X* to the record each time he didn't meet his personal goals. Later he would move to another goal, then to another, until he had reached all of them.

Was he successful? He says he was. "I was surprised to find myself so much fuller of faults than I had imagined, but I had the satisfaction of seeing them diminish."

Recording the Intensity of Emotions

So far we have presented methods for recording the A-B-Cs of a situation and for recording the frequency or duration of an act. But sometimes your target for change is an *emotional reaction,* such as anxiety or depression. In this case you want to record the *intensity* of your reaction. You'll want to discover what leads to intense reactions—positive or negative—so you can know what to do to begin to change.

A rating scale can be used to measure intensity of emotion. You assign each event a number according to a prearranged scale. For example, a psychologist asked a client to rate how distressed she felt as she tried to cope with frightening thoughts that she had (Kirk, 1989). The client used the following scale to rate her degree of distress:

0 1 2 3 4 5 6 7 8 9 10
not at all distressed — moderately distressed — extremely distressed; as bad as I could possibly feel

A second psychologist, who works with anxiety patients, asks them to use a similar scale to keep records of their anxiety (Kennerley, 1990):

0 1 2 3 4 5 6 7 8 9 10
no anxiety; really calm — moderate anxiety — absolute panic; worst possible

Another way to rate an emotion is on a scale from 0 to 100, where 0 is no emotion and 100 is the maximum level of emotion. Richard Suinn (1990) asks clients to rate their degree of stress on a scale from 0 to 100, where 0 is no tension at all and 100 is maximum tension.

You should use one of these scales to rate your intensity of emotion. For example, the goal of one young woman was to increase her feelings of happiness and make her depression less intense (Tharp, Watson, & Kaya, 1974). She invented a 9-point rating scale in which the points had these meanings:

+4 superhappy
+3 happy
+2 good feeling
+1 some positive feeling
+0 neutral
−1 some negative feeling
−2 bad feeling
−3 sad
−4 superdepressed

Her recording method included not only the rating of the feeling but also a note of the situation in which the feeling occurred. She briefly described each unit of her day's activities and then evaluated the intensity of her feelings about it. Here is a typical day's record:

Talked to Jean −2
In class −1
Took test 0
Saw Dean −2
Had lunch with Jean and Judy +1
Talked to Bill +3
Went home on bus −3
Talked to Jean on phone −3
Studied 0

Rating scales are useful in recording emotions and feelings because intensity is the crucial issue. Fears, depression, sexual arousal, jealousy, pain, joy, happiness, self-satisfaction, love, and affection can all be recorded with rating scales. You can express your goals with regard to these emotions and feelings as increases or decreases on the scale.

Stuart used the same scale and rated his feelings four times a day—at each meal and at bedtime. He also made notes about antecedents that led to feelings of depression. His records for two days looked like this:

Time	*Rating*	*Comments*
Breakfast	+1	Feel OK.
Lunch	−2	Sinking. Reason is that I ran into John, and he made a couple of "funny" remarks about my not making the basketball team.
Supper	−1	
Bedtime	−3	Had an argument with Beverly [his girlfriend].
Breakfast	0	
Lunch	−1	Had to take a test. Worried because my grades have been dropping lately.
Supper	−3	Beverly says I'm getting "paranoid and irrational" because I worry too much.
Bedtime	−3	Just want to get this day over.

After several days he reported, "I rely on external sources for approval and positive reinforcement—friends, co-workers, Beverly. Disagreements, confrontations, and disputes create tension and frustration. My mistake is that I dwell on them too long and end up either thoroughly angry or very depressed." By rating his reactions, he could discover what sorts of events made him feel bad and could begin to take steps to change his reactions to them. On another day his records were:

Time	*Rating*	*Comments*
Breakfast	+1	
Lunch	−1	At least it's an improvement, because I had another argument with Beverly. I'm staying calmer, didn't freak out over it.
Supper	−1	My grade on the test wasn't good, but I've started on a plan to increase studying.
Bedtime	+1	Randy said I seemed to be feeling better. It shows!

When your goal is to change some emotional state, you won't go immediately from discomfort to total comfort. By rating your comfort, you will be able to see that you are making progress.

As you learn more about your own behavior, you may want to change your scale to allow for distinctions that are important to your particular goal. For example, a man whose goal was to overcome nervousness about speaking in front of a group started with a scale that ranged from 1, "perfectly calm," to 5, "panic." After rating a few experiences, he noticed that he often wanted to assign a number in between two of the numbers on his original scale, so he expanded it to a 10-point scale. "In class giving a speech" was about 9; "having a speech assigned" was around 3; "preparing the speech" was 5; "waiting to give it" was 8.

If you are rating your depression over the day, you should rate four times or more. If you are rating your anxiety, you can rate it each time you confront the situation that makes you anxious. For example, if you are dealing with anxiety about interacting with the opposite sex, you might make two ratings in the morning because you have two opportunities to talk to others, then not make any ratings for several hours while you are at work, then have to make several ratings when you are off work, socializing in the dorm. Whenever you can discover the antecedents that lead to changes in your emotions, be sure to note them immediately, for that gives you important information you can use to change yourself. If one person makes you a lot more nervous than another, you'll want to know that, to see if you can figure out what it is about the one that is less anxiety-inducing.

Combining Types of Record Keeping

Often you will want to keep more than one kind of record. In a previous example, Stuart not only rated his emotions, but also kept a structured diary of the antecedents that led to various emotions. Recall that your goal for change can concern your behavior, your thoughts, or your feelings. These are so closely woven together in our lives that we often want to know about more than one of them as we formulate a plan for change.

One of our students was trying to avoid depression by fighting off her tendency to dwell on thoughts that people didn't like her. To achieve this goal, she decided to replace her negative thoughts with memories of situations in which people had obviously liked her. She used a rating scale to keep track of her feelings, but she also counted "the number of times each day that I successfully switch from thoughts that people don't like me to memories of times when people did like me." Thus, she combined rating her feeling with counting how often she was able to change her feeling.

Mitch combined keeping a structured diary and rating his emotional reactions. He wrote:

> I tend to be very self-conscious, especially when I feel I am drawing attention to myself or being evaluated by someone whose opinion I value, which is just about everybody. I tend to think too much about the consequences of my behavior before I act and to focus on the negative outcomes that are possible. This makes me uptight, and also makes me lose the timing of my actions, so they seem awkward. This happens in a lot of situations.

Mitch decided to keep track of the antecedents to being too self-conscious; his thoughts, feelings, and behaviors in the various situations; and the consequences of his actions. Pages 82–83 contain his records of the more outstanding examples.

Note that Mitch kept track of his successes as well as his failures. Note also that by recording his emotions, he saw that he could perform even when he felt uptight. This, he told us later, increased his self-confidence and actually lowered his nervousness.

See Box 3-2 for more examples of combined record keeping.

Practicalities of Record Keeping

Record your target behavior as soon as it occurs. Don't wait until the end of the day and then try to remember how many times or for how long you engaged in the target behavior. Your count will not be accurate. As soon as the target behavior occurs, stop and record it (Epstein, Miller & Webster, 1976; Epstein, Webster, & Miller, 1975). Don't wait until the end of the day to record your depression or anxiety level for the entire day, either—many people make too pessimistic a rating when they do.

You may find yourself thinking that you don't need to write something down. You're sure you will remember how much time you spent doing the target behavior, or what the situation was, or how you felt emotionally. But if you don't keep fairly strict written records, you'll find that your records are useless.

When we teach self-modification, a few students are adamant: They do *not* need to keep records. They're *sure* they know what they're doing. If you are one of these, please try this little test (Brown, 1987). Jot down your *estimated* frequencies of the target behavior—cigarettes smoked, food eaten, or

Antecedent	*Thought*	*Feeling*	*Behavior*	*Consequence*
Crossing street in front of cars.	Thought everyone would be looking at me; felt my posture was bad and I was too stiff.		Became really self-conscious and ended up fulfilling my prophecy by not walking naturally.	Felt dumb.
Saw a fantastic girl walking my way.			Wanted to smile but ended up looking at the ground as she passed.	Felt stupid because I know girls like confident guys.
Morning class, wanted to clarify a word on the board.	Pictured myself raising my hand, speaking, and mumbling—Mitch the klutz.	My heart began to pound very rapidly. Rated −1. [He was using a rating scale of +2, +1, 0, −1, −2.]	Told myself to relax, and raised my hand.	Very nervous at first, but glad I had asked the question.
Sitting down, saw a girl, from last semester's geology class, whom I never got to know. She looked right at me.			I didn't smile (I don't like my smile). I thought she would look again, but she didn't.	Felt bad, but . . .

			I got up purposely, caught her on the way out, and started to talk to her.	Felt nervous, rated −1. But I was glad I made the effort.
In the library, came to a table with a girl sitting on one side.			I was hesitant to sit down right away, so went to the restroom to make sure I looked OK. Came back, sat down, looked at my ring binder.	
	Began to think about my bad points; thought I'd make a bad impression if I spoke to her.	−2	Didn't say anything.	Left later feeling disappointed.
In class, teacher said he was going to go around the room asking for comments.		My heart started to pound. Panicked. Rated −2.	Started to rehearse what I would say.	Ended up OK, but mad at my nervousness.

BOX 3-2

A Headache Diary and Brain-Power Bowling: Examples of Combined Record-Keeping Forms

Psychologists have been creative in devising record-keeping forms that combine aspects of structured diaries, counting, and ratings of emotion. Here are two, just to give you more ideas you might use in your own recording. Note that each reminds the person keeping the records what to do, and each gives a chance to rate how well it was done.

1. *Headache Diary*

This is used by adolescents who are receiving psychological help—with the same kinds of techniques you are learning here—for migraine headaches (Lascelles, Cunningham, McGrath, & Sullivan, 1989). The teenagers learn to record their negative and positive coping reactions to stress and to rate how they feel as a result.

____ Stressful situation
____ Negative thoughts (that make it worse)
____ Tension level 0–10
____ Coping strategies (positive thoughts that make me feel better)
____ Praising myself
____ Tension level 0–10

2. *Brain-Power Bowling*

The following is a record-keeping form on which the bowler records seven different aspects of his or her bowling stance and rates how well each was carried out (Kirschenbaum, 1984).

0 = didn't do it well
1 = good
2 = very good
3 = excellent

____ *Foot position:* Same starting point each time.
____ *Stance:* Shoulders squared, elbow tucked into hip; knees relaxed.
____ *Grip:* Same grip for every shot, thumb and palm position correct.
____ *Spot:* Pick a spot and watch your ball roll into it.
____ *Approach:* Take 2–3-second delay, walk in a straight line.
____ *Push away:* Elbow tight and locked, straight pendulum-type swing near body.
____ *Finish position:* Lead foot pointed toward spot, body balanced, square at the line.

whatever—for several days. Then really keep records for an equal number of days, and compare for accuracy. If you try this, we bet you'll end up agreeing that your estimates were inaccurate. Further, you won't have the information on antecedents and consequences that record keeping can give you. Try it. If it doesn't work, you can always go back to estimates.

Making Recording Easy

The recording device has to be portable and readily accessible. A smoker can keep a note card inside the cigarette pack. Many people use a 3″ × 5″ card or some other piece of paper that will fit conveniently in a pocket, bag, or notebook. Nancy, who wanted to quit smoking, carried a 3″ × 5″ card in her pocket. As soon as she lit a cigarette, she made a note on the card in the code she had worked out for different situations—E, S, D, O. That told her she had smoked one cigarette and the situation in which she had done so.

Fit record keeping into the pattern of your usual habits. Devise your system so that it will remind you of itself. For example:

- Time management—a sheet inside your desk calendar
- Spending money impulsively—a card inside your wallet
- Too much TV watching—a chart beside the chair where you sit to watch
- Going to bed too late—a chart beside the bed
- Not studying—a record inside your notebook or at the place where you study
- Eating too much—a card beside your place at the table
- Between-meal snacks—a record sheet on the pantry or refrigerator door
- Exercising—a chart by the closet where you keep your exercise gear
- Socializing—a 3″ × 5″ card that is always in your bag or pocket

Verna had a hard time dealing with one of her co-workers. She made a list of four things she wanted to remember to do when she was with him: listen to him without interrupting, ignore his slightly rude remarks, pause before replying to him, and stop trying to figure out his motives. She kept this list in her desk. When she was about to talk with the man, she would take out the list, glance over it, and then hold it while talking to him. As soon as she finished talking, she would check off each item she had successfully performed.

In some cases, you can use a wrist counter (which is worn like a watch) or a golf counter. This helps when the target is something you do very often, such as some nervous or verbal habit. For example, Ed wanted to stop swearing and found that it happened about 200 times a day. Taking out a 3″ × 5″ card and marking it so often would have been tedious, so he used a golf counter. Use whatever sort of counter you find convenient. The easier it is to keep records, the more likely you are to keep them.

Anticipate recording problems you will have and figure out ways to deal with them. One of our students wanted to keep track of certain thoughts he had while talking with other people. To make notes on a card while talking would have looked silly. On the other hand, he was afraid he would forget if he waited until the conversation ended. His solution was to move a penny from his left to his right pocket each time he had the thought he wanted to record. After he left the person, he would count the pennies in his right pocket to see how many times the thought had occurred in the course of the conversation. Then he recorded the information on a note card.

A woman who wanted to increase the number of times she performed a particular behavior carried toothpicks in her purse and moved one into a special pocket of her purse after each occurrence. A cigarette smoker started out each day with a specific number of cigarettes (30) and counted how many he had left when he got home in the evening.

If you perform the behavior but discover that your counting device—a 3″ × 5″ card or whatever—is not there, improvise. For example, a knuckle cracker found a big leaf at the beach and tore a small hole in it each time he cracked his knuckles. Later he transferred this record to his regular chart. A smoker who left his scoring card at home kept the matches he used to light his cigarettes as a record of how many cigarettes he had smoked.

Written Storage Records

When you use 3″ × 5″ cards or other devices for keeping records, you need to transfer the information to a more permanent storage record. This storage record may not be exactly the same as the daily (or occasional) record. A woman with the nervous habit of pulling off the skin on her feet and legs kept a count like the following one:

Pulling Off Skin														
Day	1	2	3	4	5	6	7	8	9	10	11	12	13	14
Number of times per day	7	9	11	8	4	8	12	7	10	7	9	2	9	2

For her storage record, she made a graph that she posted on the wall of her room (see Chapter 8).

Our smoker, Nancy, transferred her daily record to a storage record. Her record sheet for two weeks looked like this:

	M	*T*	*W*	*T*	*F*	*S*	*S*
E	7						
S	6						
D	2						
O	3						
Total	18						

A woman who wanted to be a professional writer kept a record of the number of hours she wrote each day and the number of pages she wrote. At the end of each week, she added up the daily totals and transferred this information to a permanent chart she kept posted on the wall next to her writing desk.

	Total Hours Writing per Week	*Number of Pages Written per Week*
Week 1	14	5
Week 2	17½	20
Week 3	17½	19
Week 4	15	22
Week 5	9½	9

From this record, she could see the relationship between how much she worked and how much she produced, and she could then examine why the relationship was low at certain times.

Some people keep their storage records in terms of percentages. For example, you could keep a record of the percentage of occasions for assertion on which you actually were assertive, or the percentage of "study time" that you actually spent studying.

Sometimes you can combine your daily observations with the permanent record. For example, Allan kept his chart with his musical instrument. This way, the chart was always there when he needed it and could serve as both a daily record and a storage record. Record keeping and record storing must be adapted to each person's own behaviors and situations. If the various systems described here don't suit you, improvise one that does.

Summing Up

There are four simple rules for self-observation:

1. Do the recording when the behavior occurs, not later.
2. Be accurate and strict in your counting. Try to include all instances of the target.
3. Keep written records.
4. Keep the recording system as simple as possible. Try to fit it into your usual routine.

The Reactive Effects of Self-Observation

When a behavior is being observed, it often changes. Think what it's like to have someone closely observe your behavior. When your track coach, dance teacher, or lab instructor says, "I'm going to watch you very carefully now," don't you perform in a different way than you do when no one is observing you? You feel self-conscious; you take greater care.

Perhaps the behavior will become less smooth or automatic, as Mitch's did when he became self-conscious about the way he walked across the street. Or it may improve, just as an actor's performance can be enhanced by the presence of an audience. These effects are also produced when you are your own observer. Behavior "reacts" to observation, and the effect is known in psychology as **reactivity** (Mace & Kratochwill, 1985).

Occasionally students will complain that they are unable to work out a plan. When asked why, they explain that their problem has gone away. "I started recording my observations regularly, but then I just quit the undesirable behavior I was observing." This, of course, is the happiest form of reactivity. And in self-modification, it is the most common. Undesirable behaviors tend to diminish, and desired behaviors tend to increase, *because you are observing and recording them.*

Your values are the most important factor in reactivity. If you are recording some behavior about which you don't really care, your behavior won't be much affected (Ciminero, 1974; Fixen, Phillips, & Wolf, 1972). If you care about a behavior, however, self-recording often changes the behavior in the direction of your values. This effect has been documented in a number of case studies and experimental investigations dealing with a wide variety of problems. In fact, the effect is so reliable that clients in psychotherapy may be assigned to observe themselves as part of their therapy—a first step in changing problem behavior (Bornstein, Hamilton, & Bornstein, 1985; Gross & Drabman, 1982). The effect works only as long as you record, of course. If self-recording is the only thing you have done in your effort to change, stopping the recording may stop the improvement (Holman & Baer, 1979; Maletzky, 1974). Hal, whose office was up three flights of stairs, found that keeping records increased how often he walked up instead of taking the elevator; but when he stopped record keeping, he began to use the elevator again.

The reactive effects of self-recording can be turned to advantage. A student reported:

> For some time I felt guilty for not sharing kitchen chores with my wife. But I always seemed to have something else to do, and cooking and doing dishes were not exactly appealing, so I just continued to do nothing. Then I put a chart in the kitchen. Each time my wife cooked or cleaned up, she made an entry, and each time I cooked or cleaned up, I made an entry. It took only a week to get me moving. Now I check the chart each weekend to make sure I'm doing my share.

Another student wrote:

> I enjoy reading, and for a long time I wished I did more of it. But I'd come home from work tired and mindlessly switch on the TV. Then I bought a little notebook and began to keep a list of all the books or articles I read. I got very interested in my growing list. I enjoyed finishing reading something and making an entry in my notebook. I'd get the list out and skim it to see how I was progressing. I'm sure I read more now than I did before, because keeping track of my reading is meaningful to me. It makes me feel good.

If you are a smoker, keep long-term records of how many cigarettes you smoke per day or the amount of tar you consume. If you are overweight, keep long-term records of your caloric intake or your exercise. Reactivity alone will not be sufficient, but it will help.

Even though recording by itself is not enough, once you have changed, continued recording makes it easier to *maintain* the change. For example, a man who had to use a fairly complicated schedule of manipulating antecedents to problem drinking found that once his drinking problem had lessened, he could keep himself on the straight and narrow by keeping records of his alcohol intake. Another man who had been drinking seven to eight cups of coffee each day cut down to only two or three cups per day, and once he had cut down, he continued to keep records to be sure he didn't gradually move back up. A woman who had become a long-distance runner reported that she no longer needed to use a complicated self-change program but that she did need to keep records of her running to avoid slacking off.

You may be able to increase reactivity by changing the timing of recording (Rozensky, 1974). This works particularly well for behaviors we want to stop. For example, people who are dieting can record food intake either *before* or *after* they eat. Does it make a difference? It turns out that it does. In an experiment, some subjects first ate and then recorded the calories, whereas others reversed the order. Those who recorded *before* eating ate less (Bellack, Rozensky, & Schwartz, 1974).

Mike, who used to blow up at his children and spank them, began to record "anger" *before* rather than after he struck, and this had the desired effect. The recording itself broke the automatic chain of anger–striking, and Mike was able to discipline his children nonviolently.

During the initial stages of recording your problem behavior, record *after* you perform the act in order to provide a realistic record. Then, when you are actively trying to change the undesired behavior, record *before* you perform it. Of course, if your goal is to *increase* a behavior, then record *after* performing it (Paquin, 1982). For example, you would record jogging only after a run.

Dealing with Problems in Getting Your Records: Absentminded Behaviors

Some target behaviors are difficult to record accurately because you don't pay close attention to them. For example, you might absentmindedly pick your face while watching TV or reading. Other behaviors, such as talking too loudly or overeating, may be so well practiced that you don't notice them anymore. But if you do not get accurate records, it is more difficult to work out a plan for change.

How can you make yourself pay attention? The first step is to deliberately practice performing the behavior while consciously attending to it. This technique is called *negative practice.* Take the same approach you would for any other behavior that is not occurring—practice it.

Garrett, who habitually cracked his knuckles, spent five minutes each morning and five minutes each evening deliberately cracking his knuckles while paying close attention to every aspect of the behavior. This helped him learn to pay attention to the target behavior.

A sophomore had developed the habit of scratching her arms while sleeping. The practice had become so bad that some mornings she woke up to find her arms bleeding. How could she pay attention while she slept? Each night when she went to bed, she deliberately scratched her arms for several minutes while paying close attention to what she was doing. Being awake, she was not in danger of scratching until she bled. But the situation was similar to actually being asleep—she was sleepy, and in bed. (Note that this is not the same as so-called learning while sleeping, which is *not* an effective procedure.) After a few nights' practice, the young woman was not scratching in her sleep anymore (Watson, Tharp, & Krisberg, 1972). The case was followed up after 18 months and then again after 7 years. In the first 18 months, the woman had two relapses and used self-modification both times to correct the problem. During the next seven years she had no more relapses and remained free of nighttime scratching.

Once you have learned to pay attention to the habitual target behavior, you can begin a plan to eliminate it. The woman in the preceding example worked out a plan to replace scratching—first with rubbing her arms, then with patting them, and finally with just touching them.

Another way to deal with unconsciously performed behaviors is to ask your friends to point out instances of the target behavior. "If you see me picking my face, will you say something to me? I want to stop."

This situation is similar to asking other people to remind you of goals; here, too, be sure the reminder is not punishing. When Ed's wife said, "Ed! You're overeating!" he was embarrassed and irritated. So she changed her reminder to "Ed, dear, aren't you . . . ?" after which she dropped the subject. This incomplete, tactful way of reminding him was more effective.

Some people habitually pay little attention to themselves (Buss, 1980). If you are one of these, you may want to take steps to increase your self-consciousness, at least so that you can obtain good records of your own behavior. There are at least three things you can do to increase your self-consciousness: (1) listen to your voice on a tape recorder; (2) make a videotape of yourself; and (3) act in front of a mirror (Wegner & Guiliano, 1983). If you do one or more of these while practicing the behaviors you want to notice, you will be more likely to notice them when you perform them naturally—or fail to perform them—and that will allow you to gather good records.

Too Busy to Record?

Sometimes you are too busy doing something to record a problem behavior right when it occurs. Or perhaps other people are present, and you would be embarrassed to haul out your record notes and make an entry. A widowed man who was frankly looking for a wife found that he put off possible partners by rushing much too quickly into discussion of marriage. He wanted to learn to go more slowly, allowing the relationship to develop. His unwanted, rushing behavior occurred while he was socializing with a woman, and of course he didn't want to take out his notepad and record the event when it occurred. But he wanted to be sure to remember to record it afterward so he could think of better ways of dealing with the situation. He carried a few dried peas in his pocket, and when the behavior occurred that he wanted to stop, he would unobtrusively move a pea into his "target pocket" and say to himself, "Now remember this incident so you can record it later." The pea served as a reminder to him that something had occurred that he wanted to remember, and his self-instructions to remember helped him recall the specific event later.

A young woman who was lonely at college concluded that her negative opinions of people when she first met them were one of the main causes of her loneliness. "I judge them and find them wanting before I ever get to know them. It's a terrible habit, but I pounce on every little thing the person says and think things like, 'What a nerd.' " This habit did not endear her to others, and her loneliness was the result. To keep a record of these thoughts, she moved her pen from one part of her purse to another, to remind herself of the event later. Then, as soon as she could, she would enter the event in her structured diary.

Don't save all your reminders until the end of the day. If you must use a temporary reminder, make a full record of the incident as soon as possible.

Devising a Plan for Record Keeping

Suppose that the very act of making observations is punishing to you. You don't keep records because you can't stand the bad news. That's not an unusual situation, and if you're in it, you will be tempted to stop keeping records. Self-recording can also be punishing if you have not yet learned the skills of recording. Or you may simply forget to make your records. You can use self-direction strategies to develop record keeping. Chapters 5, 6, and 7 discuss these strategies in detail in the broader context of setting up plans for change. Self-recording is a behavior, and it follows the same principles as other behaviors. If you are failing in this step, view your failure as an appropriate goal for self-improvement, and work out a system to increase that particular behavior. In other words, *make accurate record keeping your first goal.*

Here are four techniques you can use to deal with problems in keeping records.

First, develop record keeping one piece at a time. When keeping records seems too hard, try adding just one item at a time (Hayes & Nelson, 1986). You can start with a simple plan, get used to it, and make it more complicated later. Remember Verna, who had difficulty getting along with one of her co-workers. She realized that she needed to keep track of four different aspects of her relationship with him, but this seemed impossibly complex. So she required herself to record only one aspect—ignoring his unfriendly remarks. After she had practiced this for a few days, she added a second aspect—listening carefully to him. After several more days, she was able to record both. She then added the third, and then the fourth.

A *second* technique is to provide a cue that reminds you to make records (Heins, Lloyd, & Hallahan, 1986). Powell wanted to keep records of his studying each night but often forgot to do so. He simply set the beeper on his wristwatch to go off at 11:30 to remind himself to make an entry in his record sheet. Another kind of cue is a mental one. Wallace wanted to keep records of his use of his new computer. "I just told myself to put recording in the front of my mind, so I'd remember it when I needed to. Now and then I'd remind myself: remember, make a record when you use the computer."

A *third* technique is to ask someone else to check whether you are keeping records. You don't have to show the actual records to the other person; just indicate that you are keeping records. For example, a young man who wanted to cut down on his drinking was upset when his records showed that he was drinking an average of nine beers a day. His first reaction was to stop keeping records. But he wanted to cut down, so he asked a friend to inquire each morning if he had kept records for the previous day.

A *fourth* technique is to reward yourself for keeping records (Stuart & Davis, 1972). A woman who had been overweight for several years realized that she needed to record what food she ate if she was going to lose weight. At first this seemed a burden, so she rewarded herself with $5 a week to spend on her hobby if she kept records of her food intake. Once this became a habit, she switched to rewarding herself for exercising.

Planning for Change

You are now in a phase known technically as the **baseline period.** This is a time when you make self-observations but don't engage in other efforts to change. Your present records constitute a baseline against which future changes can be evaluated. For many forms of self-observation, you'll want to know how your behavior changes from day to day or from week to week.

You may want to look for patterns in the A-B-C relationships that you observe.

You may want to know the average number of times per day or week you perform some action. For example, you could find the average number of minutes per week that you study, the average number of cigarettes that you smoke each day, or the average amount of exercise that you get each week. Once you know the average, you can see if you are gradually improving as you begin your plan for change. Important changes often occur gradually, not instantly—you don't go from a little exercise to a lot of exercise in a couple of weeks—and knowing what your average was allows you to see that you are making progress toward your goal.

You may want to know the percentage of time you perform some action. For example, you could find the percentage of time that you have a chance to be assertive that you actually are, the percentage of chances to eat junk food that you don't, or the percentage of opportunities that you take advantage of to talk to a new person.

You're not going to change from talking to possible new friends 10% of the time to 100% in a week or two. Seeing that your percentage is gradually improving is a great help in realizing that you are progressing.

A graph is another useful device for assessing your progress. Chapter 8 includes detailed instructions for constructing graphs. If you are unfamiliar with graphing, you may wish to read that section next.

Getting an Adequate Baseline Record

How long should you gather baseline data? That is, how long should you just observe yourself before trying techniques for change? The baseline period should be continued *until it shows a clear pattern.* There will be daily fluctuations, of course, but when you see a basic trend underlying the variations, the baseline can be said to be stable.

Figure 3-1 gives an example of a fairly stable baseline. From the graph, you can see that this cigarette smoker shows some variation in the number of cigarettes smoked each day. For the first few days, the pattern is not clear. By the end of the 11th day, however, it is apparent that his daily average is about 25. He also needs to discover the antecedents that lead to smoking, but he now knows his average and can begin a plan for changing.

Figure 3-2 shows the number of hours a college student studied each night. At the end of the first week, she has only the roughest idea of her

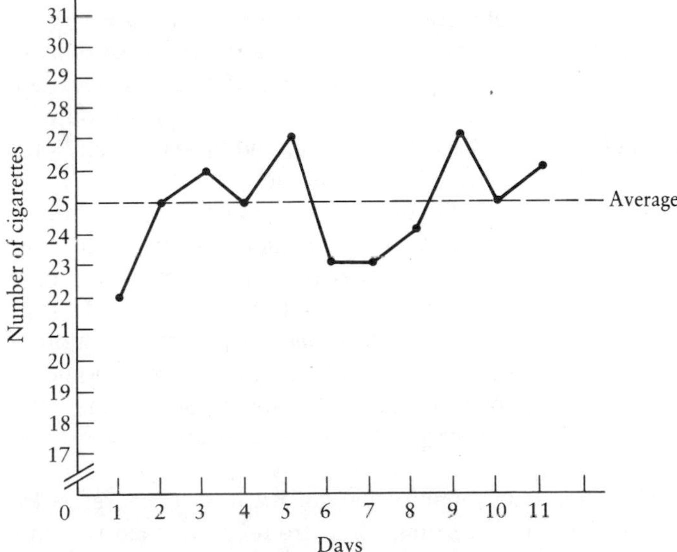

Figure 3-1 Cigarettes smoked daily

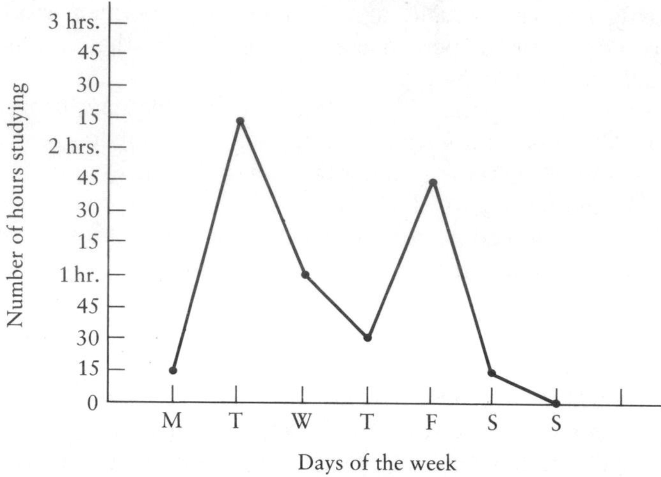

Figure 3-2 Number of hours studied daily

weekly study time because within that week her schedule varied so much. She needs to continue her baseline period for at least another week. During this time she can discover when opportunities for studying occur so that she can calculate the percentage of opportunities she is taking advantage of.

The general answer to the question "How long should you gather baseline data?" is: *long enough to have a good estimate of how often the target behavior occurs, or long enough to see the antecedents and consequences clearly, or both.* End the baseline period only when you have some confidence that you understand the actual pattern of your behavior.

You probably won't get a stable baseline in less than a week. Daily activities vary from day to day, and even for behaviors that occur quite frequently, it will take several days for a consistent pattern to emerge. Some behaviors never show a stable baseline. Complaining, for example, or outbursts of anger may be quite variable because they depend at least partly on how provoking other people's behavior happens to be.

You need to ask yourself, "Is the period of days or weeks during which I have been gathering baseline data representative of my usual life?" If, for example, you are counting the number of hours spent studying, and midterms were last week, then that week wouldn't be considered a typical week and shouldn't be used to make an estimate. If you smoke more at parties and in the last three days you went to three parties, you shouldn't use that period as a base for estimating how much you smoke on the average. (The record does have value in suggesting an antecedent that you could avoid later.)

Are your baseline data reliable? **Reliability,** in science, refers to a particular kind of accuracy in recording. Data are reliable when two or more observations of the same event result in the same recording. When you record your behavior, ask yourself, "Am I really recording each occurrence? Am I recording the same events in the same way each time they occur?" People are often a bit unreliable in their self-recording (Nelson, 1977); however, if you are very unreliable, you won't learn enough about yourself to be able to work out a good plan for change. Particularly, if you try to estimate how often you do something instead of actually counting it as it occurs, you will not get a reliable measure (Farmer & Nelson-Gray, 1990).

George was determined to improve his housekeeping behavior. Two sets of roommates had already thrown him out because he was so sloppy—left his clothes all over the place, never washed dishes, never cleaned the bathroom, and so on. He started keeping records of his behavior and established a category called "acts of good housekeeping." After two weeks, the baseline was very irregular. It turned out that his definition of "acts of good housekeeping" changed from day to day—and from case to case. Some days he gave himself a check mark for good behavior when he put his empty beer glass in the sink, but on other days he would count only what he called "major acts"—for example, making his bed or taking out the garbage. The category definition was too vague, and as a result his records were hopelessly unreliable.

You must keep relatively accurate records and self-observations in order to know how to begin to change and whether or not you are changing. If you think you tend to snack too much whenever you're at home, but in fact the problem behavior occurs only when you're watching TV or are lonely, your plan for self-change is not likely to be successful. You've got to discover the A-B-Cs of your problem behavior. If you are unsure how many hours per week you really do study, then you may not notice a small but definite improvement in your study time and may abandon a self-change plan that in the long run would have worked.

Should you ever start a change program with no baseline period? In general, it is best to make some self-observations *before* trying to change. The advantages gained through better self-understanding outweigh the disadvantage of a short delay.

If a target behavior *never* occurs, there is no point in trying to record it. If you never study, and your target is to develop studying, you already have a baseline count—zero. Yet even in this situation, there is value in self-observing in order to pinpoint the cause of your not studying. A period of self-observation in which you ask, "What are my opportunities to study?" or "What am I doing instead of studying?" or "What thoughts do I have that keep me from studying?" is valuable in formulating a plan for change. If you want to take up exercise, it is a good idea to make a schedule of your daily activities to see when you might realistically schedule exercise sessions. If you don't do this, you are likely to start with an unrealistic plan.

If your goal is to stop some unwanted behavior, it is important to record observations in your structured diary when the behavior occurs. This will help you discover the A-B-C patterns. Finding the antecedents that lead to the unwanted behavior or the consequences that encourage it is essential in devising a successful plan for change.

Tips for Typical Topics

In some cases, you won't be sure of everything you should observe until you have read Chapters 5, 6, and 7 because certain topics may require that you pay special attention to antecedents, behaviors (thoughts, feelings, or actions), and consequences. If you have already identified antecedents, behaviors, and consequences of importance, begin observing them now.

Anxieties and Stress

Not all tensions are destructive; they may heighten performance when we are especially "anxious" to do well. In psychology, **anxieties** and **stress** refer to tension, agitation, or fearfulness that are inappropriate, exaggerated, and self-defeating. It's important to realize that what makes something stressful is your reaction to it, not the event itself. One person might welcome a test as a challenge to her understanding, whereas another might find the same test quite stressful.

What situations make you anxious? Are they specific kinds of situations, such as test anxiety? Record the date, time, and situation in which you feel anxious; then rate your feelings in the situation (Deffenbacher, 1981). Use a rating scale from 0 to 10, for example, where 0 is no tension and 10 is maximum tension. Keeping track of your rated anxiety may lower it (Hiebert & Fox, 1981).

In studying the situation, note your own thoughts and reactions, as they may cue the anxiety. For example, people who become anxious about tests tend to think less about actually taking the test and more about their anxiety, or the bad things that will happen to them if they don't do well on the test, or both (Wine, 1980).

If you feel stressed, keep a daily log of confrontations with problem situations. Record your thoughts, feelings, physical reactions such as sweaty palms or rapid heartbeat, and relevant behaviors (Meichenbaum, 1985). Also record anything you do during the day to relax, as you'll want to increase this later.

Assertion

First, record instances in which you feel you were assertive. Second, note specific kinds of situations in which you *could have been* assertive but were not. Also record what you did and *its* consequences. Later, make a note of what you might have done instead.

Why weren't you assertive? Two classes of targets have been suggested for increasing assertiveness (Mizes, Morgan, & Buder, 1987). *First,* you may not know how to perform the appropriately assertive behaviors. You're not sure what to do, or you think you would do the wrong thing. What did you do instead of being assertive? *Second,* your thoughts about assertiveness may interfere. What did you fear would happen?

Keeping a structured diary will help you discover the reasons you are presently not assertive enough. Look for some or all of the following obstacles: not knowing how to assert yourself well, anxiety, thoughts about disasters that might happen, and actual reactions from others.

Being assertive is a social skill. Therefore, you'll benefit from reading the section on social skills, which appears later in this chapter.

Depression and Low Self-Esteem

By **depression,** psychologists mean a pervasive, long-lasting condition of unhappy mood, lowered energy, and loss of interest in daily events. In Chapter 1 we reported a case of self-modification of depression, and your general strategy should parallel that one.

Keep track of both positive and negative events in your life. People who are depressed tend to focus on the negatives, but you can begin to lighten things by noting positive events in your daily life (Rehm, 1982). Definitely do *not* focus on your own perceived inadequacies or negative characteristics (Kuiper & Olinger, 1986). You probably do that too much already, and doing so will only decrease your self-esteem further. *Do* record positive self-evaluations (Gauthier, Pellerin, & Renaud, 1983; Layden, 1982).

Note your self-putdowns that later lead to lowered feelings. What kinds of positive things could you be saying to yourself instead?

Rate your mood at least four times each day, using a scale you have worked out. You will probably find more fluctuation in mood, including pleasant moments, than you thought. Only rarely is a day all bad (Rehm, 1982), but when we are depressed we sometimes remember only the bad parts. Keeping a record of the better parts will correct this misremembering.

You may feel depressed because of specific problems that are worrying you. For example, are you not getting along with important others (Biglan & Campbell, 1981)? Do continuous thoughts about these problems lead to lowered mood? Counting such thoughts and later taking steps to reduce them may be the best strategy.

There are several different causes of depression (Heiby, 1987). Some people need to develop specific skills—for example, the ability to get along well with others—and others need to eliminate negative thoughts about themselves (Heiby, 1986). If you can target your plan for change to specific problems, you'll increase your chances of success (McKnight, Nelson, Hayes, & Jarrett, 1984).

The thoughts that bother depressed people often involve excessively high standards for personal behavior, self-criticism or mental self-punishment for transgressions, and overgeneralization of a single failure to the whole self-concept (Carver & Ganellen, 1983). People with low self-esteem probably suffer these same problems. Each can be recorded and targeted for change.

Exercise and Athletics

What antecedents do you need before you do your exercise? What presently keeps you from exercising? For example, how does exercise fit into your schedule? What excuses do you make to yourself? You need to discover the answers to these questions.

For many years one of us has kept daily records of exercise using a coded system:

VB Time each day playing volleyball
Ten Time playing tennis
R Number of miles jogged
su Number of sit-ups
pu Number of pushups
G Number of grip exercises
Sw Number of yards swum

The codes are entered for each day. An entry for a typical day might look like this: R 2.5, su 30, pu 10. Another entry might be: Sw 300, G 60. Coding allows you to keep your records in a compact form. The records can be displayed on a sheet of paper, perhaps taped to the closet door, so you can inspect them daily to check on your progress. We've found that, for us, just keeping the record is enough to keep us exercising; it's reactive.

Relations with Others: Social Anxieties, Social Skills, and Dating

A variety of problems fall in this category—inability to get along with others, shyness, need for better communication—but all involve monitoring the effect others have on you and increasing your skills to deal with certain social situations. Plan to record the details—the A-B-Cs—of your social interactions.

Of course, you do the recording later, not while you're with people. When you are actually interacting with others, do *not* make the mistake of paying too much attention to your own behavior and too little to theirs (Gambrill & Richey, 1985). One of the best ways to make a good impression is to pay attention to—show interest in—the other person. But we are not suggesting that you worry about what the other person thinks about you. If you are shy or socially anxious, you are already too worried about that (Goldfried, Padawer, & Robins, 1984). Just pay attention to what the other person is doing and saying; this will demonstrate your interest.

Discovering antecedents is vital in understanding shyness, because shy people often avoid social situations (Twentyman, Boland, & McFall, 1981). What antecedents lead to avoidance—physical situations, social situations, your own thoughts? For example, do you tell yourself you can't make a good impression?

Try writing down what you did in a social situation, and then write what you might have done instead. This will help you see what behaviors you want to develop. Be sure to record positive instances of good social behavior as well as negative ones.

Problems with other people often involve communication—not listening, not saying what one feels, being abusive, not communicating at all—and the way problems are solved—no solutions or poor solutions. Watch for these as you record the details of your target behavior.

Smoking, Drinking, and Drugs

Keep track of the situation you are in, and rate your emotional state when you indulge (Marlatt, 1982). Record the antecedents and consequences of your indulgence. When do you smoke or drink too much? What are you saying to yourself just before you indulge? What are the consequences? What do you get out of it? This will give you a daily count of the number of indulgences and will begin to show the reasons why you indulge. Certain situations or moods may always lead to indulgence. When you have coffee, for example, you smoke. When you are nervous, you drink. In keeping a record, you are trying to find out *why* you indulge as well as how often. Later, you will be able to use that information to formulate a workable plan for change (O'Connor & Stravynski, 1982). For example, if you find that you often indulge as a way of relaxing, you may start a plan to learn to relax in other ways.

Be sure to record urges to indulge that you resist. If you want to have a cigarette but resist the urge, then record it (O'Banion, Armstrong, & Ellis, 1980). You might also want to record how satisfying it is to give in to an urge (Gordon & Marlatt, 1981). Some cigarettes or some drinks, for example, are more satisfying than others. You can rate the satisfaction—on a scale, for example, where 1 is "no satisfaction" and 7 is "maximal satisfaction." This will remind you later which situations are the most tempting. You might then avoid these situations or require yourself to indulge only in less satisfying behaviors.

Once you have quit, plan to continue keeping records. It's been shown that it helps you keep abstaining. (Kamarck & Lichtenstein, 1987).

Studying and Time Management

Before establishing a full time-management schedule, you'll need to know how you currently use your time. Prepare a daily log, and mark the beginning and the ending time for each change of activity. Buy a small daily appointment book for this purpose, or make your own daily sheets. Mark when an activity begins and when it ends. For example:

7:00 A.M. Woke up and got ready to go to school
7:42 A.M. Watched television while I ate breakfast
8:15 A.M. Left the house

For studying, record how much time you were in a position to study and how much time you actually spent studying. This will allow you to find the percentage of time you're on target. For times when you did not study, record what you did instead and the consequences.

Also record your actual studying behaviors. The quality of your studying is as important as the quantity. Do you read and underline? Do you make notes? We've emphasized percentage of time on target, but the kinds of study techniques outlined in Box 1-1 also improve one's learning. You can begin to record your use of those techniques.

Weight Loss and Overeating

Successful weight loss requires observation of several kinds. Keep track of everything you eat and list the time, place, and social situation (Campbell, Bender, Bennett, & Donnelly, 1981). Record the antecedents—your feelings, the locations, and whether you were alone or with particular people. What did you say to yourself just before you overate? Also record the consequences: What did you get out of your overeating? You may eat to relax, to celebrate, or to get some reward from life. If you do, you want to find out so that later you can consider seeking rewards or relaxation in other ways.

Remember that you don't have to eat less now; you only have to record what you do eat. Recording the actual food consumed is probably the best form of daily record. For your weight, a weekly record is sufficient. Also keep track of your exercise. This will become an important part of your eventual plan.

Chapter Summary

Structured Diaries

Self-observation is the first element of self-direction. Recording your behavior provides the basis for self-observation.

Situations can be divided into antecedents and consequences of behavior. To identify both, keep a structured diary in which you record the behavior, its antecedents, and its consequences:

Antecedents (A)	*Behaviors (B)*	*Consequences (C)*
When did it happen? Whom were you with? What were you doing? Where were you? What were you saying to yourself?	Actions, thoughts, feelings	What happened as a result? Was it pleasant or unpleasant?

An entry should be made as soon as possible after the event. The diary will tell you what situations affect your actions, thoughts, and feelings. Use entries to figure out how to change your behavior by changing the situation.

Recording Frequency and Duration

You can count either the amount of time you spend doing something or the number of times you do it. You can also compute the percentage of time you do something. Record positive events as well as negative ones.

Make definite plans for how you will carry out your self-observations. Anticipate what problems may come up, and figure out how you will deal with them.

Recording the Intensity of Emotions

Rating scales allow you to gauge the intensity of an event. They are particularly useful for recording feelings and emotions. A good technique is to combine the use of rating scales with counts of actual behaviors.

Practicalities of Record Keeping

Four rules for self-observation are:

1. Do the counting when the behavior occurs, not later.
2. Be accurate and strict in your counting. Try to include all instances of the behavior.
3. Keep written records.
4. Keep the recording system as simple as possible. Try to fit it with your usual habits.

Observing what you do may change what you do. Sometimes the very act of recording your behavior is enough to produce change; most often, it helps. Use the reactivity of self-recording to your advantage.

If you perform the problem behavior absentmindedly, practice performing it while paying close attention so that your attention is switched on whenever the behavior occurs. Ask others to point out instances of the target behavior. For behaviors that are difficult or impractical to record immediately, find some way to make a mark, and instruct yourself to remember and record the incident later.

If you are failing to self-observe, your *first* plan for change should be to work out a system to increase accurate self-observation. Develop record keeping one step at a time. Reward yourself for keeping records, and have others check on your record keeping.

Planning for Change

Data recorded before you begin a plan can serve as a baseline against which you measure future progress. You should continue the baseline record until a stable pattern emerges. This almost always requires at least a week.

The data should be as reliable as possible. You can increase reliability through specific definitions, careful attention, simple recording procedures, and practice. Other techniques for improving reliability include soliciting the help of someone else and rewarding yourself for good recording.

As a general rule, you should not begin a plan for self-change until after you have established a stable, reliable baseline because only then will you really know the extent of the problem and its exact nature.

YOUR OWN SELF-DIRECTION PROJECT: STEP THREE

You should now begin self-observation for the behavior-in-a-situation you chose in Step Two. For your self-observation, use a structured diary, a frequency count, a rating scale, or a combination of the three.

Make record keeping easy, and build it into your daily schedule. Don't go directly into an attempt to change; first observe the target behavior as it is now occurring.

Collect baseline records for at least one week. Be as accurate as you can.

While you are gathering data, read the next five chapters, which deal with the principles of behavior and the techniques of change. When you have an adequate number of self-observations, you will be ready to begin your plan for change.

4

The Principles of Self-Regulation

Outline

- Regulation Theory
- Regulation by Others and Regulation by Self
- Language Regulation
- Consequences
- Antecedents
- Respondent Behavior and Conditioning
- Modeling
- *Chapter Summary*
- *Your Own Self-Direction Project: Step Four*

Learning Objectives

Regulation Theory

1. According to cybernetics, what are the four basic elements in all self-controlling systems?
2. What are the limitations of cybernetic theory?
3. How do regulation theories attempt to improve on cybernetics?

Regulation by Others and Regulation by Self

4. What are the developmental stages in learning new behaviors?
5. What is subvocal speech?
6. What is learned resourcefulness?
7. What is rule-governed behavior?

Language Regulation

8. Describe the process by which verbal control by others becomes self-control.
9. What does it mean to say that subvocal speech "goes underground"?

Consequences

10. What is operant behavior? What affects it?
11. What is a positive reinforcer?
12. What is a negative reinforcer?
13. Explain the concept of contingency.
14. Describe escape and avoidance learning. How do they differ?
15. What effect does punishment have on the frequency of behavior?
    a. What are the two types of punishment?
    b. What is the difference between negative reinforcement and punishment?
16. What is extinction?
    a. What is the effect of intermittent reinforcement on extinction?
    b. How can maladaptive behaviors sometimes be explained by the idea of intermittent reinforcement?
17. What are your beliefs on the issue of freedom and determinism? What is the text's position?

Antecedents

18. What role is played by the cue, or antecedent, in operant behavior?
    a. When does an antecedent become a cue to behavior?
    b. What guides avoidance behavior? To what does the person respond?
    c. What is stimulus control?
    d. Why is avoidance behavior resistant to extinction?

Respondent Behavior and Conditioning

19. What is respondent behavior?
20. Explain respondent conditioning.
    a. What is higher-order conditioning?
    b. How does emotional conditioning occur?
    c. After a reaction has been conditioned, what effect does the stimulus—or antecedent—have?

Modeling

21. Describe learning through modeling.
22. List the principles presented in Box 4-2.

You have taken several steps toward self-change: selected a goal, identified the behaviors that need to be adjusted, and begun to keep records of your present behaviors. These steps are giant ones. Establishing goals and collecting self-observations are in many instances sufficient to bring about behavior change. This is often astonishing to people who find that they are somehow changing a problem behavior after failing before, and the only apparent difference is that they are keeping records. This phenomenon has also puzzled psychologists. But in the past 25 years, psychologists have begun to solve the mystery. The power of setting goals and keeping records is now well explained by **regulation theory.**

Regulation Theory

Regulation theory is a body of thought in psychology; it is derived partially from **cybernetics** (Wiener, 1948). Cybernetics, or the science of self-regulation, has had a major impact on contemporary scientific thought, from physics to sociology, and has produced all manner of self-regulating machines, from automatic pilots to the self-tuning radio. Cybernetics has also influenced several psychological theories of self-regulation, each with different emphases, but all sharing certain basic cybernetic principles (Bandura, 1986; Carver & Scheier, 1982; Kanfer, 1975; Kanfer & Stevenson, 1985; Miller, Galanter, & Pribram, 1960). What are these basic, highly influential principles? What is cybernetic regulation theory?

The thermostat of your home heating system is a simple example of the mechanisms discussed in cybernetic theory. The thermostat has very few parts and functions. It has a *standard* to be set, by which the desired temperature is indicated. It has a *sensor,* a thermometer, that responds to actual temperature. It has a *comparator,* a device that compares what the temperature is with what it should be. And finally, it has an *activator* that—when the discrepancy between actual and desired temperature is too great—closes the circuit and turns the heater on, or opens the circuit and turns it off. Thus, a reasonably good fit between actual and desired temperature is maintained. These few elements are at the core of all self-regulating machines, from self-guiding rockets to home robots.

Most self-regulation of human behavior contains the same elements: we each have *standards* for our behavior; we have *sensors* to gauge what our behavior actually is; *comparisons* are made between the desired and actual behavior; and when we perceive a discrepancy, we *activate* to change. Now you can see why your own first steps toward self-direction—setting standards and collecting observations—may bring about significant change. If you collect those observations and compare them with your standards, you may well activate for change. Simple *attending* to a problem area can clarify goals and standards and can energize us for careful observation and comparison.

This theory is a very powerful tool for the understanding of all human behavior, even when behavior is not going well. For example, we know that not all behavior is effectively regulated. The reason for this, according to cybernetic theories, is that when standards are lacking, when we do not notice our own behavior, when we do not compare our behavior to our standards, or when we do not have the skills that would bring our behavior into line with our standards, no change would be expected. Regulation theories account for much emotion as well as action. When one compares one's own behavior to a standard, a favorable comparison produces feelings of optimism or happiness; a disappointing comparison evokes negative feelings, such as frustration, discouragement, or depression (Carver & Scheier, 1990; Curtis, 1991).

Regulation theorists vary in the "purity" with which they use cybernetic formulations. Carver and Scheier (for example, 1982, 1986, 1990) are among the most influential contemporary social psychologists; their *control theory* is strictly based on cybernetic formulations. Bandura (for example, 1986) is a powerful voice in *social learning theory*. Although he uses aspects of cybernetic formulations, his own theory focuses equally on such considerations as thinking, planning, and judgment. Kanfer (for example, 1975), an influential figure in *self-regulation theory*, incorporates considerations of reward, punishment, learning, and thinking. And others, such as radical behaviorists, do not use cybernetic concepts at all (for example, Zettle & Hayes, 1982). What are the difficulties regarding cybernetic theories that lead many regulation theorists to consider other concepts? Even though an individual may have clear goals and standards and may have observed his or her behavior closely, activation for change may not come about. How can that be explained by cybernetic theories, which seem to assert that the human being is constructed so that sensing and comparing with standards "automatically" produces action? In effect, the proponents' argument is that human beings are "hard-wired" to behave that way, and no further explanation is needed on the psychological level. While much evidence supports this view of human nature, it cannot be seen as complete, for three reasons.

First, psychological and behavioral systems are infinitely more complex than are mechanical systems (Bandura, 1986). A thermostat activates by either "opening" or "closing." When a person discovers a discrepancy between standards and actuality, he or she must choose among a thousand alternatives, and cybernetic regulation theory does not guide us in understanding these choices.

A second limitation is that the correct action may not be available. We may never have learned the appropriate action that would bring our behavior closer to standard. The rest of this chapter discusses the ways in which alternative behaviors are learned and kept at ready strength.

There is a third limitation to cybernetic theory that we will address in the following section. *Not all human behavior is self-regulated.* This is particularly obvious in very young children, who are closely regulated by others, but it is also true for adults. Some behavior is under the regulation of the environment, not the self. Even for the most self-determining person, behavior is intimately connected to the setting in which it occurs. Much self-regulation is actually learning to control the environment that controls us.

Therefore, the next step in understanding the principles of self-regulation is to examine the relationship between regulation by others and regulation by self.

Regulation by Others and Regulation by Self

All behavior, as it develops, passes through the following sequence: (1) control by others, (2) control by self, and (3) automatization. Thus, not all behaviors, much less all persons, are self-regulated. Self-regulation is a stage of development that lies between the point where assistance is required from other people and the point where the behavior becomes automatic and no further regulation is needed. It is important to realize that we are discussing specific behaviors, not the person as a whole. That is, even for the most self-actualized adult, each new learned behavior passes through this same sequence (Tharp & Gallimore, 1988).

Try to recall what learning to drive was like. Your instructor is beside you. The traffic is moderately heavy as you approach an intersection, and you are concentrating on staying in your lane, at a safe distance from the car ahead. Twenty yards from the intersection, the traffic light snaps from green to amber. "Stop!" your instructor says. "There won't be enough time to get through." You stop slowly and safely.

Approaching the next intersection, you watch the traffic light more closely. When it changes to amber, it is likely that you'll say to yourself "Stop!" and do so. You may actually speak to yourself aloud; more likely, it will be a "mental" message—subvocal speech. In either event, this is self-regulation—a self-instruction that helps you come to a smooth, safe stop. Soon you need no regulation. Braking at the sight of the amber light is now so automatic that you need no instructor or self-instruction—you just stop.

Each new behavior that you develop through your self-modification project will go through that same sequence. In most instances, either this text or your instructor or other advisor will provide the needed regulation, assistance, or "control" by others. The second stage of the sequence will be represented by your own acts of self-regulation: refining your standards, inventing observational methods, or using self-instruction. In the last stage, your new behavior will become as automatic as driving your automobile, and you will need to think about it as little as you think about your driving.

This sequence of behavior development is widely discussed in contemporary developmental psychology (Rogoff, 1982; Rogoff & Lave, 1984; Tharp, Gallimore, & Calkins, 1984; Tharp, Jordan, et al., 1984; Vygotsky, 1978; Wertsch, 1985). All the details of this theory do not concern us here. The main point is that each new competence added to your repertoire passes from regulation by some outside source to regulation by yourself. At the point that competence is fully developed, the behavior becomes automatic—consciously regulated neither by others nor by you.

Does automatic, fully developed behavior run free, entirely disentangled from the world around? Not at all. When behavior has become fully automatic, it has come under environmental control. But it is possible at any time to retrieve automatic behavior and bring it back under your own self-regulation if it does not meet your standards. Once self-regulation has produced the desirable balance between environment and behavior, the behavior will come under the control of new environmental stimuli—that is, it will become automatic again. This recurring cycle is typical of the self-directing, well-adjusted individual (Karoly & Kanfer, 1982).

Learned resourcefulness is the bundle of skills that allows us to retrieve our behaviors from an automatic, "mindless" state. Rosenbaum (1988) has discussed how learned resourcefulness is activated when "mindless" sequences are disrupted. The resourcefulness you will learn will allow you to self-consciously disrupt your unsatisfactory, mindless sequences and bring them under self-regulation.

In beginning to understand this recurrent cycle, it is important to understand the basic principles of regulation. Regulation of behavior, whether by others or by the self, takes place through the same basic mechanisms: language regulation, consequences, antecedents, respondent behavior and conditioning, and modeling. Each mechanism operates first by control from the outside and then through control by the self.

Language Regulation

The most common method of controlling behavior is through language. We give orders: "Platoon, halt!" or "Take out your driver's license, please!" We make requests: "Please pass the salt." We give hints: "I suppose it's a good movie, but I'm so tired tonight. . . ." We coach: "Good, good; a little more to the right; that's better. . . ." Hundreds of examples occur in everyone's daily life. Of all forms of antecedents, the language of others (both spoken and written) may well have the strongest and most immediate effect on our behavior. Of course, we do not always comply. We may refuse, ignore, argue, resent, or laugh. But the effects are there. Language is a pervasive, inescapable influence on our reactions. In charting chains of events, you will find that the language of others represents the immediate antecedent of many of your behaviors, desirable ones as well as problematic ones. The human environment is in many ways a language environment, and the environment controls behavior largely through language.

"Talking to oneself," or self-directed speech, is often considered comical, if not aberrant. It conjures up a picture of an old man muttering to himself on a city street or even of someone in a mental hospital. Actually, self-directed speech is common, useful, often highly adaptive, routine, and normal. For most adults, however, self-directed speech is subvocal. What is the relationship between talking to oneself aloud and talking to oneself subvocally (that is, silently, covertly, or "mentally"—thinking in words)? In fact, the effects of these two forms of self-speech antecedents are virtually identical.

As very young children develop, a first task of their parents is to bring them into the language community. Children learn to heed language and use it. Psychologists Luria (1961) and Vygotsky (1965, 1978) have studied this developmental process in detail and found a regular sequence that is roughly linked to the child's age. Some aspects of this sequence are illustrated in the following example.

"Don't kick over the wastebasket!" the father shouts to the 2- or 3-year-old. Too late; the trash is on the floor. The father rights the wastebasket and says again, this time more gently, "Don't kick over the wastebasket now." Next day, the child approaches the basket, draws back the foot for a happy kick—and stops midway through. "Don't kick over the basket!" the child says, and walks on by. The sight of the wastebasket may for some time cause the child to mutter the instruction aloud. For a while longer, the father may see the child's lips moving in a silent self-instruction. Eventually, all traces of speech disappear, and the child merely walks by, leaving the basket unmolested. No external evidence of self-speech remains. In all likelihood, subvocal speech itself drops out, and the behavior becomes "automatic."

In transferring from control by others to self-control, very young children imitate and incorporate adult speech. First the father says, "Don't kick!" Then the child says the same thing, often imitating emphasis and inflection. Control of the child's behavior is passed from parent to child. But notice this: the control by language instruction is maintained. Regardless of who says it, the antecedent "Don't kick!" affects the child's behavior. It is normal for young children to use imitated, spoken-aloud self-instructions for self-control (Tharp, Gallimore, & Calkins, 1984; Vygotsky, 1965, 1978).

At a certain point, around the age of 5, this self-controlling speech "goes underground," in Vygotsky's (1965) apt phrase. That is, the use of self-controlling language becomes subvocal—steadily more silent, rapid, and condensed. Many psychologists would argue that this is when thinking begins, because so much thinking can be seen as subvocal speech. During earlier stages, before language "goes underground," self-instructing aloud helps children perform tasks more efficiently (Luria, 1961).

Even in adulthood, the power of self-directed speech as an antecedent is not lost; it is merely not used as often. Donald Meichenbaum (1977) has demonstrated that verbal self-control can be reinstituted for older children and adults when new skills are being learned, when self-control deficiencies are present, or when a person is in a problematic situation. Self-directed speech (vocal or subvocal) is a powerful controlling antecedent of behavior. It is particularly useful and natural in new or stressful situations.

It was useful and natural for you to say "Stop!" to yourself when you were learning to drive. You probably no longer do so. But the next time you are driving in a strange city, when the amber light stays on a much longer or shorter time than you are accustomed to, you may need to talk to yourself again. When the smooth flow of behaviors is somehow disrupted, conscious self-regulation comes into play (Kanfer & Karoly, 1972). Difficult situations make us more likely to use self-speech. This is one way in which we "rescue" automatic behavior when it no longer meets our standards.

Thus, you probably talk to yourself in precisely those situations that you find most fearful, most depressing, or most difficult to cope with. This self-speech is likely to be "underground"—probably no more than a mutter, or only a quick "speech in the mind." Regardless of the form it takes, this self-speech antecedent has a powerful influence over your responses to difficulties. Have you ever said to yourself, "This is probably one of those situations in which I make a fool of myself," and walked away, lonely and depressed? This kind of self-speech can perpetuate shy responses.

A more general and powerful form of verbal self-regulation is seen in what psychologists call **rule-governed behavior** (Hayes, 1989). People establish rules of conduct for themselves, often by adopting rules taught to them by others, and often distilled from their own experiences. These may be general rules of a high moral abstraction, such as a rule to always be kind or loyal. Other rules concern daily schedules (always rising early) or never having a late assignment. Even children, when doing schoolwork, say rules aloud to themselves to cope with difficult tasks or stress (Berk, 1986). Each rule is actually a verbal statement, self-spoken, that guides interpretations of events and sets standards with which people compare their actual conduct. These rules are powerful regulators of behavior; indeed, they often insulate our habits from almost any other influence (Catania, Matthews, & Shimoff, 1990). In the self-change procedures presented in this book, self-established rules will play an important role.

In your self-observation, observe yourself carefully as a problem situation begins to unfold. Try to detect the things you are saying to yourself; they act as instructions.

Principle 1: *From early life to adulthood, regulation by others and the self (particularly through verbal instructions) acts as a powerful guide to behavior.*

Consequences

A child walks up and kicks a wastebasket. Her mother scolds her and makes her replace the trash. This consequence makes it less likely that the child will upset the basket again.

Another child walks by the basket and does not kick it. "Good, Ginny!" her mother says. "What a good girl!" This rewarding consequence makes it more likely that Ginny will leave the basket unmolested in the future.

Two groups of workers in a furniture company decided to form "quality circles"—discussion groups that management consultants recommend as a way of increasing employee production and morale. One group's supervisor was resentful and accused the group of trying to "go union." The workers dropped the idea. The other supervisor encouraged his subordinates and praised them for their initiative. That group formed its quality circle and put real energy into it.

Different consequences in the form of supervisors' reactions had strongly affected each group's behavior. Within the quality circle, when the discussions became difficult, the workers encouraged themselves with reminders that their initiative was valued by their supervisor. In this way, they transferred the positive consequences from the supervisor to themselves and moved into the stage of self-regulation.

Operant Behaviors

Behaviors that are affected by their consequences are called **operant** behaviors. The dictionary defines *to operate* as "to perform an act, to function, to produce an effect." An effect is a consequence. Through operant behaviors, we act, function, and produce effects on ourselves and on our environment. Through the effects—the consequences—the environment acts once again on us. Much of our behavior is operant. Operant behavior includes all the complex things we do as we weave the fabric of our daily lives. Our bad habits are operant behaviors we want to eliminate. The things we don't do but wish we did are operant behaviors we want to develop.

We develop operant behaviors—that is, we learn them—through the consequences of our actions. Operant behaviors are changed—learned or unlearned—as a result of their consequences.

Principle 2: *Operant behavior is a function of its consequences.* No matter what we are learning to do—type, speak, write, study, eat, kiss, or compose a string quartet—our skills will be strengthened or weakened by the events that follow them. A child learning to speak, for example, will become more verbal if praised than if scolded for talking. A composer will be more or less likely to write a second quartet depending on the events that follow the first attempt.

Consequences That Strengthen Behavior

The *strength* of behavior refers to the chances that a particular behavior will be performed. The best practical index for gauging the probability of a behavior is its frequency. We usually infer the strength of a behavior from its frequency. That is, we count how often the behavior occurs. This is why the chapter on self-observation placed so much emphasis on counting occurrences of a behavior.

Reinforcers

If a consequence strengthens a behavior, it is called a **reinforcer.** How reinforcers strengthen behavior depends on the nature of the consequence.

Principle 3: *A positive reinforcer is a consequence that maintains and strengthens behavior by its added presence.* Positive reinforcers may be anything—kisses, food, money, praise, or the chance to ride a motorcycle. What is a positive reinforcer for one person is not necessarily a positive reinforcer for another. The list is inexhaustible and highly individualized.

A little boy goes to his father and shows him a picture he has drawn. "That's lovely, son," the father praises him. "I really like it. Hey, what's this part?" he asks, giving the child attention. The father's praise and attention are probably positive reinforcers for the child. They increase the chance that in the future the child will continue to draw and will show his pictures to his father.

A positive reinforcer is anything that, when added to the situation, makes the behavior that preceded it more likely to recur. The composer is more likely to attempt a second quartet if the first act of composing is positively reinforced. This positive reinforcement might consist of one or more consequences: applause from the audience, the pleasure of hearing the work performed, a sense of satisfaction in knowing that the work meets high standards. It is important to note that praise from critics or friends has positive reinforcing effects. Thus, language acts as a reinforcing consequence, as well as an antecedent.

Principle 4: *A negative reinforcer is a consequence that strengthens behavior by being subtracted from the situation.* If you are standing outside and it begins to rain hard, you might put up your umbrella to keep the rain from falling on your head. The act of putting up the umbrella is thus negatively reinforced by the removal of the unpleasant consequence of getting wet. The act that took away the unpleasant situation is reinforced—that is, made more likely to happen again.

Picture a person talking to a friend. The friend seems bored. The more the person talks on a particular topic, the more bored the friend seems to be. So the speaker changes to a new topic. Immediately the friend appears less bored. The act of changing topics is negatively reinforced by the fact that the friend is no longer bored. In other words, changing topics has removed the unpleasant consequence—the friend's boredom.

Just as with positive reinforcers, what is a negative reinforcer for one person is not necessarily so for another. The saying "One person's meat is another's poison" expresses this concept.

Contingency

The conditions necessary for a reinforcer to strengthen a behavior are expressed in the concept of **contingency.** For any stimulus to function as a reinforcer, it must occur after, and only after, a certain response. If you gain a reward whether or not you perform some behavior, the "rewarding" stimulus will not actually reinforce the behavior; in fact it probably will not affect it at all. If instead you can gain the reward only by performing the behavior, that behavior will be reinforced and strengthened—that is, it will be more likely to occur again. It is the *contingent* relationship that is important, not the reinforcer alone. This same principle applies to punishment, as we will discuss later: both reinforcement and punishment must be contingent in order to function.

Escape and Avoidance

The principle of negative reinforcement explains how we learn to escape or avoid unpleasant consequences. Suppose a mother says, "Come here, please," to a child who is in a rebellious mood. The child does not come. The mother reaches over and swats the child. The child still does not come. The mother raises her hand again. The child comes. The mother drops her hand. By complying, the child has escaped or avoided a second swat.

Technically, **escape learning** refers to behaviors that terminate an unpleasant consequence. The mother keeps spanking until the child submits and comes along. **Avoidance learning,** on the other hand, refers to behaviors that remove the possibility of an unpleasant consequence. The next time the mother says, "Come here," the child obeys, thus avoiding a spanking like the one he got in the past. In escape learning the unpleasantness is actually delivered, but in avoidance learning it is avoided.

When you begin to analyze your own behavior, you may discover that you do things for which you get no apparent reward. People sometimes think of these behaviors as being "unmotivated," but they are often avoidance behaviors. For example, you may tend to go off by yourself rather than to places frequented by your friends, even though being by yourself is not reinforcing. You might ask, "What am I responding to?" You may have learned an avoidance behavior. An important characteristic of well-learned avoidance behaviors is that often they are performed in an unemotional, even blasé, way. Such behaviors are not motivated by anxiety. Until it is called to your attention, you may be totally unaware that some of your behaviors are based on the avoidance of discomfort.

Reinforcing Consequences

You can see why an analysis of consequences is an important part of a plan for changing. You may find that you are *not* in fact positively reinforced for the behavior you want to perform. You may even find that you are being positively reinforced for some action that makes the desired behavior difficult or impossible. For example, one student wrote in a self-analysis: "I would like to be nicer to my roommate and be able to solve our little difficulties in a friendly way. But I usually fly off the handle and shout at him. The terrible thing is that I get reinforced for that: he gives in!"

By understanding how reinforcing consequences work—positively or negatively—you can form better plans for changing your behavior. In self-change, sometimes you learn new behaviors—for example, an overeater learns to deal with tension in some new way instead of eating—and sometimes you arrange to be reinforced for acts you already know how to perform—for example, a nail biter is reinforced for not biting his nails.

Reinforcements are important for both learning and performance of actions. Theoretical psychologists argue whether, strictly speaking, reinforcement is necessary for learning or only for performance. But it is clear that your *performance* of behavior is affected by the reinforcement you get. You do what you are reinforced for doing.

Punishment

Principle 5: *Behavior that is punished will occur less often.* Psychologists distinguish two kinds of punishment. In the first kind, after a behavior has been performed, some unpleasant event occurs. For example, a child says a naughty word and is immediately reprimanded by her parents. An adult says something rude and immediately receives disapproval from friends. If these disapprovals are unpleasant enough, the naughtiness and rudeness are less likely to happen in the future. They have been punished.

In the second kind of punishment, after a behavior has been performed, something pleasant is taken away. For example, a child who is playing with her parents says a naughty word and is put in her room by herself. A man says something rude, and his friends go away. In both cases, it is the *loss* of something pleasant—playing with parents, being with friends—that punishes the behavior that preceded it.

What is the difference between punishment and negative reinforcement? In negative reinforcement, an act that allows the person to escape or avoid some event is reinforced by *removing* the unpleasant event. In punishment, behavior probabilities are reduced in one of two ways: (1) an unpleasant event follows a behavior, or (2) a pleasant event is withdrawn following a behavior.

The following summarizes the difference between negative reinforcement and punishment:

	What Your Behavior Leads to	*Effect on Future Behavior*
Negative Reinforcement	Escape or avoidance of a (usually unpleasant) consequence	Behavior is strengthened
Punishment, Type 1	An unpleasant event	Behavior is less likely to recur
Punishment, Type 2	The loss of something pleasant	Behavior is less likely to recur

Note that punishment, like reinforcement, must be delivered contingent on the behavior in order to work; that is, both must occur when and only when the behavior occurs.

The strong effects of punishment on behavior have been demonstrated in animal laboratories throughout this century. Punishment's effects on human behavior remain problematic and continue to be debated (Axelrod & Apsche, 1983). Should punishment be used to regulate human behavior? Punishment creates strong emotional reactions, its side effects are volatile and unpredictable, and it creates aggression. Strong punishment can brutalize both the victim and the punisher. "Punishing" others is often only a justification for releasing anger and frustration. However, mild punishment—keeping lazy children in from an occasional recess; quick, quiet scolds or objections—is characteristic of all human relationships.

The effectiveness of punishment for humans has one very serious limitation: punishment has no effect if the punishing situation can be escaped (Azrin, Hake, Holz, & Hutchinson, 1965), and in a free community, it usually can—often merely by apologizing or lying. This succeeds only in teaching people to apologize and lie.

In self-directed behavior change, punishment can always be avoided. For these and other reasons, to be explained in detail in Chapter 7, we urge you not to include punishment in your plans for self-change unless you consider it very carefully. The same advances can be made through the use of other learning principles, such as extinction.

Extinction

Suppose you first learn to do some act because you are reinforced for it, but then, on later performances, no reward follows. What was once reinforced no longer is. As a consequence, your act begins to lose some of its strength. This is called **extinction.**

Principle 6: *An act that was reinforced but no longer is will begin to weaken.* Two people have been going together happily for several months. But then a new pattern begins. He calls her, but she's not home. He leaves a message, but she doesn't call back. Or she drops by to see him, and he doesn't seem very interested. Life, alas, changes, and acts that were once reinforced may no longer be. He will be less likely to call in the future. She will be less likely to drop by.

Extinction occurs all around us, continuously. It is the process by which we adjust our behavior to a changing world. If the woman never returns the man's calls, he wouldn't want to keep calling back forever. Nor would the woman want to keep dropping by to see an uninterested man. Behaviors that are no longer productive are gradually dropped.

Extinction and punishment are not the same, incidentally. In extinction there is *no* consequence to an act. In our example, the calls are simply ignored. If the woman said, "Don't call me anymore. I don't want to talk to you," that would *punish* the act of calling. If she simply didn't return calls—that is, she did nothing—that would *extinguish* the act of calling.

Do all acts extinguish equally? No.

Principle 7: *Intermittent reinforcement increases resistance to extinction.* Reinforcement that follows each instance of a behavior is called **continuous re-**

inforcement. This can be described as a 100% schedule of reinforcement. But most behaviors in the real world are not reinforced at each instance. Sometimes they are reinforced, and sometimes they are not. This is called **intermittent reinforcement.**

As you might expect, continuous reinforcement provides for rapid new learning. But intermittent reinforcement has a most interesting effect: *it makes behaviors more resistant to extinction.* The behaviors weaken more gradually. A behavior that has been reinforced randomly but on an average of every other time (a 50% schedule) will persist longer when reinforcement is withdrawn than if it had been reinforced continuously.

Let's go back to the example of the spurned lover. Suppose the woman has been careless about returning the man's calls, and he has been reinforced about half the time for calling her. Finally, she loses interest in him entirely and no longer responds at all to his telephone messages. (Each telephone call sequence is called an *extinction trial.*) The intermittent reinforcement schedule he was on before (when she returned about half his calls) means that it will take *longer* for his calling behavior to be extinguished than if he had been reinforced 100% of the time. If her nonreinforcement continues, of course, extinction will eventually occur. But the number of trials to extinction is affected by the previous reinforcement schedule.

This effect of intermittent reinforcement is significant for self-change because it helps explain the persistence of maladaptive behaviors. Why do you do things you are apparently not reinforced for or things you don't even want to do? You may not notice the rare reinforcement—perhaps 1 in 50 or 100 times—that is keeping your behavior going. Or you may have been intermittently reinforced for maladaptive acts in the past, so now they are very resistant to extinction. A casual observer, not realizing the effect of intermittent reinforcement, might label such behavior "stubborn" or "foolish." Many maladjusted behaviors you see in yourself or other people persist because they are reinforced on intermittent schedules.

Incidentally, changing from reinforcement to extinction often produces an initial increase in the behavior before the gradual decline begins. At first, when the woman does not return the calls, the man calls more often; then his telephoning gradually tapers off and is finally extinguished altogether.

Antecedents

We now turn to a general consideration of *antecedents* and how antecedent control of behavior develops. Regardless of the power of consequences, your behavior can never be stimulated by its consequences alone. Consequences, after all, occur after a behavior is completed. Antecedents, on the other hand, are the setting events for your behavior. As such, they control it, in the sense of calling it up or stimulating it. When an antecedent calls up a behavior that is subsequently reinforced, the behavior and the environment are in good balance. When a behavior is firmly integrated with its antecedents and consequences, we experience a smooth flow. No thought or self-regulation intervenes, and the behavior has become "automatic."

Antecedents and Positive Reinforcement

Throughout our lives, most of our actions are controlled by **cues** (signals). For example, when the bell rings or the lecturer says, "That's all for today," students leave their seats and move toward the door. Each student knows perfectly well how to leave a classroom, but ordinarily no one does so until the cue is given.

Principle 8: *Most operant behavior is eventually guided by antecedent stimuli, or cues, the most important of which are often self-directed statements.* The interesting question is "How do we learn the cues?" In any hour of our lives, the environment provides thousands of cues. The world is rich with stimuli—conversations, sounds, sights, events, smells—and our behaviors are orchestrated into this complexity. Cues that evoke a particular action are called **discriminative stimuli.** This technical term is useful because it helps us understand how a cue works. A cue identifies the conditions in which an action will or will not be reinforced. It is a cue that helps us *discriminate* conditions when the behavior will be followed by reinforcement from other conditions when the behavior will not be followed by reinforcement. In college you soon learn that when the lecturer says, "That's all," you can leave in good conscience. You also learn that in the absence of that cue, it would be wiser to stay in your seat.

An antecedent, or stimulus, becomes a cue to a behavior when the behavior is reinforced in the presence of that stimulus and not reinforced in the absence of the stimulus. When a stimulus and a behavior occur and the behavior is reinforced *only* when stimulus and behavior occur together, the stimulus will become a cue for that behavior.

This process can be studied in the laboratory by reinforcing a hungry mouse with food for pressing a lever when a light is on and by not reinforcing it for pressing the lever when the light is off. The mouse will learn to press the lever only in the presence of the light. In our everyday lives, this process occurs continually. For example, couples who date regularly can "tell" when it is time to leave a party. Each has learned that when one partner gives certain cues—perhaps becoming quieter or acting edgy—the other will be reinforced for preparing to leave. In the absence of that cue, neither is likely to be reinforced for leaving.

Role of Antecedents in Avoidance Behavior and Extinction

To avoid an unpleasant outcome, you have to know that such an outcome is about to occur. This means that your avoidance behavior is guided by the antecedents—the cues—you get from your environment. If your avoidance behavior is successful, the unpleasant event does not occur.

Principle 9: *An antecedent can be a cue or signal that an unpleasant event may be imminent. This is likely to produce avoidance behavior.*

Suppose that when you were in your early teens, you weren't adept at social niceties and often made a poor impression on others. This may have led to unpleasant experiences, and you may have gradually learned to avoid certain social situations. You learned to be shy. Now, several years later, you are much more adept at social behaviors. But you continue to avoid particular kinds of social events—parties, for example, or dancing—and other situations that in the past would have been unpleasant. You continue to respond to the antecedent as a cue to avoidance, even though the actual unpleasant event doesn't take place anymore. Why?

Avoidance learning is highly resistant to extinction because the antecedent stimulus evokes the avoidance behavior, and the person who has learned the avoidance response has no opportunity to learn that the old, unpleasant outcome is no longer there.

Children and teenagers are often punished for their sexual behavior, and this punishment is likely to produce various kinds of avoidance behavior. Some will simply learn to avoid being caught, but others may learn to avoid sex. As children grow older and marry, the situation changes. Parents are unlikely to punish their married children's sexual behavior. What was formerly punishable behavior is now permissible. And yet, the person who has learned to avoid making love as a way of avoiding punishment may continue to avoid, even though the situation has changed and the punishment is no longer a threat.

This is how much "neurotic" or maladjusted behavior is learned. Because you were once punished—in childhood, for example—in the presence of a particular stimulus, you continue to engage in old habits of avoidance that to someone else might seem quite "foolish." You may avoid situations that could be pleasant for you, because the signals that control your avoidance behavior continue to operate. One of the techniques of self-modification is to gradually make yourself engage in previously avoided behaviors and situations that now seem desirable. Only then can you know whether you will still be punished for the behavior.

Stimulus Control and Automatic Behaviors

Now we are in a position to return to our discussion of the ways in which behavior evolves from regulation by others, through self-regulation, to automatic stimulus control. How can we reduce maladaptive automatic behavior and bring it back under self-regulation?

When an antecedent has consistently been associated with a behavior that is reinforced, it gains what is called **stimulus control** over the behavior. We respond in a seemingly automatic way. As an experienced driver, you no longer slow down at lights while yelling "Stop!" to yourself, or even while saying it subvocally. You slow down and brake when the amber light appears even though you are singing, listening to the radio, or thinking about last night's movie. Because of its previous association with a variety of reinforcements, the amber light has stimulus control over your stopping the car. Coming to a halt at the amber light has repeatedly allowed you to avoid collisions, escape fear, earn the praise of your driving instructor, and even elicit your own self-congratulation. In the normal processes of performance, language control is dropped because immediate recognition of and response to specific situations is much more efficient. In most situations, excessive self-speech is undesirable, because it can actually interfere with our performance. Like Hamlet, we become "sicklied o'er with the pale cast of thought." It is better that we run on the automatic pilot of stimulus control.

Better, that is, when we are running well. Unfortunately, those undesirable behaviors that you now wish to change are very likely under stimulus control, and that stimulus control must be broken and rebuilt. For some people, the stimulus control is so strong that it seems almost irresistible, in spite of the fact that it evokes an undesired behavior. One of our students wrote:

> I have been losing some weight, but there is one situation I just can't resist. That's when people who work in my office bring in doughnuts from King's Bakery. They are too much. When I get to work, as soon as I see that King's Bakery box, I know I'm in trouble!

Many overweight people have the same problem. The sight of certain foods automatically stimulates them to eat whether they are hungry or not. Their task, therefore, is to reduce the automatic control of certain stimuli.

A most important tactic for rescuing behavior from an undesirable automatic condition is to insert new antecedents at the very time the old antecedents are about to begin their work. Self-speech antecedents are particularly useful when the "automatic" cue is also self-directed language. For example, you might stop saying to yourself, "I can't resist eating this," and say instead, "You can do it. Hang in there!"

Stimulus control can be the goal of a self-modification plan even when no automatic sequence exists. An antecedent can be set up, a desirable behavior arranged to occur in its presence, and reinforcement programmed to follow. In this way, a new automatic sequence can be created. One of our students, for example, wanted to be more efficient. She wrote:

> I always do my planning as soon as I get off the bus that takes me to school. This puts the planning under the control of that antecedent. I go straight from the bus to an empty classroom and spend a few minutes planning the day, then reinforce myself for the planning.

For this student, getting off the bus had gained stimulus control over the act of planning.

Respondent Behavior and Conditioning

Not all learning is based on reinforcement of operant behavior. Some behaviors are automatically controlled by antecedent stimuli. These behaviors have built-in, nonlearned triggers. For example, when the knee tendon is struck lightly, leg extension follows automatically. The antecedent stimulus of striking has control over this reaction. A fleck on the eyeball is the controlling stimulus for eye blinking. Milk in the mouth produces salivation automatically from the earliest hours of life. Behaviors for which original, controlling antecedent stimuli exist are sometimes called **reflexes.** Humans have fewer of these automatic behaviors than do organisms with less complicated nervous systems, but we do have reflexes, and they are important.

Here is a small experiment that will illustrate one of your reflexive responses. Have someone agree to surprise you with a sudden loud noise sometime in the next few days. For example, ask a friend to slam a book onto a table when you seem to expect it least. Observe your reactions: you tense, whip around, and blink. This is a reflexive response; the stimulus alone is sufficient to cause it. Only repeated familiarity with the stimulus will allow the behavior to fade. But notice, too, that there is an *emotional* component to your reaction—a feeling of arousal and emotional fullness, a discomfort that is much like a small fear reaction that reaches its peak a second or two after the stimulus and then gradually subsides.

This experiment illustrates the control that the antecedent stimulus has over emotional reactions. Behaviors of this type have certain properties in common: For example, they are largely controlled by the autonomic nervous system, they involve smooth muscles, and they are highly similar among individuals of the same species. These behaviors are sometimes called **respondent** behaviors because they occur originally in response to the antecedent stimulus.

The most important characteristic of all respondent behaviors is that the antecedent stimuli are adequate to produce the behavior. This kind of antecedent control over reactions is important because, through this basic process, many emotional reactions become associated with particular antecedents so that the antecedent comes to elicit them.

A person who is very shy may experience considerable anxiety when meeting strangers. Some people become very upset if they have to stay in an enclosed place. Others are extremely afraid of heights, or airplanes, or snakes. How do these stimuli come to gain control of the person's reaction so that an emotion such as anxiety is elicited? One explanation is that antecedent stimuli gain control of a person's reactions through the process of **respondent conditioning.**

Respondent Conditioning

Respondent conditioning involves pairing a stimulus that elicits some response with one that does not, in such a way that the two stimuli occur together. The individual reacts automatically to the original stimulus in the presence of the new, or *conditioned,* stimulus.

After a number of such pairings, the person will react to the new, conditioned stimulus by itself and in nearly the same way that he or she reacted to the original stimulus. In this way, automatic reactions can be transferred to what was originally a neutral antecedent (that is, an antecedent with no stimulus control over a reaction). What was once a neutral stimulus becomes a conditioned stimulus—a stimulus that has control over a reaction—by being associated with an antecedent that already has stimulus control. A new stimulus control is developed.

Schematically, first you have an antecedent—call it A_1—that elicits a response. If A_1 is always preceded by another antecedent—call it A_2—then, after a few such associations, A_2 will develop nearly the same stimulus control over the response that A_1 has. If the response is some emotional reaction, through this process of respondent conditioning the new antecedent (A_2) will develop the capacity to elicit the emotional reaction even if A_1 does not occur.

This conditioned stimulus (A_2) can then be paired with a new neutral stimulus (A_3), and A_3 will then come to elicit that emotional reaction. This pairing of A_2 with A_3 (and A_3 with A_4, A_4 with A_5, and so on) is called **higher-order conditioning.** The following chart summarizes respondent-conditioning processes and explains how we develop emotional reactions to so many antecedent stimuli.

Reflex	$A_1 \rightarrow$ Response	Automatic, unlearned, triggered response.
Respondent conditioning	$\begin{cases} A_1 \\ A_2 \rightarrow \text{Response} \end{cases}$	Pairing the "trigger" stimulus with some new neutral stimulus.
Conditioned response	$A_2 \rightarrow$ Response	In the absence of A_1, A_2 produces the response.
Higher-order conditioning	$\begin{cases} A_2 \\ A_3 \rightarrow \text{Response} \end{cases}$	A_2 (conditioned stimulus) is now paired with a new neutral stimulus.
Higher-order conditioned response	$A_3 \rightarrow$ Response	Now A_1, A_2, and A_3 can all elicit the response, frequently an emotion.

Emotional Conditioning

More than 75 years ago, John Watson and Rosalie Rayner (1920) demonstrated how an emotional reaction can be conditioned so that it comes to be elicited by an antecedent that was previously neutral. From the earliest days of our lives, a sudden loud noise is an adequate stimulus for a fear reaction. To associate that stimulus with one that was neutral, Watson and Rayner followed this procedure: a baby was presented several times with a white rat; the baby showed no signs of fear. Then he was presented with the rat, and a few seconds afterward, a very loud, unexpected noise was made behind him. The baby reacted automatically to the startling noise with fear. After several experiences in which the rat was presented just before the frightening noise—so that fear was experienced while seeing the rat—the rat became a conditioned stimulus. The rat itself became sufficient to elicit the fear, even if the noise did not occur. Thus, what had been a neutral stimulus became a frightening one.

Once a conditioned reaction has been established, a new stimulus may be associated with the conditioned stimulus so that the new antecedent also acquires stimulus control over the emotional response (higher-order conditioning). For example, if the experimenters were to play a certain tune every time the rat were presented, through higher-order conditioning, the baby would come to fear the music.

In a similar way, emotional reactions can be transferred to many new stimuli in your life. As you have new experiences, you may undergo new associations between conditioned emotional reactions and new stimuli so that the new stimuli will come to elicit the original emotional reaction.

Principle 10: *Through conditioning, antecedents come to elicit automatic reactions that are often emotional.*

In most everyday situations, conditioning and operant learning are going on at the same time. For example, a student who is trying to study but hates it and is not reinforced for it not only suffers the effects of not being reinforced but may also develop a conditioned boredom reaction to studying (Watson, 1992).

Most chains of events contain both behavioral and emotional components (DiCara, 1970; Miller, 1969; Staats, 1968). For example, think of a person who, having failed a driver's test once, goes back for a second try. The person is, at the same time, walking into the testing station (the observable behavior) and experiencing feelings of anxiety or tension. Many environmental circumstances produce *both a behavioral and an emotional reaction.* That is, antecedents have an effect on both your behavior and your feelings.

Respondent Conditioning and Language

Many, if not most, conditioned stimuli are words. Parents deliberately try to condition emotional reactions to language as they teach their children that the street is "Dangerous!" or that the burner is "Hot! Hurt you!" As we explained earlier, both a behavioral and an emotional reaction come to be cued by the same stimulus. The child both withdraws from the dangerous situation and develops an emotional response not only to the stimulus but also to the word for it. For adults, too, emotional reactions are often conditioned to words. If we are told that a spider or snake is "poisonous," we have a different emotional response to it than if we are told that it is "harmless."

This effect is also present when we use language to ourselves. A situation that we tell ourselves is dangerous or depressing can produce fear or depression even before we actually experience it. Some fears are "cognitively learned" (Wolpe, 1981). Therefore, many situations affect us not so much because of their consequences but because of the way we define the situations to ourselves.

Negative self-statements—for example, "I can't cope with this situation"—actually produce higher cardiac levels and respiration rates than do positive self-statements (Schuele & Wiesenfeld, 1983). Goldfried (1979) has developed strategies for restructuring self-statements to produce more adaptive emotional reactions as well as more effective coping with problems.

Modeling

Much human learning occurs by simply observing what others do. This is called learning through **modeling.**

Principle 11: *Many behaviors are learned by observing someone else (a model) perform the actions, which are then imitated.* Golf, dancing, chess, and bridge; expressions of love and of anger; even fears—all are learned through modeling. By simply observing a model, you learn behaviors. This kind of learning allows you to develop wholly new behaviors and to modify old ones.

You learn both desirable and undesirable acts this way. For example, you may have grown up with hardworking, ambitious parents. Now you realize that you, too, have these characteristics. Your parents may also have been rather irritable and inclined to blow up when frustrated. To your chagrin, you see that this description fits you as well. Of course, in your life hundreds of people have set different kinds of examples for you. Your present behavior is not a carbon copy of any one person. Rather, you have borrowed a bit of this from one, a bit of that from another, and blended them together to make the unique you.

Learning through observation follows the same principles as direct learning. The consequences of your model's behavior will determine whether you will imitate the behavior. Reinforced model behavior is strengthened *in you,* and punished model behavior is weakened *in you.* We learn cues and signals from models. We can even gain emotional conditioning from seeing models frightened by stimuli such as snakes or spiders (Ollendick & King, 1991; Rachman, 1977). And there is evidence that we learn to be calm, at least to a certain degree, by watching models behave calmly before stimuli of which we are afraid.

In your own self-change project, you can deliberately use this ability to learn through modeling to develop new behaviors. For example, a young man who wasn't very sure of himself on dates asked a friend if they could double date; then he could see how his friend behaved. A woman who had an unreasonable fear of birds accompanied a friend who didn't have that problem in order to see how her friend dealt with birds.

These examples also illustrate that behavior learned through modeling follows the same developmental sequence as all other behavior. In developing their dating behavior and relaxation around birds, both people were first having their new behaviors regulated by *others* (the models). Soon they were able to move to the stage of self-regulation through self-modification programs that included practice and self-reinforcement. And eventually both of them developed automatic competence and relaxation.

This concludes the discussion of the 11 principles of self-regulation, which are listed in Box 4-1.

The search for the basic principles of self-regulation continues and will continue so long as there is human society that wants to understand itself. We do not believe that the 11 principles are likely to change, but with each passing year, the way these principles are understood evolves, adds details, and becomes more inclusive. This evolution proceeds by discovery and by debate, sometimes heated! The hot edges of the current debate are described in Box 4-2.

BOX 4-1

The Principles of Self-Regulation

Principle 1:	From early life to adulthood, regulation by others and the self (particularly through verbal instructions) acts as a powerful guide to behavior.
Principle 2:	Operant behavior is a function of its consequences.
Principle 3:	A positive reinforcer is a consequence that maintains and strengthens behavior by its added presence.
Principle 4:	A negative reinforcer is a consequence that strengthens behavior by being subtracted from the situation.
Principle 5:	Behavior that is punished will occur less often.
Principle 6:	An act that was reinforced but no longer is will begin to weaken.
Principle 7:	Intermittent reinforcement increases resistance to extinction.
Principle 8:	Most operant behavior is eventually guided by antecedent stimuli, or cues, the most important of which are often self-directed statements.
Principle 9:	An antecedent can be a cue or signal that an unpleasant event may be imminent. This is likely to produce avoidance behavior.
Principle 10:	Through conditioning, antecedents come to elicit automatic reactions that are often emotional.
Principle 11:	Many behaviors are learned by observing someone else (a model) perform the actions, which are then imitated.

BOX 4-2

Thinking and Behavior

Science progresses through a series of arguments—often vigorous, frequently fierce—that are ultimately resolved through new information, superior logic, or deeper and broader argumentation. Today psychology is embroiled in such an argument over the role of thinking in determining behavior. The debate is about the question "What guides our behavior, our thoughts or habits?" If it is our thoughts, then psychologists should look mainly inside the person for the causes of behavior. If it is our habits, then the psychologist should look outside, in the environment that guides our habits. These days "cognition" (the study of thinking and mental operations) is "in," just as "behaviorism" was the enthusiasm of the preceding period.

Actually, this is a resurgence of the same tension that defined the first half of the century in psychology, when psychology attempted to imitate the physical sciences by concentration only on what could be objectively observed and measured: behavior itself and the environmental events that preceded and followed it (Antecedents-Behavior-Consequences). Thoughts were ignored. This enormously successful theoretical position subdued those psychologists who believed that humans' overt acts are expressions of the basic reality of the human mind.

Today, behaviorists themselves have reintroduced into science "mental events," such as thoughts, plans, beliefs, and interpretations. Indeed, such "unobservable" events are generally acknowledged to be necessary for understanding people's acts and lives. Two prominent behaviorists have recently made "attributions" (beliefs about causation) central to their new theories (Bandura, 1989; Kanfer & Hagerman, 1987). Cognitive behaviorists (for example, Kanfer & Hagerman, 1987; Rescorla, 1988) emphasize that even "conditioning" provides information on which the world can be predicted and behavior decided. Thus, thoughts and habits have been combined, and psychologists now examine both.

But how are these "cognitions" to be handled theoretically? Here, the battle rages. Are the connections between environmental events and behavior to be understood as mechanistic and "automatic," or is there, between antecedents and behavior and between consequences and behavior, something in the thinking mind that makes sense, makes predictions, and decides? Do our thoughts ultimately guide our behaviors?

Ironically, two of the more intellectually lively books published since our last edition of this text are (1) *Rule-Governed Behavior: Cognition, Contingencies, and Instructional Control* (Hayes, 1989), a reinterpretation of the "cognitive" events of rules largely in terms of the basic constructs of B. F. Skinner, the patriarch and patron saint of radical behaviorism; and (2) *Action Control: From Cognition to Behavior* (Kuhl & Beckmann, 1985), which injects a heavy dose of cognitive theory into the debate. Some participants ignore the others or reject the opposite position completely. Morris (1991) is not alone in being equally irritable toward the extremes on both sides, which he calls "cogniphobia" and "cogniphilia."

Karoly (1991) analyzed all the self-change theorists and observed that many (including this textbook's authors) have retained the A-B-C analysis because of its great practical value. That is accurate: We organize this book that way because it works. We have treated beliefs, expectations, thoughts, rules, and plans very seriously indeed, primarily as statements we make to ourselves about ourselves and the world. We have classified these statements principally as antecedents because they most often affect what people do next, frequently in just the ways that behaviorists have studied.

And we continue to enjoy the debate. How do our lives run: according to our thoughts and beliefs or to our habits? Nothing is more fun in science than this kind of intellectual tennis match.

Chapter Summary

Regulation Theory

Merely setting goals and collecting observations on behavior can often bring about behavior change. This process is explained by regulation theories, all of which include some principles of cybernetics. Just as a thermostat regulates temperature, setting a standard and comparing real information to that standard can regulate behavior. To some extent, human beings can be "hard-wired" to self-regulate in this way, like the robots we have created in our own image. Other aspects of self-regulation are not as well explained by cybernetics. Human beings make choices that are not anticipated. Sometimes we cannot "automatically" self-regulate because we do not know how to perform the required behavior. Further, not all our behavior is self-regulated; much of it is controlled by the external environment. In particular, much of our behavior is strongly affected by other people.

Regulation by Others and Regulation by Self

All behavior, as it develops, passes through this sequence: (1) control by others, (2) control by self, and (3) automatization. Control by others is exercised by parents, instructors, models, books, bosses, spouses, friends. When a new behavior is being learned, it is regulated by these external sources. As we gradually become more skillful in a behavior, we take over self-regulation—by reminding ourselves, practicing, setting goals, and collecting observations. When a behavior is fully learned, it becomes automatic. In this stage, it is under environmental control. That is, it is a smooth response to situations and does not even require any thought. When this smooth flow is interrupted—by a change in the environment or a change in our goals—it is possible to retrieve behavior from this automatic condition and bring it back under self-regulation. The skills we use in retrieving and regulating these automatic behaviors are called learned resourcefulness. Learned resourcefulness includes skills in managing language, consequences, antecedents, respondent conditioning, and modeling.

Language Regulation

The most common method of controlling behavior is through language. Children gradually incorporate the speech of their parents and teachers and give themselves the same kinds of instructions they have heard from others. Even as adults, we are controlled by the speech of others. In difficult situations, or when we are retrieving behavior from automaticity, our own self-directed speech powerfully regulates our own behavior. Even when behavior is automatic, it may occur in response to subvocal speech. What we say to ourselves, particularly self-statements that are rules for our conduct, controls what we do.

Consequences

Operant behaviors are strengthened or weakened by what follows them. Behavior is said to be "stronger" if it is more likely to occur in a particular situation.

A positive reinforcer is a consequence that strengthens behavior by its added presence. A negative reinforcer is an unpleasant consequence that strengthens behavior by being removed from the situation. You learn to escape or avoid unpleasant consequences.

What is a reinforcer—positive or negative—for one person is not necessarily so for another and is not necessarily a reinforcer at all times. Some people dislike pastrami; even those who like it would not find a pastrami sandwich reinforcing immediately after a Thanksgiving feast.

Behavior that is punished will occur less often in the future. Punishment means either taking away a positive event following a behavior or adding a negative event following a behavior. Both kinds of punishment decrease the likelihood of the behavior. Both reinforcement and punishment must be contingent on the behavior to affect it; that is, they must occur if and only if the behavior occurs.

An act that is no longer reinforced, either positively or negatively, will weaken. This is called extinction. In this process, the behavior has no reinforcing consequence and therefore weakens. Intermittent reinforcement, however, increases the resistance of a behavior to extinction.

Antecedents

Eventually, most behavior is guided by antecedents. These guiding antecedents, called discriminative stimuli or cues, come to control behavior that has been reinforced only when the cues were present. Many cues signal that danger is imminent. Escaping from those cues is reinforced by a reduction in anxiety, and we learn to avoid them. Avoidance behavior is highly resistant to extinction. Thus, many problem behaviors continue even after real danger has disappeared because the cue causes us to act as though something we used to fear were still a threat. (This is a description of many "neurotic" behaviors.)

It is normal for behavior to develop to the point that it is automatically controlled by antecedent stimuli. When these sequences are undesirable, automatic behavior can be retrieved and brought back under self-regulation. Tactics that can be used include inserting new antecedents, narrowing the behaviors that follow an antecedent, and constructing entirely new sequences of Antecedents-Behavior-Consequences.

Respondent Behavior and Conditioning

Respondent behavior refers to those behaviors that are originally controlled by antecedent stimuli. In respondent conditioning, a neutral antecedent is associated with a stimulus that can elicit an automatic reaction; after a series of associations, the once neutral stimulus becomes capable of eliciting the same reaction. In higher-order conditioning, another neutral event is paired with this antecedent, and it, too, acquires the capacity to produce the reaction.

This process is important because many emotional reactions may be conditioned to particular antecedents in this way. Various emotional reactions, such as joy or depression, may come under the control of antecedent stimuli so that just encountering the antecedent elicits that reaction. Normally, both operant learning and respondent conditioning are going on at the same time.

Conditioned stimuli are frequently words. Thus, language—even language we address to ourselves—produces emotional reactions. Because operant and respondent processes are both present when language is antecedent to behavior, what we say to ourselves affects both behaviors and emotions. Many self-change programs require a change in our self-speech.

Modeling

Many behaviors are learned simply by observing a model. Learning through observation follows the same principles as direct learning. The consequences of the behavior for the model will determine the strength of the behavior in the observer. Even emotional conditioning can be learned by watching models who are frightened or calm.

YOUR OWN SELF-DIRECTION PROJECT: STEP FOUR

This chapter has presented background material you need in order to embark on a successful self-modification project. It's important, therefore, that you have a good grasp of the principles that govern your behavior. To make sure, answer the learning-objectives questions at the beginning of this chapter.

If you can answer these questions, you can feel confident that you understand the principles that explain your behavior and that you are ready to apply these principles toward self-understanding. If you cannot, reread the chapter. Find the answers, and write them down. Then answer the questions again.

Now think about your behaviors that you have been observing, get out your observation notes, and answer the following questions about your own target behaviors.

First, consider the antecedents of your behavior:

1. What stimuli seem to control the behavior? In what situations does the behavior occur?
2. Do you react automatically to some cue with undesirable behavior?
3. Do you react to some cue with an unwanted emotion? What is the conditioned stimulus for it?
4. What are you saying to yourself before the behavior?

Second, look at the behavior itself:

5. Is it strong and quite frequent, or is it weak and not very frequent? What does this tell you about what you can do to change it?
6. Is any element of your problem due to something you are avoiding, perhaps unnecessarily?
7. Are you aware of models in your past whose behavior (or, perhaps, some aspects of it) you may have copied?
8. Does any part of your goal involve changing behaviors that are resistant to extinction either because they are intermittently reinforced or because they are avoidance behaviors?

Third, examine the consequences of the behavior:

9. Are your desired behaviors positively reinforced?
10. What actions make the desired behavior difficult? Are they reinforced?
11. Is it possible that the desired behavior is being punished?
12. Is your own self-speech rewarding or punishing your behavior?
13. Are the consequences for some behaviors difficult to identify, perhaps because of intermittent reinforcement?

Answer these questions carefully. In the next four chapters, we discuss various ways to move toward self-change by using techniques that solve different problems. Some techniques are designed for the person who is not being reinforced for a desired act. Others are for the person who needs to develop stimulus control for a desired act. Still others are for the person who already has inappropriate stimulus control over undesired acts. Also, some techniques are for those who are showing conditioned emotional responses. Your answers to the preceding questions will tell you which kinds of techniques you should use in your own plan for self-change.

5

Antecedents

Outline

- Identifying Antecedents
- Modifying Old Antecedents
- Arranging New Antecedents
- *Tips for Typical Topics*
- *Chapter Summary*
- *Your Own Self-Direction Project: Step Five*

Learning Objectives

Identifying Antecedents

1. How do you identify antecedents? What are three possible points of difficulty in identifying them?
2. What two kinds of self-statements can be antecedents?
   a. Explain self-instructions.
   b. How do beliefs and interpretations serve as antecedents, and how can you identify them?
   c. What are two common maladaptive beliefs?

Modifying Old Antecedents

3. In the first steps of a self-change plan, how can you avoid the antecedents of problem behavior?
4. What are some of the situations in which indulging in consummatory behaviors is most likely?
5. Explain the strategy of narrowing antecedent control.
6. Explain reperceiving antecedents. What are "hot" and "cool" cognitions? How does distraction work?
7. Explain the strategy of changing chains.
   a. What is the advantage of building in pauses?
   b. Explain pausing to make a record.
   c. How do you unlink a chain of events?
   d. At what part of the chain is it best to try breaking the chain?

Arranging New Antecedents

8. How can you use self-instructions to promote new, desired behavior?
   a. Which are best—precise or general self-instructions?
   b. How can you use self-instructions to remind yourself of beliefs or long-range goals?
   c. When you use self-instructions, which is more effective—saying them to yourself or thinking about them?
9. What are negative self-instructions? How can they be eliminated?
10. Explain the thought-stopping procedure. In addition to or instead of stopping the unwanted thought, what else should you do?
11. Explain how you can build stimulus control to cue a desired new behavior, such as concentrating while studying.
12. What is stimulus generalization? What can you do to develop it for a new, desired behavior?

13. Explain the precommitment strategy. How can you use other people's help in precommitment?

At this point, you have a clear understanding of the principles that govern your behavior, and you should have gathered data about your behaviors, the situations in which they occur, and their consequences. Each of the next three chapters discusses one of the A-B-C components. The present chapter discusses the A issues—ways of arranging antecedents so that desired behaviors become more likely. Chapter 6 treats the B issues—how behaviors themselves can be changed, replaced, and originated. Chapter 7 is devoted to the C issues—ways of rearranging the consequences of behavior to gain better self-direction. Finally, Chapter 8 discusses ways of organizing and incorporating all these ideas into an effective plan.

The separation of these topics is unfortunate, but unavoidable. It is not possible to present them simultaneously on the same printed page. But remember: You cannot design a full self-direction plan until you have read *all* the material in these four chapters. A, B, and C units are all required for full analysis and planning, although each person may emphasize one or the other somewhat differently. A good self-change plan is based on all three. Continue to work at your self-direction project as you read these chapters. The material is organized so that each chapter allows some planning and analysis, but a full plan will require all elements.

Identifying Antecedents

In Chapter 4 we explained how antecedents come to control behavior, thoughts, and feelings. Self-regulation principles 8, 9, and 10 summarized the way in which any antecedent, when it occurs in regular patterns before or with behaviors, thoughts, or feelings, can begin to stimulate those behaviors, thoughts, and feelings. Because of previous conditions of learning, even logically unrelated antecedents can become discriminative stimuli or conditioned stimuli. In everyday language, these controlling stimuli act as **cues,** and we will use the terms *cues* and *antecedents* as synonyms in this chapter. An effective plan for self-improvement depends on accurate discovery of your current system of cues. Discovering antecedents is the first task in designing an effective plan.

A married couple had been quarreling. In the past, they had had constructive arguments in which they tried to solve their differences. Lately, however, the man had found himself flying off the handle in the middle of an argument, calling his wife names, and swearing. We suggested he keep a record of what happened just before he lost his temper. He thought about what had happened in the past and made current observations for several days. As a result, he discovered a consistent antecedent of his anger: "It's a particular expression on her face. I think of it as her holier-than-thou expression, and it makes me angry."

In this case the unwanted behavior was cued by a single stimulus. For other behaviors, there may be several antecedents that have stimulus control.

When any one of them occurs, so does the problem behavior. "Hurt feelings" was the concern of one young woman, who discovered all these antecedents:

> (a) her mother or brother questioning specific decisions or behaviors, (b) her roommate asking her not to be around for a while, (c) her ex-husband questioning her dating or implying that the separation was her fault, and (d) her boyfriend failing to meet her as planned or flaunting the fact that he dated her acquaintances. (Zimmerman, 1975, p. 8)

Do you understand the antecedents of your own problem behavior? There are three possible points of difficulty in doing so. First, have you been recording fully and accurately? Not keeping complete, accurate records is the most common (and most self-defeating) error. Many fine students have told us, "You can't seriously mean that I'm supposed to write all that stuff down. I know what the problem is, and I do notice the situations. Writing them down is just a made-up exercise for a course." But we are very serious. Only the most experienced self-analyzer can do without written records. Written records force you to keep your attention on problem situations, in which perceptions tend to rush by and become blurred. Cues to problem behavior are often those that make you anxious, the ones you don't like to notice and remember.

The second most likely difficulty in recognizing antecedents is not beginning early enough in your chain-of-events analysis. If you begin recording at the moment your problem is clear and overt, you can be nearly certain that you have not begun early enough in the chain. This point is illustrated by one student who became alarmed at his increasing amount of beer drinking. "It happens at night," he reported. "I stay home, cook a little something, turn on the TV. I'm bored, get depressed, start popping the beer cans. The antecedent seems to be that I feel lonely." Recognizing his feelings of loneliness was a giant step forward, but those feelings were clearly not the first link in the chain. We suggested he work further backward: What chain of events produced the loneliness? He wrote:

> I've had three disastrous love affairs in the past year, self-confidence—zero. Every time I meet a woman, I tell myself not to bother. I've been staying home. Even telephone invitations become occasions for feeling worse. Twice last week I could have gone out, once to an auto show and once on a blind date. I declined. The next time a chance like that comes up, I'll try to notice what I'm saying to myself. It's probably some self-putdown.

Not every antecedent is so far removed from the behavior as this self-putdown made a week before. But this student saw the long chain that linked his refusal of a date last week to his lonely drunkenness this week. Discovering this distant antecedent allowed him to design a self-modification plan for a more stimulating social life. The student's discovery of the role his own feelings played in this chain of events was certainly important.

Feelings should always be examined to see if they are cues for problem behavior. Overeating, for example, is often triggered by feelings of restlessness, tension, irritability, anger, depression, or frustration. Many people feel unable to control their eating under such conditions (Glynn & Ruderman, 1986). You should identify those feelings and record them.

The third most likely difficulty with discovering antecedents is that of identifying self-statements; this will require a lengthier discussion.

Discovering Self-Statements

Self-directed messages and thoughts are among the most powerful influences on subsequent behavior. There are three types: (1) self-instructions, (2) beliefs, and (3) interpretations.

Self-instructions. Self-instructions can be obvious: "Get out of here!" "I've got to study tonight!" "Go three blocks and turn left." "Be calm, be relaxed." However, self-instructions are sometimes difficult to identify because they occur in a "still, small voice," so swiftly that only careful attention reveals them. The task is to amplify the words until they are loud and clear. It's like bringing self-directions back from the underground so that they can be consciously controlled. Once this principle is understood, most self-instructions *can* be detected. You need only pay careful attention during antecedent conditions. What are you telling yourself?

The first task in designing a plan for self-improvement is to discover whether or not self-instructions are the antecedents of your problem behavior. To make that discovery, turn up the amplifier of your still, small voice. Hear yourself thinking. Then record your thought as an antecedent.

Beliefs. Beliefs may be more difficult to discover. Belief statements may occur so rarely that they are not often observable. You must infer them by logically analyzing your self-observations. By beliefs, we mean the underlying assumptions on which your self-speech and other behaviors rest.

Recall the example of the young woman with "hurt feelings." All the instances in which she felt hurt—whether by mother, brother, roommate, ex-husband, or boyfriend—presented a common theme. If she had discussed her records with us, we would have asked her, "What is common to all these situations? Why does each of these events hurt you? What belief can you see operating here?" She might have answered,

> I guess I'm telling myself that no one loves me. It seems as though I want approval from everyone all the time. I suppose I believe that I must be loved by everyone and that each disapproval means I'm not loved.

The conversation might have continued as follows:

"Do you really believe that?"

"I suppose so; it's the way I behave."

"Is it logical?"

"Not really. People can disapprove of some things their loved ones do."

"Must everyone love you, constantly?"

"No. That's absurd."

"What would be a preferable belief?"

"That it is acceptable to be disapproved of sometimes, even by those one loves."

People torment themselves with an infinite number of self-destructive belief statements. Many of these statements are so habitual that they become abbreviated and no longer even fully stated: "I'm just . . . !" and the sentence remains an unfinished insult. These are some of the reasons why belief statements are often difficult to discover. But however great the variety, these statements tend to fall into certain predictable groups.

For example, Albert Ellis (1979; Ellis & Dryden, 1987) has identified three basic kinds of destructive self-statements and beliefs:

1. *"Awfulizing"* ("No one likes me!")
2. *I-can't-stand-it* ("I'm coming to pieces and can't stand one more minute!")
3. *Self-damnation* ("No wonder she turned me down, I'm repulsive!")

Another way of classifying these statements is according to their basic logical organization. According to Marvin Goldfried (1988), two basic assumptions appear to underlie all the detailed maladaptive beliefs that influence our self-talk. The first is the belief that *constant love and approval from everybody is a necessity.* The second is that *all our important undertakings must be performed with perfection.* Not surprisingly, those who hold these beliefs are more likely to suffer from low self-esteem (Daly & Burton, 1983).

Changing beliefs often leads to widespread benefits, emotionally and behaviorally. For instance, a group of unassertive people believed that standing up for themselves would be followed by disapproval and embarrassment. They came to see that they let themselves be mistreated by waiters, cashiers, and even friends because of these illogical, imagined outcomes. Once they began to anticipate different outcomes—greater respect and comfort—their assertiveness increased (Goldfried, 1977).

In examining your self-observations for relevant antecedents, don't overlook the possibility that a maladaptive belief may be contributing to the problem (Arnkoff & Glass, 1982). Be systematic in searching out these beliefs. Consider each instance of your problem. Look for some common theme, some assumption that underlies all these instances. Write out that theme as precisely as possible, and examine it. Is it rational? Is it adaptive? Do you really believe it, now that it is explicit?

In our experience, after bringing maladaptive beliefs to light, many people find that they can then readily accept a quite different belief. One doesn't have to be always perfect. One can do very well with some disapproval. By accepting a more reasonable belief, you can change a controlling antecedent and begin a new pattern of self-direction (Thorpe, Amatu, Blakey, & Burns, 1976).

Examining her journal records allowed a graduate student, Kathy, to see that her frantic social activity was based on a belief that she had to make very frequent contacts with her friends or she would lose them. She realized that this belief was highly exaggerated. This realization allowed her to contact friends only when she wanted to. She reported that she was *less* lonely because the times she spent with her friends became more satisfying.

We are not suggesting that every negative thought about the self should be replaced. Rather, it is a question of balance. Some evidence exists that people who are effective in situations have about 68% positive thoughts about themselves and 32% negative thoughts; less effective people have about equal numbers of positive and negative self-statements (Schwartz, 1986; Schwartz & Garamoni, 1986). Some negative thoughts are natural and provide accurate feedback. However, poor coping often results from self-criticism that leads away from situations that could be mastered. Such self-statements can be identified and replaced with a more adaptive and balanced internal dialogue (Kendall & Ingram, 1987).

Interpretations. The way we interpret events contains self-instructions. For example, the person with a problematic bad temper will interpret a situation as an affront, a putdown, an insult, or a loss of face. Each of these interpretations can be discovered by listening to the self-statements that result: "I won't let that SOB get away with that!" or "Nobody puts me down like that!" One of the key elements in bringing anger under control is changing the self-statements that trigger angry reactions (Masters, Burrish, Hollon, & Rimm, 1987).

The first task of self-modification is to use the power of antecedents to reach goals. The strategies you can employ to accomplish this task fall under two main headings: (1) modifying old antecedents (including avoiding antecedents, narrowing antecedents, reperceiving antecedents, and changing chains); and (2) arranging new antecedents.

Modifying Old Antecedents

Avoiding Antecedents

If all you have in front of you is two pieces of celery and a bowl of soup, you have already avoided some antecedents of overeating—the sight of an open box of chocolates, for example. Chronic alcoholics who successfully control drunkenness often do so by never confronting the crucial antecedent of overdrinking—the first drink. Most people who stay off cigarettes also follow a policy of not having the first one. If you are a habitual overeater, smoker, or drug user, sometimes almost nothing is as reinforcing as your "habit." For such behaviors, perhaps the most promising type of self-modification plan is one in which you *avoid* the antecedents that set the time and place for your **consummatory behavior**—behavior that is consummated, or climaxed, by its own ends, such as eating, drinking, or sexual activity. The smoker avoids cigarettes, the drinker avoids drinks, and the overeater avoids fattening foods. They all know that if they are exposed to those stimuli, they will very likely perform the undesired behavior again. Therefore, people with this kind of problem can work out self-direction plans in which they avoid the antecedent.

A middle-aged, overweight man wanted to diet but reported that his progress was always followed by disaster. So he began to record the antecedents of his eating binges and realized that, although he normally stayed on his diet quite regularly, in one situation he always ate too much: when he and his wife were invited to someone else's house for dinner. Their friends were good cooks! He solved his problem by setting a simple rule, to which his wife agreed. Until he had lost 20 pounds, they wouldn't accept any dinner invitations. He would explain to his would-be host or hostess that he had to lose weight and that he couldn't possibly resist such fine food, so he must regretfully decline.

Self-control becomes most difficult when you are around others who are indulging. Marlatt and Parks (1982) have conducted extensive research on people with addictive behaviors, particularly consumers of drugs, such as alcohol, heroin, marijuana, or tobacco. They report that relapse in persons resisting addictive behaviors is very likely to occur when in the presence of others who are engaging in that behavior.

A person may need to avoid social cues for a variety of behavioral goals. For example, Heffernan and Richards (1981) studied students who had initiated attempts to improve their poor study behaviors. Those who had succeeded were more likely to use the simple procedure of studying in an environment where they would *not* have to interact or talk with other people.

In other circumstances, a private environment can be the cue for problem behavior. A young man was concerned with what he felt was "excessive" masturbation, an activity in which he indulged three times a day. The reinforcer was fairly obvious here—the sexual pleasure itself—although by masturbating he also gained some temporary relief from social anxieties. The young man avoided the antecedent—the place in which masturbation usually occurred. He began to use a less private campus restroom.

Avoiding antecedents for drinking, drugs, smoking, or overeating is particularly important when you are emotionally upset. Feelings of anger, fear, depression, or disappointment are certain to make indulgence more tempting, and thus more likely. Even the excitement of unusual happiness tends to make abstainers more likely to violate their resolutions, but negative emotions are the most dangerous conditions for relapsing into indulgence (Marlatt & Parks, 1982; Shiffman, 1982). Therefore, avoiding your problem antecedents is especially wise during periods of emotional arousal.

This strategy of avoidance is one you can begin immediately. Later you will learn how to develop new behaviors for situations in which you cannot avoid the antecedent. After all, you can't avoid parties all your life. But avoiding the antecedents to unwanted, indulgent behaviors will allow your self-controlling responses to be strengthened before they are again tested in tempting situations. By the time you return to parties, you will know when you must say "no" and how to do it.

Narrowing Antecedent Control

Undesired behavior can be deliberately linked to a gradually narrower range of antecedents. The idea is to narrow the range of situations that control the behaviors down to a fine point, or to narrow the behaviors that occur in a situation.

For example, Goldiamond (1965) helped control sulking behavior in a client by a program that allowed the client to sulk, but only on a particular "sulking stool." Nolan (1968) reports a case of restricting smoking to a certain uncomfortably located chair. Even unpleasant thoughts can be restricted to a certain "worry chair" and to a certain half-hour per day (Borkovec, Wilkinson, Folensbee, & Lerman, 1983).

This technique has been studied best in the control of insomnia. The insomniac wants the situation of being in bed to produce sleep, but instead it stimulates tossing, turning, thinking, reading, turning the radio on and off, and everything but sleep. Bootzin & Nicassio (1979) recommend narrowing the stimulus control of the bed. Except for sex, nothing else should be done there—no reading, television watching, conversation, or worrying. If the insomniac is still awake after ten minutes, he or she should leave the bed and not return until sleepy. This system of narrowing appears to be the best self-modification technique for insomnia, even in severe cases (Lacks, Bertelson, Gans, & Kunkel, 1983; Turner, 1986).

A similar strategy for making studying more automatic is for the person to leave the study desk when he or she is daydreaming, eating, or chatting (Spurr & Stevens, 1980).

Reperceiving Antecedents

Some antecedents cannot be avoided or narrowed. Sometimes tempting situations are unexpected or are an inescapable part of daily routine. A useful strategy is to change the nature of the situation by changing the way you think about it.

An Olympic fencer often hurried her warm-up because officials had delayed her from getting to the fencing strip on time. Her self-defeating reaction was to think, "I'm holding everyone up, they're mad at me, I shouldn't take any more time." Without a decent warm-up, she would also think, "I'm not really ready to fence . . . I haven't even warmed up, I can't possibly perform well . . . oh, well, let's get it over with." With help from her coach, she began to reperceive this situation and change her thoughts: "I have a right to warm up. They kept me waiting, so now they can wait a little for me. If I'm taking up too much time, it's the judge's obligation to tell me and not my responsibility" (Suinn, 1989).

Another way to reperceive a situation is by attending to some specific parts of the situation and not to others. For example, it is possible to attend to either the "hot" or the "cool" aspects of any situation. In Chapter 2 we told of the work of Walter Mischel and his associates on the ways that children learn to resist temptation (Cantor, Mischel, & Schwartz, 1982; Mischel,

1981). By the sixth grade, children are aware that attending to the "cool" rather than the "hot" qualities of tempting things will help them resist unwise choices. A "hot" perception of marshmallows would be, "They taste yummy and chewy." A "cool" marshmallow perception would be, "They are puffy like clouds" (Mischel, 1981). A "yummy" marshmallow is more likely to be snatched and eaten than is a "cloudlike" marshmallow.

Adults as well as 12-year-old children know this technique, but in indulgent responses we often err by letting hot perceptions dominate our attention.

A cool perception does not include any attention to the experience of actually smoking a cigarette or a joint, its pleasures or effects. Transforming an antecedent condition by concentrating on its cool qualities will reduce arousal, frustration, and, ultimately, the likelihood of succumbing to temptation.

A dieter who successfully used a reperceiving strategy reported that she initially was very attracted to fatty foods like hamburgers, cheese, and butter. She focused on the fat, however, and began to imagine that when she was eating something fatty, she was actually injecting fat into her bloodstream.

As another example, faithful lovers and mates are more likely to focus on the least desirable features of other attractive people; perceiving alternate partners as desirable increases the strength of the temptation (Johnson & Rusbult, 1989). And in resisting tempting situations for alcohol or drugs, successful people are more likely to focus on the unattractive features of those who are drunk or stoned (Brown, Stetson, & Beatty, 1989).

Changing Chains

Another strategy that can be used to control antecedents is to change the chain of events that produces the undesired behavior.

Many behaviors are the result of a fairly long chain of events. An antecedent produces some behavior that leads to a particular consequence, which is itself the antecedent of yet another behavior, and so on. Thus, the end behavior, which may be an undesired act, is the result of a long series of antecedent–behavior–new antecedent–new behavior. By the time you reach the end of the chain of events, the impulse to perform the final, undesirable behavior is so strong that it is very difficult to restrain.

Such chains are always present in any form of substance abuse—in the problem drinker who transfers buses just in front of the liquor store, the ex-smoker who buys cigarettes to keep around the house for his friends, or the reformed drug user who decides to go to the party just to be cordial to his druggie friends. These mini-decisions are formed into chains that lead to violations (Cummings, Gordon, & Marlatt, 1980).

A good strategy is to interrupt the chain of events *early* (Bergin, 1969; Ferster, Nurnberger, & Levitt, 1962). An interruption at an early, weak link in the chain can prevent the occurrence of the final behavior.

Annon (1975) reports the case of a problem drinker who used a complex "scrambling" of previous chain links to stop drinking. This person had consumed up to a pint of vodka before bedtime each night for several years and could no longer sleep without it. He analyzed the links of the usual chain of events that led to drinking: coming home, turning on the TV, going to the refrigerator, putting ice in the glass, pouring and drinking the vodka, going to the bathroom, undressing, showering, going to bed, pouring another drink, and so on. The man reorganized this chain into a different order. For example, he moved showering to immediately after coming home, delayed going to the refrigerator until after showering, and substituted cola for vodka in the glass. This scrambling of links had the effect of decreasing the vodka-drinking probabilities because it broke up much of the antecedent control.

Building in pauses. When a chain is well established, you may find yourself responding without thinking, whether the antecedent is a rude statement or a plateful of food. A helpful technique for dealing with this automatic quality of chained antecedents is to pause before responding.

The pause technique is particularly useful for indulgent behaviors. For smoking, gradually increasing pauses between the urge and lighting up, or between puffs, is an effective technique for reducing the number of cigarettes smoked (Newman & Bloom, 1981a, 1981b). For excessive drinking, a pause between feeling the urge for another and allowing oneself that next drink is highly recommended. The same is true for eating problems. A two-minute pause in the middle of each meal is one of the most effective techniques dieters can use (Sandifer & Buchanan, 1983). This may be because the pause allows time to form a clearer perception of whether you are really still hungry. In fact, one goal for people who want to control their eating is to learn to take longer to eat.

Whether smoking, drinking, or eating is the problem, a two-minute pause is often enough for the urge to pass. During that pause, the body can be read more accurately. Does it really need that cigarette? Are you getting drunk? Are you really hungry? Merely asking these questions during the pause will break up the automatic sequence of consume, consume, consume.

The pause technique is useful for a variety of problems and combines well with other tactics. One of our students wrote:

> I began by looking at the situations that I got angry in. For each situation I would ask myself three questions: (1) Why did I get angry? (2) Was it reasonable to be angry in this situation? (3) How could I have handled the situation differently? I found that it was unreasonable for me to get angry, for example, at someone on the street whom I would never see again. I used self-instructions to tell myself that people are a certain way and will do things that I don't like and I could make my life easier if I would just accept them. But the technique that helped most was pausing. When I was in an actual situation where I was an-

> gry, I would pause for a couple of minutes and think about what I should say, or maybe not say anything at all. This helped, because sometimes when I was angry I would say something that I would really regret.

What you do during the pause makes a difference, of course. A young father was upset because he often spanked his children.

> I know that I hit them when they disobey me—particularly when they bicker with each other and I tell them to stop and they don't. So I tried just pausing for a second before spanking them. Sometimes that worked, but sometimes it didn't. I just waited a second and then hit the child anyway. So I started saying to myself, "Now, think. Don't just stand here being angry and then hit. Think. What should I do right now to get the children to behave?"

What that man did during his pause was to give himself instructions.

Pausing to make a record. Recording an unwanted behavior *before* you do it may reduce its frequency. If you require yourself to make a record early in the chain of events, you gain greater control over later events than if you wait until the last links in the chain to record the behavior (Kazdin, 1974b). For example, as you feel the first signs of panic coming over you, stop and rate the degree of panic you feel. That gives you time to realize that your reaction is (probably) out of proportion to the actual event and that there are ways in which you can cope.

In general, the earlier in the chain of events you make the interruption, the more effective your plan will be. A couple who had developed a destructive pattern of arguing learned to recognize the first signs of such a pattern and arranged to stop immediately to make entries in their structured diaries. Usually this pause was sufficient to break the chain of their destructive arguing.

Unlinking the chain of events. A young woman had a problem with excessively frequent urination. She reported that she went to the bathroom an average of 13 times a day. She was upset by this personally, and sometimes socially, embarrassing situation. She had seen a physician, who assured her that there was no medical problem.

In gathering the baseline data, she realized that two separate antecedents led to urination. First, she almost never went into a bathroom (for example, to wash her face or comb her hair) without using the toilet. Second, she went to the toilet at the first hint of bladder pressure. To break up the control of the first antecedent (entering a bathroom), she used this simple plan. She would go into a bathroom, perform some behavior that didn't involve using the toilet, and walk out. For example, she would enter, wash her hands, and leave. Or she might comb her hair or put on lipstick and then leave. In this way, she broke up the inevitable relaitonship between going into a bathroom (the antecedent) and using the toilet (the behavior).

To break up the control of the second antecedent (the initial hint of bladder pressure), she used the pause technique. Upon feeling the first hint of pressure, she required herself to pause for five minutes before urinating. This technique was sufficient because five minutes later she was usually busy doing something else.

Suppose your problem is that you eat too many between-meal snacks. What chain of events leads to this final step? First, you may feel slightly bored or have nothing to do for a couple of minutes. Second, you move toward the kitchen. Third, you open the refrigerator or pantry and search for food. Finally, you eat the food. If this is your chain, you may be able to interrupt it by having an intervention plan that calls for performing at step 2 some behavior other than moving toward the kitchen. It can be *any* behavior—for example, making a phone call.

This strategy of unlinking a chain is necessary whenever problem antecedents cannot be avoided. The old antecedent must lead to a new, desired behavior instead of the old, undesired act. The next case illustrates an unusual use of this strategy.

A depressed young woman discovered through her A-B-C analysis that her "down" feelings were preceded by interactions with other people that made her feel uninteresting, ignored, and even rejected. These feelings would quickly turn into almost obsessive thoughts about her worthlessness, and a deep depression would set in. The chain looked like this:

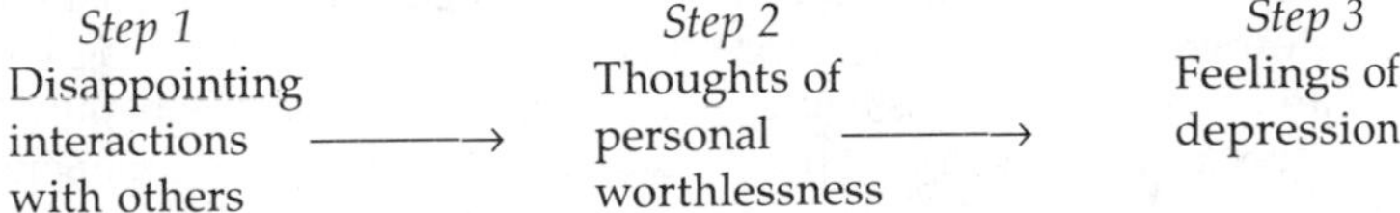

She reasoned that not every interaction with others could turn out perfectly for her. Her plan called for changing the second link of the chain. Whenever she felt disappointed by an interaction, as soon as she got home she would insert a new, pleasant event—sewing. This was an entirely new activity for her, and she began with no previous interest in or skill at dressmaking.

She said, "I never thought of sewing as something good, but I've discovered that those simple things can have a lot of meaning. And now I'm much less dependent on other people." At the end of her program, she felt much more mature, and her depressions were no longer a problem (Tharp, Watson, & Kaya, 1974).

Long chains can be altered most effectively by intervening at both ends. The research and theory supporting this position have been presented by Frankel (1975), who also reported the case study in Box 5-1. As you read this case, notice three features in particular. First, the antecedents were changed both at the beginning and at the end of the chain. Second, the father had to learn a new behavior to be inserted in the chain. Third, the outcome of the new chain had to be reinforced. This illustrates how a well-developed plan will often require a combination of strategies.

BOX 5-1

A Family's Chain

Chains of events are often composed of the behaviors of several people. This case illustrates a chain of family behaviors that produced unhappiness for all three members.

The Chain

1. Mother asks Bobby to do something at home. (When Father asks him, there is usually immediate compliance.)
2. Bobby refuses.
3. Mother gets very irritated and screams at Bobby, or hits him, or both.
4. Bobby screams back and rarely complies.
5. When Bobby does not comply, either Mother goes and gets Father or Father hears the incident occurring and barges in. (Or Father is told of the incident on returning home.)
6. Father and Bobby yell at each other. Usually Father hits Bobby or physically forces him to get moving on task. In any case, Bobby eventually complies.

This chain of events lasted from a few minutes to several hours, ending when the father, on coming home, learned of the incident and forced Bobby to comply. The incidents didn't always go all the way through the chain. When Bobby complied with his mother's demands or when she didn't tell her husband about an incident, the incident ended at those points.

The Plan

It seemed that Bobby had learned to use one of his parents to get to the other one. A simple analysis of the problem behavior might have stopped after step 3, when Mother screams at Bobby, or hits him, or both. The time lag between steps 3 and 6 was sometimes hours, and the whole behavior chain didn't always occur because sometimes the incident ended without Father's intervention.

To achieve modification of this sequence, Mother was instructed to extinguish her behavior in response to Bobby's noncompliance (step 3). She agreed to either remain calm or leave the room until she could respond to Bobby calmly. In no case was she to call Father or was he to come in. Father also agreed to spend three hours a week with Bobby doing something of Bobby's choosing. At the three-month follow-up, the parents reported that Bobby's incidents of aggression and noncompliance in the home had been reduced to a level not considered a problem. They rated Bobby's aggression at a raw score of 65 (compared to 80 initially). At the one-year follow-up, the parents reported that Bobby's behavior at home continued not to be a problem.

In the old chain, Bobby was receiving a strong reward for his misbehaviors—interaction with Father, even though it was an aggressive kind of interaction. It turned out that Father had never learned to play with his little boy. In the new chain, the three hours a week of play with Dad were strongly rewarding to both Bobby and his father.

SOURCE: Adapted from "Beyond the Simple Functional Analysis—The Chain: A Conceptual Framework for Assessment with a Case Study Example," by A. J. Frankel, 1975, *Behavior Therapy, 6,* pp. 254–260. Copyright 1975 by Academic Press, Inc. Reprinted by permission of the author and Academic Press.

Arranging New Antecedents

So far we have spoken of avoiding, narrowing, or rearranging antecedents, but a critical factor is often creating *new* antecedents that will cue desirable outcomes. New antecedents can be inserted at the beginning of a chain or at any point within it. In this section, we will discuss verbal antecedents (self-instructions) and other forms of stimulus control.

Eliminating Negative Self-Instructions

When you begin to perform some self-defeating behavior, you may actually be instructing yourself to do it. Your self-observations can show this pattern. For example, a young woman who didn't seem to be able to relax when she was with men reported that as soon as a man started talking with her, she would say to herself things like, "He's not going to like me," or "I'm going to be shy," or "I'm not going to make a good impression." These "self-instructions" made her tense and made her act in a less attractive manner.

A man whose job was less than perfect said that while at work, he would say things to himself such as, "This is so boring. How depressing! This is awful!" which made him like his job even less. A dieter confided in us that when she got a bit hungry, she would say to herself, "I'm starving," or "I *must* have something to eat," and then rush off to eat as if she were really starving.

In these kinds of situations, *replace the self-defeating thoughts with incompatible ones, including thoughts that contain positive self-instructions.* For example, when the shy young woman realized that she was thinking, "He's not going to like me; I'm going to be shy," she said instead, "No, not this time. Now remember: smile, make eye contact, stay calm, listen carefully to what he is saying." She was substituting "self-coaching" for the unwanted self-defeating thoughts.

The dieter who said "I'm starving" corrected herself by saying, "No, I'm not. I'm just a bit hungry, and that's good, because it means I'm losing weight." The man who didn't like his job substituted thoughts like, "It's not so bad. I need the money, and it's an easy job."

Words guide your actions. They are antecedents you produce for your own behavior. Thus, it is important you notice negative words and change them to desirable self-instructions.

Suppose a newly hired salesperson fails to make a sale to her first customer. If she says to herself, "I was never cut out to be in sales," or "I'll never learn to do this," her future disaster is already clear. If, on the other hand, she says to herself, "I'm going to learn how to do this," then there is the possibility of future success. Those two ways of speaking to the self will produce very different actions—and two very different levels of success (Rehm, 1982).

Initiating Positive Self-Instructions

As you discover the role of self-speech antecedents in your problem situations, it is very likely that one of two conditions is present: (1) either you are giving yourself instructions and assigning labels that cue undesired reactions; or (2) your problem behavior is "automated," and you can't identify any self-statements.

In either event, the same strategy is called for. *Insert into the chain of events new self-instructions that will guide the desired behavior.* Almost every self-modification plan should include the use of some new self-instructions (Meichenbaum, 1977). They are very effective and can help overcome a variety of problems (Dush, Hirt, Schroeder, 1983).

Designing a self-instruction plan is very simple. The strategy is merely to substitute new instructions for the self-defeating ones you now use. Stop telling yourself, "I can't do this!" Say instead, "I can" (and then tell yourself how). Decide what you want to do, and tell yourself to do it. The instructions should be brief and clear (see Box 5-2).

Here are the self-instructions a shy man used to talk himself through approaching a new acquaintance: "Go up to her and say hello. Don't forget to smile. Make eye contact. Face her directly. Be open." If you are explicit, giving yourself instructions can guide you through a new, unfamiliar behavior by reminding you of some steps you might forget in the stress or excitement of the situation.

BOX 5-2

Talking through the Music

Even learning how to improvise can be improved by self-directing talk. Jazz pianist David Sudnow has written a book describing how he learned improvisational jazz piano.

Here are his words—the ones he said to himself as he played:

I did nudgings to myself, taking an inner course of action to help the outer one . . . I perked up with the assistance of saying to myself:

Springboard—
get the beat right—
keep the hand loose and flexible—
bounce around on a place—
breathe deeply—. . .
relax—. . .
be careful—. . .
get those shoulders moving—
keep that hand from tripping—
get especially bebopical—
play beautifully—
get down on it—
do it.

SOURCE: *Ways of the Hand: The Organization of Improvised Conduct* (p. 146–147) by D. Sudnow, 1978, Cambridge, MA: Harvard University Press. Reprinted by permission.

As a further example, the following are changed self-instructions for reducing angry outbursts. Instead of saying, "Nobody treats me that way!" substitute a coping statement such as, "This is rough, but I can handle it"; "Chill out, this will soon be over"; or "I'm in control" (Deffenbacher, in press; Deffenbacher, McNamara, Stark, & Sabadell, 1990).

State your new belief aloud as a reminder before you enter a difficult situation (Kanter & Goldfried, 1979). A young student who had just moved into her own apartment (against her parents' wishes) reminded herself while driving back home on Saturdays, "Remember, I can tolerate their disapproval. They continue to love me. I have made the right decision. I don't need to have approval constantly." Even during a problem situation, statements of belief or judgment can guide your reactions. When the topic of living alone comes up once more, this student can say to herself, "I'm overreacting; I don't need to feel upset," and then add a precise self-instruction: "Relax now. Try to change the subject."

Making absurd statements is of little use. One study of women who had attempted to cope with depression discovered that both the successful and the unsuccessful women used encouraging self-instructions. But the successful ones *believed* the positive things they told themselves (Doerfler & Richards, 1981). Telling yourself, "I am the most brilliant woman in the state of Illinois!" will not affect your behavior much—unless, of course, you believe it's true. Prepare a list of true positive statements about yourself. Use those statements regularly, at moments of quiet as well as moments of stress.

Self-instructions can also remind you of your long-range goals. Before approaching a woman, the shy man described earlier said to himself, "Remember, this is important to me. I've got to learn how to talk to women or I'll die a hermit." This kind of self-statement will bring your long-range goal forward in your mind and increase your incentive to perform the next new behavior.

Couldn't you get all these benefits by just "remembering" what to do without actually saying the words? Perhaps, but unless you say the words, your "remembering" may be too vague to be useful. Actually saying the words—in your mind, in your imagination, or even aloud—brings up self-speech from the underground and allows it to exercise full power. In our experience, beginning students most often fail to harness the power of self-instructions because they don't truly self-instruct. They "figure it out," decide that saying the words is "silly," and skip over the crucial behavior—actually saying the words in the critical situation. Saying the words makes all the difference (see Box 5-3).

Thought Substitutions

Intrusive or unpleasant thoughts, in their extreme forms, are called *obsessions.* In their milder forms, self-degrading and self-defeating thoughts—such as, "I'm no good" or I'm a loser"—are unfortunately common. They may be visual as well as verbal and may take the form of some unpleasant image that, like a persistent tune, you can't seem to get out of your mind.

BOX 5-3

Self-Instructions for Studying: A Self-Experiment

A college student's instructors reported the following case:

> Betty was 19 years of age, enrolled as an undergraduate student at a large urban university, and currently sharing an apartment with two students. Although Betty always studied (read) at home, she described the process as a "hassle" in that she frequently talked on the telephone, snacked on "junk foods," conversed with her roommates, and/or listened to music while reading. Because she was enrolled in a class that required a great deal of reading, she wanted to decrease these behaviors.

Behavior Observations

Betty made observations of her studying once every five minutes for approximately one hour per evening, five evenings per week. She would note whether or not she had been studying in the previous five minutes. Because the length of time spent studying varied, the number of observed time samples ranged from 6 to 15, with the majority equaling 12 per session. Studying was defined as "sitting in a chair, reading a textbook, underlining important facts and/or taking notes on a separate sheet of paper." All data were transcribed onto an 8½" × 11" paper that was divided into squares, each square representing a five-minute time sample.

Experimental Phases

Baseline. During this ten-day phase, Betty continued to study in the living room. Although most studying occurred during the early evening hours, on two occasions Betty read during the afternoon. Other than recording data according to the described procedures, Betty was asked not to attempt to alter her studying behaviors.

Experimental demands. Betty wrote a series of instructions on an index card:

> It's important to study to get good grades. I need to study to understand new material. I'm not going to talk to my roommates, because it's important that I learn this material. It's important that I learn this material; therefore, I will not talk on the phone. I will remain studying even though I feel the urge to eat or drink something. Because listening to music distracts me and it is important that I learn this material, I will not play the stereo.

Betty read the card once immediately prior to reading. She did this for 13 days.

Self-instructions. Then Betty constructed a second card, listing an additional series of instructions:

> OK. I've got my books out, and I'm turning to the right page. This is what I am supposed to be doing, because it will help me to be a better student and earn good grades. Studying also helps me understand new material, which is important in getting good grades. Because I need to learn this material, I will not talk to my roommates or talk on the phone. Even

though I feel the urge to get up and get something to eat or drink, I will not, because it is important for me to learn this material. Therefore, I will keep reading the textbook and take good notes.

During the next 6 days, Betty read the second card once every 15 minutes throughout the studying hour. She continued to read the first card prior to studying. All other procedures were similar to the initial baseline phase.

Withdrawal. During the next ten days, Betty was asked by her experimenting instructor not to read either card. This was done to test whether the instructions were still needed.

Self-instructions 2. This six-day phase was similar to the previous self-instruction phase; she read both cards to herself again.

Results

Figure 5-1 represents graphically the percentage of time Betty studied. Studying percentages were computed by dividing the number of times Betty recorded herself as reading by the total number of observations taken during that session. Baseline rates for studying averaged about 59%. Under the demand-phase condition, studying increased to about 73%. After the self-instruction phase was implemented, studying increased to approximately 96%. During the withdrawal phase, the percentage fluctuated widely, but leveled out again at about 96% after the treatment was reinstated.

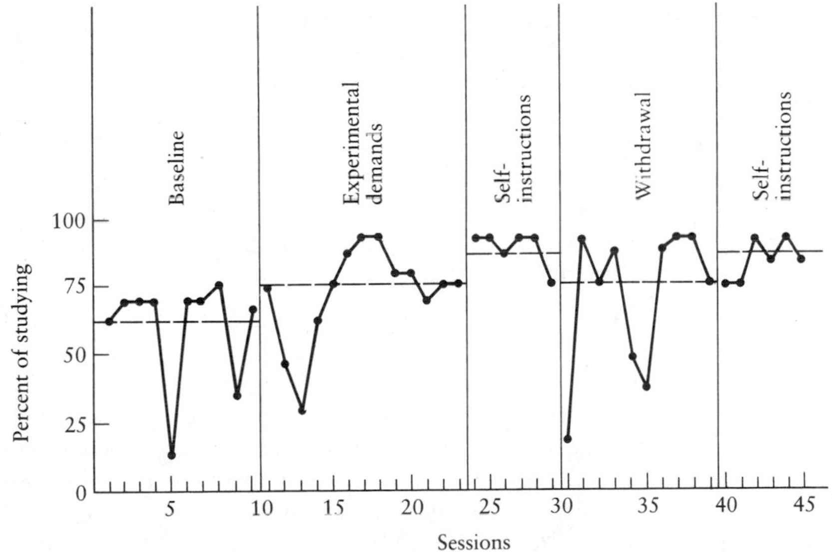

Figure 5-1 A record of Betty's studying across experimental conditions

SOURCE: Reprinted with permission of the authors and publisher from Cohen, R., De James, P., Nocera, B., and Ramberger, M. Application of a simple self-instruction procedure on adults' exercise and studying: Two case reports. *Psychological Reports,* 1980, *46,* 443–451.

Such unwanted thoughts have been problematic since the dawn of time. Early Buddhism, since at least the fifth century B.C., has prescribed several techniques for ridding oneself of unwanted thoughts. One technique is to forcibly restrain and dominate the mind, with teeth clenched and tongue pressed hard against the palate, like a stronger man forcing a weaker man, driving the thought from the mind (de Silva, 1985). Does this technique really work? That question continues to plague modern versions of self-control of thoughts.

The most detailed modern version is called **thought stopping** (Wolpe, 1958). Thought stopping is simple. As soon as the unwanted thought occurs, say to yourself, "Stop!" Say it sharply, and if not aloud, say it clearly in your mind. As in the case of other self-instructions, it is vital that you actually verbalize "Stop!"

Does it work? Perhaps; perhaps not. Some research suggests that driving a thought from your mind only causes it to rebound and come back more vigorously later (Clark, Ball, & Paper, 1991; Wegner & Schneider, 1989). Particularly, suppressing thoughts of things like sex tends to produce more emotional reaction than actually thinking of them does (Wegner, Shortt, Blake, & Page, 1990).

What about using thoughts of something else to distract the mind from the unwanted thought? That seems to work better (Wegner & Schneider, 1989). As soon as some unwanted thought occurs, immediately substitute another thought. If possible, the substituted thought should be the opposite of the unwanted one (Cautela, 1983; Turner, Holzman, & Jacob, 1983). If you think, "I'm going to screw this up," substitute, "No, I'm not." Then give yourself instructions on how to perform adequately.

Also, learn to relax in the situations in which you have the unwanted thoughts. A tennis player, for example, who is losing a match tells himself, "Okay, just relax. Relax. Now remember, short stroke on the backhand." One of our students suffered from embarrassing and repeated sexual fantasies. She substituted images of being alone, on a beach, in deep relaxation.

Amy, one of our students, reported:

> Whenever I was late, I would increase my nervousness by thinking, "I'm always late. Someone will be mad at me. I'm letting them down." During the project, I attempted to stop those thoughts and replace them with others, especially when I was hopelessly late! I would tell myself, "They probably won't even notice. They'll forgive you. Try harder next time. Getting stressed about the situation won't help. You can change." Many times I was on the bus or walking to class, so these statements, just a few of them, would be sufficient to stop the negative thoughts.

Building New Stimulus Control: The Physical and Social Environments

You can also arrange new physical antecedents, or cues, to stimulate desired behavior. The simplest instance of this procedure can be illustrated by expanding our discussion of narrowing antecedents of intellectual work—

studying or writing. A good way to begin developing the habit of increased studying or writing is to increase the environmental stimulus control over concentrated writing. You can arrange a special "writing" environment so that (1) whenever you are in that situation, you are concentrating; and (2) while you are in that situation, you are not doing anything else. Thus, you begin by learning to concentrate while writing at a certain place in which you *never do anything else* but write.

If you don't have a place you can reserve for this one behavior, you can set up a particular *arrangement* of cues. For example, a man had in his room only one table, which he had to use for a variety of activities, such as writing letters, paying bills, watching TV, and eating. But when he wanted to do concentrated studying or writing, he always pulled his table away from the wall and sat on the other side of it. In that way, sitting on the other side of his table became the cue associated only with concentrated intellectual work.

Suppose that no matter how diligent you are in removing yourself from your desk when not concentrating, the concentrated work still does not come? Using other people as supporting stimuli can provide the necessary first step. Brigham (1982) suggests that the first environment you choose for studying should be one in which studying is a high-probability response—such as the library. He suggests:

> A change in behavior could be accomplished by identifying a friend who regularly studies in the library and asking to study with that person. . . . [You should] reinforce the friend for being a study partner. Such reinforcement will . . . increase the likelihood that the friend will reinforce [your] studying behavior. (p. 55)

One of the most powerful cues to behavior is seeing that same behavior performed by other people in the same environment. This effect can be used to positive advantage when you have difficulty "priming" that first behavior step. A woman who wanted to increase her exercise required herself to go to an exercise class, and a man who wanted to jog required himself to meet with members of a jogging clinic each Sunday morning. Placing yourself in an environment where others are performing your desired behavior can provide a powerful antecedent for your own similar performance.

It's important to ask yourself if changing some of your social interactions could help you change. Friends, family, and acquaintances interact with us in habitual ways, and these interactions can build cues that are not always desirable. Frequently, the responses are emotional. People who are depressed often find themselves unable to "break out" of frustrating and unrewarding patterns with their associates. Doerfler and Richards (1981) studied a group of women who had initiated efforts to control their mild depression. Of those who were successful, 67% had made dramatic changes in their social environments, whereas few unsuccessful subjects had done so (14%).

In beginning a difficult self-improvement program, such as giving up tobacco, alcohol, or drugs, it is important that you experience early success in order to increase your feelings of self-efficacy. For this reason, it is often wise to choose one situation or cue condition in which you feel confident that you can resist temptation. Begin by not smoking or drinking in that situation, and when you have experienced that feeling of self-efficacy, expand to more difficult situations (Nicki, Remington, & MacDonald, 1984).

These are all examples of deliberately establishing antecedent stimulus control so that you can perform a desired behavior reliably in at least one situation. For some goals, only one situation is necessary. For other goals, however, you will want to perform the behavior in many situations. For example, Fo (1975) found that students are better off if they can study in many situations so that each opportunity to study can be seized. In this and many other cases, it is desirable to broaden the range of effective antecedents for a desired target behavior.

Stimulus Generalization

Many behaviors, such as studying, writing, abstaining from drugs, improving social skills, and refraining from overeating, will have to be performed eventually in a variety of environments. **Stimulus generalization** is the process by which a behavior that has been learned in the presence of one antecedent is performed in the presence of other, similar antecedents.

The more similar the new situation is to the original situation, the easier it is to generalize your newly learned behavior. Therefore, you will want to think about the similarity between other situations and the one in which you can already perform the desired behavior. You should begin generalization by performing the target behavior in the situation that is most similar to the original one.

A middle-aged woman suffered from a very strong fear of speaking in front of groups. Through self-modification, she developed the ability to speak to a group of three or four friends. Having accomplished that, she wanted to generalize the newly acquired ability to new groups. She thought it would be easier if the new group contained at least a couple of friends from the old one because the new situation would then be very similar to the one in which she first practiced. She arranged things so that such an opportunity would come up. When it did, she performed the target behavior and then reinforced it.

Once you have developed a behavior that you can perform in certain situations, you should gradually move into other, similar situations. Use self-instructions. A great strength of self-instructions is that they can be used in many situations, thus creating a bridge from familiar to unfamiliar circumstances. Self-instructions are portable cues. They can be taken with you from party to party, from home to library. Thus, self-instructions enhance the development of a broad skill base, just as stimulus generalization does.

Precommitment and Programming of the Social Environment

Precommitment means arranging in advance for helpful antecedents to occur. This arrangement can be made when some problem situation is anticipated, especially for those moments of maximum difficulty.

A smoker had been off cigarettes for about two months. He had stopped several times in the past, but each time he had gone back to smoking. He had been successful this time because he had identified those situations in which he had relapsed in the past and had taken steps to deal with them. One of the problem situations was being at a party. The drinks, the party atmosphere, and the feeling of relaxation represented an irresistible temptation to "smoke just a few," although in the past this had usually led to a return to regular smoking. One night, as the man and his wife were getting ready to go out to a party, he said, "You know, I am really going to be tempted to smoke there. Will you do me a favor? If you see me bumming a cigarette from someone, remind me of the kids and that I really don't want to go back to smoking." (One of the reasons he wanted to quit was that he knew he was setting a bad example for his children.)

This man arranged in advance to be reminded. He precommitted himself to facing the knowledge that he would end up smoking again if he tried to have just a few, and he made this precommitment at a time when he was not strongly tempted—*before* going to the party.

This intelligent strategy was possible because he had profited from previous mistakes. Each time a smoker returns to smoking, it is a relapse, but it is also a source of *information* about what kinds of situations are most tempting (Hunt & Matarazzo, 1973). The man used this information to cope better with the problem situation by enlisting his wife's help.

Asking other people to cue or remind you can be an effective way of arranging antecedents. You are not asking to be nagged, of course, but simply to be reminded of what you wanted to do back when you were not being so sorely tempted. You can encourage family and friends to help you achieve your goals by asking them to provide cues and reinforcers for the behaviors you want to develop and by asking them not to support undesired behavior (Stuart, 1967).

A student of ours wrote:

> With the help and cooperation of my family and friends, an agreement was made not to smoke cigarettes in front of me for one month. If they were going to smoke, they would let me know, so I could leave the room until the smoke cleared. My girlfriend and parents were especially helpful (though occasionally irritating) when they reminded me about my project. During situations that encouraged smoking, such as mealtime, driving, parties, and so on, they would remind me of my goal. This was very encouraging, because it showed that they were concerned and wanted to help. As they continued with their support, I began to feel more determined and obligated to quit.

Many antecedents to problem behaviors are created by family or friends. The dieter whose roommate presents her with a box of chocolates or whose mother bakes her a pie is placed in a situation in which overeating becomes more likely. Loved ones cannot always know exactly what you need; be specific in telling others what kind of helpful antecedents they can provide.

Precommitment, in the form of reminders, can also be arranged without the help of others. Setting an alarm clock is one obvious way. Preparing a

BOX 5-4
The Odysseus Box

A letter from a reader:

> Dear Drs. Watson and Tharp:
> A brief note to tell you how much I enjoyed and profited from *Self-Directed Behavior.* Terrific!!
> I have a box with a timer and spring mechanism in it arranged so that I can set the timer, put various keys into the box (a padlock on the refrigerator, doors, car, etc.), close the box, and it will spring open at predetermined times. I've found it very helpful. Others might also. I call it the *Odysseus Box.* . . .
> With best wishes,
> . . .

daily or weekly schedule of obligations is another. A man who had a bad tendency to "forget" to pay his monthly bills tacked a list of them over the toilet in the bathroom and checked them off each month when they were paid, so that each time he used the toilet he would see whether he had paid or not. An overweight student began to plan the day's meals each morning and found she was better able to diet by not having to make any decisions when mealtime came. Tempting situations can be avoided; tempting substances can be locked away (Ainslee, 1987). Box 5-4 contains an example of how one person used an innovative method of avoiding temptation.

Tips for Typical Topics

Anxiety and Stress

No doubt you are avoiding all the stressful situations you can. But many situations that induce anxiety are not "objectively" dangerous. What are the antecedents to which you react? Many situations induce anxiety, depending on how you interpret them to yourself.

Feelings of anxiety are most often preceded by thoughts, feelings, or interpretations that a personal threat is present (Beck & Emery, 1985; Sewitch & Kirsch, 1984). Note the worrisome things you tell yourself. Are they true? For example, "I'm failing this test. This is a catastrophe!" First, are you actually failing? Second, is it a catastrophe? Compared to an earthquake? Statements that suggest extreme personal threat—catastrophizing statements, such as "Oh, God, I can't stand it!"—lead to less adequate coping (Steenman, 1986). Particularly watch for thoughts in which you tell yourself that the anxiety-provoking situation is uncontrollable (Barlow, 1988). Almost certainly the situation *is* controllable—by those who have learned how. You are more likely to learn how if you tell yourself, "It is possible."

Include in your self-contract very specific self-statement analysis. For example, Altmaier, Ross, Leary, and Thornbookrough (1982) suggest the following items for your contract:

- In order to cope more successfully, I will pause when I notice my stress signals of __________.
- I will examine my feelings, images, and self-statements, such as __________.
- If I am using negative self-talk, I will switch to telling myself: __________.

Assertion

The assertive person is one who (1) behaves appropriately in social situations, (2) is honest, and (3) is able to express thoughts and feelings straightforwardly while taking into account the feelings and welfare of others (Rimm & Masters, 1979).

The difference between assertion and aggression is that one is appropriate, the other is not. Many nonassertive people become very angry before they finally speak up, so when they do act, they are more likely to be verbally aggressive than if they had asserted themselves earlier (Linehan, 1979). Therefore, it is desirable to act assertively early in the chain of events. Increasing assertive behavior has been shown to reduce feelings of anger (Moon & Eisler, 1983).

Early intervention in the chain can be approached through *beliefs* or *self-instructions* or both. Goldfried (1979) and his associates have shown that timid people often believe that others will reject or punish them for the slightest bit of standing up for themselves, but objectively this is rarely true. Search out such beliefs. Change them to positive self-instructions. Self-instructions are particularly useful in coaching yourself through unfamiliar behavior: "Remember, be firm. That's right, you needn't be unpleasant. Just state your position firmly. Good."

Depression and Low Self-Esteem

The single most effective antidote to depression is probably a new environment—one that has more pleasant activities available and offers more opportunities for rewarding social interactions. Changing environments is often a sufficient plan for lifting mood and self-esteem (Doerfler & Richards, 1983). When such a change is impossible or insufficient, attend to the following issues in your self-change plan.

Depression and low self-esteem are closely tied together, even in childhood (Kendall, Stark, & Adam, 1990). If we think about a cybernetic model of depression, depressed people perform just as well as those who are not depressed, but depressed people have much higher standards than nondepressed people do. Thus, after equivalent events, depressed persons will be more down on themselves for not meeting their own too-high standards (Rehm, 1988). Look for such distorted self-statements as too many *shoulds* ("I should visit my family more"), *perfectionisms* ("I must do everything perfectly; otherwise I will be criticized and be a failure"), and *comparisons* ("Compared with ________, I am really flawed") (Freeman & Zaken-Greenburg, 1989).

These excessive standards suggest two strategies. First, you can reexamine your goals and standards and try to make them more realistic. Second, you can closely examine your self-statements, thoughts, and judgments of your own performance.

When you notice a change in your mood, try to discover what thoughts have led to it. Thoughts such as "I'm a loser" or "I never do anything right" will certainly depress your mood and should be replaced by more positive self-statements (Rehm, 1982). Prepare positive self-statements in advance, even rehearse them, so that you can use them immediately as replacements. This is especially important if you are depressed. Depressed people tend to distract themselves from negative thoughts with other negative thoughts (Wenzlaff, Wegner, & Roper, 1988). When you are depressed, you may even criticize yourself for criticizing yourself: "I just thought that I'm a loser. What a stupid thing to think" (Hollon & Beck, 1979). Have a replacement thought ready: "I'm a los—No I'm not. Actually I'm a loyal and sensitive friend."

Be especially vigilant about negative self-statements after some disappointment. When depressed, you will be likely to overgeneralize and tell yourself that you are worthless in general (Carver & Ganellen, 1983). Prepare positive self-statements, and expect to use them immediately after disappointments.

Another major tactic for antecedent control of depression is the scheduling of pleasant activities (Hollon & Beck, 1979). This powerful antecedent of good mood is not often used by depressed people (Fuchs & Rehm, 1977). The type of activity—entertainment, socializing, exercise, fantasizing, or handicrafts—is not crucial so long as it is pleasant for you. Schedule these activities regularly and frequently, and stick to the schedule.

Exercise and Athletics

In beginning a lifestyle-change program, such as adopting a schedule of regular exercise, one of the first hurdles to overcome is the pain. Stiff muscles, aches, and weariness in the early stages of running or aerobics can punish the new behavior out of existence. However, self-instructions during exercise-induced discomfort can be very helpful. It is better to use self-instructions that *distract* from pain rather than those that urge you on in spite of the pain. Tell yourself to "smell the flowers" or "watch the clouds." This is more effective for beginning exercisers than such instructions as "You can do better!" or "You can make it!" (Martin et al., 1984).

If you are a more experienced athlete who is attempting to increase performance, altogether different strategies may be appropriate (Suinn, 1987). Serious runners, such as marathoners, improve performance by careful monitoring and self-instructions about their form and fatigue levels, even their levels of pain. No smelling the flowers for them! However, if events occur that produce anxiety—such as seeing other runners gaining, or feeling fear of the hill to come—then distracting self-instructions may help even seasoned athletes, who might tell themselves to count the clouds or find the biggest tree.

Relations with Others: Social Anxieties, Social Skills, and Dating

Antecedents for social anxiety often include meeting new people, carrying on a conversation with people you don't know well, being the center of attention, speaking in front of a class, or being evaluated by others. All these conditions have one thing in common: You want to manage your self-presentation to others and be perceived in positive terms. It is completely normal to experience some tension in these situations. But those who suffer from high social anxiety engage in very different kinds of self-talk when they prepare for social interactions. They are more likely to tell themselves that the situation is threatening and that they will be seen as incompetent and unattractive (Carver & Scheier, 1986).

Discover your own self-talk in approaching social interactions. Make sure you are not using catastrophizing statements. Plan for more adaptive, skill-related, and confident self-instructions.

Self-instructions are also very useful as antecedent control in strained relationships. If relationships are severely distressed, you may wish to use avoidance for a time, limiting interaction to certain situations.

In what specific situations do you have problems? Consult the list in Chapter 3. Many students, for example, feel they don't know how to ask for a date, or they fear rejection so much that they never ask. Do certain situations cue you to avoid social interactions? What negative self-instructions, such as "He'd probably just laugh if I asked him out," do you give yourself? Can you discover any self-defeating beliefs, such as, "If I ask her out and she refuses, it's a disaster," "If there's a lull in the conversation, it means we are bored, and that's terrible," or "I really need to impress him, so I'd better show off"?

Use self-instructions to coax yourself through particular situations, such as making conversation. "Remember, talk about what she wants to talk about. Ask her what she is interested in, then talk about that. Express interest in her."

You may feel you don't know what to do in certain social situations, or you become fearful in them. These problems can be dealt with after you read the next chapter.

Smoking, Drinking, and Drugs

Early success is important in controlling the use of harmful substances. Select one situation in which you are confident that you can resist smoking or drinking. Begin with that situation so that you can have the experience of success and self-efficacy (Nicki, Remington, & MacDonald, 1984).

If your problem occurs frequently at home, change the antecedents by changing the geography of your area—rearrange the furniture; move the television set or the bed where your indulgence occurs. For public locations, as an immediate first step, avoid the antecedent situations that are the cues for your indulgence, particularly those where others will be indulging—for example, a smoker's cigarette cravings are stronger and more frequent around other smokers (Rickard-Figueroa & Zeichner, 1985). Avoiding such situations is particularly important when you are emotionally upset (Marlatt & Parks, 1982). If you fail to avoid a situation, then escape from it (Shiffman, 1984). If you cannot escape, distract yourself with other thoughts or activities. If you cannot be distracted, concentrate on the abstract, cool qualities of indulging. As a rule, keeping company with nonsmokers can serve as a form of positive antecedent control for people trying to stop smoking (Carey, Snel, Carey, & Richards, 1989).

Caffeine and alcohol are very frequent cues for smoking (Zimmerman, Warheit, Ulbrich, & Auth, 1990). Avoidance of caffeine and alcohol will make stopping smoking more likely (Berecz, 1984).

Analyze the chains that lead to the problem behavior. The chains often lead as far back as shopping. Not buying the marijuana in the first place is the most effective point at which to break the chain. Don't order a pitcher of beer or wine; order only a single glass (George & Marlatt, 1986).

However, a complete plan should address both ends of the chain. For instance, interfere early in the chain by reducing or eliminating the supply of cigarettes—rationing them if you are cutting down, not buying or carrying them if you are stopping. Interfere late in the chain, right at the moment of the strongest urge, by asking goal questions:

1. Why do I want to smoke this cigarette (or joint), when I have started a program to quit smoking (or using pot)?
2. Whom am I fooling by smoking this cigarette (or joint)?
3. Do I want to keep on being a smoker (or a drug user)?
4. Do I want to indulge more than I want to break my habit?

For alcohol, drugs, and tobacco, taking a two-minute pause between the urge and the indulgence is an effective technique for reducing violations. Substance cravings have a particular form, like a wave: They rise in intensity, crest, and subside. George and Marlatt (1986) suggest that you "surf" those urges. Ride them out—feel them rise, then feel them fall. Even a two-minute pause can be enough to let the wave pass under you.

Studying and Time Management

Five specific forms of antecedent control have proven effective:

1. Write out a planned schedule, and keep it as a reminder in some obvious place. Plan at least a week at a time (Kirschenbaum, Humphrey, & Malett, 1981).

2. Use self-reminders of goals and values. Ask several times a day, "Is this the best use of my time right now? If it's not, what would be?" (Lakein, 1973).

3. Substitute more adaptive self-speech while studying. Do not tell yourself that studying is boring. Do not remind yourself of things you'd rather do. Clarify your goals for the study period, and tell yourself to reach them.

4. Do not interact with other people while you study (Heffernan & Richards, 1981). Studying can sometimes be facilitated by studying with an effective partner or in the library where others are also studying, but do not interact with others except before and after your study time.

5. Your study time will be more effectively used if your nonstudying activities are also well organized. Each day, make a "to-do" list of all the things you need to fit into your scheduled time blocks. If necessary, arrange the items by priority, and select your activities accordingly (Lakein, 1973).

Weight Loss and Overeating

All behavioral programs for weight loss have certain features in common that concentrate on antecedents of eating. These common features are:

1. Self-monitoring of eating behavior and activity levels
2. Instructions to control environmental influences on eating
3. Attention to thoughts and self-speech that interfere with the necessary behavior changes (Agras, 1987, p. 31)

Your own self-directed program should also include these features.

Overeating is likely to have multiple antecedents—many chains, all leading to excessive eating. You may eat when you are bored, sad, angry, or happy. You may always eat what is offered to you, even if you are not hungry. You may eat because the food is there or because you want to relax. Learning to eat properly requires careful observation of all those antecedents—emotional, social, and physical (Leon, 1979; Stuart & Davis, 1972).

Analyze the chains that lead to the problem behavior. You can interrupt the overeating chain at several early points—for example, by shopping when you are *not* hungry (to prevent overbuying), by taking a list of fattening foods *not* to buy, by avoiding the cookie-and-cracker aisle, and by not allowing yourself to become so hungry that you will gorge.

Interfering at the end of the chain—right at the moment of the overwhelming urge to eat—can often be done with a recommitment strategy. Require yourself to write answers to these questions before you give in to the urge (Rosen, 1981; Youdin & Hemmes, 1978):

1. Am I really hungry? Why am I eating?
2. Whom am I fooling by eating this food?
3. Do I want to be overweight?
4. Do I want this food more than I want a normal weight?

All weight-loss programs should include a two-minute pause in the middle of every meal.

Finally, it is highly important to have a social support system that can help you plan to avoid or to better handle high-risk situations. Your significant others can help make poor food choices less accessible and provide cues and encouragement during times when your environment is tempting or unpredictable (Fitzgibbon & Kirschenbaum, in press).

If your problem is infrequent but excessive "binge eating," you should take two additional steps. First, note your self-destructive beliefs, particularly those of the "perfect love from everyone" and "perfect performance from me" types. Binge eaters appear to be especially burdened with these extremely high standards for pleasing others. When they (naturally) cannot always live up to those standards, they react with "self-damnation" statements, and then with eating splurges. Second, replace those beliefs with more reasonable ones; replace your negative self-evaluations with positive ones. This may be just as important as a direct attack on daily eating habits (Heatherton & Baumeister, 1991).

Chapter Summary

Identifying Antecedents

Identifying current antecedents requires careful record keeping. Be sure to trace the chain of antecedents to its logical beginning. Discovering self-instructional antecedents involves carefully observing and amplifying the quiet thoughts that instruct you. You can discover self-defeating beliefs by writing down all instances of your problem behavior and identifying their common theme.

Modifying Old Antecedents

The first strategy for achieving antecedent control is to avoid the antecedent for the problem behavior. This is particularly appropriate for consummatory behaviors, such as overindulgence in food, drugs, or sex, because they automatically strengthen themselves on each performance by producing their own reinforcements. Particularly avoid situations where other people are engaging in your indulgent habit. This is especially important when you are in a highly emotional state.

You can sometimes avoid antecedents by narrowing the problem behavior down to a very restricted antecedent. Thus, you should leave the special desk if you are not studying, or leave the bed if you cannot sleep. Antecedents can also be changed by reperceiving them—by attending to their "cool," abstract qualities rather than their "hot," pleasurable features. You can also lessen temptation by distracting yourself with thoughts of something else.

Chains of behavior develop as one act becomes the cue for the next, which in turn becomes the cue for the next, and so forth, with the entire chain being reinforced by the final reinforcement. Although it is the final act that is likely to be seen as the problem, the entire chain is implicated. Changing the chain can interrupt the automatic, "uncontrollable" nature of the problem. A chain can be scrambled, interrupted by pauses or record keeping, or changed by substituting one or more links. For long chains, it is advisable to change elements both at the beginning and at the end of the chain.

Arranging New Antecedents

A most effective way to arrange new antecedents is through self-instructions. Before an occasion for a desired behavior takes place, instruct yourself clearly and incisively. These instructions can pertain to actions or to beliefs; that is, you can instruct yourself about the details of the action you plan to take, or you can instruct yourself about your own good qualities and competence.

Self-defeating or unpleasant self-statements can be replaced with more positive ones. A key to success in suppressing negative thoughts is to substitute new, adaptive self-statements. You should actually say self-instructions aloud or subvocally, as clearly as possible and as close as possible to the moment of the actual behavior.

The physical environment can be rearranged to increase stimulus control over desired behavior. The technique is to restrict the desired behavior to a particular environment. You can arrange the social environment to stimulate desired behavior by being in the presence of others who are performing the behavior you desire.

Most behaviors that you want to acquire will be useful in several situations, so that techniques of stimulus generalization are recommended. Desirable behaviors should gradually be extended to similar situations, thus broadening the range of controlling antecedents. If you use self-instructions to bridge between situations, then the self-instructions will become portable, reliable cues, thus allowing self-regulated behavior in many situations.

Precommitment—arranging in advance for helpful antecedents to occur—is especially useful when moments of maximum difficulty are anticipated. When you know that cues to your undesired behavior are going to be present in a situation, precommit to having cues present that will assist your new performance—reminders from others, the ring of an alarm clock, or self-reminders of your goals.

YOUR OWN SELF-DIRECTION PROJECT: STEP FIVE

By examining your structured diary or your self-recording or both, identify the antecedents of any problem behavior relevant to your goals. Devise a plan for either increasing or decreasing antecedent stimulus control. As one procedure, use new self-instructions, but use at least one other technique as well.

Write this plan out, just as you have done for those in the previous steps. Don't implement your new plan yet; Chapters 6 and 7 are likely to contain ideas that you'll want to incorporate in your final plan.

6

Behaviors: Actions, Thoughts, and Feelings

Outline

- Substituting New Thoughts and Behaviors
- Substitutions for Anxiety and Stress Reactions
- Relaxation
- Developing New Behaviors
- Shaping: The Method of Successive Approximations
- *Tips for Typical Topics*
- *Chapter Summary*
- *Your Own Self-Direction Project: Step Six*

Learning Objectives

Substituting New Thoughts and Behaviors

1. What is the best approach to ridding yourself of an unwanted behavior?
2. What is an incompatible response?

Substitutions for Anxiety and Stress Reactions

3. What are some activities that are incompatible with anxiety? How would you use them in a self-change program?
4. How do you meditate?

Relaxation

5. What are the different types of "relaxation"?
6. Describe the tension-release method of relaxation.
   a. Where do you practice relaxation?
   b. When should you practice?
   c. How is relaxation used as an incompatible response?
   d. How is it combined with self-instructions?
7. What are common problems in mastering relaxation?

Developing New Behaviors

8. What is the fundamental way of mastering a behavior?
9. Explain *imagined rehearsal.*
10. How are imagined rehearsal and relaxation combined?
11. How does one use models in developing new behaviors?
12. Explain *imagined modeling.* What are the recommended procedures?
13. What is the value of practice in the real world?

Shaping: The Method of Successive Approximations

14. Explain the general procedure for shaping.
15. What are the rules for shaping?
16. How can relaxation be combined with shaping?
17. What are some common problems in shaping?

Any plan for self-modification involves developing some new behavior. The principles for developing new behaviors in self-modification programs are the same as those that govern learning in all settings. Self-modification techniques have been devised and refined by psychologists to assist in the self-conscious use of these principles.

This chapter is organized into five main units. The first section discusses procedures for *substituting* a more desirable behavior for a less desirable one. Bringing a new behavior into position—in place of an undesired one—can be a ready solution to some problems. The second section discusses substitutions for anxiety and tension. The third section concentrates on a particular new behavior—*relaxation*—because it is such a useful response to substitute for anxiety and worry. Many readers can already relax effectively but will need to bring this "new" behavior into the chains that now produce worry and anxiety. The fourth section is devoted to techniques for developing new behaviors in general, particularly when the behavior is genuinely new or unknown to you. The principal techniques are *modeling* and *rehearsal*. Finally, we will discuss a fundamental strategy for acquiring new behaviors and bringing them into self-modification programs: *shaping*, or the method of successive approximations.

Substituting New Thoughts and Behaviors

Substituting positive self-statements for negative ones, substituting new self-instructions, and substituting new elements into chains are all examples of a general principle of self-modification. *The task is always to develop new behavior, not merely to suppress old behavior.* Simply eliminating some undesired habit has been likened to creating a behavioral "vacuum." If something is not inserted in its place, the old behavior will quickly rush back in to fill the void (Davidson, Denney, & Elliott, 1980; Tinling, 1972). Eventually, some new behavioral development is necessary. Beginning immediately with the tactic of substitution is economical because the effort of developing the new may automatically suppress the undesired thought or behavior.

Andrea, a young woman who was bothered by too frequent arguments with her father, began to observe her own behavior. She discovered the following chain of events: Her father would make a comment about some aspect of her behavior that seemed to bother him (for example, he disapproved of her career goals). Usually Andrea would respond with a frown and the comment that he should mind his own business. This would enrage him, and they would be off to another bitter argument. Andrea knew that her father basically loved her and that he was simply having a difficult time adjusting to the fact that she was now an adult. She reasoned that if she substituted kind remarks and a smile when he opened up some topic about her behavior, they might be able to discuss it in a friendlier fashion. Instead of setting out to *decrease* frowning and unkind comments, she set out to *increase* smiling and kind comments.

Thereafter, when her father made some remark about her behavior or goals, Andrea would smile at him and strive to disagree as pleasantly as possible. (Of course, she kept a record of her responses and also used other techniques to maintain them.) Increasing the desirable behavior had the effect of calming her father, and they progressed through a series of amicable conversations to a new understanding.

Ron, a college junior, used the same tactic of substituting new behaviors for undesirable ones. Ron's girlfriend had told him very clearly that his long daily telephone calls were becoming oppressive. Ron wanted to keep the relationship, and he genuinely wanted to please his girlfriend. He set out to reduce his telephone calls to no more than one every other day. For the first few days, he did suppress the urge to call, but he found himself brooding and telling himself that her attitude proved that he was a distasteful person.

Ron then adopted a plan that used two substitute behaviors. First, he substituted more favorable (and more realistic) self-statements. At 9:00 on nights he did not call, he said to himself, "I am able to be thoughtful and generous in adopting her preferences." Second, Ron systematically substituted another behavior for that time block. Because he was an able student, he substituted an hour of studying for the phone call. Note that merely suppressing the phone calls not only left a vacuum but allowed feelings of worthlessness and anger to slip in. The substitution strategy allowed him a more realistic self-appraisal, increased his study time, and made him a more desirable friend.

Distracting Behaviors

Another strategy—employed even by very young children—is to distract yourself from the temptation to violate your resolutions. This is not a suggestion to avoid thinking about the general issue. But when temptation, discomfort, or pain is present and inescapable, think about something else; it will make giving in less likely. Not only children use this tactic. Beginning joggers who included distracting thoughts while running were much more likely to still be following their running program three months later (Dubbert, Martin, Raczynski, & Smith, 1982). For more experienced and able runners, this was not true. For experts, careful attention to actual performance was correlated with success (Okwumabua, Meyers, Schleser, & Cooke, 1983). But in early stages of mastery, distracting yourself from the temptations to smoke, eat, drink, take drugs, or stop running is a good device.

The early Buddhists taught self-control of unwanted thoughts by this tactic of self-distracting—by recalling some doctrinal passage; by concentrating on a concrete object, such as a cloud or tree; or by concentrating on a physical activity, such as darning a sock (de Silva, 1985). In using distractors for thoughts, select a single distractor as a replacement and always use it instead of using several different distractors (Wegner & Schneider, 1989).

Incompatible Behaviors

Whenever possible, it is a good tactic to select a substitute behavior that is *incompatible* with the undesired one.

An incompatible response is a behavior that prevents the occurrence of some other behavior. Smiling is incompatible with frowning. Sitting is incompatible with running. Going swimming is incompatible with staying in your room. Being courteous is incompatible with being rude. For many undesired behaviors, several incompatible ones may be available.

The use of incompatible behaviors in controlling unwanted thoughts has a long history in religious instruction. The following is paraphrased from Buddhist advice of the fifth century:

> If an unwanted cognition is associated with lust, one should think of something lustless; if it is associated with hatred, think of something promoting loving kindness. If you are confused, think of something of great clarity. Substitute these thoughts like a carpenter driving in a new peg. (de Silva, 1985, p. 439)

A student active in campus politics was elected to the council of the Associated Students. In the meetings, he found he was talking too much and losing his effectiveness because he was irritating the other members. He felt the impulse to talk, he said, with "the force of a compulsion." He first tried simply being silent. He had some success, but after considering the use of incompatible responses, he reasoned that he could do better by choosing a more active and positive alternative behavior. He chose "listening." This was a genuinely new act, not merely the suppression of an old one. It resulted in less talking, which he wanted, and also in greater listening, which he came to value more and more.

Habit reversal for annoying or self-destructive habits and tics involves substituting an incompatible behavior. After you have focused your attention on the habit (perhaps through negative practice; see Chapter 2), the basic technique is to substitute a similar but harmless response. For example, substitute grooming of the nails and cuticles for biting them (Davidson, Denny, & Elliott, 1980). This proves more effective than any technique aimed only at reducing biting.

It is useful to choose an incompatible behavior even though it is of no particular value in itself. A man who wanted to stop cracking his knuckles all the time decided that whenever he felt like cracking his knuckles, he would *instead* make a fist. A young woman who sometimes scratched her skin until it bled substituted patting for scratching. (For an illustration of some incompatible responses for replacing nervous habits, see Figure 6-1.) The research evidence for the effectiveness of these techniques is excellent (Azrin, Nunn, & Frantz-Renshaw, 1982; Finney, Rapoff, Hall, & Christophersen, 1983). A full habit-reversal program, of course, involves several methods: record keeping, incompatible responses, relaxation, and self-reinforcement (Azrin & Peterson, 1990).

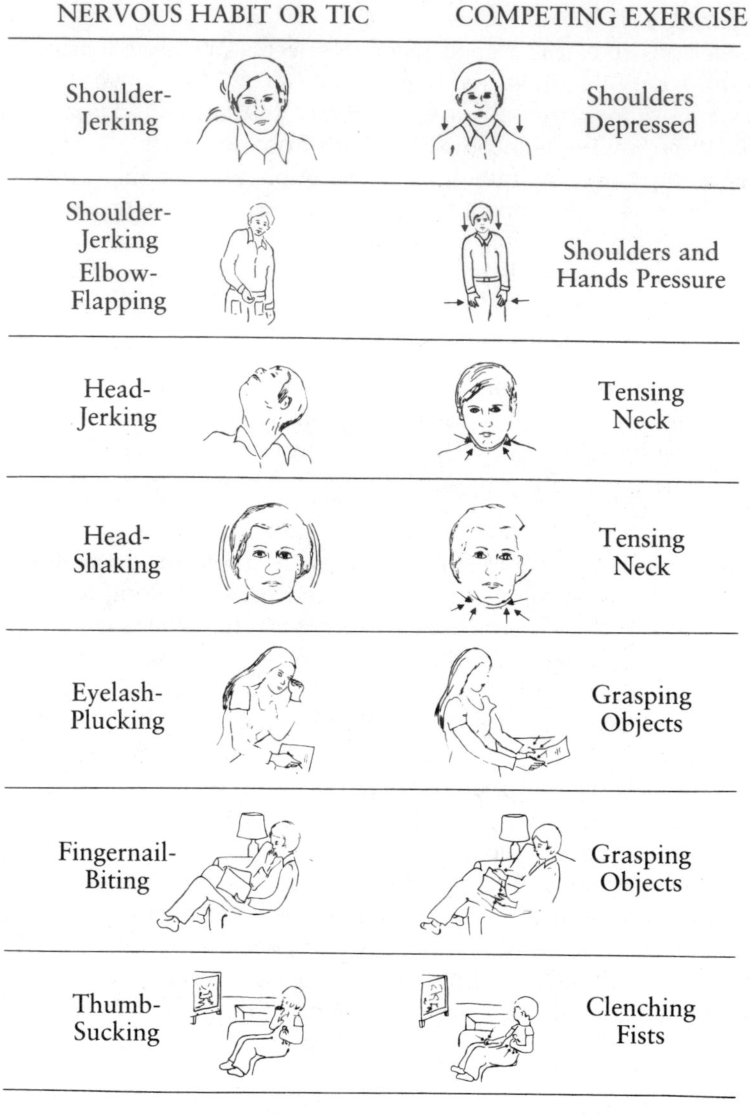

NERVOUS HABIT OR TIC	COMPETING EXERCISE
Shoulder-Jerking	Shoulders Depressed
Shoulder-Jerking Elbow-Flapping	Shoulders and Hands Pressure
Head-Jerking	Tensing Neck
Head-Shaking	Tensing Neck
Eyelash-Plucking	Grasping Objects
Fingernail-Biting	Grasping Objects
Thumb-Sucking	Clenching Fists

Figure 6-1 A pictorial representation of the various types of nervous tics or habits. The left-hand column illustrates the different tics or habits. The adjacent illustration in the right-hand column illustrates the type of competing exercise used for that nervous tic or habit. The arrows in each of the Competing Exercise illustrations show the direction of isometric muscle contraction being exerted by the client.

SOURCE: *"Habit Reversal: A Method of Eliminating Nervous Habits and Tics," by N. H. Azrin and R. G. Nunn, 1973,* Behaviour Research and Therapy, 11, *619–628. Copyright 1973 by Pergamon Press, Ltd. Reprinted by permission.*

The substitution of positive self-statements for negative ones is an element in almost all contemporary treatments for depression (Beck, Rush, Shaw, & Emery, 1979; Lewinsohn, Biglan, & Zeiss, 1976; Rehm, 1982). Negative self-evaluations are always a part of being depressed. The following are typical depressed self-statements (Rehm, 1982):

1. After a minor quarrel with a friend: "I'm just that way. I can't get along with anyone."
2. After being praised by the boss: "He's just doing that to make me feel better because he criticized me last week."
3. After making an "A" on an exam: "It was an easy test. I'll fail a hard exam."

None of these statements tells the whole story. Equally true (but incompatible) self-statements could be substituted. For each negative statement, try to think of substitute statements that emphasize the positive aspects of the events. You should then make these statements in place of the self-critical ones (see Box 6-1 for an example).

When you select an incompatible behavior you want to increase at the expense of some unwanted act, be sure you keep a record of how often you do the one instead of the other. It's a good idea to select an incompatible behavior as soon as possible and begin to count it, even if you are still doing a baseline count on the unwanted target behavior. Keeping a record of the incompatible behavior will encourage you to perform it (Kazdin, 1974b).

Substitutions for Anxiety and Stress Reactions

A student complained to us,

> I don't see how this system [substituting incompatible responses] will work for me. I really don't need to learn anything new. I just need to get rid of my fears. When my husband wants to make love, I want to make love too, very much, but when the crucial moment comes, I get so nervous that I can't carry on.

In fact, substituting an incompatible response is probably the best strategy for her. A goal common to many plans for self-modification is to achieve mastery over fears, anxiety, nervousness, tension, or other stress reactions. In this section, we will discuss a variety of responses that are incompatible with anxiety, and we will discuss how to arrange their substitution.

Phobias, Fears, and Avoidance Behavior

There are people who are so afraid of dogs that they will not enter a house until they are certain no dogs are there. Others fear open places so much they will not leave their own homes. An unreasonable fear of heights may

BOX 6-1

Relieving Depression with Incompatible Thoughts

"My problem is that I get depressed, and then I think about death and suicide, and this frightens me. Sometimes I just don't care what happens." This young woman tried a plan of listening to music or talking to friends when depression began, thinking that they would produce feelings incompatible with depression. Although she kept to this plan for 48 days, no real improvement occurred.

Then, "I thought why not fight fire with fire—use good-feeling thoughts to combat depression thoughts. This would be an incompatible behavior (in the mind)."

She selected a fantasy, which she called "my good dream." Whenever a depressed thought or feeling began, she immediately substituted her "good dream" and held the dream in her mind until her feelings moved "back up at least to neutral."

Here is a typical entry from her journal, which she kept along with her frequency counts and mood ratings:

> The bus driver was in a foul mood and, just as I was going out the front door, shouted "Go to the back!" This made me feel like a fool and really started my depression. Ten minutes had gone by when I reached my job, and by then I was really starting to sink. So I took 15 minutes to try and counter my depression with my good dream. I went in 15 minutes late, but it worked.
>
> It worked remarkably well. The graph of her declining depression shows that her depressions dropped from three hours a day to virtually zero (see Figure 6-2). After day 67, she stopped using any self-modification plan. We never found out what her "good dream" was.

prevent a person from using an elevator. Others, like the young woman above, fear sex so that they are unable to respond with any pleasure. These **phobias**—strong, irrational fears that interfere with normal life—produce avoidance behaviors, and the avoidance is reinforced by reducing the anxiety that would come from dogs, open spaces, heights, or sex.

Many milder, common stresses also cause people to avoid the cues that produce them. Some students feel anxious during tests. The anxiety can grow strong enough to produce extreme avoidance, even to the extent of dropping out of school.

Coping with an unreasonable fear by substituting an incompatible response is the best way to deal with the feared situation (Goldfried, 1977). The basic form of this plan is to develop a new behavior that is incompatible with anxiety and then substitute it for the anxiety as you gradually approach the feared situation.

From Sex to Kung Fu: Substitutions for Anxiety

Many behaviors are incompatible with anxiety. Simple *attention* to a different aspect of the situation can interfere with anxiety. For example, Frederick

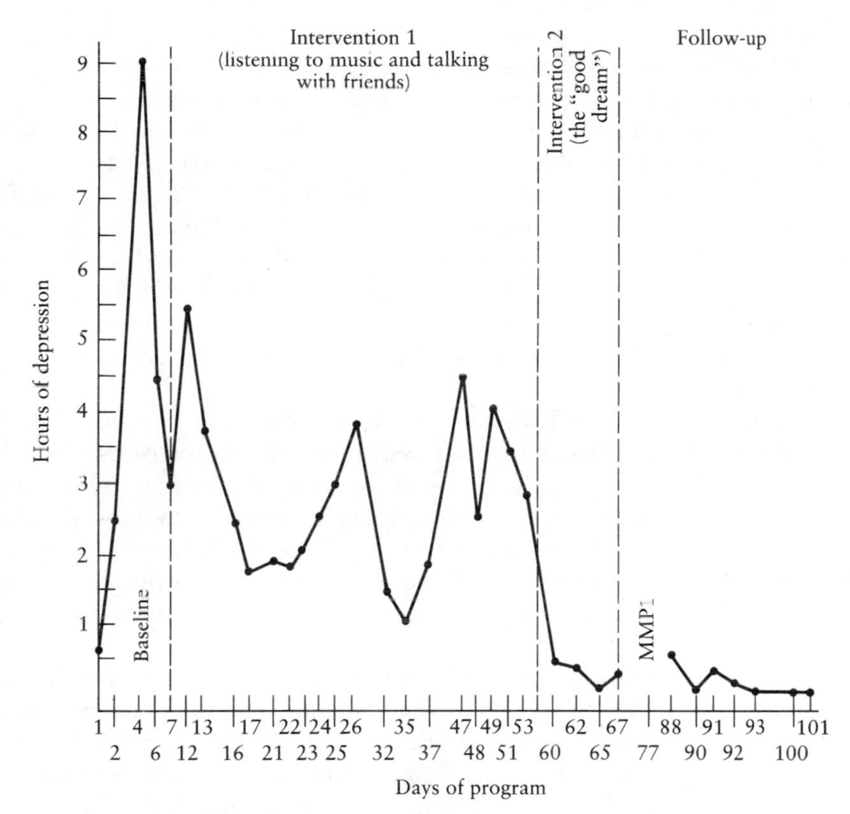

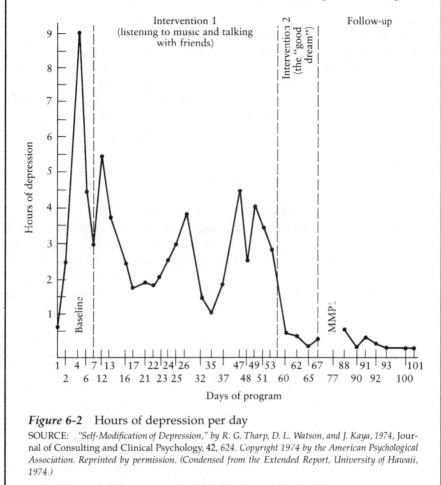

Figure 6-2 Hours of depression per day

SOURCE: *"Self-Modification of Depression," by R. G. Tharp, D. L. Watson, and J. Kaya, 1974,* Journal of Consulting and Clinical Psychology, 42, *624. Copyright 1974 by the American Psychological Association. Reprinted by permission. (Condensed from the Extended Report, University of Hawaii, 1974.)*

Kanfer (1975) has suggested that an extremely withdrawn person go to a drugstore for a cup of coffee and specifically record for 15 minutes the number and types of interactions among people sitting at the counter. A shy, insecure woman might feel less anxious at parties if she made a point of making notes about the occupational background of a certain number of guests. In other words, if you are attending to the task of recording and interviewing, you will be less influenced by the anxiety-provoking aspects of the situation. This also allows the natural reinforcement of social gatherings to take effect.

Concentrating the attention has been used to reduce test anxiety. Focusing on the test itself (not on the fears, the grade, the consequences, other people, or the instructor) can reduce anxiety in an examination (Sarason, 1980).

Sexual arousal, too, can be used to combat anxiety because the two are incompatible. There are limits to the use of this substitute, but, when feasible, it can be helpful. Gary Brown (1978) reported a case in which a client suffered extreme anxiety whenever he had to drive past a cemetery at night. Usually he avoided driving at night, but if he did have to drive past a cemetery, he had "an overwhelming compulsion to stop the car, turn the inside light on, and look at the back seat." The client was instructed to practice driving past a cemetery near his home while imagining scenes of sexual activity with his wife. He began the imagined scenes when he was far enough from the cemetery that anxiety would not interfere and arranged to be maximally aroused just as the tombstones appeared. He did this 30 minutes each day for several days. His anxiety at the cemetery dropped to zero, and after a few days he was able to drive past without sexual arousal *and* without fear.

Vigorous *exercise* is a behavior incompatible with many forms of anxiety (Johnsgard, 1989). Marlatt and Parks (1982) recommend exercise as a substitute behavior for drinking, drug use, or smoking. As tension begins, you could substitute a session of vigorous running, aerobics, or racquetball. This can effectively replace the tension that cues indulgence in drugs. One of our students used jogging to replace the stress he experienced during marital difficulties. He found that the reduced anxiety allowed him to do better thinking and problem solving.

Gershman and Stedman (1971) have reported cases in which Oriental defense exercises were used as behaviors incompatible with anxiety. Their "Mr. P." feared closed places, such as elevators, locked rooms, and trains, and had begun to feel anxiety when wearing tight clothes and even his wedding ring. Their plan had Mr. P. going into a large closet and, as soon as the door closed, engaging in kung fu exercises (at which he was already adept). His anxiety disappeared after no more than 20 seconds. After several such trials, he was able to stay in the closet for up to an hour without doing his exercises or feeling any anxiety. He then began to practice in elevators, and it took him only two sessions to feel comfortable there, too. All his anxieties disappeared, and a six-month follow-up showed no signs of recurrence. These same investigators reported similar results for Mr. R., who used karate exercises to inhibit his anxieties.

Headphones and a favorite CD or tape may also help in a feared situation. Highly valued music has demonstrated effects on reducing the anxiety associated with high-stress situations, such as being near feared animals (Eifert, Craill, Carey, & O'Conner, 1988).

Rational Restructuring

Self-defeating statements and irrational beliefs often define conditions in ways that cause stress. When stress reactions, particularly anxiety or anger, begin, it is likely that these self-statements are playing a role. Actually, replacing them with effective coping statements is a form of substitution that will work like other incompatible responses (Goldfried, 1988).

This kind of reevaluation of a situation has been called *rational restructuring.* Here is an example:

> I'm standing here at a party where I know relatively few people. Everybody seems to be talking in small groups, and I'm not feeling part of things. I'm starting to become tense. On a scale of 0 to 100% tension, I'm about at a level of 40. OK, what is it that I'm thinking that may be creating this anxiety? I think I'm worried that I won't do so well in this situation. What do I mean by that? That I might not know what to say or might not come across well. And *that* would bother me because . . . I would look foolish to these people . . . and that would bother me because . . . they would think badly about me. And why does that upset me? That would upset me because . . . because that would mean that there is something wrong with me. Wait a minute. First of all, what are the chances that they think that of me? I don't know that they would actually think that I was inadequate or anything. At worst, they might think that I was a quiet person. Second of all, even if they did think badly of me, that doesn't necessarily mean that that's the way I am. I just don't show the best side of me in groups. I would still be me. Now that I think this way, I don't feel quite as anxious as I did, perhaps more at an anxiety level of about 20. (Goldfried, 1988, p. 62)

Meditation as a Substitution for Anxiety

Meditation produces physical and mental conditions that are incompatible with anxiety. When a person practices meditation just before contact with a feared situation, it can produce relaxation. Boudreau (1972) reported the case of a college student who "expressed fears of enclosed places, elevators, being alone, and examinations. His avoidance behavior to these situations was extreme, having started when he was 13. The physiological sensations he experienced gave him the additional fear of mental illness" (pp. 97-98). The man was instructed to practice meditation for half an hour every day after imagining some fear-inducing scenes and *also at the actual appearance of fear-evoking situations.* Boudreau states:

> Marked improvement followed. . . . Within one month, the avoidance behavior to enclosed places, being alone, and elevators had all disappeared. Once his tension level had decreased, he did not experience abnormal physiological sensations, and this reassured him as to his physical and mental state. (p. 62)

In general, the continued practice of meditation and its use in many situations is associated with a better capacity to cope with a variety of stresses (Shapiro & Walsh, 1980). Marlatt and Marques (1977) found that meditation led to less alcohol drinking, and Throll (1981) found that it produced improvement on a variety of psychological tests measuring general stress.

Current research indicates that meditation is as effective as any other way of producing relaxation as a response incompatible with anxiety (Delmonte, 1985; Woolfolk, Lehrer, McCann, & Rooney, 1982). In the next section of this chapter, we will present specific training instructions for learning another way to relax, called the **tension-release method,** or **progressive relaxation.** Select the method that is most pleasant for you. The technique is less important than the amount of practice you devote to it. For that reason, it is important to enjoy it (Throll, 1981).

How to meditate. There are several ways to meditate; every world culture has developed one or more techniques. J. C. Smith's *Relaxation Dynamics* (1985) is a useful compendium of nine world approaches to self-relaxation. Here is one method that has proven useful to our students.

Sit in a comfortable chair in a quiet room away from noise and interruptions. Pay no attention to the world outside your body. It is easiest to do this if you have something to focus on in your mind. For example, concentrate on your breathing or use a mantra—a word you say softly over and over to yourself. Here are three different mantras: *mahing, shiam,* and *wen.* Choose one. Don't say the mantra aloud, but think it, silently and gently.

When you first sit down and begin to relax, you will notice thoughts coming into your mind. After a minute or two, begin to say the mantra in your mind. Do this slowly, in a passive way. As you say the mantra to yourself, other thoughts will come. As a matter of fact, after a while you may realize that you've been so busy with these thoughts that you haven't said your mantra in several minutes. When you become aware of this, just return gently to the mantra. Don't fight to keep thoughts out of your mind; instead, let them drift through. This is not a time for working out solutions to problems or thinking things over. Try to keep your mind open so that as thoughts other than the mantra drift in, they drift out again, smoothly as the flowing of a river. The mantra will return, and you will relax with it.

It is important to make this a gentle process, a relaxing time. Don't fight to keep thoughts out of your mind. Don't get upset if you are distracted. Merely let the mantra return.

It is best to meditate in preparation for activity—for example, before you go to work—rather than after you are already tense. If used as soon as you begin to feel tense, it is a good coping reaction. People often nod off to sleep while meditating. If you do go to sleep, usually you will find that five minutes of meditation afterwards will make you wide awake. Some people notice that meditating makes them feel very awake—so much so that if they meditate before bedtime, they can't get to sleep.

Relaxation

Relaxation is a behavior that can be used to cope with a wide variety of problem situations. According to the dictionary, relaxation is "the casting off of nervous tension and anxiety." It is both a mental and a physical response—a feeling of calmness and serenity, and a state of muscular release and passivity.

One of the simplest methods of self-relaxation is called **integrative breathing** (Smith, 1985). It involves a quiet contemplation of your own breathing.

> Think about your breathing. Notice the passage of air through your nose, into your lungs, the swelling of your chest. Forget all else; consider only the air and the quiet. As you breathe out, feel the air flow gently over your lips; imagine it moving a feather softly and gently. You are your breathing, forget all else. Concentrate on the breath moving easily in and out. You have nothing to do but breathe, and feel the air refreshing you.

Relaxation is easily learned, if one is willing to practice it. The method used is not important (Barrios & Shigetomi, 1979, 1980; Lewis, Biglan, & Steinbock, 1978; Miller & Bornstein, 1977)—the relaxation is. If you are already adept at some technique for inducing relaxation, there is no reason for not using your own. For example, preliminary evidence exists that a good program of muscle stretching may have effects similar to the relaxation techniques discussed in this chapter (Carlson, Collins, Nitz, Sturgis, & Rogers, 1990). If you are already adept at stretching exercises, you might try them as a relaxation technique. Any form of relaxation will do as long as you can produce it quickly, thoroughly, and at your own instructions. But don't use alcohol, drugs, tobacco, or any other substance to achieve relaxation. If you do, you won't learn the independent self-direction of relaxation you need to overcome real-life anxieties.

A reliable method for learning to relax is to use deep muscular relaxation. As you read this sentence, try relaxing your hand and arm or your jaw muscles. If you can do so, you will realize how much energy you tie up in excess muscular tension. You can also experience subtle mental changes as your muscles "cast off their tensions" (I. Evans, personal communication, 1976).

Once you have learned relaxation, you will use it to replace anxiety responses in situations in which you are now uncomfortable or that you now avoid. The basic idea is to learn to produce relaxation *at the first sign of tension.* That is the reason for the *tension-release method,* which calls for *tensing* muscles and then *releasing* them. You will learn to recognize the signs of tension so that when you feel them later in real-life situations, you can quickly produce the release that is relaxation. In this way, you can use the first signs of tension (for example, before taking tests or talking to strangers) as the cue to relax and interrupt the tension process early in its sequence. This method of recognizing tension and producing relaxation is a very effective strategy for coping with any form of anxiety (Goldfried, 1971, 1977; Goldfried & Trier, 1974; Snyder & Deffenbacher, 1977).

A renewed debate is under way about whether the tension phase is really necessary or desirable. There is some evidence that *not* tensing before relaxing produces a deeper muscle relaxation (Lucic, Steffen, Harrigan, & Stuebing, 1991). This has been the position for many years of the originator of the relaxation procedure, Edmond Jacobson (for example, 1938). On the other hand, most influential psychologists (for example, Bernstein & Borkovec, 1973) continue to advocate tension *and* release. In our view, Jacobson is correct: The contractions are not a necessary part of the mature skill of relaxation and need not be repeated in actual use of relaxation in real-life situations. But the tension-release sequence is an excellent training and practice technique that helps us learn to recognize tension. For that reason, we include the tension-release as the way to learn the skill. As it is mastered, the muscle tensing can be eliminated.

The mastery and use of relaxation will be discussed in three steps: (1) how to use the instructions, (2) where to practice, and (3) using relaxation as an incompatible response.

How to Use the Relaxation Instructions: Step 1

The tension-release instructions (Box 6-2) are like a set of exercises, one for each group of muscles. The final goal is to relax all groups simultaneously to achieve total body relaxation. Each muscle group can be relaxed sepa-

BOX 6-2
Relaxation Instructions

Muscle Groups	*Tension Exercises*
1. The dominant hand	Make a tight fist.
2. The other hand	
3. The dominant arm	Curl your arm up; tighten the bicep.
4. The other arm	
5. Upper face and scalp	Raise eyebrows as high as possible.
6. Center face	Squint eyes and wrinkle nose.
7. Lower face	Smile in a false, exaggerated way; clench teeth.
8. Neck	a. Pull head slightly forward, then relax. b. Pull head slightly back, then relax.
9. Chest and shoulders	a. Pull shoulders back until the blades almost touch, then relax. b. Pull shoulders forward all the way, then relax.
10. Abdomen	Make abdomen tight and hard.
11. Buttocks	Tighten together.
12. Upper right leg	Stretch leg out from you, tensing both upper and lower muscles.
13. Upper left leg	
14. Lower right leg	Pull toes up toward you.
15. Lower left leg	
16. Right foot	Curl toes down and away from you.
17. Left foot	

rately. Relaxation cannot be achieved all at once, so you should follow a gradual procedure in learning it. First you learn to relax your arms; then your facial area, neck, shoulders, and upper back; then your chest, stomach, and lower back; then your hips, thighs, and calves; and finally your whole body.

The general idea is to first tense a set of muscles and then relax them, so that they will relax more deeply than before they were tensed. You should focus your attention on each muscle system as you work through the various muscle groups. This will give you a good sense of what each set feels like when it is tense and when it is well relaxed. The exercises may take 20 to 30 minutes at first. As you learn, you will need less and less time.

Choose a private place, quiet and free of interruptions and distracting stimuli. Sit comfortably, well supported by the chair, so that you don't have to use your muscles to support yourself. You may want to close your eyes. Some people prefer to lie down while practicing. You may find it especially pleasant to practice before going to sleep.

The basic procedure for each muscle group is the same: *Tense* the muscle, *release* the muscle, and *feel* the relaxation. You may want to memorize the

First, for each muscle group:

Tense the muscles and hold for five seconds.
Feel the tension. Notice it carefully.
Now release. Let the tension slide away, all away.
Feel the difference.
Notice the pleasant warmth of relaxation.
Now repeat the sequence with the same group.
Repeat again. Do the sequence three times for each group of muscles.
Tense. Release. Learn the difference. Feel the warmth of relaxation.

Then for the whole body:

Now tense all the muscles together and hold for five seconds.
Feel the tension, notice it carefully, then release. Let all tension slide away.
Notice any remaining tension. Release it.
Take a deep breath. Say "relax" softly to yourself as you breathe out slowly.
Remain totally relaxed.
Repeat breathing in and out slowly, saying "relax," staying perfectly relaxed.
Do this three times.
The exercise has ended. Enjoy the relaxation.

In your daily life, in many situations:

Notice your body's tension.
Identify the tense muscle groups.
Say "relax" softly to yourself.
Relax the tense group.
Feel the relaxation and enjoy it.

SOURCE: Adapted from *Insight vs. Desensitization in Psychotherapy*, by G. L. Paul. Copyright 1966 by Stanford University Press. Reprinted by permission.

specific muscle groups and the exercises for each. For example, the hands are exercised by making a first; the forehead, by raising the eyebrows. You will want to know the instructions by heart so you can relax quickly, at any time or place, according to your own self-instructions. This is the reason for the final exercise—saying "relax" slowly and softly as you breathe out while totally relaxed. You can then transfer this self-instruction into your natural environment and produce relaxation instead of anxiety (Cautela, 1966).

Where to Practice Relaxation: Step 2

As soon as you have practiced enough that you can tense and relax some muscle groups, it's time to begin doing the exercises in other situations. You can practice tension release of some muscle groups while driving, riding the bus, attending lectures or concerts, sunbathing at the beach, sitting at your desk, or washing dishes. Relax whatever muscles are not needed for the activity you are engaged in at the moment. Choose a wide variety of situations. It is best not to begin with a situation that represents a particular problem for you.

It's not necessary to use all muscle groups during this practice. Exercise those groups that you've learned to control in your private sessions. If you detect tension in one group—your face or your throat, for example—practice relaxing those muscles.

This phase of practice has three purposes. First, you learn to detect specific tensions. You will discover that you are prone to tension in particular muscle groups. For some people, it's the shoulders and neck that tense up most often; for others, the arms or the face. Relaxing these specific groups will decrease your overall tension.

Second, you learn to regulate the *depth* of relaxation. Although it is crucial to learn total, deep muscle relaxation—even to the point of physical limpness—it is not necessary or desirable to use this full response to combat all tensions. Relaxation is a physical skill, just as weight lifting is. The strong man does not use his full strength to carry eggs, although he has it available for moving pianos. As we will discuss shortly, you can use *deep* relaxation as a response incompatible with anxiety in specific situations that you find difficult. But *graduated* relaxation of muscle groups is a highly valuable skill, and you can begin to learn it by practicing both shallow and deep relaxation. You will be fully skilled when you can totally relax without using the tension technique. Tensing the muscles before relaxing them is only a training method, and it should be dropped as soon as you can relax without it. Then, just saying "relax" to yourself or simply deciding to relax will produce the relaxation at the depth you want.

Practicing relaxation in many situations will prepare you to use it as a general skill for self-direction.

As the next step, it is particularly important to *practice while you are experiencing some tension.* Use tension as a cue for your practice sessions. When you feel the signs of anxiety—whether as mental discomfort or as muscular tension—immediately substitute a relaxation practice session.

If anxiety-producing occasions do not occur during the time you are practicing, you can imagine scenes that have caused tension in the past. While imagining them, go through your complete relaxation practice (Suinn, 1977).

If it is simply not possible to discover the specific moments of heightened anxiety, you can use one of two strategies: (1) practice relaxation before and during a situation that you judge ought to be difficult. (2) If you cannot detect increased tensions from moment to moment, practice relaxation at several predetermined times of day no matter what the situation.

The third purpose of practicing relaxation in other settings is to learn to relax in as many situations as possible. Even if you set out to combat a specific anxiety in a specific situation, the odds are high that you will find additional situations in which relaxation is useful (Goldfried, 1971; Goldfried & Goldfried, 1977; Zemore, 1975). Sherman and Plummer (1973) trained 21 students in relaxation as a general self-direction skill. All but one reported at least one way in which they had benefited from the training; the average was 2.1 ways per person. The most common situations in which the students used relaxation were social situations, sleep problems, test anxiety, handling of interviews, and efforts to increase energy and alertness. Sherman (1975) reported that two years after training, the students still used the strategy. Deffenbacher and Michaels (1981) found that students who learned to use relaxation as a coping skill for test anxiety stayed less anxious in tests even after 15 months. Further, they demonstrated a reduction in their overall experience of anxiety. A review of 18 controlled-outcome studies shows that applied relaxation succeeds, that improvements are maintained, and that further improvements are often obtained (Ost, 1987).

Relaxation, then, should be considered a general coping skill. It can be used both as a counter to specific stressors and as a general strategy to prevent maladaptive reactions to stress. A dramatic example of relaxation as a general strategy is demonstrated in a recent study of the symptoms of genital herpes. As many as 20 million Americans suffer from this incurable, sexually transmitted disease, the painful symptoms of which recur unpredictably, but apparently in response to general life stress. Progressive relaxation, practiced regularly at home, sharply decreased the recurrence of these symptoms for 60% of treated patients (Burnette, Koehn, Kenyon-Jump, Hutton, & Stark, 1991).

Using Relaxation as an Incompatible Response: Step 3

Susan, an 18-year-old freshman, was extremely nervous while taking tests. She studied long and effectively but made only D's and F's on examinations, even though she could answer the questions after the exam was over. She came from a small rural high school, where the teachers overlooked her poor exam performances because she was one of their brightest students and excelled in projects and reports. In the large university, she lost this personal understanding and support.

Susan's counselor first gave her some brief paper-and-pencil tests to measure her anxiety and also three subtests of a well-known IQ measure. She then attended four training sessions, one per week, to learn how to relax. The method Susan followed was the same one you are learning in this book. She first practiced at home and then extended her practice into real-life situations in which she was reasonably comfortable. After her fifth session, she had to take a number of course examinations. Using her cue word "calm" (like our "relax"), she relaxed during the examinations and performed remarkably well. Before her relaxation training, her average test score was 1.0 (on a 4-point system). After Susan underwent the training, her scores averaged 3.5. She completed the term with a 2.88 grade point average.

Susan then repeated the anxiety and IQ tests she had taken before her relaxation training. When compared with her first scores, the test results indicated that her test anxiety was reduced and that her general level of tension was also lower. She even improved on two of the IQ measures. Obviously, relaxation cannot improve "intelligence," but replacing anxiety with relaxation allowed Susan to perform closer to her real potential (Russell & Sipich, 1974).

Susan's case is a good example of the use of relaxation as a response incompatible with test anxiety. Susan followed exactly the same procedures we have suggested for you, except that she had some assistance from her counselors in the initial stages of her relaxation training. But basically her counselors gave her the advice we are giving you. Susan's success is by no means unique. Research has indicated that "cue-controlled relaxation" is particularly helpful to test-anxious students (Denney, 1980; McGlynn, Kinjo, & Doherty, 1978; Russell & Lent, 1982; Russell, Miller, & June, 1975; Russell, Wise, & Stratoudakis, 1976). It has also been used to correct many other specific anxieties, such as fears of the dental chair (Beck, Kaul, & Russell, 1978).

The usefulness of relaxation as a substituted response is not limited to anxieties. Other problems that have been alleviated by relaxation include insomnia (Turner, 1986), tension headache (Blanchard, Crailler, Carey, & O'Connor, 1991), and pain (Levendusky & Pankratz, 1975). Ernst (1973) reports a case in which relaxation was used to stop "self-mutilation" by a woman who repeatedly bit the insides of her lips and mouth, causing tissue damage and pain. She learned deep muscle relaxation during a baseline period in which she recorded with a golf counter the frequency of her self-biting. Then she began to relax, using the golf-counter click as the cue. She paid particular attention to relaxing the muscles of the jaw and lower face. As Figure 6-3 indicates, she almost totally stopped her self-mutilating behavior. That happy outcome continued through months of follow-up.

One of our students reported:

> I want to reduce spacing out in class; that is, I want to increase the number of times my attention is on what the lecturer is saying. My mind wanders to all sorts of things, such as feelings I've been having about people or escape fantasies—you know, like backpacking or get-

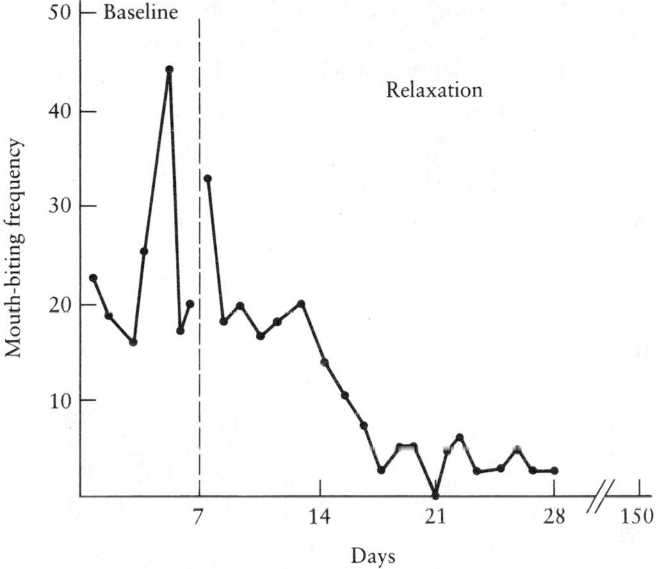

Figure 6-3 Daily self-recorded mouth-biting frequencies
SOURCE: *"Self-Recording and Counterconditioning of a Self-Mutilative Compulsion," by F. A. Ernst, 1973,* Behavior Therapy, 4 *144–146. Copyright 1973 by Academic Press, Inc. Reprinted by permission.*

> ting 20 acres of land and living on it with my friends. Another way I have of not being there is one I learned in grammar school, where I felt the teachers were powering me around. I'd find something ridiculous in what they said and laugh to myself about it or tell the person next to me. My plan is to use deep muscle relaxation to feel easy, instead of using my old tricks. That way my mind will wander less. I'll come into the lecture hall five minutes early, relax, and then try to listen to what's going on.

This student's plan was very successful; he reduced the frequency of mind wandering by 50%.

You may notice that both the spaced-out student and the mouth-biting woman used two forms of behavior incompatible with their problem behavior—self-recording and relaxation—which may account for their success.

As a rule, you should use relaxation just before the time you expect your anxiety to begin—just before the plane takes off, while you are waiting to walk to the front of the room to give your talk, during the earliest stages of sexual foreplay, immediately before you go in for an interview or an exam, or while you sit in the dentist's waiting room.

You may be thinking, "But I can't always predict exactly when tension will begin." Right! This is why you must learn the tension phase of the relaxation program. You will then be able to recognize the beginning stages of tension and use that information as the cue to relax. Typical cues that tension and anxiety are beginning include neck and shoulder tightening, upset stomach, clenched fists or jaws, and teeth grinding (Deffenbacher & Suinn, 1982).

Combining Relaxation with New Self-Instructions

New self-instructions should be combined with relaxation. In an experiment, students using relaxation during examinations were compared with students who combined relaxation with a series of encouraging self-instructions. The combined group performed better on geology multiple-choice and fill-in-the-blank tests (Collins, Dansereau, Garland, Holley, & McDonald, 1981).

An education major used this combined approach when she began her student teaching. The slightest sign that she was losing control over her pupils caused her to tense, and she responded by scolding. She wanted to be gentler and more positive with the children. Her plan called for giving the self-cue "relax" at the first sign of muscular tension. She also added self-coaching during the relaxation, saying to herself, "You can stay in control," and "Be gentle." The most effective procedure involves combining relaxation with correction of self-defeating thoughts (Deffenbacher & Hahnloser, 1981).

Problems in Relaxation

The most frequent problem encountered in developing a relaxation program is simply not doing it. This is particularly true in the early stages of developing the skills and habits of relaxation—whether the chosen method is meditation, breath concentration, stretching, or progressive relaxation of tension-release. In general, we recommend practicing about 30 minutes a day for the first two weeks, then including relaxation at frequent times during the regular course of life, both at home and in the larger world. If you are not giving that 30 minutes, examine these possibilities. Are you telling yourself something? Do the following excuses sound familiar?

I don't have a place to relax. You do need quiet and privacy. Plan ahead. Negotiate for the time and space. Make relaxation practice a priority because of its wide-ranging benefits.

The whole thing is too boring. Relaxation is, in fact, not boring in the least. But your own level of agitation or anxiety may be so great that you can't get to the relaxation pleasure. Try listening to some quiet music you value in order to induce a slower pace of thoughts and a pleasant mood. Listen at low volume as you begin to relax. Use the mood-enhancing effects of music as a bridge to the pleasures of relaxation itself (Eifert Crailler, Carey, & O'Connor, 1988).

There is not enough time in the day. There is never enough time for everything; it is an issue of priorities. Remind yourself of the benefits relaxation can bring to your health, your social life, your success in school and work. Reassert your goals. Try *rational restructuring* to talk yourself through the self-defeating prioritizing of less important activity.

And remember the power of self-observation. Set up a record sheet that will not only prompt you to do the exercises but will establish a record of your improvement.*

Date & Hour of Practice	Duration of Practice	Body Areas Easily Relaxed	Body Areas with Tension	Tension Level 0–100 Before	After

*0–100 scale:
0 = No tension
100 = Maximum tension

Developing New Behaviors

The fundamental way of mastering a new behavior is simply to rehearse it over and over in the situations in which you want it to occur. All the other methods this book teaches are merely ways of making that rehearsal more likely to take place. Practice does make perfect. Actually performing the desired behaviors—that is, rehearsing them—is the final technique for attaining your goal.

Often, however, it is difficult to arrange actual rehearsals. You can't always rehearse relaxation in the presence of some feared object, such as snakes, because (fortunately!) snakes are not always around. You may not be able to rehearse enough for relaxing in examinations because no exams may be scheduled for several weeks. And many avoidance behaviors are so strong that approaching them for rehearsal is more than your current anxiety level will allow. Imagined rehearsal may solve these problems.

Imagined Rehearsal

Rehearsing behavior in one's imagination is called **imagined** (also called **mental** or **covert**) **rehearsal.** There is convincing evidence that imagined rehearsal can improve physical skills for competitors in almost every sport (Suinn, 1983). The same principles apply to high achievement in the workplace, for salespeople, and in all fields of endeavor (Seligman, 1990).

Research evidence points to the fact that in reaching your goals, actual events and behaviors are much more effective than imagined ones. Therefore, actual practice and performance are the final strategies. However, be-

*SOURCE: Adapted from *Anxiety Management Training: A Behavior Therapy* (p. 331) by R. M. Suinn (1990), New York: Plenum Press.

cause imagined events and behaviors can influence actual behavior, using imagined events has many advantages. Imagined events and behaviors can be practiced quickly and easily. Most important, they can be controlled: Imagined snakes are less likely to move suddenly toward you than real ones.

Imagined rehearsal can be used to provide *preliminary* rehearsals, to provide *extra* rehearsals, and to provide rehearsals that *emphasize* certain features of a behavior or situation. Thus, imagined rehearsal can often speed up your journey toward your goal. It is a form of visual self-instruction. For example, in 1976 the U.S. Olympic ski team, before making difficult downhill runs, would rehearse the entire run in their imaginations, thinking of each bump and turn and how they would cope with it. They turned in better runs than they had before, and the United States won some surprising medals (Suinn, 1976). These techniques were then used to train athletes for the Summer and Winter Games of 1980 and 1984 (Suinn, 1985). Imagined rehearsal has been used to correct "loss of confidence"; for example, that of a wide receiver who, having missed an easy pass once, developed a fear of dropping the football. Imagined rehearsal of successfully eluding the defensive back, gathering in the ball, and scoring a touchdown restored his confidence in actual games (Cautela & Samdperil, 1989).

To use imaginary practice, try to imagine the situation and your behavior in complete, minute detail. For example, if you imagine an introduction to a stranger, you should visualize how the imaginary person looks, the expression on his or her face, what the person says, how you react, and all the other details of the physical situation. You may have to imagine the situation in its component parts in order to concentrate separately on imagined sounds, textures, and other elements.

It is important that you attain a vivid picture (Paul, 1966; Wisocki, 1973). It doesn't have to be as clear as if you were watching a movie, but it should be as clear as a very vivid memory. Sometimes your imaginary scenes become more vivid with practice. A good way to check the vividness of an imagined behavior-in-a-situation is to compare it with that of some scene you recreate in your imagination, a scene you know and can visualize very well—for example, what it looks, feels, smells, and sounds like to be lying on your bed in your room. First, visualize the scene of your room. Then compare the visualized behavior-in-a-situation with the scene of your room. The two should be nearly equally vivid. You should also be able to start and stop an image at will.

Imagined rehearsal is particularly appropriate when you are preparing to cope with high-risk situations. Earlier, we mentioned that the dangers of relapse into substance abuse are highest when other people around you are drinking, smoking, or taking drugs. At the first stage of self-modification, these situations should be avoided. But eventually, you will encounter a high-risk situation, and you will want to have coping skills ready. Imagining these high-risk situations—for example, a restaurant, bar, party, or banquet—and rehearsing in your imagination your coping responses to them can be useful in building skills to prevent relapse (Marlatt & Parks, 1982).

In imagined rehearsal, use the coping skills you intend to use in real life, whatever these skills might be. Religious individuals, for example, have profited more from imagined rehearsal of coping skills when they used religious imagery that was important to them. Nonreligious imagery of coping, such as saying, "I see myself coping with that difficult situation," was less effective for religious Christians than imagining, "I can see Christ going with me into that difficult situation" (Propst, 1980).

Actively imagining yourself in a coping situation is probably the key element in this kind of rehearsal. One technique for getting a good image of yourself coping is to remember a time when you coped well and then to transfer it to the imagined problem situation. Test-anxious students who used this tactic actually raised their grade point averages. The students remembered a previous situation in which their coping skills were high (running a radio broadcast, tending a busy bar, playing in a recital). They then transposed that competent self-image into an imagined test situation (Harris & Johnson, 1980).

Do not drift into imagining failure or focus on factors that could impair performance. This will diminish subsequent actual performance and confidence, whereas positive rehearsal and focusing will improve both (Cerone, 1989; Seligman, 1990).

Imagined Rehearsal and Relaxation

One of the best uses of imagined rehearsal is in the practice of relaxation. In this technique, a form of **desensitization,** you imagine yourself remaining calm and relaxed in different situations, and you carry out the imagined rehearsal while actually being in a state of deep muscle relaxation.

You may find it necessary to approach feared situations gradually, maintaining your state of calm relaxation. It is important that you succeed in the early trials at relaxation because success breeds success.

Suppose that you become tense when you take tests. You know, of course, that there are different kinds of tests, some worse than others, ranging from unimportant, simple quizzes to make-you-or-break-you final exams, and some make you more anxious than others. You might write down situations in hierarchical order from easiest to most difficult, as in the following example:

Taking a test that doesn't count for very much
Taking a test when I am not prepared
Taking a surprise test
Taking a test when the professor watches me all the time
Taking a midterm exam
Taking a final exam that determines my grade in the course

It would be most unusual if these situations happened to come along in exactly that order. In imagination, though, you can rehearse them in any order and as many times as you wish.

Liza, one of our students, used the preceding list with imagined rehearsal plus relaxation. Because her courses had only midterms and finals, she wanted to prepare in advance for those situations and to proceed gradually. After learning deep muscle relaxation, she lay on her couch with a pillow, just as she had done when practicing relaxation. While deeply relaxed, Liza imagined the first item in the list—taking a minor test—while being just as relaxed as she was at that moment. She held that scene for a minute or two, imagining all sorts of details—feeling the hardness of the desk at which she sat, putting the end of the pencil in her mouth while thinking of an answer, going back over each answer—and all the while remaining perfectly calm. Then she cleared her mind, checked herself for any signs of tension, relaxed again, and went on to the next item on her list. She tried to do one of these sessions each day.

Liza spent about 10 to 15 minutes on the exercise, although the length of time varied with her mood and ability to relax deeply. In general, she went down her list in order—from least to most difficult. But she sometimes changed the sequence, occasionally trying to begin with a difficult situation. If she couldn't visualize it and stay calm, she relaxed again and moved back to an easier level.

About five weeks into the semester, Liza had to take a quiz, entirely unannounced, in her geology class. She was so surprised that she nearly panicked. However, she was able to induce relaxation by going through a rather hasty tension-release exercise. Liza relaxed enough to do well on the quiz, although she barely finished in time.

This incident illustrates the only error Liza made in her plan. During the same weeks in which she was using imagined rehearsal, she should also have been practicing the relaxation response in many outside situations. Then she would have been better prepared to relax in the geology lecture hall.

The pop quiz motivated Liza to continue the imagined rehearsals. By the time midterm exams arrived, she had been able to imagine being relaxed throughout her entire hierarchy and had used relaxation several times in her actual lecture halls. Both steps were probably important. Imagined rehearsal with relaxation gave her some practice in situations before they came up. Actual rehearsal of relaxation in various physical surroundings gave her practice in the situations in which she would later face the tension-producing tests.

Simply exposing yourself to a tension-producing situation will slightly reduce your tension in it (Goldfried & Goldfried, 1977; Greist, Marks, Berlin, Gournay, & Noshirvani, 1980). But you will achieve better results if you can practice your relaxation while in the situation. Thus, imagining yourself in tension-producing situations while being relaxed is a good way to get ready to cope with the reality.

There is only one caution for the use of imagined rehearsal. If you are imagining an incompetent performance, it will cause you to perform in an incompetent way. Imagined rehearsal will not help unless you are imagining an effective performance. If you are uncertain about exactly how to perform an activity—whether it is social skills or a tennis backhand—there is one excellent way to identify the right skills: find a model.

Modeling

Learning through observation of models is one of the basic processes by which learning occurs—for adults as well as for infants.

Finding and imitating good models is an extremely important part of self-regulation because models help us identify effective behaviors. No amount of rehearsal will benefit your learning if you are rehearsing the wrong behaviors. Remember the benefits that Olympic-quality athletes experienced from imagined rehearsal of their skills. These results were achieved because the athletes knew exactly what to do; their imagined rehearsals were of a correct performance. But novice athletes' performance may be made worse by imagined rehearsals because they do not know what to rehearse. One study found that imagined rehearsals of tennis serves improved accuracy for experienced tennis players but made novices less accurate (Noel, 1980; see also Suinn, 1983). Imagined rehearsal is useless or even harmful when the goals are poorly defined. Merely imagining being "a better public speaker" or "trying harder" or "being more assertive" will not lead to improvement. Imagined rehearsals must be precise and correct (Suinn, 1983).

Where can you discover these specific, correct behaviors? You can discover them by observing models—those who already are expert. Whether your goal is better tennis, better social skills, or any other behavior, a fundamental strategy is to identify a model, analyze the model's skills, and use those skills as your standard.

If you find someone who has the very skills you want, don't hesitate to try straight imitation. None of us minds using imitation when we are learning tennis or driving, but you may be embarrassed to think of imitating others' social or personal behaviors. As we counseled the student who watched how his friend dealt with women:

> If you decide to smile when you meet someone, as he does, you will be smiling your own smile, not his. You will be answering with your own comments, not his. You will do everything in your own style. You'll be yourself, but yourself smiling and answering.

One of our students set out to improve his public speaking skills. He wrote:

> I made use of models, observing both their good and bad habits to use or not while speaking in class. I noticed the effects of eye contact and gestures in communicating, and the importance of a loud and clear voice. However, I feel that the most important effect of observing good, relaxed models was the feeling that if they could do it, so could I. Therefore, these vicarious influences boosted my self-efficacy expectations.

If observation doesn't reveal the crucial part of a model's performance, ask your chosen model to explain something. A talented young swimmer asked her heroine, a conference champion, how she managed such sustained and disciplined practice. The answer was clear and provided an excellent model. "*Preschedule* your practice times and your goals for the day," she said. "Never make your decisions on the way to the pool! If we did that, no one would ever practice hard."

Our student Dunston was a pleasant person, but his stooped posture lowered his self-esteem. Dunston's plan for self-improvement was to improve his 6'4" posture to a straight, tall, confident bearing. His plan included the memory of a model, a friend from high school who Dunston remembered as having a self-confident bearing. But he thought the main feature of his plan should be exercise and back-strengthening exercises, using precommitted punishment and self-reward. While he made some progress, his plan stalled. Here is his report:

> In an unexpected telephone call from Illinois, I spent about half an hour talking to the model I chose for my project—Mark L. I asked him to go back to our high school years, and describe how exactly weight lifting helped him to achieve good posture. To my surprise, he told me his strength had little to do with his posture. His main drive [to improve his posture] was a result of trying to model after a girl he saw around the tenth grade! She had the greatest influence on his posture, and in his opinion, his back strength played a minor role. . . . Mark became even more important of a model to me after I learned that his posture was a result of modeling, and I began to rely on that more than on my faith in the exercises—they were just a myth, but the model was real. They are an essential part of good posture, but I also see that the strength attained by exercise needs to be put into practice, or it won't be used at all.

We see him often across campus, his head well above the crowd.

Imagined Modeling

In using imagined rehearsal, some people have difficulty imagining themselves doing acts they cannot perform in real life. For instance, imagining that you are sending back your overcooked steak may seem so unrealistic that you lose the scene or end up imagining yourself eating the steak anyway. If this happens, you might use the technique of imagined modeling.

This process is similar to imagined rehearsal, except that you imagine someone else, instead of yourself, performing the behavior, being reinforced for it, and so forth. This technique has been found effective in a variety of applications (Cautela & Kearney, 1986; Kazdin, 1984). Athletes who have problems with losing their tempers have used imagined rehearsal to visualize staying cool and in command of their skills when being goaded and baited (Cautela & Samdperil, 1989). Students using this technique actually demonstrated improved grades as well as reduced anxiety during tests (Harris & Johnson, 1980).

When you use others as imagined models, you don't have to use real persons who are known to you, although you may do so. Here are some recommended procedures for imagined modeling, based on Alan Kazdin's (1984) summary:

1. Imagine a model who is similar to you in age and of the same gender.
2. Imagine different models in each situation rather than one person only.
3. Imagine a model who begins with the same difficulties you have—one who must cope with the problem rather than one who has already mastered the problem. For example, your model should also be afraid of pigeons, although able to approach them; your model is also tempted by fattening food; your model also has to muster up some courage to send the steak back.
4. Imagine your model being reinforced for successful coping, preferably with desired natural outcomes.
5. Imagine your model self-instructing during the performance. Make those self-instructions the ones you will use in your eventual real-life performance.

Imagined modeling can be used as a first step in preparing yourself for imagined rehearsal. But increase the degree of *your* imagined performance, not that of someone else. If you imagine only others as models, the technique is not likely to be effective. There is no need to use imagined modeling if you can effectively use rehearsal, either actual or imagined. If you can successfully imagine yourself rehearsing behaviors, it is probably better to use yourself as your own model. And most effective of all is to move from imagined modeling into actual practice. For individuals learning to be more assertive, for example, those who combined imagined modeling with actual practice showed the greatest improvement in social situations requiring assertive behavior (Kazdin, 1982). As you progress in imagination, begin to practice, at the lower end of the scale of difficulty, in the real world.

Mastery in the Real World

We cannot emphasize too much that, no matter how valuable all the imagined techniques are, they are only bridges to performance in the real world. Imagined rehearsal and all its supporting tactics can help you prepare for real-life situations. *But you must rehearse your developing behaviors in the actual situations in which you want them to occur.* Therefore, no plan is complete without tactics for transferring your behavior from imagined rehearsal into real life.

For example, Gershman and Stedman (1971) had one of their clients use karate exercises as the incompatible behavior for anxiety about his flying lessons. The client constructed a hierarchy of items such as "gaining altitude," "saying to myself, 'How high *am* I?'" "passing over treetops too low," and so on. He went through the various items while vigorously engaged in his karate exercises until he was able to consider the items without anxiety. Then he began to transfer the plan into real life. He rehearsed before going to the flying field and again in the men's room before reporting to his instructor. He developed confidence and eventually became able to fly without anxiety.

In a long series of studies, Jerry Deffenbacher has demonstrated considerable benefit from programs that include relaxation in real anxiety-producing situations. Specific target anxieties reduced have included test anxiety, fear of flying, fear of public speaking, and fear of cats. In addition, a general reduction in anxiety occurs, so the person is less tense and uncomfortable in ordinary daily activities. There are other side benefits as well: People who use relaxation in real problem situations also become less depressed, less hostile, and more assertive. Relaxation, when well practiced in real situations, becomes a general coping skill (Deffenbacher & Suinn, 1982).

Whether you have used imagined relaxation rehearsal for dieting, being assertive, test anxiety, fear of birds, or fear of being outdoors, the next step is planning to transfer these behaviors into real life. Often we do need to begin in our imagination, but the real-life situation is a far more effective learning arena than its imagined substitute (Flannery, 1972; Goldstein & Kanfer, 1979; Sherman, 1972). *When one learns new responses, even from models, it is the rehearsal in the actual situation that brings about long-lasting change* (Bandura, Jeffery, & Gajdos, 1975; Blanchard, 1970; Thase & Moss, 1976). When you can bring yourself to exposure to the feared situation and stay there, you will have taken the last necessary, effective step (Emmelkamp, 1990).

Shaping: The Method of Successive Approximations

Whatever your goal behavior may be, you should anticipate that you will not be able to master it at the first effort. Even if you have a perfect model, the expert behavior may have to be acquired a piece at a time. Even though you have become competent in relaxation, you may have to approach the feared situation by taking small steps toward it. A general procedure for behavioral improvement is this: Start from the point in your current store of behaviors that most closely approximates your eventual goal. Practice this approximation, and it will become the basis from which the next (improved) step can be taken. Move toward full mastery in a process of steady, successive approximations. This method is known as **shaping.**

Shaping involves the gradual raising of standards. This method avoids the greatest hazard to learning—failure and discouragement in the early stages. Early failure and discouragement very frequently are due to the setting of unrealistically high standards for improvement. This is typical of dieters who violate their standards by going on eating "binges." Excessively strict standards for dieting, in the absence of success experiences, is the condition most likely to produce binge eating. Those dieters who set careful shaping steps for reducing calories—steps gradual enough that they can experience success in each step—are more likely to develop self-control (Gormally, Black, Daston, & Rardin, 1982; Hawkins & Clement, 1980).

A steady experience of success reinforces and strengthens gradually improving performance. The belief in your own competence—self-efficacy—is one of the strongest predictors of eventual success (Bandura, 1986). Given two people of equal skill, the one who believes he or she can succeed is more likely to do so. The use of intelligent shaping steps will bring success experiences, thereby increasing belief in self-efficacy, and thus leading to greater success.

How Shaping Works in Self-Modification

Your baseline indicates your *current* level of performance. And at that level—or just beyond it—is where the shaping process should begin.

There are two simple rules for shaping: (1) *you can never begin too low,* and (2) *the steps upward can never be too small.* When in doubt, begin at a lower level or reduce the size of the steps. This makes it simple to perform the desired behavior because you feel that your movement upward is easy. And this is very important, for it increases your chances of success.

One of the most common reasons for failure in self-directed projects is the lack of shaping. Some students resist using shaping because they believe they "should" perform at certain levels and don't "deserve" to be reinforced for performance that falls below that level. This is a maladaptive belief because it makes learning impossible. Shaping increases your ability to do what you believe you should do. If you find shaping at a very low level embarrassing, keep it a secret, but do reinforce yourself heavily for starting.

Here is the shaping schedule of a student who wanted to attain the goal of studying many hours per week.:

Baseline: I am now actually studying an average of 40 minutes per day.
Level 1: I will begin my reinforcement for studying 45 minutes per day, five days a week. This should be easy to do, since I have done it several times in the past.
Level 2: I will require myself to study 60 minutes per day to get the reinforcer.
Level 3: One hour, 15 minutes.
Level 4: One hour, 30 minutes.
Level 5: Two hours.

Notice how carefully the student followed the two rules for shaping: start low, and keep the steps small. This allowed her to move, slowly but inevitably, toward her goal.

Notice also that the first steps were smaller than later steps. This is generally a good idea because very small initial steps will ensure that some progress is made, whereas later it may be possible to progress more quickly.

When you are following a shaping schedule, you must remain flexible. *Be ready to change your schedule.* You may have to do so, for example, if some of the projected steps turn out to be too large. What you plan on paper may not work in practice, and you may have to reduce the size of the steps. You may have to stay at the same level for a longer time, or you may have to return to an earlier level if some setback occurs. This is highly intelligent problem-solving: Be guided by your own actual experience, and move backwards when you have gone forward too rapidly (Barlow, 1988).

The basic rule for these and all other problems in shaping is: *Don't move up a step until you have mastered the previous one.* Notice that the student's plan outlined earlier in this section is not tied to specific dates for changing levels.

These rules for shaping won't work if you don't follow them. The primary reason students do not use shaping is that they don't think they de-

BOX 6-3

Shaping Away School Phobia

by Harriet Kathryn Brown

The most complex "project report" turned in by any student in the many classes in self-modification that I've instructed was this. This shaping program was almost entirely self-invented. The student wrote:

> I was 28 years old, separated from my husband, and wanted to return to the university. But I experienced anxiety attacks when just physically present on the campus—rapid heartbeat, cold sweat, shaking, acid stomach, skin rash, and a mindless urge to flee. A long way to go! I started a plan to shape my way back into school.

Step 1: Drive onto campus through the east gate, around the mall circle, and out the west gate. Do this two or three times a week for three weeks. This meant three to five minutes of anxiety, but it was bearable. I was then ready for the next shaping stage.

Step 2: Park on campus, and walk around for ten minutes. Do this two or three times a week for three weeks. I had to avoid particular buildings where I felt the most uncomfortable, but I made it, and upped the shaping step. I gradually improved, and the next steps lasted one or two weeks each.

Step 3: Walk around 20 to 30 minutes.

Step 4: Walk around, then sit in an empty classroom for ten minutes while reading a book.

Step 5: Sit in the classroom reading for an hour. By then it was January, and I wanted to sign up for a noncredit writing class. I knew that I wrote reasonably well, and there were no grades involved. This was the least threatening class I'd ever find—except that the class was scheduled for a building that I still avoided. There were two weeks till class began.

Step 6: Sign up for the class. For three days in a row, drive on campus, park outside the scary building, and walk around the outside of it.

Step 7: Walk through the building once without stopping—three days in a row.

serve to gain some reward for such a low level of performance. "Now listen, I need to cut out smoking *all* the time, and you're telling me I should start out just cutting it out in one particular, easy situation? I ought not to get reinforced for that. It's too easy." The word *ought* is the operative word; it is what will keep this person from succeeding. A second reason for not using shaping is impatience to get on with total self-change. It makes taking a small step seem too little. So you try for a big step and stumble. Stop telling yourself what you "ought" to do, and start at a level you *can* do. Stop yearning to start at the top, and start where you can really get started. A journey of a thousand miles begins with a single step.

Box 6–3 illustrates the steps of a long and successful journey made by a woman who had far to travel before she could become a student at all.

Step 8: Sit in the actual classroom. Start with ten minutes, increase each day as much as possible until I can do one hour.

Once I was relaxed enough to actually stay in the classroom, the course was really no problem. In fact, I enrolled in another noncredit writing course during the following semester. Now I was ready to attempt my first class for credit. I checked out the room, and felt comfortable enough in it. I was on my way!

The text for that course was [this book]. As a result, my next steps used more techniques. Up to this point, I'd been using food to reward myself for each of these shaping achievements. That was doing my weight no good, so I found a variety of better reinforcers. My favorite is to let myself put on rock music, stand in front of the mirror, and lip-synch while pretending to be a star like Linda Ronstadt. But there are others, too—like picturing myself wandering in a beautiful garden.

I reinforced myself each day for keeping to my study schedule, with a separate reinforcer just for going to class.

Step 9: Go to class each day. Reinforcement daily. Study each day. Reinforcement daily. Use relaxation exercises daily. I enjoyed them; no reward needed. Use relaxation before and during tests. Use positive self-statements before and during tests. Got an "A."

I won't write down all the rest of the steps. I took another credit class the following semester, and after that two at once. I no longer needed to check out the classrooms in advance. Gradually I dropped the reinforcement for attending class; I was falling in love with school, and am now a full-time student. Success on exams was high enough that my test anxiety got killed. I continued to use reinforcement for a regular study schedule; in fact, I still do. My attendance record is now 100%, compared to only 75% in that first noncredit course. I've gone from school-phobic to school-fanatic!

Occasionally I like to look back to my records of those early "walking around" stages. It's all in my journal, which I have kept since I was 12 years old.

Relaxation and the Method of Approximations

Often relaxation plans require successive approximations. For example, several of our students have been unable to maintain relaxation when going abruptly into a major examination. They have used graduated steps in approaching the dreaded situation, such as going into the examination room two or three days before a test and practicing in the empty hall.

Some of our students have used detailed schedules of steps along a shaping continuum. Linda, a college senior, wrote:

> I am really very afraid of birds, under almost any conditions. This sometimes makes me look like a fool—for example, I won't go to the zoo because there are so many birds around, loose as well as in cages—and often causes me unnecessary fear and trepidation. My life would be more pleasant with fewer fears!

Here is Linda's hierarchy:

A. When *one or two birds* are 15 yards away:
   1. Turn and face the birds.
   2. Take one step toward the birds.
   3. Take two steps toward the birds.
   4. Continue until I have walked a total of 5 yards toward the birds.
   5. Begin step B.

B. When *more than two birds* are 15 yards away:
   1. Turn and face the birds.
   2. Take two steps toward them.
   3. Take four steps toward them.
   4. Continue until I have walked a total of 5 yards toward the birds.

She then repeated the procedures, beginning at a 10-yard distance, first from a single bird and then from a group of birds. Next, she repeated the procedure beginning at 5 yards. In the last stages, she would begin at 3 yards from the birds and move to within 3 feet of them, then gradually increase the amount of time, in seconds, that she spent close to them.

At first Linda had difficulty, but she reported that by getting her boyfriend to hold her hand, her anxiety was considerably lessened. This worked well until, perhaps out of boredom, the boyfriend gave her a "playful push," and she found herself frighteningly close to the birds, which set her back about three weeks. (It also set their romance back a bit.)

Using friends, as Linda did, is a good idea (Moss & Arend, 1977). But be sure to tell them not to give you a playful push. Having a friend around when you are coping with nervousness in a social situation is particularly appropriate, so long as the helper has a serious desire to be helpful.

The use of friends to gradually shape advancing steps is a general strategy well worth considering, especially if your goal is behavior in a social situation. For goals such as public speaking, successful employment interviews, improved conversation, or asking for dates, the conditions of rehearsal can be shaped. The first step might be to rehearse in your imagination. The second step should be to rehearse in actual behavior, but privately. The third step can then be rehearsal in the presence of someone you trust; the final step, rehearsal in the actual goal situation (Goldstein, Sprafkin, & Gershaw, 1979).

Examples of Shaping Schedules

Alan, a young man whose goal was to have more dates, had followed chain-of-events reasoning and decided that the chain he needed to follow was: (1) go where women are, (2) smile at them, (3) talk with them, and so on. Step 3 could be broken down into talking with women about "safe" subjects, such as school or the weather, and then he could progress to more adventurous conversational topics. After achieving the first steps in the chain, Alan decided to shape his behavior according to the degree of controversy he would bring into the conversation. He chose this dimension because conversational disagreements made him very uncomfortable.

Alan's baseline showed that he did very little talking with women on any subject whatsoever. He reasoned that it would be a mistake to move immediately into conversations on controversial issues.

Therefore, for level 1 he chose to increase only talking about school. After he could comfortably perform at level 1, he would raise his sights and try a foray into more exciting but (for him) dangerous topics, such as whether a movie was funny or not. That was level 2. Level 3 was at an even higher level of potential controversy—university politics. Level 4 was interpersonal relationships and sex, and level 5 was the most difficult of all for him—national politics, personal philosophy, and the like.

Shaping in this fashion has two advantages. First, as with all shaping procedures, you can perform at a level that allows you to succeed. Second, it encourages analysis of the component parts of a situation—analysis that can result, for example, in seeing that there are levels of difficulty in handling a conversation or that being attractive is the result of several different behaviors. You can work on one part at a time instead of trying to deal with all levels of difficulty at once.

Here are some other examples of shaping. A young woman who wanted to be a writer remarked that she could write only a few paragraphs at a time. She would then "clutch up," unable to go on. She kept records of how many paragraphs she wrote on the average and started off requiring herself to do *one* more than that. Then she raised it to two more, three more, and so on.

A very withdrawn woman who felt she needed to become assertive "in about seven or eight different kinds of situations" started by requiring herself to practice assertiveness in two of the easiest situations and then added the others one at a time.

Problems in Shaping

You can't expect the course of learning to be smooth all the time. The important thing is to keep trying—staying within a shaping program—even if it is the 39th revision of the original schedule.

Encountering plateaus. When you follow a shaping schedule, you are likely to encounter plateaus. You may make excellent progress week after week and then suddenly stop. Moving up all those previous steps seemed so easy; then, all of a sudden, a new step—the same size as all the others—seems very difficult. The easiest way to continue upward when you reach a plateau is to reduce the size of the steps. If that is not possible, continue the plan for a week or so. The plateau experience is so common that you should expect it and "ride it out." This is particularly true for dieting, where physiological changes in your body can lead to less weight loss for a period of time (LeBow, 1981).

Losing "willpower." You now know enough about the principles that govern behavior/environment relationships to know that there are many reasons why you don't perform a given behavior. In our experience, the loss of self-control in the middle of intervention is most often due to some failure in the shaping program.

For example, a student will say:

> To hell with it. I can't do it. I want to get into that library and stay there, but I just can't make it. I haven't got enough willpower. Besides, this whole idea of self-change is ridiculous because the whole problem is really whether I have the willpower to improve myself. I don't, so I quit.

In our terms, this may be a shaping problem. For example, two hours in the library may be much too severe an increase over current performance. Instead of two hours, this student should have set his first approximation at only 30 minutes. Some students with a near-zero baseline might, as a first approximation, merely walk to the library and go up the steps, then return home to get their reinforcer. But many self-modifiers are simply too embarrassed to perform such elementary steps. Instead, they increase the step to a "respectable" level, which is often outside their performance capacity, and finally quit altogether in a huff of "willpower" failure.

You may experience this failure of self-control in two ways. First, you simply may not start on a self-modification project. You would like to achieve the final goal but somehow cannot get around to starting toward that goal. This is a shaping problem, and you need to start with a very low step. Remember, if it's embarrassingly low—"I jog around my living room three times every day"—then don't tell anyone, but do it.

Second, you may have started but find that you are not making progress. This may also be a shaping problem, and you need to use smaller steps.

The whole point of shaping is to make it as easy as possible to start and to continue. Therefore, you require yourself to do so little more than you can presently do that it is easy to perform the target behavior. Then, after practicing a bit, it becomes easy to move up one more short step. With each step, self-confidence will increase.

Not knowing how to begin. By referring to the baseline, you can determine your capability for certain tasks. For others, however, you may not know how to begin. You may not know exactly which acts come first in a chain-of-events sequence. In this case, you could use someone else as a model to get an idea of a starting point.

A young woman chose as her model another woman who was effective in getting acquainted with new people. The model's first behavior was merely to smile responsively. So our young woman used "smiling responsively" as the first step in her shaping plan. Observing models is especially appropriate when you are uncertain about the exact behaviors you should choose to develop.

Mark Twain knew about shaping, although he didn't use that word. In *Pudd'nhead Wilson's Calendar,* he wrote: "Habit is habit, and not to be flung out of the window by any man, but coaxed downstairs a step at a time." Coax yourself.

Tips for Typical Topics

Anxiety and Stress

Stress almost certainly is related to negative long-term effects on health. For that reason, it is important that you include a sound exercise program in your overall plan. For example, you could integrate walking into your life in several ways: walk to go shopping, to school, or to work; at the end of the day; when talking with friends; instead of lingering over a big lunch (Johnsgard, 1989).

Recent evidence shows that physical fitness buffers the negative health effects of life stress (Brown, 1991), reduces general anxiety, and improves self-efficacy (Long & Haney, 1988).

Stress reactions—whether anxiety, tension, anger, frustration, or general exhaustion and impaired health—all respond to the same general strategy outlined in this chapter. For reducing these reactions and the irritabilities of daily hassles, use the following steps:

1. Select a method of relaxation, and practice it thoroughly.
2. Notice the tightness, tension, anger, or frustration that you can feel in your shoulders or in your gut when you are under stress. Identify this as the first sign of your stress reaction.
3. Begin your own self-directed program in this way: First relax. Then imagine those feelings of anxiety, anger, or frustration that you experience in daily life. Instruct yourself to relax. Relax again.
4. When you have mastered this simple sequence, practice it in the ordinary traffic and hassles of daily life (Deffenbacher, in press; Deffenbacher & Craun, 1985).

For any specific anxiety or stress situation, develop a plan that includes practicing an incompatible behavior (usually relaxation) and gradually approaching the feared situation. Incorporate improved self-instructions, first in imagined rehearsal and then in the actual situation. Some evidence shows that the best order of practice is: (1) learn the relaxation process, (2) practice the self-instructions, (3) use imagined rehearsal while relaxing and instructing, and (4) perform the same process in the actual situation (Knowlton & Harris, 1987).

For anxiety about public speaking, it is important that the imagined rehearsal also include the material to be spoken. Being well prepared includes practicing the performance itself as well as the relaxation. Don't focus on yourself (Barlow, 1988). Instead, focus on getting your message across.

For test anxiety, imagined rehearsal that includes images of competence, such as detailed images of successful test-taking, should be combined with relaxation (Harris & Johnson, 1983). Self-instructions should also be combined with relaxation so that during tests self-defeating thoughts are replaced with active, coping self-instructions (Deffenbacher & Hahnloser, 1981). In fact, self-defeating negative thoughts about performance play a larger role in underachievement than does test anxiety itself (Smith, Arnkoff, & Wright, 1987). Replace those thoughts with statements of competence and calmness, and use your relaxation. Studying enough to be well prepared helps, too.

Assertion

You need not wait to practice new assertive skills until real opportunities occur. Use imagined rehearsal as a first stage in developing assertive behavior. When imagining the scenes, use relaxation as a prelude (Shelton, 1979). Be sure to imagine the full scene, including a favorable outcome (Kazdin, 1984). The following assertive responses can be useful to practice in imagination:

1. Imagine a scene in a restaurant, where smoke from a cigarette at the next table is making you uncomfortable. Imagine yourself saying to the waiter, "Please move me to a nonsmoking table."
2. Imagine being in your dorm room, unable to sleep because of the noise coming from a room down the hall. Imagine going to that room and saying, "Please try to be quieter; it's late, and others need to sleep."

Scenes such as these, drawn from your own daily hassles, should be imagined fully, with the sounds, smells, and feelings of real life. If you cannot imagine yourself giving these assertive responses, begin by imagining someone much like yourself doing so.

Begin your actual rehearsals in the most familiar and comfortable surroundings, at home or with good friends. You may even tell them that you are going to play the role of a more assertive person. A study of 58 female college students at the University of Kansas showed them to be more assertive in role-playing situations than in actual ones (Higgins, Frisch, & Smith, 1983). "Playing the role" can be a good place to begin developing the exact statements and skills that you can then transfer to more unfamiliar situations. Role-play and practice particular skills, such as positive self-statements, eye contact, and remarks that begin with "I."

After several days of this practice, you might use the following as the next step in the shaping schedule: Pick five different people, in different places, and state your opinion to them. Do this for about five days (Shelton, 1981a, 1981b). Those who engage in overt practice make consistently greater gains in assertion, and the gains are maintained for longer periods (Kazdin, 1984).

Depression and Low Self-Esteem

Two basic approaches to the self-improvement of depression have been researched, and they are equally effective (Rehm, Kaslow, & Rabin, 1987). These are (1) increasing specific new behaviors, and (2) increasing positive self-statements.

Specific new behaviors. The new behaviors needed to combat depression are those that lead to pleasant activities. Your plan should be aimed at increasing pleasant activities drastically. Do not overlook small pleasures. Fuchs and Rehm (1977), who have developed an effective self-control program for depression, encourage depressed people to set three subgoal activities for each major goal and to make those activities personally pleasant, no matter how modest they are—calling a friend for a chat or going to the library to get a book. Our students have used an enormous range of activities: engaging in the "good dream," sewing or embroidering, reading travel folders, cactus gardening, or browsing in the gourmet section of the market.

Notice the good things that happen to you. Keep a record of them. Increasing the attention paid to pleasant events can have the same effect as adding new ones.

And by all means, *increase your exercise.* Exercise is a reliable, well-demonstrated corrective for depression (McCann & Holmes, 1984; Rush, 1982; Simons, McGowan, Epstein, Kupfer, & Robertson, 1985). Beneficial exercise need not be extreme; even walking, briskly and regularly, can have startling effects on depression and anxiety. The benefits come from both aerobic exercise, such as running, and nonaerobic activities, such as weight lifting (Doyne et al., 1987). Exercise, even if it is the only element of a plan to alleviate depression, can be very effective. But because depressed people are often more sedentary than others, it may be useful to plan for structured programs or social encouragement to make sure you actually follow the program (Martinsen, 1990). Build this new activity into your plan, using the techniques for building in any new behavior.

If the depressed mood itself is troubling—feelings of sadness or sorrow—temporary relief can be gained by concentrated work; deep absorption in a task appears to reduce the emotions of mood (Erber & Tesser, 1991).

Positive self-statements. Make an effort to make clear, specific self-statements that recognize the positive things you do. You need not fear praising and encouraging yourself excessively. If you are now suffering from low self-esteem, it is almost certain that you are too heavily balanced toward negative self-appraisal and self-criticism.

Exercise and Athletics

To achieve the eventual goal of true physical fitness, most experts say, you must expend about 2000 calories per week in vigorous exercise (Stockton, 1987). For various sports, this translates approximately as:

Tennis	1 hour per day	5 days per week
Aerobics classes	40 minutes per day	5 days per week
Running, 10-min. miles	3 per day	6 days per week
Walking, 12-min. miles	5 per day	5 days per week
Swimming	30 minutes per day	6 days per week
Cross-country skiing	30 minutes per day	6 days per week

In adopting a new program for a healthier lifestyle, the gradual, shaped increase of exercise is an important element. Setting goals for performance—in reasonable shaping steps—leads to increases in performance and fitness (Ferretti & Hollandsworth, 1987). These goals should be reasonable, realistic, and gradual. Do not set goals for yourself that are punishing; that only leads to dropping out of your program (Selby, DiLorenzo, & Steinkamp, 1987). For some sedentary people, exercise should be increased as slowly as merely parking farther away from their destination. Two sessions per week of vigorous exercise—low-impact aerobics or brisk walking—may well be a wise first (or even second) step (Dubbert, Martin, & Epstein, 1986).

Skilled and novice athletes should use different approaches to increasing skill level even more. Imagined rehearsal, after relaxing, has been shown to help performance levels of experts in many sports—running, skiing, basketball, golf. In this technique, a successful competitive event is used as the imagined scene. But imagined rehearsal actually makes novices' performance worse! This is because the wrong skills are being practiced. Modeling and actual practice are more effective in the earliest stages of skill building (Suinn, 1987).

Relations with Others: Social Anxieties, Social Skills, and Dating

If social anxiety prevents you from making friends, develop a full plan as discussed for specific anxieties. Some form of relaxation is the incompatible behavior to choose.

Some students feel that their problem is not only feeling anxiety with others, but also not knowing what to do. Making friends with others of the same or the opposite sex is much the same. To be pleasant to others, a few general rules are especially helpful in the early stages of getting to know another person. For example, psychologists teach people to improve their social skills by using more appropriate body language. We suggest you use the acronym SOLER to remind yourself of what to do (Egan, 1977):

S Sit facing the person
O with an Open posture (no crossed arms, for example),
L Lean slightly forward,

E make Eye contact,
R and Relax.

Conversational skills are also of great importance in making friends, and the skills themselves are surprisingly simple.

1. Focus on the other person. Open a conversation with something that conveys an interest in her or him—pay a compliment, ask for an opinion or advice.
2. Remember to keep the conversational ball moving back and forth over the net, with special attention to keeping it in the other person's court.
3. Avoid insincere remarks. Silence is better than slick.
4. Think about the conversation from the other's point of view. Don't ask yourself, "Does he like me?" Instead, ask yourself, "Is he comfortable in this conversation?" (Farber, 1987)

These common social skills are also vital to good intimate relationships. Gottman and his co-workers (Gottman, Notarius, Gonso, & Markman, 1976) found that married people are ruder to each other than to complete strangers. Gottman's group set up rules for people involved in quarrelsome relationships: Be polite; really listen to the other person, without assuming that you know what she or he is going to say; be willing to compromise; express your feelings, and expect the other person to do the same. Any or all of these rules would make excellent goals for improving relationships.

If these lists are not sufficient and you don't know what to do, ask someone who is successful, or watch carefully. Modeling is especially important in improving social skills (Lipton & Nelson, 1980). If your problem is initiating conversations, for example, observe someone who does it better than you do. It is vital to select some effective behaviors, from the preceding lists or from your own models, and rehearse them before you begin to expose yourself to problem situations.

If these behaviors seem alien or difficult, use imagined rehearsal with relaxation as a preliminary stage.

Applying your relaxation in social situations is very helpful, but those who combine new social skills with relaxation improve significantly more (Cappe & Alden, 1986).

Smoking, Drinking, and Drugs

Those who resist the temptation of situations highly risky for abusing alcohol are more likely to engage in alternative behaviors to drinking, such as dancing, playing games, or having soft drinks (Brown, Stetson, & Beatty, 1989).

For all consummatory behaviors, the development of alternative responses is crucial. Choose one or more alternatives, and perform them at high-risk moments or in response to urges to indulge. Distraction from the urge will result. Distraction and substitute behaviors are among the most effective methods for resisting temptations to smoke (Shiffman, 1984). When you are in the early period of nonsmoking, the experience of craving can be an appropriate time for alternate behavior. Eating a flavorful noncaloric mint is a good substitute; drinking water is probably the best because of its flushing action.

Relaxation is an extremely valuable alternative behavior. Tension or anxiety often leads to overconsumption—of alcohol, tobacco, drugs, and even food. Include relaxation in your plan. Learn to relax, and apply relaxation at the first cue that you are tense. Also apply it at the first sign of your craving.

There has been a great deal of controversy on the best way to stop smoking, especially on whether it is better to quit "cold turkey" or to cut down gradually (Bernard & Efran, 1972; Flaxman, 1978). A review of the research literature (Pechacek & Danaher, 1979) concludes that the best way is a fairly rapid cessation. Abrupt quitting should be delayed for two weeks or so (Flaxman, 1978), until self-directional skills have been organized and practiced. You can, for example, set a date two weeks away and use this period for conducting self-observation, designing the plan, thinking how you will cope with urges to smoke, and practicing your plan.

On the other hand, some evidence exists that shaping is a reasonable approach. For example, heavy smokers are less likely to quit altogether, so a first goal might be to cut back on frequency; one way to do that is to gradually lengthen the time before the first cigarette in the morning (Cohen et al., 1989).

Regular exercise is a potent antidote to the use of drugs, alcohol, and tobacco—particularly if you substitute exercise for the usual end-of-the-day snack, cocktail, or drug (Marlatt & Parks, 1982; Murphy, Pagano, & Marlatt, 1986).

Studying and Time Management

In your record keeping, include some notation about the *effectiveness* of the study time. For example, our student Frances found her studying plan to be a disaster. Although she had sharply increased her study time, she wrote:

> I was a walking robot ready to explode! Then I developed a plan where I would study for one hour and meditate for the next. This plan worked magnificently and actually gave me more energy. I increased my previous high level to two additional hours of studying.

Her meditation worked both as a relaxation and a reward. Finding the right balance between mental efficiency and time spent on mental work is a trick that good records can help you perform.

Three specific new studying behaviors should be developed:

1. Make *written outlines* or summaries to organize the material.
2. *Rehearse* these outlines or summaries by repeating them aloud (without looking at your notes).
3. *Practice for tests* by asking yourself questions and answering them (Robinson, 1970).

What you do within a scheduled block of study time does make a difference.

For other parts of your time management—housecleaning, cooking, writing letters, or doing volunteer work—you may know well enough how to perform the behavior. For your self-change goal, the issue is that of actually sticking to the schedule. Thus, motivation is crucial; the next chapter will address that problem.

Weight Loss and Overeating

Trying to lose weight simply by cutting down on the calories you consume each day often fails, and worse yet, can actually lead to weight gain if you become so famished or stressed that you binge. If you're going to take weight off and keep it off, you will have to change some of your behaviors and attitudes. All successful behavioral programs for weight loss have certain features in common that concentrate on specific behaviors related to eating, diet, and exercise. (see Box 6-4). These common features are:

1. Procedures designed to decrease the rate of eating
2. Alterations in dietary content, reducing fat and alcohol intake and increasing consumption of complex carbohydrates
3. Increase in structured and unstructured exercise (Agras, 1987, p. 31)

Using a preliminary "practice" period is a good principle to follow with dieting as well. Choose a moderate reduction of calories as your first shaping goal, and for two weeks or so practice the general skills of self-control. Then steadily cut the calorie level to your actual shaping-step goals. Learn to substitute less caloric foods; for example, eat fruit instead of other desserts, or drink water instead of soft drinks or beer.

Try shaping by eliminating overeating in a few situations at a time. For example, if your regularly overeat in eight different situations, start by trying to eat correctly in one or two of them. Once those are under control, move on to the others.

A regular program of exercise is vital to weight control. The evidence is overwhelming: Dieting should be combined with exercise (Perri, McAdoo, McAllister, Lauer, & Yancey, 1986; Stalonas & Kirschenbaum, 1985). Supervised exercise programs are more likely to continue, and thus weight loss in the long term is more likely to be maintained (Craighead & Blum, 1989). Exercisers do not compensate by eating more; in fact, they tend toward the opposite—exercisers eat less (Dickson-Parnell & Zeichner, 1985).

If you are a binge eater, you should focus on an additional issue. Because binge eating is so strongly associated with negative self-statements, some means of replacing these negative thoughts with positive ones should be a central part of your program, even though it may appear not to be directly related to eating issues. When you are about to binge, examine your self-speech very carefully, and note self-criticisms. Use techniques of thought-stopping and/or thought-replacement (Heatherton & Baumeister, 1991).

BOX 6-4

The Best Possible Weight-Loss Program

The American College of Sports Medicine (1983) has released a position stand on "Proper and Improper Weight-Loss Programs." The following is a summary of that position:

1. Prolonged fasting and diet programs that severely restrict caloric intake are scientifically undesirable and can be medically dangerous.
2. Fasting and diet programs that severely restrict caloric intake result in the loss of large amounts of water, electrolytes, minerals, glycogen stores, and other fat-free tissue (including proteins within fat-free tissues), with minimal amounts of fat loss.
3. Mild calorie restriction (500-1000 kcal less than the usual daily intake) results in a smaller loss of water, electrolytes, minerals, and other fat-free tissue, and is less likely to cause malnutrition.
4. Dynamic exercise of large muscles helps to maintain fat-free tissue, including muscle mass and bone density, and results in losses of body weight. Weight loss resulting from an increase in energy expenditure is primarily in the form of fat weight.
5. A nutritionally sound diet resulting in mild calorie restriction, an endurance exercise program, and behavioral modification of existing eating habits are all recommended for weight reduction. The rate of sustained weight loss should not exceed 1 kg (2 lb.) per week.
6. To maintain proper weight control and optimal body-fat levels, a lifetime commitment to proper eating habits and regular physical activity is required.

SOURCE: *"American College of Sports Medicine Position Stand, Proper and Improper Weight Loss Programs" (1983). In* Medicine and Science in Sports and Exercise, *Vol. 15, No. 1, 1983. Copyright American College of Sports Medicine 1983. Reprinted by permission.*

Chapter Summary

Substituting New Thoughts and Behaviors

Substituting a desired behavior for an undesired one is preferable to following a plan that merely suppresses the bad habit. Substitution of overt behaviors, self-statements, and thoughts should be considered; these can often be effectively combined. Selecting an *incompatible* behavior is generally a good tactic. If the incompatible behavior is itself desirable, so much the better. But even when the substituted behavior has no intrinsic merit, it is better to substitute a neutral response than merely to suppress the old. Keeping records of the substitution will help strengthen the new behavior.

Substitutions for Anxiety and Stress Reactions

You can reduce fears and anxieties by (1) identifying carefully the situations in which you are uncomfortable, (2) choosing a behavior that is incompatible with anxiety, and (3) practicing the behavior in the situation that produces anxiety. Several behaviors that are incompatible with anxiety have been discussed, including distraction of attention, sexual arousal, martial arts, exercise, rational restructuring, and meditation.

Relaxation

Whenever you want to eliminate an undesired behavior, choose an alternative behavior for that same situation. When emotional reactions are the problem, relaxation is a useful incompatible response.

At the beginning, relaxation should be practiced privately, then quickly employed in many real-life situations. As soon as relaxation is a well-developed skill, it should be practiced in those situations that produce anxiety. Ideally, relaxation should be practiced immediately before the time when anxiety usually begins. You may combine relaxation with positive self-instructions.

Developing New Behaviors

Rehearsing a behavior repeatedly in the actual situation is the best way of mastering that behavior. When rehearsals are difficult to arrange in real life, you can use imagined rehearsal in the initial stages. Imagined rehearsals must be vivid and must include both situation and behavior. When you imagine behaviors in feared situations, use relaxation. But imagined rehearsal is only a prelude, a bridge to actual rehearsal in real-life situations. Your ultimate plan must include actual performance in actual situations. You can identify effective behaviors by observing models who are achieving the goals you want. Identify a model, analyze the model's skills, and use those skills as your standard. Don't hesitate to ask your model's help in explaining or even coaching those skills. If you have difficulty imagining yourself rehearsing your goal behaviors, imagine your models performing. Imagine more than one model in the situations that are difficult for you. Imagine them coping, self-instructing, and succeeding. This should be only the first step, however. Next, imagine rehearsals with yourself as the performer. The third step is the most important: Transfer those behaviors into real life. It is the rehearsal in the actual situation that brings about long-lasting change.

Shaping: The Method of Successive Approximations

Most self-direction plans, particularly those that call for developing some desired behavior, require shaping. Shaping means that instead of requiring yourself to perform the complete new behavior, you require yourself to perform only a part. Then, in a series of successive approximations to the final goal, you gradually increase the size of your steps. The two main rules of shaping are (1) you can never begin too low, and (2) the steps can never be too small. You can shape your behavior along any desired continuum.

Common problems in shaping include *plateaus*—progress stops and you find it hard to go on—and *lack of "willpower"*—you are either requiring yourself to start too high or using steps that are too large.

In the next chapter, which discusses self-reinforcement, you will learn methods for rewarding each step along the way.

YOUR OWN SELF-DIRECTION PROJECT: STEP SIX

You should now be able to draw up another version of your plan for self-modification, taking into account the methods for developing new behaviors. Consider your own goals, and write plans for reaching them. At this stage, try to include each of the basic tactics discussed in this chapter:

- Substituting new thoughts and behaviors (especially relaxation)
- Overt and imagined modeling and rehearsal
- Shaping

Later, you can choose the most effective total package. For now, specify ways you might use each of these tactics.

One of our students, Edward, wrote a fine plan incorporating these suggestions. Here is his letter to us:

> Last semester, I took a course in self-modification using your text *Self-Directed Behavior.* Even then I really wanted to do something about my speech anxiety which had been a problem for me ever since I could remember. But it wasn't until this semester that I actually had to give a speech in a course. Just thinking about it made me nervous, but I remembered the techniques I had learned in the book and set out to use them. I used imaginary rehearsals while in a state of deep relaxation, picturing the room and people with as much detail as possible. Whenever I felt myself getting too nervous, I would stop, do the muscle relaxation exercises until I was calm, and start over again. I also used the principles of shaping by practicing alone, with my sister, and finally with friends. Realistic positive self-statements to "psych" myself up were also useful. When the time came to give my presentation, I told myself to relax and proceeded. I couldn't believe how relaxed I felt! As a result, I could concentrate a lot better on what I was saying and not what I was feeling. I now feel quite confident that I can give an informative speech.

Write your plan now, but remember—it is not yet complete. The next chapter discusses methods of self-modification through control of consequences. Your final plan will include all three elements: antecedent control, new behavior development, and consequence control.

7

Consequences

Outline

- Discovering and Selecting Reinforcers
- Using Others to Dispense Reinforcers
- Self-Administered Consequences
- Techniques of Self-Reinforcement
- Self-Punishment and Extinction
- Reinforcement in Plans for Self-Modification
- *Tips for Typical Topics*
- *Chapter Summary*
- *Your Own Self-Direction Project: Step Seven*

Learning Objectives

Discovering and Selecting Reinforcers

1. What is a contingent reinforcer?
2. What is the simple formula for self-modification using reinforcers?
3. How can intermittent reinforcement schedules and avoidance behaviors make it difficult for you to discover your reinforcers?
4. How do you use activities, things, or people as reinforcers?
   a. What is the Premack principle?
   b. How do you pick reinforcers to use?

Using Others to Dispense Reinforcers

5. How do you use mediators to reinforce self-change behaviors? What does the mediator do?
   a. Should you ask for praise?
   b. How can you reinforce the mediators?
   c. What should you do if you share reinforcers with the mediator?

Self-Administered Consequences

6. Can people self-administer rewards contingently? What affects whether they do it or not?
   a. When people administer their own consequences, do behaviors actually change?
   b. Does the change occur according to the principles of reinforcement?
   c. If a self-administered reward is not a reinforcement, what is it?
   d. Is self-reinforcement really reinforcement, or is it feedback? Describe the experiments on that question.

Techniques of Self-Reinforcement

7. How soon after the desired behavior should reinforcement come?
8. Explain how to use token reinforcers. What is their main purpose?
9. How do you use imagined reinforcement?
10. Explain how to use verbal self-reinforcement.
    a. Why do people sometimes not use self-praise?
    b. What is the relationship of self-reinforcement to depression?
11. Should you ever get noncontingent positive events? When?

Self-Punishment and Extinction

12. Can you count on using extinction to change your own behavior? What is a better procedure?
13. Why is self-punishment usually insufficient?
    a. Is losing a positive event punishment enough? Or should you try to arrange to add on some negative event?
    b. Explain precommitted punishment. Is it properly a punishment or a deterrent?

Reinforcement in Plans for Self-Modification

14. How is reinforcement used in conjunction with antecedent control of behavior?
15. How is it combined with developing new behaviors? For example, how is it combined with imagined rehearsal or shaping?
16. What kinds of self-modification plans should include self-reinforcement?

One of the basic formulas for self-regulation is the arrangement of rewards for desired behaviors.

How is positive reinforcement used in self-modification? *The basic principle is that a positive event is made contingent on the desired behavior.* As discussed in Chapter 4, the idea of **contingency** is very important. A reinforcer is delivered after, and only after, a certain response. If you gain a reward whether or not you perform some behavior, that reinforcer will not affect the behavior. If, instead, you can gain the reinforcer only by performing the behavior, that behavior will be strengthened—that is, it will be more likely to occur again. It is the contingent relationship that is important, not the positive reinforcer alone.

The use of reinforcement was one of the first techniques studied in the field of self-directed behavior. Twenty-three years ago, when we wrote the first edition of this book, reinforcement was the cornerstone of all self-change plans because it was the best understood technique. As psychology's understanding of self-control processes has deepened, many new procedures have emerged, and these often seem more sophisticated than simple reinforcement. Ten years ago, many writers seemed ready to put reinforcement out to pasture. More recently, however, there is a new consensus: reinforcement is still the most reliable horse in the stable.

Contingent rewards, when delivered by the social environment, will strengthen the behaviors they follow. Very little in psychology is more certain than that.

Discovering and Selecting Reinforcers

The simple formula for self-modification is to rearrange the contingencies so that reinforcement follows desirable behavior. To do so, you need to know what reinforcers you have available for rearrangement. This section discusses ways of discovering and cataloging reinforcers so that you'll be able to select reinforcers you can use.

Direct Observation of Reinforcing Consequences: Possibilities and Problems

Ramon kept careful baseline records of his studying behavior. He recorded the situations and opportunities for studying (for example, "at library, 42 min."). He also recorded his actual study time ("4 min.," "15 min.," and so on). The baseline rate of actual study time was very low—less than 20% of the time he was in an appropriate study situation. What was the reinforcer for all this inattention while in a study situation? Ramon was able to report it instantly: Instead of reading, he spent his time talking with the friends who sat near his usual table.

This reinforcer, incidentally, was not only clear but very available for rearrangement. Ramon designed an intervention plan that required him to spend at least 60 minutes studying in his room, a behavior he would then reinforce with a trip to the library, where he could converse with single-minded devotion. He reported that this plan increased both his study time and his socializing.

It is likely that in this kind of situation you will have discovered the reinforcer for your undesirable behavior while observing yourself. The easiest kind of intervention plan is simply to rearrange the reinforcers that you are already getting so that they are used to reinforce some desirable behavior rather than some undesirable behavior.

Of course, situations are not always so simple. In some cases the reinforcers, although evident, cannot be so easily detached from the problem behavior and rearranged in an intervention plan. This is the case with *consummatory responses,* such as eating or drinking. Problems can also arise when the reinforcing consequences of behavior are not so obvious. Sometimes the most careful observer can't discover what they are. Two conditions that commonly obscure reinforcers are *intermittent reinforcement schedules* and *avoidance behaviors.*

Intermittent reinforcement schedules. If each instance of your problem behavior were followed by reinforcement, careful observation could reveal the reinforcer in question. But some of your more persistent actions are followed by reinforcement only part of the time. Remember that intermittent reinforcement leads to greater resistance to extinction. Thus, you might expect to find that an intermittent reinforcement schedule is responsible for maintaining especially persistent problem behaviors. But it might take months of observation to discover the pattern.

Avoidance behaviors. Avoidance behavior creates even worse problems for the person trying to discover reinforcers because the aversive consequence may not occur at all. When you have been punished for a behavior in the presence of a cue, that cue will come to elicit avoidance of the behavior.

Thus, you will not be punished again and therefore will not be able to observe the negative reinforcer because it will not occur. Although avoidance learning probably accounts for many problems, you might keep observing forever and not detect the specific unpleasantness you are avoiding.

Bill, a sophomore, wanted to go out for his dormitory's intramural basketball team. He had not played competitively in high school and had not even played many pickup games since he was about 14, although he enjoyed shooting baskets alone. Bill told us that he really had a baseline; during three semesters of college in which he had wanted to go out for a team, he just couldn't make himself do it. He wanted to know how he could discover the reinforcer for not going out. Of course, he couldn't discover such a reinforcer, and neither could a professional. In a case like this, we suspect a pattern of avoidance learning. During high school, some unpleasant consequence probably followed Bill's efforts to participate in organized basketball. That consequence might well be lost in his history of learning. Even if Bill had been able to remember the punishment he once received, he would have needed new positive reinforcers to strengthen the behavior he now wanted—joining the dormitory team.

In summary, if you can discover the reinforcers that are supporting some undesirable behavior, you may be able to rearrange them so that they will reinforce some desirable behavior. Three conditions can interfere with this process:

1. The behavior may be unalterably attached to the reinforcer.
2. The problem behavior may be on an impossible-to-detect intermittent reinforcement schedule.
3. You may be engaging in avoidance behavior.

Your strategy, then, must be to discover reinforcers that *are* controllable. The reinforcers don't need to be those that are actually maintaining your problem behavior. You can use *any* pleasant event, as long as it increases the frequency of your desired behavior.

Positive Reinforcers

If you cannot rearrange or even discover the reinforcers for a particular behavior, you can still modify your behavior by selecting some reinforcer and making it contingent upon a desired behavior.

A positive reinforcer is anything that will increase the occurrence of the behavior it follows. Reinforcers can be things, people, or activities. A "thing" reinforcer might be a doughnut, a $5 bill, a new dress, a fancy shirt, a compact disc—anything you want or would like to have. A "people" reinforcer might be praise or approval, going on a date with your girlfriend, or talking with your boyfriend on the phone—spending time with someone you enjoy. An "activity" reinforcer is any event you enjoy—playing a game, going to a movie, or having dinner out. Even "doing nothing"—talking with friends or loafing—can be a reinforcer. Usually these kinds of potential reinforcers are not limited to any one behavior or situation. You may just feel like going out for a beer or a pizza. Any kind of special occasion like that can be used as a reinforcer. *The task is simply to connect contingently the occurrence of the reinforcer with the target behavior.*

The most important reinforcers are those that will eventually help you maintain your new behavior once it is solidly in place. You can use those reinforcers to support the steps along your way. For example, one of our students aspired toward membership in the scholarly society Phi Beta Kappa. That meant harder work, with the reward of higher grades. She used the reinforcer of "grades awarded" to increase her studying time, except that she awarded the grades herself on a daily basis. She entered an "A" for excellent, a "B" for good, and so forth, beside each day's entry in her study record. If she had studied very well, she gave herself an "A"; if fairly well, a "B," and so on. Another student wanted to increase her range of friends. She reinforced making friendly overtures to new people with the reward of phone chats with her best friend.

Using logical reinforcers—ones similar to the rewards you are striving toward—is highly desirable. But if you cannot arrange logical reinforcers, any pleasant event can reinforce behavior. The range of reinforcers is potentially as wide as the range of objects in the world—as wide as the range of human activities. To illustrate this variety, here is a partial list of the reinforcers our students have used:

praising oneself
taking bubble baths
making love
going to a movie or a play
going to the beach
mountain climbing
spending time at a favorite hobby
spending money
playing records
listening to the radio
eating favorite foods
going out "on the town"
playing sports
getting to "be the boss" with a boyfriend
pampering oneself
taking long breaks from work
taking a "fantasy break"
window shopping
putting on makeup
not going to work
"doing anything I want to do"
going to parties
being alone
"doing only the things I want to do, all day"
"not doing my duty sometimes"
goofing off
watching TV
gardening
making long-distance calls
playing with the parrot
buying a present for someone
spending extra time with a friend
reading erotica
reading mystery stories
lip-synching (pretending to be a rock star in front of a mirror)

Activities are excellent reinforcers. Actually, *any activity that you are more likely to perform can be used to reinforce any behavior that you are less likely to perform (when you have a free choice).* This is known as the **Premack principle,** after the psychologist who studied the phenomenon most systematically.

The Premack principle tells you that you can use any one of certain behaviors you engage in every day—such as taking a bath, going to work, eating, watching TV, or talking to friends on the phone—to reinforce the goal behavior by connecting its occurrence to the goal behavior. The object of the plan is to require yourself to perform the goal behavior *before* you perform the behavior that occurs frequently.

Shirley wanted to increase her exercise time to 15 minutes each day. Taking a shower was one of her preferred behaviors. Following the Premack principle, she simply arranged not to take a shower until she had done her exercises.

Select for a Premack-type reinforcer some behavior that is not aversive. The behavior can be simply neutral. For example, although not many people find brushing their teeth wildly pleasurable, probably very few find it really unpleasant. The point is to select a behavior that is (or can be) frequent in free-choice conditions. Thus, you might also select an activity that you do not perform as frequently as you would like. For example, one student chose "dreaming about my trip to Europe" as a reinforcer, in spite of the fact that this daydreaming generally occurred less than once a day. She liked to lie quietly and picture the different routes she might take on her trip, the hotels in which she might stay, and the different museums she might visit. This activity required quiet, a relaxed atmosphere, and time enough to get thoroughly into the fantasy. She reasoned that this was a good Premack-type reinforcer because, given the opportunity, she would engage in this behavior very frequently.

A good strategy is to use the behavior that you usually perform *instead* of the target behavior as the *reinforcer* for that target behavior. For example, a man who wanted to spend some time in the evening reading serious literature instead spent all his time reading "whodunits." He did this very frequently and it interfered with his reading the cultural material. So he used the whodunit reading as a Premack-type reinforcer. If he spent a certain amount of time reading serious material, then he would reinforce that behavior by allowing himself the more frequent activity—reading mystery stories.

Examples of Premack-type activities used in published cases of self-directed behavior change include eating, urinating (Johnson, 1971), sitting on a particular chair (Horan & Johnson, 1971), smoking, making telephone calls (Todd, 1972), and opening daily mail at the office (Spinelli & Packard, 1975).

Given the tremendous scope of any list of possible reinforcers for any one individual, how can you decide which are the potentially effective reinforcers for yourself? Answering the following questions may help you.

1. What will be the rewards of achieving your goal?
2. What kind of praise do you like to receive from yourself and others?
3. What kinds of things do you like to have?
4. What are your major interests?
5. What are your hobbies?
6. What people do you like to be with?
7. What do you like to do with those people?
8. What do you do for fun?

9. What do you do to relax?
10. What do you do to get away from it all?
11. What makes you feel good?
12. What would be a nice present to receive?
13. What kinds of things are important to you?
14. What would you buy if you had an extra $20? $50? $100?
15. On what do you spend your money each week?
16. What behaviors do you perform every day? (Don't overlook the obvious or the commonplace.)
17. Are there any behaviors that you usually perform instead of the target behavior?
18. What would you hate to lose?
19. Of the things you do every day, which would you hate to give up?
20. What are your favorite daydreams and fantasies?
21. What are the most relaxing scenes you can imagine?

Wherever you are in your own self-direction project, stop at this point and take a few minutes to think about the preceding questions. You should be able to give specific answers to each question. If you can, you will have a good-sized catalog of possible reinforcers. Eventually you will choose one or more reinforcers from this list.

Consider each reinforcer in these terms: *Can I stand withholding it from myself one or more times if I don't earn it?* Putting a reinforcer on contingency means that you may have to withhold it. Don't choose a reinforcer that you simply will not give up. How potent is this reinforcer? Choosing a trivial reward will bring trivial results. The trick is to strike a balance between too important and trivial. The ideal reinforcer should be something you could stand losing (temporarily) if you had to, but you would be very disappointed if you did.

Using Others to Dispense Reinforcers

Using important other people to dispense reinforcement has proven beneficial in a wide variety of problem behaviors, such as reducing delinquent acts (Tharp & Wetzel, 1969), complying with health-care practices (Becker & Green, 1975; Blackwell, 1979; Brownlee, 1978), dieting (Brownell, Heckerman, Westlake, Hayes, & Monti, 1978; Weisz & Bucher, 1980), and smoking cessation (Coppotelli & Orleans, 1985). When your family, friends, or associates become involved in reinforcing your self-change behavior, long-term maintenance of the behavior is much more likely (Hall, 1980; Shelton, Levy, & contributors, 1981; Stokes & Baer, 1977).

For example, using money to reinforce good eating habits increases weight loss, but when the money is dispensed by the dieter's spouse, the long-range effectiveness of the program is even greater (Israel & Saccone, 1979; Saccone & Israel, 1978). The praise given by the husband in the case in Box 7-1 dramatizes this point.

BOX 7-1

Social Reinforcement by the Spouse in Weight Control: A Case Study

The subject, Mrs. L., was a 44-year-old female, 5 ft. 6 in. tall and weighing 174 lb. She had made numerous unsuccessful attempts to lose weight over the past ten years employing treatments ranging from "do it yourself remedies" to an assortment of fad diets and then drug therapy administered under a physician's care. Her husband had also tried a treatment of verbal abuse during which he routinely made statements such as "You are so fat I am ashamed to be seen with you." He also offered to buy Mrs. L. a new wardrobe if she would lose 30 lb. The most weight [Mrs. L.] ever lost was 12 lb in six weeks with drugs. She remained at the new weight for 12 weeks of treatment, and gained the weight back within one month when medication was discontinued. With all treatments the consistent pattern was weight loss for a few weeks followed by a return to old eating habits and weight gain again. Mrs. L. frequently snacked while cooking or shopping, remarking that she did not have the necessary willpower to lose weight.

During an initial phase of self-observation and the arrangement of new antecedents, she lost less than one-half pound per week. Then a plan involving social reinforcement was added. The subject stated that Mr. L.'s verbal abuse of her weight was highly aversive. Therefore, the frequency of these comments was made contingent on weight loss. If Mrs. L. lost 2 lb a week, Mr. L. was to compliment his wife two or more times each evening for progress being made on her diet. No derogatory comments about her figure were allowed. If the weekly criterion was not reached, Mr. L. was to use verbal abuse of Mrs. L.'s figure as frequently as desired. A contract was signed by both persons with each spouse serving as a reliability check for the other. Mr. L. was to assure accurate weighins, and Mrs. L. made sure no verbal abuse of her weight was used inappropriately. When the contract was violated, the offended spouse used a verbal reminder such as "You just called me a fat hog; this violates the contract we made."

Greater weight losses were reported during the social-reinforcement phase (39 lb). Mrs. L. attributed her success to self-confidence created primarily by praise she received from her husband. She indicated that maintaining weight at or below the goal (135 lb) during follow-up was due to praise and gradual weight loss resulting in altered eating habits (i.e., eating only at the dining table and consuming smaller portions).

Mr. and Mrs. L. stated that social reinforcement resulted in better social interactions at home. Both were pleased with the weight loss and increased affection shown toward each other. They indicated that this positive behavior would continue in other aspects of their relationship.

SOURCE: "Social Reinforcement by the Spouse in Weight Control: A Case Study," by J. L. Matson, 1977, *Journal of Behavior Therapy and Experimental Psychiatry, 8*, 327–328.

One of the most effective weight-control studies ever reported used spouses as mediators. Spouses modeled good behavior: They paused while eating, did not eat snacks in the partner's presence, avoided buying high-calorie foods, rewarded habit change, and assisted in record keeping (Brownell, Heckerman, Westlake, Hayes, & Monti, 1978). Help this elaborate may not be necessary, but spouses must not sabotage a dieter's efforts (Pearce, LeBow, & Orchard, 1981). When spouses successfully mediate a program of weight loss, excellent side benefits are likely. Women whose husbands cooperated showed significant improvement in marital happiness and a drop in depression (Weisz & Bucher, 1980).

Evidence from ex-smokers is similar: Social support from friends, companions, partners, and spouses is associated with greater likelihood of quitting smoking (Coppotelli & Orleans, 1985; Gritz, 1978; Mermelstein, Lichtenstein, & McIntyre, 1983; Wood, Hardin, & Wong, 1984). The most recent evidence seems to indicate that it is not the absolute number of reinforcements delivered by a spouse or partner that makes the difference; rather, it is the *proportion* of reinforcing to punishing events that predicts successful quitting and staying off cigarettes. The authors of this study point out that this proportion reflects the general climate of the partner's support; it's not necessary for the partner to praise you effusively and frequently. What makes the difference is the partner's being more supportive than not (Cohen & Lichtenstein, 1990).

If your reinforcer is something tangible, such as money, you can give it to another person and explain what you must do to get it back. If the reinforcer is some activity, you can arrange to get permission from those who are present, stipulating that permission should be granted only if you perform the target behavior. For example, Carmen, a college freshman, wanted to increase her studying time. She arranged with her daily aerobics classmates that they wouldn't let her join in unless she reported at least an hour's studying already that day.

Setting up a fund that will be returned to you as reinforcement for meeting goals has been shown to add to the effectiveness of good programs for weight loss and smoking cessation (Jeffery, Hellerstedt, & Schmid, 1990). As an example, our student Loren wrote:

> I gave a good friend five dollars to hold for me. He would give it back to me one dollar at a time after he had checked my records once a week to see if I had spoken up in class according to my goals. Two other friends, Caleb and Joe, displayed a lot of interest in my self-modification plan, and this put some social pressure on me. They would also compliment me when I reported my results for the week. The use of my friends in my plan was quite effective. They seemed to set off a positive emotional response in me that was very motivating.

Carmen—who apparently liked the system of using mediators—felt guilty about her infrequent letters and phone calls to her parents, who were thousands of miles away from her campus. She arranged with them that they would send her monthly allowance only after she wrote or called in the last week of the month. Everyone was delighted. Carmen wrote more letters, and her parents raised her allowance by $10!

Mediators can also provide praise. The power of praise coming from those we care about cannot be overestimated. In all likelihood, praise—for increasing studying, losing weight, staying on a good health regimen, or stopping smoking—is much more effective than material reinforcers. And the more important the mediator is to you, the more powerful that praise will be. A good self-modification plan should almost certainly contain this element. Arrange with your important others to praise your reaching each shaping step. Don't hesitate to call attention to your changed behavior, prompting others to respond with encouragement (Stokes & Osnes, 1989).

An instructor of a course that uses this book as the text organized her students into special self-supporting groups. For example, those students whose goal was weight loss met regularly and worked out mutual-reinforcement plans for improved eating habits. In such groups, reinforcement can be even more powerful if the group earns (or loses) rewards *as a group* (Jeffery, Gerber, Rosenthal, & Lindquist, 1983).

Such support groups can be extremely helpful, especially when mediators in natural relationships are difficult to find. For long-term benefits, though, whenever possible the reinforcement plans should involve people who will be close to you in your regular and continuing life. This becomes even more important after the novelty and early enthusiasm of your self-modification plan diminish (Fisher, Lowe, Levenkron, & Newman, 1982). Exercisers who stick with their programs long enough to experience real health benefits are more likely to have a regular aerobics partner (Lawson & Rhodes, 1981) or a supportive spouse (Heinzelmann & Bagley, 1970).

Whenever you use a mediator, it is important that the person understand exactly what he or she is supposed to do—namely, to reinforce contingently and not to punish you. If you fail to perform the target behavior and the mediator withholds the reinforcer, that is unpleasant enough. You don't need further punishment such as scolding, which may even cause you to discontinue your plan altogether. Nagging by people in a smokers' network leads to failure (Wood, Hardin, & Wong, 1984).

The effectiveness of mediated reinforcement depends on the mediator's actually delivering the reward, of course. Only failure can be expected if the reinforcement is not produced—as in the case of a husband who repeatedly failed to reward his wife's improvements by the dinner dates he had agreed to; a mediator who could not find the promised dress in the shops of a small town; or a careless instructor who gave a grade of "D" despite greatly improved study habits (Peterson, 1983). These failures caution us to choose mediators wisely. Make sure the mediator can and will cooperate, or it may harm the relationship.

If your behavior change will affect others, consider the issue fully with them, and decide together how they might serve as mediators for you. For example, Ellen's husband and children warmly applauded her decision to finish her college degree. But when she began a program to increase study time, her family began to punish her by comments that housework was being neglected (Peterson, 1983). An excellent plan here would be for Ellen's husband and children to reinforce her studying by doing some extra housework.

The "good" mediators' tasks are really very simple: They should give you your reinforcement when you are meeting your standard and withhold it when you're not. But you must appreciate that this can put them in a different relationship to you, and it can sometimes be awkward—especially when they have to withhold your reinforcer. So reinforce *their* good mediating. Simple praise and expressions of thanks—especially at awkward moments—can help to keep their help.

Sharing Reinforcers

Sometimes the reinforcers you select are shared with other people or affect them as much as they affect you. Even in such a case, it is *your* behavior that establishes the contingency. For example, a young woman chose going to the movies with her boyfriend as a reinforcer. She needed his cooperation in her intervention plan because if she failed to perform the target behavior, she would have to miss seeing the movie with him. But if she did miss the movie, *so would he.* The pleasurable experiences we have with other people—being together, doing favorite things, loving—are often very powerful reinforcers and thus are ideal choices for an intervention plan. But if you want to use them, you must have the other person's cooperation.

Many times one person will decide to modify a particular aspect of his or her behavior because a friend or lover is concerned about it. A man might smoke, for example, and his friend might disapprove. It is often possible to use the other person, who is not changing his or her behavior, as a partner in the process of change. This is particularly true when the partner values your goals. The change in your behavior becomes the reinforcer for the partner's behavior of cooperation. Or the partner may simply care enough to be willing to share a reinforcer. We know of a woman who agreed with her student husband not to talk with him until he had spent so many minutes on a paper he was writing.

Using activities with others as reinforcers is effective not only because the reinforcer is a powerful one but also because it brings another force to bear in your intervention plan. The other person, who may stand to lose if you fail to perform the target behavior, will pressure you to perform it. If your determination begins to lag, your friend may say to you, "You better do it! I want to see that movie!"

A special situation arises when a couple undertakes the same plan together. Before deciding on such a course, both partners should make sure they are equally committed to the plan and goals. When two partners both try to lose weight, for example, and one or both subtly sabotage the other's efforts, they may be less successful than if only one were trying to lose weight (Zitter & Fremouw, 1978).

The people who will help you in your self-change plan sometimes need a little help themselves to know just what to do. Box 7-2 contains a letter we've written to them explaining what you need them to do. Copy this or show it to anyone who is going to help you.

BOX 7-2

Dear Helper

Dear Helper:

__________ will soon be discussing with you a new program of self-improvement that will probably please you. Because it may also affect you, we are writing this note with some tips on how you can be most helpful.

The details will be worked out with you in conversation. It is very important that you understand exactly what you are being asked to do so that you can follow the plan closely. So make sure your conversation is clear and precise.

Your role will be to provide three kinds of help: *reminders, rewards,* and *general companionship and support.*

The plans will concentrate on the positive. These plans should increase the pleasant aspects of life for you both. If reminders are called for, be sure to remind—*but don't nag.* If rewards are called for, be sure to provide them if they are earned. If they are not earned, no reward—but no scolding either.

To make things really clear, here are some examples of positive behaviors you could perform:

Compliment small successes
Help the person think of substitutes for an unwanted behavior
Celebrate successes together
Help the person calm down when feeling stressed
Encourage the person to stick with it
Express confidence that the person can stick with it
Express pleasure that the person is changing

The following are examples of things you should avoid doing:

Nag the person
Criticize the old behavior
Get involved in every little decision the person makes
Comment on your friend's lack of willpower
Mention being bothered by the old, bad habit
Express doubt about the person's ability to change

Success in the plan will be strongly affected by a general climate of helpfulness and a positive overall atmosphere of encouragement. With your help, more can be achieved in many ways.

Sincerely yours,
David L. Watson/Roland G. Tharp
Authors, *Self-Directed Behavior*

SOURCE: Adapted from "Partner Behaviors That Support Quitting Smoking" by S. Cohen and E. Lichtenstein, 1990, *Journal of Consulting and Clinical Psychology, 58,* pp. 304–309.

Self-Administered Consequences

Reinforcement dispensed by mediators is a powerful technique for increasing behavior strength, frequency, and probability. But can contingent reward administered by the *self* have the same effect? After all, the idea of contingency is that the rewards are *not* freely available. They appear only when a standard is met and otherwise are not available. If the self administers rewards, they are presumably available whether or not the standard is met. If you know that the reward is there for the taking, whether or not you meet your standard, will self-reward actually reinforce the behavior? This is one of the liveliest questions in contemporary psychology. Because it is so important to self-regulation, it is important that you understand something of the issues.

Actually, there are two interrelated questions: (1) Can people actually self-administer rewards contingently? In self-control terms, can people abstain from taking immediate rewards in favor of gaining long-term rewards? (2) If people do administer consequences contingently, do these consequences really reinforce and punish behavior? We will discuss these two issues in turn.

Learning Self-Reward and Self-Control

The answer to the first question is actually quite clear: yes, people can and do self-administer rewards contingently. People can and do abstain from taking immediate rewards in favor of gaining long-term, more desirable ones. One can learn self-reinforcing by imitating others (Bandura, 1971), by following instructions (Kanfer, 1970), by receiving rewards for self-reinforcing (Speidel & Tharp, 1980), or through classlike lectures (Heiby, Ozaki, & Campos, 1984). Bandura and his associates have taught even pigeons, monkeys, and dogs to "self-reinforce"—that is, to not take freely available rewards until after they have performed the desired behavior. These animals were taught by an experimenter who removed the food trays if the animals tried to take the reward before performing. Once learned, self-reinforcing persisted for some time (Bandura & Mahoney, 1974; Mahoney & Bandura, 1972; Mahoney, Bandura, Dirks, & Wright, 1974).

Cantania (1975) argues that this isn't really self-control, any more than refraining from shoplifting is self-control. If there were no external punishment for shoplifting (or taking the food), everyone would eventually walk out with whatever reinforcers he or she wanted.

Theoreticians who make this kind of argument point out that there has to be some external reason to self-reinforce and to stick to the planned contingencies. Rachlin (1974) correctly points out that a student would not make moviegoing contingent on studying unless the external reasons for studying—grades and career success—were meaningful.

In self-modification, the external contingencies are provided by your goals. You choose your goals because achieving them will improve your life.

When you are working for goals that you genuinely value, self-rewarding and self-punishing can certainly be carried out. Competent self-directors do so all the time. Thousands of students who have used this textbook have done so. Not every student does, of course; and some do better than others in holding to accurate, contingent self-rewarding. But *can* people self-control and self-reinforce? Of course they can.

Do Self-Administered Consequences Actually Reinforce and Punish?

After 25 years of puzzling over this issue, psychologists are beginning to phrase the questions as two separate issues: (1) When people administer their own consequences, does behavior actually improve? (2) Does this improvement occur according to the conditioning principles of reinforcement and punishment or according to the principles of feedback and cybernetics?

The first question has been addressed by a multitude of studies (see review articles by Ainslee, 1975; Bandura, 1971; Catania, 1975; Kanfer, 1970; Morgan & Bass, 1973; Rachlin, 1974; Sohn & Lamal, 1982), and the answer here, too, is yes. When people self-administer contingent consequences, their behavior is indeed likely to improve. Successful self-controllers, regardless of the problem area—overeating, studying, dating, or smoking—are three times more likely to use self-reward procedures than are unsuccessful self-controllers (Heffernan & Richards, 1981; Perri & Richards, 1977; Perri, Richards, & Schultheis, 1977). Though not every study reports this result for every behavior, the vast majority of research supports this conclusion for a wide range of specific programs—weight loss, smoking, assertiveness, and many others. Yes, self-administered consequence programs are very likely to improve behavior.

But that does not end the debate. Does self-reward operate as *reinforcement?* Do the principles of conditioning described in Chapter 4 explain the positive effects of self-reward?

The logical problem is this. We have already established that self-reinforcement will not occur at all unless the person is motivated to change and unless the external world eventually provides encouragement. Therefore, self-reinforcement can only be found embedded in a context of external reinforcement.

Bandura (1981) argues that self-reinforcing plans create incentives along the way to the eventual goal. Ainslee (1975), Catania (1975), and Rachlin (1974) point out that self-reward is a very complicated process that contains *many* effective elements: You are teaching yourself to discriminate between correct and incorrect performances. You are reminding yourself of your long-term goals and of your rules for getting there (Nelson, Hayes, Spong, Jarrett, & McKnight, 1983). You are learning *self-awareness* (Catania, 1975).

Regulation theorists who work within the feedback/cybernetics model point out that when you reinforce your behavior, you are calling your own attention to it and making the behavior more vivid, even more vivid than by self-recording alone. Thus, you are able to give yourself clearer feedback to compare with your standards and goals (Castro & Rachlin, 1980).

B. F. Skinner (1953) himself, the father of the operant-conditioning movement, expressed doubt that "operant conditioning" alone is the best explanation for the effects of self-administered contingent reward; the undoubted effectiveness must also come from a different route. That route has been described in detail by Brigham (1989): Self-direction plans change the environment so that the environment reinforces behavior the individual is motivated to achieve.

Box 7-3 contains a further example of the continuing debate on whether self-reward and punishment operate according to the principles of reinforcement or of feedback.

So although theoreticians continue to argue about the mechanism, there is really no dispute on the following formulation. You can change the way you relate to your environment. You can learn to change it more effectively. You can assist that learning by the use of contingent rewards as you go along. In the long run, success in changing will depend on your setting up a new, improved reciprocal relationship with the world and people around you (Brigham, 1989).

Techniques of Self-Reinforcement

Prompt Reinforcement

When should you get reinforcement? The ideal situation is one in which the reinforcement occurs immediately after you perform the desired behavior. The longer a reinforcement is delayed, the less effective it is, partly because it must compete with other reinforcement that is occurring immediately.

Whatever your goal, it will be reinforced at some *later* time, when it is achieved. The dieter is reinforced immediately *by* overeating. Only weeks from now, when a new, thinner image is reflected in the mirror, will this person be reinforced for *not* eating. At nine o'clock in the morning, shortly after a nice breakfast, a dieter will choose to diet. At noon, walking through the cafeteria line, our same dieter may choose to ignore the diet. For this reason, self-reinforcement systems are a vital part of self-directed strategies. By providing yourself with extra immediate reinforcement, you can tip the balance and cause yourself to choose behaviors that contribute to your long-term goal. If the dieter arranges the reinforcement of, say, watching an enjoyable TV program immediately after (or even during) self-restraint, dieting is more likely to be observed than if he or she depends entirely on the long-range rewards of being slim someday. In other words, it is the TV program that competes right now with an extra bowl of spaghetti, not the dim dream of slimness in what, at the moment, may appear as a faraway future (Bandura, 1981).

A student who was wild about women chose exercise as his goal. So he enrolled in an aerobics class that contained almost all women. He reported that just being in that atmosphere provided all the reinforcement he needed

BOX 7-3

Self-Reward and Punishment: Reinforcement or Feedback?

Here is an important and amusing example of research strategies and logic in the field of self-directed behavior. Rachlin (1974) has argued that self-rewarding works not by reinforcing, but by clearly *marking* behavior, making people more *attentive,* and so increasing accurate *self-observation* and self-monitoring. To test this hypothesis, Castro and Rachlin (1980) had people who attended a weight-reduction clinic pay the clinic *more* money if they lost more weight. These dieters lost as much weight as another group that took money as a "reward" for losing weight. Castro and Rachlin concluded that if these contingencies worked as reinforcement and punishment, then those who paid for losing weight should have lost less because they were punished, and those who took money should have lost more because they were reinforced. Therefore, contingencies work as *feedback* (as in cybernetic theory) and not according to conditioning principles.

Bandura (1981) attacked this study by pointing out that of course consequences are evaluated according to usual social standards. It is not "punishing" to pay a professional for effective services; we happily pay accountants who save us money, dentists who save our teeth, or clinics that help us lose weight. Therefore, no "punishment" had been studied at all.

The debate heated up and moved to Bogotá, Colombia, where Castro and his colleagues (Castro, de Pérez, de Albanchez, & de León, 1983) resolved to "punish" their weight losers in a way that had no correspondence to ordinary professional life. One group of clients that came to their weight-reduction clinic agreed to a bizarre plan. For each pound lost, each person either mailed one dollar (equivalent) to his or her most hated political party or cut the money into tiny pieces in the presence of the clinic staff. This group lost *more* weight than another one that took the same amount of money per pound lost to spend on a special treat! The Castro group concluded that contingencies do not operate as reinforcement and punishment.

Castro and his colleagues do not argue that self-reward is ineffective; the self-reward group also lost weight. But they do insist that self-reward and self-punishment operate primarily by providing information—making people pay more attention to their own behavior.

Bandura replied that if this game with the money were actually punishing, then the weight loss would have stopped; therefore, the "punishment" was not punishing at all (Bandura, 1986). He did not mention it, but surely there was some rewarding effect in playing this bizarre game with the clinic staff. Would you find it "punishing" to be told to cut money up into little pieces, especially if you were led to believe that it would help you lose weight? Doing something outrageous can be a lot of fun.

Whatever the conclusion, the Rachlin/Castro/Bandura debate illustrates the complexity involved in self-administered contingencies. All agree on one point: Contingent consequences work. But how?

to keep to his goal. A year later, he was a strong and enthusiastic aerobicizer. His new feelings of health and attractiveness were reinforcement enough, and he exercised regularly without women present (though he still liked doing it better when they were around).

Another student had developed the habit of swearing excessively. His baseline average was more than 150 swearwords per 8 hours. He worked out a plan in which he received strong reinforcers from his wife if he reduced his daily average of swearwords by 10% for one week. Unfortunately, he never made it to the end of the week. After one or two days of good language, he would revert to his old habits. We advised him to reduce the delay of reinforcement. His new contract, agreed to by his wife, called for *daily* reinforcement if he reduced his undesired language by 10%.

The general principle is that the reinforcer should be delivered as quickly as is reasonable after the desired behavior is performed. In some cases, *it is vital that the delay be extremely short.* This is especially true when the undesired behavior consists of consummatory or fear responses. For example, a cigarette in the mouth *right now* is more reinforcing than the thought of cleaner lungs six months from now. A bite of pie in the mouth *right now* feels a lot better than that remote picture of the scales, weeks or even months from now, showing a drop of several pounds. Biting your nails *right now* is more rewarding than the thought of the movie you will go to as a reinforcer Saturday night.

The same kind of problem exists for people who are afraid of some situation, such as talking in front of an audience or going into the water to swim. It feels much better to avoid the feared situation *right now* than to think about how good it will feel to get a reinforcer at the end of the week.

Whenever the target behavior has to do with very strong habits or feared objects, provide yourself with positive reinforcement immediately after performing the desired behavior. For example, a smoker asked his wife to praise him immediately each time he resisted the impulse to light a cigarette.

Tokens

When you cannot arrange to have the reinforcer follow quickly after the behavior, **token reinforcers** are appropriate. A token is a symbolic reinforcer—symbolic because it can be converted into real reinforcement. Money, for example, is our major token reinforcer, for it is the things money can buy that make money attractive and thus represent the real reinforcement. Such devices as poker chips, gold stars, check marks, ticket punches, and dollar bills have all been used as tokens.

Many people choose a *point system* of token reinforcement to modify their behaviors. The performance of a desired behavior earns a specified number of "points" that can be "spent" for reinforcement. The cost of reinforcement—so many points per reinforcer—is specified in the point-system contract.

The main function of tokens and points is to bridge the delay between the time you perform the desired behavior and the time you can take the reinforcer. For many people, the chosen reinforcer is something they are going to do at the day's end. They may use a particularly nice supper, an opportunity to watch TV, or a talk with friends in the evening as a reinforcer contingent on their having performed the target behavior earlier in the day. For all these delayed reinforcers, tokens can be used during the day to provide immediacy.

A man who wanted to substitute being nice to friends for being rude to friends selected watching TV in the evening as his reinforcer. He couldn't be sure when the opportunity to be nice to his friends would arise during the day and couldn't rush off to watch TV as soon as he had performed his target behavior, so he decided to use a token system. He carried a 3″ × 5″ card in his pocket and made a check on it when he performed the target behavior. Then, later in the evening, he would allow himself to watch TV if he had earned the number of points his shaping schedule required for that day. He used his tokens cumulatively. The more points he earned during the day, the more TV he could watch at night. His "menu" looked like this:

1 token	30 minutes of TV watching
2 tokens	60 minutes
3 tokens	90 minutes
4 tokens	as much as I want

This is a simple point system. By adding behaviors and rewards, a point system can be expanded into a complex token "economy." A group of five students who lived together had difficulty in arranging their household duties fairly and reliably. The three men and two women devised a *group* self-modification plan, using the point system that follows. It specified each important household task, along with the points to be awarded for doing each one, and it specified the reinforcers that the household had to offer, along with the number of points that each would cost. Each member was free to choose both tasks and reinforcers.

Tasks	*Points*
Prepare evening meal	150
Do laundry	200
Prepare sandwiches	80
Plan meals	40
Prepare extra snacks	80
Plan shopping	60
Wash up dishes (major)	30
Weekly shopping	200
Wash up dishes (minor)	10
Minor shopping	30
Dry up dishes (major)	30
Record prices (major)	60
Dry up dishes (minor)	10
Record prices (minor)	10
Clean living room	30
Write down recipe	25
Clean kitchen	30

(continued)

Tasks	*Points*
Write diary	25
Clean bathroom	30
Empty fireplace	10
Tidy living room	10
Put out milk bottle	5
Take in milk	30
Pay milk bill	30
Tie refuse sack	5
Put refuse out	30
Tidy sink	10
Reinforcers	
Evening meal	50
Lunch	20
Film	50
Drink	50
Meeting etc.	50

SOURCE: "The Use of a Token Economy to Regulate Household Behaviours," by J. F. Masterson and A. C. Vaux, 1982, *Behavioural Psychotherapy, 10,* 65-78. Copyright 1982 by the British Association of Behavioural Psychotherapy. Reprinted by permission.

The group members kept careful records and were convinced that the point system made their household run more smoothly. More tasks were performed on time, and the members all felt that the work and benefits were distributed fairly. In fact, it was typical that more points were earned than were ever spent. They concluded that their mutual encouragement and verbal reinforcement provided rewards in addition to the points (Masterson & Vaux, 1982).

Notice also that the group's list of reinforcers included several items, from food to watching films. This illustrates another advantage of point systems: You can use a variety of reinforcers for the same behaviors; this will help keep reinforcement fresh and desirable. If you can exchange your earned points for watching TV, having a snack, or playing with the dog, you can choose the reinforcer that is most attractive to you at the moment. One of our students included as the last item on his reinforcement menu: "Every Saturday morning, *anything* I want to do!"

A point system can be adjusted to surgical precision. One of our students, who was trying to lose weight, wrote:

This was my first point system:

Eating a light, balanced breakfast	1 point
Eating a light, balanced lunch	1 point
Eating a light, balanced supper	1 point
Eating no more than two light snacks per day	1 point
Daily exercise	1 point

When I got 35 points, I could buy an art poster.

Then I noticed where I was failing most often—too much snacking on weekends. So I added an item:

On Saturday and Sunday, no more than two light snacks

My second big insight was that I would earn 3 or 4 points each day, and then pig out on a snack or supper and blow the calorie count for the rest of the day. So I added another item:

Bonus for a perfect day	3 points

That did it!

Box 7-4 presents an excellent self-modification plan that incorporates three of the principles discussed so far in this chapter. To increase exercising, this woman used self-reinforcement (a small amount of money), a husband/mediator to dispense larger rewards, and a point system to bridge the gap between performance and the delayed larger rewards. Good self-modification plans integrate several techniques.

Imagined (Covert) Reinforcement

If things, people, or activities act as reinforcers, imagining them may also be reinforcing (Ascher, 1973; Blanchard & Draper, 1973; Cautela, 1972; Cautela & Samdperil, 1989; Epstein & Peterson, 1973a, 1973b; Krop, Calhoon, & Verrier, 1971; Marshall, Boutilier, & Minnes, 1974; Wisocki, 1973). **Imagined reinforcers** have been traditionally called **covert reinforcers** by behavior analysts.

Imagined reinforcers are probably not as powerful as their actual counterparts. But imagined reinforcers have the advantage of being completely portable and easily accessible. Although you may be unable to travel or to go skin diving during the winter, you can imagine doing so. Imagining pleasant and relaxing scenes, such as a lazy swim on a hot day, can be used to reward yourself for performing a desired behavior (Cautela, 1973).

Imagined reinforcement is used the same way as any other kind of reinforcement: It is arranged to follow a desirable behavior.

You can record the frequencies of your thoughts and fantasies and select imagined reinforcers as you would other reinforcers. Cautela (1983) insists that imagined reinforcers need not always be based in reality—you can imagine riding in a spaceship or winning a gold medal. Or you can imagine any of the reinforcers you discovered when you answered the 21 questions in the section on positive reinforcers.

The best imagined reinforcement is an anticipation of rewarding, realistic outcomes. Dieters can use images of themselves after losing weight—slim, attractive, athletic, fashionably dressed, or whatever image of themselves reflects the wish they want to fulfill by losing weight (Horan, Baker, Hoffman, & Shute, 1975)—to reinforce their dieting (Cautela, 1972). This kind of reinforcer has the advantage of being realistic and logical and of representing a

BOX 7-4

Self-Modification of Exercise Behavior

While regular exercise itself can be reinforcing to some persons, for [this woman] it was not. In order to establish and maintain an exercise habit, an attempt at self-directed behavior change seemed appropriate.

Method

A prior attempt to establish an exercise routine using the Premack principle (tooth brushing at night contingent upon the completion of a series of calisthenics) had not been successful, for the contingency was ignored. Therefore, the present plan placed control of the reinforcers in the hands of another person. The husband was the logical choice, and the intervention plan was put into a written contract that he and she signed. The plan had the following features:

1. The form of exercise was jogging.
2. Money and social activities of the woman's choice (for example, going to a movie or eating at a restaurant) were the reinforcers. She received 25¢ immediately after jogging. At the end of each week, if she had jogged every day (and earned $1.75), she could select and engage in one of several possible social activities with her husband. Otherwise, none of the social activities was permitted.
3. The husband dispensed the reinforcers and tabulated points.
4. In addition, points were earned for jogging. The long-term goal was set at 40 points per week . . . where 4 points could be earned by jogging 1 mile within 9.59 min. and . . . more earned by increasing the distance . . . and reducing the time. This was approached through a series of intermediate steps. The plan was to begin with the jogging of 1 mile, with gradual increments of 0.25 miles.

Results

The results of the intervention plan can be seen in Figure 7-1. At the end of the first week of intervention, 20 points were earned, representing a sharp increase in exercise activity from a baseline of zero. After this initial spurt, progress slowed but increased to 23 points in the second week. Jogging had occurred on only four days, but, because of the increased distance run, more points were earned. The third week showed a drop in total number of points to 19. Jogging had occurred on four days, and again during the fourth week of intervention occurred on only four days of the week. Up to this point, the social-activity reinforcer had not been given, because jogging had not occurred daily during any of the four weeks. A change in the program was adopted at the start of the fifth week. The activity reinforcer was made available after earning 25 or more points per week (rather than running every day), and the 25¢

bridge to the world of actual contingencies. Not only will reinforcement benefits be present, but long-range goals will be brought to mind, and thus commitment will be strengthened again. The depressed person can use anticipation of feeling good to reinforce efforts to overcome low moods; the smoker can imagine better health and breath to reinforce efforts to stop payment was eliminated. This was followed by an increase in total points to 27 for the fifth week. The twelfth week showed the highest level of activity, with 38½ points earned—only 1½ points short of the long-term goal, even though the activity reinforcer had been eliminated at the beginning of the tenth week.

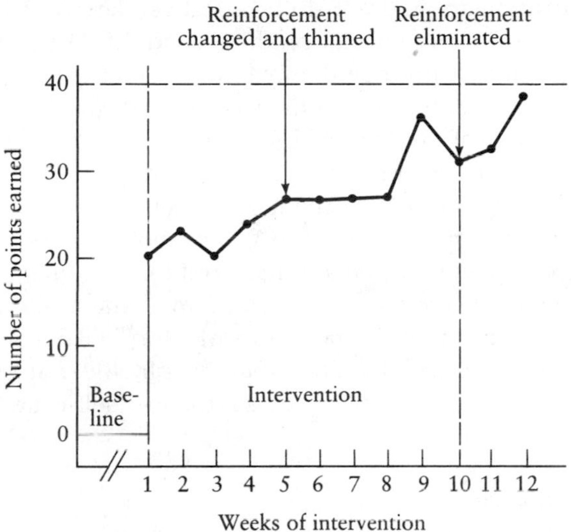

Figure 7-1 Number of points earned by exercising

Formal reinforcement was terminated before the long-term goal (40 points per week) was reached, for two reasons. First, the subject had become satiated with the activity reinforcer. For two weeks prior to its elimination, she had earned enough points to gain the reinforcer but had not bothered to "collect" it. Second, the natural positive results of regular physical exercise were being noticed. She felt better and more energetic than when she began the program. She had lost several pounds without any change in eating habits. With these natural reinforcements, the long-term goal was soon reached. As the natural environment had taken over and begun to maintain the desired behavior, the program was judged to have been successful.

The key to the success may have been the placement of control of the program with another person. The mediator, the husband, was firm in his commitment to the plan and the rules agreed upon. The contingency between the behavior and the reinforcers was maintained rigorously.

SOURCE: "Self-Modification of Exercise Behavior," by M. L. Kau and J. Fischer, 1974, *Journal of Behavior Therapy and Experimental Psychiatry, 5,* 213–214. Copyright 1974 by Pergamon Press, Ltd. Reprinted by permission.

smoking; the test-anxious person can imagine being able to take tests calmly and getting back an "A."

It is also possible to imagine unrelated reinforcers, such as some favorite pleasant scenes. Particularly in anxiety-producing situations, such as test taking, this kind of unrelated reinforcer may have some advantage if the imagined scene helps to produce relaxation. Such relaxation can produce a respondent conditioning effect, increasing relaxation in the test-taking situation (Bajtelsmit & Gershman, 1976).

Although there are many advantages to using imagined reinforcement, a few words of caution are in order. To be effective, the images must be vivid (Wisocki, 1973). Not everyone can produce vivid, lifelike images; therefore, it is necessary that you practice the imagined reinforcement until you can almost feel the water, almost touch the clothes, or hear the music almost as clearly as if you were at the concert. Use many senses in imagining—smells, sounds, sights, physical feelings (Cautela & Samdperil, 1989). To practice, begin by calling up scenes from memory, which may produce more vivid images than purely imagined scenes. If you cannot produce images as vivid as memories, you should not rely on imagined reinforcement.

Imagined reinforcement has been studied most intensely in combination with thought stopping: after saying the word "stop," take a deep breath and relax while exhaling through the nose; then imagine the reinforcing pleasant scene. Cautela (1983) refers to this sequence as the "self-control triad."

Verbal Self-Reinforcement

Praise is one of the fundamental methods of control in all human society. Parents, teachers, coaches, politicians, and lovers all encourage behavior by praising. **Verbal reinforcement** is only a technical term for praise and an acknowledgment that praise is a powerful reinforcer. Here we discuss verbal *self*-reinforcement—that is, self-encouragement following desired behavior. Recall the discussion of the power of bringing self-directions up from the underground. That same technique can be used to increase the reinforcing power of self-speech as well. Every individual experiences pleasure at meeting a goal and at behaving according to his or her own standards. But if that pleasure can be made verbal, brought up from the underground, it takes on stronger reinforcing properties.

The technique is merely to tell yourself, "Good! I did it." Say it either covertly or aloud, but say it clearly. Say it after each instance of your desired behavior (Meichenbaum, 1977; Shelton et al., 1981).

Self-praise is often omitted from self-modification plans for three reasons. First, you may think it sounds silly or absurd. It is not. Don't underestimate the power of language. Second, you may think self-reinforcement is conceited or "bragging." That is also incorrect because bragging is an effort to get reinforcement from others. Verbal self-reinforcement is a way of marking off your successes justly and privately (Rehm, 1982). Third, self-praise may be omitted from self-direction plans because of a long habit of self-criticism and generally low self-esteem. In such cases, the problem is interfering with the solution: because you are depressed, you are perpetuating depression.

Some individuals reinforce themselves less than others do regardless of their situations or activities. Depressed individuals have a lower frequency of self-reinforcement than do nondepressed people (Heiby, 1981), and depressed people use verbal self-*punishment* frequently (Rehm, 1982). Does low self-reinforcement "cause" depression? Not necessarily, but those who are low self-reinforcers may be at higher risk for depression. When external reinforcement is lost, low self-reinforcers are more likely than others to become depressed (Heiby, 1983a, 1983b).

The loss of external reinforcement and support—a run of bad grades, the loss of a friend or a loved one, the loss of a job—can make anyone depressed. But those who have the skill to reinforce, encourage, and support themselves are less likely to be pitched into a severe depression. Self-reinforcers are better able to ride out periods when external reinforcement is taken away.

If you have difficulty in praising yourself contingently, make that goal a part of your plan. Positive self-statements can themselves be increased by reinforcement (Krop, Calhoon, & Verrier, 1971; Krop, Perez, & Beaudoin, 1973). Giving yourself reminders (cues) to make positive self-statements and then following the statements with some form of reward is an effective procedure (Epstein & Hersen, 1974).

Noncontingent Positive Events

Are there ever any conditions when positive events should be added to your life freely, richly, and noncontingently? Indeed there are, and the discussion of depression leads naturally into this topic. A life that is empty of pleasant events is almost certain to be a depressed life. Psychologists, as well as depressed people, have puzzled for years as to whether or not simply increasing pleasant events will cause depression to lift. There is now evidence that increasing pleasant events increases positive aspects of well-being in general (Reich & Zautra, 1981). Peter Lewinsohn's influential theory suggests that depression is brought about by the loss of external reinforcement, and his suggested treatment includes increasing pleasant activities (for example, MacPhillamy & Lewinsohn, 1982).

Most psychologists recommend that pleasant events be arranged to follow some behavior that will contribute to decreasing depression. Pleasant events can be used to reward making new social contacts, to reward assertive responses, to reward better study habits, and the like. But *in addition* to these tactics, merely increasing pleasant activities in general is a wise course for those suffering depression.

In fact, a general change in the balance of pleasant to unpleasant events is advisable for people wrestling with a variety of problems. Binge eaters, as an example, are known to lack sufficient "self-nurturance" and to be good to themselves only through eating (Lehman & Rodin, 1989). Marlatt and Parks (1982) discuss this in terms of getting the "wants" in balance with the "shoulds." A life that is too filled with duties that are felt as "shoulds," with little time for enjoying the things that are "wants," is a life set up for problems. Problems are likely to erupt in destructive binges of consumption: food, drink, drugs, or escapism. For such situations, Marlatt and Parks (1982) suggest a change in lifestyle, including time for relaxation each day: time for meditation, time for exercise, or especially "free time"—the opportunity to do whatever is pleasant and available at the moment. Box 7-5 illustrates that plans for increasing behavior through this kind of reinforcement will produce a higher quality of experienced life.

The irony is that those people who most need to increase pleasant events are the ones least likely to do so. In fact, increasing free pleasant events may have to be taken as a goal for self-modification, and that plan will require reinforcement for increasing pleasant events!

Marsha, one of our 19-year-old students, was struggling to stay in school. She had registered for morning classes starting at 7:30 because at 2:00 each weekday she reported to the bakery where she was a salesclerk. She worked until 10:00 each night. Then she had papers to write, exams to prepare for, and all the tasks of personal life. She lived with her partially disabled mother, so housework, laundry, and shopping occupied most of her time on the weekends. She dated very rarely, and Sundays she slept, exhausted and dull.

Marsha's first step toward self-modification was to create her catalog of reinforcers. It included such things as new clothes and a new stereo, but it became clear to her that she had no time to wear new dresses and no time

BOX 7-5

Increasing Honest Thoughts by Reinforcement

A student suffered from persistent depression. She believed that she would be far less depressed if she could be honest with herself and others. Thus, her target behavior was to increase the number of "honest, authentic statements made to myself and other people." Examples she gave of "honest, authentic statements" were the following:

- That made me angry!
- Even if she is my sister, I don't like what she is doing.
- I just put on an act—a good act, but totally phony.
- I don't agree. Pro football is brutal.

Figure 7-2 shows the frequencies of this student's honest statements. After 20 days of baseline self-observation, she began her first intervention plan. She called it "autosuggestion" and required herself each morning to "*will* myself to feel better, psych myself up, just not indulge my black morning moods." For about three weeks, the plan worked. Her number of honest statements climbed, and so did her mood. Then both quickly tumbled. At that point, she began the following full program of tokenized reinforcement.

> For each verbal expression of feeling or opinion (talking to myself included), I will award myself 1 point, to be redeemed on the following schedule: For each 5 points, I'll have 15 minutes of free time to do anything I choose; *or* each point will be paid in money at the rate of 1 cent per point, and this money can be spent on "luxury" things I usually wouldn't buy. Bonus for attaining a new high will be rewarded by a special event of equal value. Also, for each time my morning autosuggestion

to listen to new tapes. Each reinforcer she listed required time for its enjoyment, and what Marsha did *not* have was time.

Where was it to come from? Where could any pleasant events fit into that life crowded with "shoulds"? On analysis, she realized that the weekend might be rearranged: Saturdays were stuffed with all the duties, Sundays were a dead loss of sluggish sleep and dullness.

There were three things Marsha wanted to do but had never managed to arrange: visit a favorite aunt, practice yoga, and attend a discussion group. How could she motivate herself to rearrange her weekends to allow for these pleasant events? For several weeks, she never "got around" to it. Her final plan involved the use of the Premack principle. Of all her duties, the one she enjoyed most was housekeeping, which she performed vigorously and with pleasure. So she selected one behavior, cleaning the bathroom, and did not allow herself to perform it until after she had done at least one of her desired pleasant activities. The outcome of this plan was an increase in the three desired activities, less sleeping and moping on Sunday—and the bathroom stayed as clean as ever.

works, I will get 5 points. My morning coffee will also be contingent on getting myself into a better mood.

Her honest statements quickly jumped to more than 30 a day. There were ups and downs, but the average stabilized at more than 20. She terminated the plan after about a month and a half. Psychological tests, and her own report, showed that her depression was remarkably improved (Tharp, Watson, & Kaya, 1974).

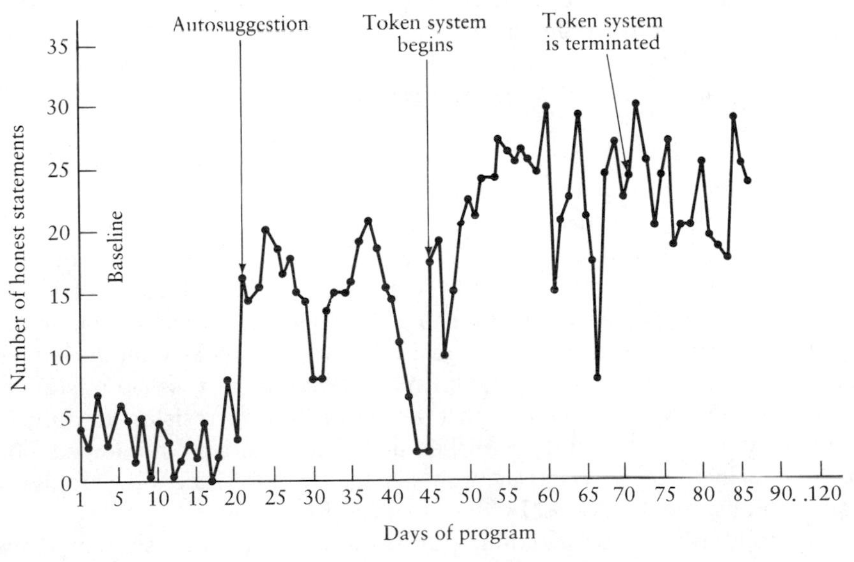

Figure 7-2 Number of honest statements per day

The point of Marsha's case is this: Although it is often desirable to make changes in your lifestyle so that free, noncontingent pleasant activities are increased, it may be necessary to use reinforcement plans to bring that about.

Self-Punishment and Extinction

Extinction

Extinction is the weakening of a behavior by withdrawing reinforcement from it. This is a simple strategy when used in the laboratory. If an experimental animal is no longer given food pellets, it will eventually quit pressing the bar. In self-direction, however, extinction is more complicated. When real-life reinforcers are withdrawn, an immediate burst of the undesirable behavior may occur. Following that, even when the behavior is reduced, other behaviors will certainly rush in to fill the vacuum, and if those new behaviors are not planned for, they may be as problematic as the original. When used alone, extinction is very rarely an effective self-directing strategy.

The following case illustrates the point. A student wanted to reduce the frequency of cutting his trigonometry class. His midterm grade was "D," and it was obvious that poor attendance was the reason. His A-B-C analysis clearly showed that class cutting was being reinforced by shooting pool and playing pinball because he was going to the Billiard Palace instead of the classroom. His plan called for withdrawing this reinforcer: When he cut class, he would go home immediately. But this plan didn't result in less class cutting; instead, he found himself listening to the stereo in his room. The correct procedure here would have been to reinforce class attendance, perhaps by making going to the Billiard Palace contingent on it. *When you withdraw reinforcement from an undesired behavior, you should simultaneously increase reinforcement for the alternative, desired behavior.*

Why Punishment Alone Is Insufficient

Punishment alone is usually an undesirable strategy. This is true for either kind of punishment—adding an aversive stimulus to a situation or removing a positive event. Most plans that rely solely on punishment don't work. For example, people who used self-punishing statements and thoughts for smoking transgressions were less able to resist the urge to smoke than those who used any other kind of strategy (Shiffman, 1984). In fact, self-punishment can make things worse. One way that behaviors become resistant to punishment is by being first mildly punished and then positively reinforced. You might actually increase the behavior's resistance to punishment by supplying a small punishment followed by the usual reinforcement.

A second reason for avoiding punishment is that punishment alone doesn't teach new behaviors. Punishment suppresses the behavior it follows, but what happens *instead* is determined by the reinforcement that follows the behavior that is substituted. Your plan should provide for designating and reinforcing desired alternatives to your problem behaviors. Otherwise, the plan is incomplete.

One of our students had three part-time jobs plus a full load at college. Her first plan consisted of punishing herself for *not* performing a desired behavior by depriving herself of one of the few things in her life that she enjoyed. She had somehow managed to keep two hours free every Friday afternoon, and she always used them to go to the beach with a close friend. In her plan, she proposed to punish excessive eating by giving up this weekly pleasure. We strongly disagreed with that idea. Her life needed enrichment, not a further impoverishment of positive reinforcers. We suggested that she reward dieting by adding another social activity—if necessary, at the expense of her quite adequate study time. To lose her one weekly contact with a friend would have made her even more dependent on her only other real pleasure—food. Besides, her overall happiness required a broader spectrum of pleasant events. Punishment would have restricted her life and would also have made dieting less likely.

The third reason for not including punishment in your plan is that you will be less likely to carry out your plan. In a course in behavioral self-control, Worthington (1979) found that only one-third of the students actually inflicted self-punishment when their plans called for it.

When you are performing some undesired behavior, you should be able to positively reinforce an incompatible behavior instead of punishing the undesired behavior. Reinforce nail grooming instead of punishing nail biting. Before you decide to use punishment, search for an incompatible behavior that you can positively reinforce instead.

The Loss of Positive Events as Punishment

If you insist on using punishment, it should involve giving up something pleasant. This is better than using an aversive stimulus as punishment (Kazdin, 1973).

Here are some examples of punishment in the form of giving up usual pleasures. One person might not allow herself to take a customary bath if she has not studied enough. Another might not allow himself to eat certain preferred foods if he has performed some undesired behavior. If you are accustomed to going to a movie on Saturday night, you could punish yourself for your nonperformance of a target behavior by staying home. Many people use the general category of "things I do for fun" to require themselves to perform some target behavior before they allow themselves to engage in the "fun" activities. Another student, who was in love with a man in another state, used the daily letters she received from him. Each day she handed the unopened letter to a friend. If she performed her target behavior, she got the letter back unopened. If she did not perform the target behavior, her friend was instructed to open and read the love letter.

A few of our students have had success with such plans, but a better strategy is to combine positive reinforcement with punishment so that you lose *additional* rewards, not customary ones. A plan to increase studying could call for an extra movie per week if your goal is met, but only if your goal is met.

A token system can be used for a combination program. Lutzker and Lutzker (1974) reported a program used by a dieter with the help of her husband. She could earn several reinforcers for losing a half-pound or more each week, but the most effective part of the plan involved a "household duties" punishment. Before beginning the plan, she and her husband divided the household chores into "his" and "hers," with the husband taking on more chores than he had before. Each week, after her weigh-in, if she had lost weight or stayed even, he continued doing the chores on his list for the next week. If she had gained weight, she had to do his chores in addition to her own. She lost weight.

Precommitted Punishment

Precommitment refers to making some arrangement in advance so that you will be more likely to choose behaviors that are in your long-term best interest. **Precommitted punishment,** therefore, means arranging in advance that some particular punishing event will take place if you perform a certain undesired act. Precommitted punishment may be appropriate when the undesired behavior is so rewarding that no new reinforcers can be found to counter it. A woman who was trying to stop eating late-night snacks would tell her daughter, who lived with her, "If I eat anything after 8:00 P.M., I'll give you $20."

You can arrange advance control of yourself by giving over some kind of forfeit to a helper. For example, you can require yourself to study for two hours before going to a movie. To enforce this behavior, you can give a friend $10 and instruct the friend to call you every half hour from 7:00 to 9:00. If you don't answer the telephone, the friend is to mail the money to your worst enemy (Rachlin, 1974). One of our students wanted to completely eliminate using sugar, no longer adding it to coffee, cereal, or other foods. So she selected a cup from her treasured collection of handmade coffee cups, marked it with a piece of tape on the bottom, and instructed her husband to break it if she used any sugar.

In these precommitment strategies, the trick is to make the penalty so heavy that in fact you never apply it. Precommitment should work as a *deterrent,* not as a *punishment.* In this way, precommitment is consistent with our general recommendation that you should not actually punish yourself. In precommitting, you must arrange for penalties that would be so unpleasant that you simply won't incur them. The woman who offered to pay her daughter if she ate late at night only had to pay once in six months. That one time was enough to keep her out of the kitchen.

A heavy forfeit, however, presents problems of its own. The specter of a great loss may create new anxieties, and the helper who holds the forfeit may begin to seem a menace. A middle-aged man was determined to stop smoking. His wife, who had recently stopped, was willing to cooperate to almost any extent. The husband was an avid collector of cacti and other small succulent plants. Over the years, his garden had grown down the wall and into the lawn, and even the kitchen counter often held young plants as a kind of incubator. His precommitment plan arranged that for every cigarette he smoked, his wife was to destroy one young cactus. The precommitment worked, in the sense that he smoked no cigarettes for seven days. But the threat was intolerable. He prowled the house and garden wondering which plant would be sacrificed if he smoked. And how would they die—drowned in the toilet or crushed under his wife's heel? After one week, he canceled the agreement and felt at ease with his wife once again.

Any form of self-punishment, even when used as a deterrent, brings about problems and should be approached carefully. Precommitted punishment should be used only temporarily and only when you can quickly bring desirable behavior under the control of positive reinforcement or natural rewards (Rachlin, 1974).

Punishment as a Temporary Solution

Punishment can be a temporary, partial tactic for achieving some goals. But, remember, it is only temporary and only partial. There is no point in using self-punishment except when it leads to positive reinforcers.

One form of self-punishment can perhaps be recommended in the early stages of self-direction—"punishment" of facing up to the negative consequences of a problem behavior. Imagining the real consequences of shoplifting, for example, can be a powerful deterrent: prison, publicity, and the loss of contact with family and friends (Gauthier & Pellerin, 1982). Imagining the continued loneliness and frustration of social withdrawal can provide strong motivation to persevere in building social skills. A systematic plan for reminding yourself of these long-range punishments can keep you from drifting from your goals. Force yourself to read the latest figures on cancer and smoking. Youdin and Hemmes (1978) recommend to dieters that they stare at their naked bodies in the mirror for 60 seconds a day while thinking about overeating. Rosen (1981) reports a successful program for weight loss in which dieters agreed that if they decided to overeat, they would do so while watching themselves in a mirror, with as few clothes on as possible. The dieters found the vision "disgusting" and commonly stopped the eating session. One of our colleagues told us she succeeded in eliminating fat from her diet by imagining that she was injecting fat directly into her bloodstream whenever she ate some fatty food. Both of your authors have imagined themselves as pot-gutted and too slow on the tennis court and thus have found strength to push the dessert aside.

Ancient Buddhist systems of thought control have also emphasized that unwanted thoughts can be controlled by considering their consequences.

> If you are burdened with distasteful thoughts, be like young men and women who want to be clean and well-dressed, and then find the carcass of a snake or dog around their necks. See the effects on you! Immediately get rid of it! (paraphrased from de Silva, 1985, p. 439)

Reminding yourself of the negative consequences of some problem behavior can be considered not only as punishment, but also as another way of building and maintaining commitment.

Reinforcement in Plans for Self-Modification

Now we must consider the place of reinforcement in the A-B-C sequence. Powerful as reinforcement may be, it must be organized into a total intervention plan that involves antecedents, behaviors, and consequences. As you read this section, bear in mind the preliminary plans you have developed in Steps five (antecedents) and six (developing new behaviors) of your own self-direction project. By adding reinforcing contingencies to these plans, you will bring them to full potential.

For example, as you begin to adopt self-reinforcement plans, and observe yourself carrying them out, then, observing the improvements, include new self-statements about the reinforcement. Tell yourself, "I did it," and, "I can control it." Increasing your felt ability at self-directed reinforcement will have its own good effects on your behavior change.

Reinforcement and Antecedent Control

In Chapter 5, we described several methods for achieving antecedent control: avoiding antecedents, narrowing them, and building new ones by performing the desired behavior in new situations. *Each of these tactics involves a behavior change that should also be reinforced.*

For example, avoiding old antecedents was recommended as a first tactic for reducing undesirable consummatory responses. Thus, avoiding the morning cup of coffee can reduce the temptation to smoke; avoiding parties, at least for a while, can help bring overeating, pot smoking, or drinking under control. But this tactic involves a sharp decrease in reinforcement because old reinforcers are lost. Therefore, new reinforcement is needed—reinforcement gained for avoiding the old antecedents.

The dieter who refused dinner invitations for a month arranged with his wife that they would go to a movie on the nights when the parties were held. A student who was smoking marijuana reinforced her avoidance of pot parties by having a long telephone chat with a friend the next morning. The young man who avoided excessive masturbation by choosing a busier restroom carried a paperback mystery with him and read it only while using the new facility. Each of these plans replaced the lost reinforcement with a new one, made contingent on avoiding an antecedent.

The same principle applies to behaviors performed in the presence of new antecedents: reinforcement should follow.

Reinforcement and the Development of New Behaviors

The necessity of reinforcing most new behaviors is a general principle, which we will illustrate with a discussion of two topics: imagined rehearsal and shaping.

Imagined rehearsal. Imagined (covert) rehearsals influence real performances. In rehearsing a desired behavior in your imagination, it is useful to follow it with an imagined reinforcement (Kazdin, 1974a).

Cautela (1972, 1973) gives several examples of imagined reinforcers, such as swimming on a hot day and hearing good music. Suppose you are a dieter who wants to practice control of overeating. Sometime during the day, wherever you happen to be, you imagine you are "sitting at home watching TV. . . . You say to yourself 'I think I'll have a piece of pie.' You get up to go to the pantry. Then you say, 'This is stupid. I don't want to be a fat pig.' " You should follow this imagined scene with the imagined reinforcement—the swim or the music. Here is another scene you can rehearse in imagination: "You are at home eating steak. You are just about to reach for your second piece, and you stop and say to yourself, 'Who needs it, anyway?'" (Cautela, 1972, p. 213) and then imagine your reinforcer.

Imagined rehearsal can be a way of practicing when your own behaviors are not yet firm enough to earn reinforcement in the real world. A young man who had almost no experience or skills in approaching young women was taught to imagine the following scene and to self-reinforce it with imagined swimming in a warm river.

> Say to yourself "I think I'll call Jane for a date." As soon as you have this scene clearly, switch quickly to the reinforcement. As soon as you have the reinforcement vividly, hold it for two seconds. Then imagine that you walk to the phone and start to dial (reinforcement). You finish dialing. She answers. You say hello and ask her if she is free Saturday night. You tell her that you would like to go out with her. . . . Now do the whole sequence again. Make sure that the image is vivid. You can see the kitchen, feel the telephone. This time try to imagine that you are comfortable and confident as you call. (Cautela, 1973, p. 30)

A similar example, adapted from Kazdin (1974a), is for the person who wants to become more assertive.

1. Imagine that you are eating in a restaurant with friends. You order a steak and tell the waiter you would like it rare. When the food arrives, you begin to eat and notice that it is overcooked.
2. Imagine that you immediately signal the waiter. When he arrives, you say, "I ordered this steak rare, and this one is medium. Please take it back and bring me one that is rare."
3. Imagine that in a few minutes the waiter brings another steak, rare, and says he is very sorry this has happened.*

When imagining assertiveness—saying no when a person asks for a favor you really don't want to do, protesting against being shortchanged, objecting when someone cuts in front of you in a line, sending an undercooked steak back—let the positive reinforcement grow naturally out of the rehearsed be-

*SOURCE: "Effects of Covert Modeling and Model Reinforcement on Assertive Behavior," by A. E. Kazdin, 1974, *Journal of Abnormal Psychology, 83*, 240–252.

havior: You get the steak you want! If you are rehearsing in your imagination how to deal with a persistent door-to-door salesperson, you can follow your imagined firmness by imagining the person leaving quickly and your own feelings of competence and self-assurance. Whenever possible, use a desirable "natural outcome" as your reinforcer. The advantage of using brief, independent scenes is that you can reinforce the various stages along the way.

Shaping. The technique of shaping also illustrates the necessity of reinforcing all new behaviors. There is one remaining rule for correct shaping: Each step must be reinforced.

The definition of each shaping step is actually a standard or criterion. For example:

Step 1:	2000 calories per day
Step 2:	1800 calories per day
Reinforcer:	One hour of television per evening

For step 1, the reinforcer is taken when the standard for that step is met (2000 calories). For step 2, the standard becomes 1800 calories daily, and only then will television be watched.

Shaping steps are no different from any other behavior. If their natural consequences are not yet strong enough, they require arranged reinforcement. The case of Linda (Chapter 6), who feared birds, is a good illustration. As she built a schedule of steps closer and closer to the birds she feared, she didn't use any extra reinforcement at first because she received strong rewards from her pride in mastering the fear. But when her schedule brought her quite close to the birds, she got stuck. At this point, Linda introduced a token system. For each step in her shaping schedule, she earned so many points, which she could turn in at the end of the day to "buy" certain privileges, such as allowing herself extra dates, doing "idiot" reading, and so on. Her goal was to increase her total positive reinforcements so that she would gain something for getting really close to the birds. In Linda's case, two separate forms of reinforcement were employed. One was the formal token system. The earlier, less obvious reinforcement was the presence of her boyfriend. She originally elected to include him because his presence made her feel more relaxed. But his walking beside her also had reinforcing value for the approach behavior.

Cheating. Taking the reinforcer without having performed the target behavior is a fairly common occurrence in self-modification. Almost everyone does it sometimes. You should watch yourself very carefully, however, because cheating more than occasionally—say, more than 10% of the time—indicates a shaping problem. In that case, you should redesign your shaping schedule so that you will be reinforced for performing at some level that you find realistic. As long as you are able to provide a contingent reinforcement, you are building toward the final goal, no matter how small the steps are or how low you begin. If you cheat, don't abandon the project—redesign it.

A young man whose final goal was to save $7 each week began by requiring himself to save 50¢ each day (he put it in a piggy bank), even though he had almost never saved any money before. He used the reinforcer of eating supper only after he had put the money in his piggy bank. After three days, he skipped his saving for one day but went ahead and ate supper anyway. This was the beginning of a two-week period during which he skipped more often than he saved but ate his supper anyway. He realized that this kind of cheating was due to a problem in his shaping program. So he wrote a new contract in which he required himself to save only 25¢ each day—a more realistic place to begin, in his case—in order to gain the reinforcer.

When to Include Self-Reinforcement in Your Intervention Plan

Now that we have discussed methods for adding reinforcement to self-change projects, both for antecedent control and for developing new behaviors, the questions to be answered are: When should self-reinforcement be included in the project? When can it be omitted?

We suggest the following rule of thumb: During the process of learning, make sure that any *new* behavior is followed promptly by some reinforcement. Some behaviors will be reinforced naturally and immediately, merely by being performed, and require no contrived reinforcement. For example, a tennis player who coaches herself with self-instructions will be reinforced by the swift consequences of her improved play. In social interactions, the game is also swift, and improved behaviors are likely to produce their own rewards. In such situations, inserting self-reinforcement after each performance of the behavior can be distracting.

Ten to fifteen years ago there was a flurry of research on the **overjustification** hypothesis—the idea that tangible rewards can actually reduce motivation for behaviors that people already enjoy and perform well (Barrera & Rosen, 1977; Heatherington & Kirsch, 1984; Lepper & Greene, 1975). But there is no evidence for this effect in the use of social reinforcement or of self-encouragement and self-praise. For any behaviors that require shaping, and for those that need strengthening, self-reinforcement remains a strong, reliable technique.

And for many new behaviors natural reinforcement can be a long time coming—for the dieter, the beginning exerciser, the fearful, the shy, or the academically disadvantaged student who is just beginning to learn study skills (Green, 1982). Therefore, our rule of thumb—that new behavior should be followed by some reinforcement. This may not always be necessary. But don't exclude reinforcement unless you are confident that the environment itself will provide the necessary immediate reinforcement.

Objections to Self-Reinforcement

If you are encountering the idea of control through consequences for the first time, you probably find it peculiar. Some students object. They don't believe that a desired behavior *should* be deliberately self-rewarded. Virtue should be its own reward. We agree. The goal is to make your desired behavior so smooth and successful that the natural consequences of daily life will sustain it. When you reach that stage, self-reinforcement (and all the rest of your plan) can go underground: only your skill will be left showing. Self-reinforcement is a temporary strategy, like verbal self-control, to be used only until behaviors have become automated in their settings. But like talking to yourself, reinforcing your behaviors will continue to be a useful, temporary device whenever virtue again fails to reward itself enough.

Some of our students have continued to object "Even if we grant that point," they say, "you can't learn—really learn—under these conditions of self-bribery. It's all an act, not real behavior." Well, we reply, bribery is reinforcement for *inappropriate,* not desirable, behavior. Further, what is real, and what is an act? If you could put on an act of playing tennis well enough to win real matches, would you feel embarrassed because "it's just an act"? Skill is a real thing, however you learn it. But if you mean that "self-bribed" behavior cannot sustain itself, you have a point. If you are motivated to perform your new behavior only by the artificial rewards in your plan, you probably won't continue once you tire of playing the game. Remember that we cautioned you to select a behavior-change project you really value. If your changed behavior will bring greater self-respect and a happier life, then these rewarding consequences will sustain you over the long haul. Self-reinforcement is to be used only now and at those times in the future when a stronger push is needed to get you rolling again.

And remember this: *You* did it. The plan, the self-reinforcement, the changed behavior—you did it all. Take credit, take pride.

Tips for Typical Topics

Anxiety and Stress

Two basic strategies for using consequences in reducing anxieties and stress reactions are (1) avoiding reinforcement for escape, and (2) adding reinforcement for your emerging coping reactions.

By escaping a stressful situation, people stop that punishment, but the learning that results has serious disadvantages: new, successful coping skills are not learned, and new life opportunities are lost. Escaping stress by leaving social situations, by not trying out for a play, or by not attempting to join in class discussions is "self-reinforcing" in the sense that it reduces anxiety. Unfortunately, these escapes also become habitual. To escape anxiety through drinks, dope, or food creates a short-term advantage with disastrous long-term results. How can this strategy of escape and avoidance be interrupted?

From previous chapters, you have learned how to gain better control over the antecedents of anxiety and stress and how to make your new behaviors more competent and better organized. Now it is time to consider the careful reinforcement of these new behaviors. Provide reinforcement for your new coping skills, and you will be less likely to seek reward in the old escape and avoidance.

Reinforcement should be part of every plan for coping with and mastery of feared situations or for reducing the hassles of daily life. Use shaping schedules backed up by rewards from your menu of reinforcements. Particularly when dealing with anxieties and stresses, follow every instance of your new behaviors with the covert reinforcement of self-encouragement, positive statements of praise, and positive images of your new, more competent self. These quick, private thoughts and images can provide the bridges from moment-to-moment coping to the longer-term reinforcements of the earned movie or mystery book; and those reinforcements from your menu can provide the bridges to the longer-term rewards of a happier and richer life.

Assertion

Most nonassertive people suffer from the unreasonable expectation that some awful consequence will necessarily follow from their attempts to assert themselves: "If I do, he won't be my friend anymore." Instead, use imagined positive reinforcement, and anticipate favorable outcomes. If you assert yourself early, moderately, and politely, the actual consequences are likely to be pleasant. However, if you realistically expect to be punished by someone for asserting yourself (for example, by a hostile waiter who doesn't want to take your steak back), you can take steps to minimize the effects of that punishment by practicing being assertive in your imagination, by relaxing, and by concentrating on the positive consequences of your behavior (Shelton, 1979).

Use shaping and reinforcement, beginning with assertive behaviors that are likely to produce success. As you risk more, you may feel guilty or hurt after having been assertive. If these feelings persist, they will decrease your chances of maintaining the gains you have made. Try to eliminate those feelings by using thought substitution and by concentrating on the positive consequences of your newly learned assertiveness.

Some of our students have abandoned improving assertion as their goal because they were punished by others for being too "aggressive." Women in particular sometimes meet with disapproval for behavior that is interpreted as "aggressive" (Leviton, 1979), so you may want to tailor your behavior to the situation. The line between assertiveness and abrasiveness is different for every person, depending on his or her own values and the values of friends and associates.

Our own advice is to use your A-B-C journal analysis. Think over the A-B-C elements of the situations in which you felt too passive. Then reconstruct those situations as you wish you had behaved. Anticipate the consequences as they are likely to occur in your real social world, and take those into account in establishing goals. For whatever goals you choose, reinforce those gradually practiced behaviors in the ways this chapter suggests. Anticipate that others will respond to you differently. If their response is unfavorable, think again. Have you gone too far? Or is it *their* responsibility to change?

Depression and Low Self-Esteem

Use self-reinforcement to increase the frequency of your desired behaviors. Your plan should have this general form:

1. *Schedule* pleasant activities frequently.
2. *Reinforce* yourself for engaging in the activities. Be very liberal. Reinforce only on contingency, but begin with shaping steps that you can meet (Fuchs & Rehm, 1977). The goal is to increase pleasant events, not to squeeze even more pleasure out of your life. Do not make your reinforcement plans too severe, complicated, or difficult (Kornblith, Rehm, O'Hara, & Lamparski, 1983). Reward yourself!
3. *Replace* denigrating self-speech with realistic self-praise. Be sure to include verbal self-reinforcement for each desired behavior.

An effective technique for increasing the number of pleasant events in your life is to make sure you notice the ones that do occur. Keeping daily records of pleasant events is a reliable way to bring them to your attention. These may include such things as seeing a rainbow, talking with friends, receiving a smile from someone of the opposite sex, savoring the taste of an excellent olive.

It is almost certain that you are receiving less reinforcement than you need from other people. To increase those rewards, you will probably have to build new habits—making yourself more available to others, or being more skillful in your interactions. Therefore, some problem solving and social-skill building should be a part of your overall plan (Lewisohn, Sullivan, & Grosscup, 1980).

Exercise and Athletics

If your exercise program is a solitary one, try to get social support and reinforcement from your friends, family, or partner. Participation in group exercise programs, either in formal "classes" or with informal groups of friends, can provide mutual reinforcement and the increase in motivation associated with public goal setting. Reinforcement is vital, especially in the earlier stages of exercise development, when soreness and tiredness can provide automatic punishment. For successful exercisers, soreness and tiredness actually become positive reinforcers. This is more likely when a coach, class leader, or friend is present to help you identify these feelings and help you associate them with the improvement they represent (Lees & Dygdon, 1988). This is another advantage for beginning your program in some structured, assisted way.

Reinforcement of your new exercise patterns will help make them solid. You can use all forms of reinforcement: pleasant activities made contingent on completing the shaping steps, material things as rewards, and especially the covert reinforcement of self-praise and imagined scenes. Sato (1986) showed that joggers who self-reinforced increased their mileage. Her runners used such self-statements as the following:

- This will make me healthier.
- I am doing something really good for this body!
- I am happier and more alert after running.
- Sweat means burning calories and building strength!
- My lover is going to love my good mood!

The following punishing self-statements were to be avoided:

- I'm sweaty and sore.
- My husband is going to bitch about my running.
- I'm conspicuous.
- This is boring and stupid.

For improving performance in golf, tennis, team sports, or any skilled athletics, the most effective consequence can often be information. Whether we think of information about our performances as reinforcement or as feedback, positive self-monitoring can bring about improvement in skill.

Attending carefully to one's performance and comparing it with a standard makes performance more skillful than not self-monitoring. These benefits can be strengthened by the use of videotapes or mirrors (Johnston-O'Connor & Kirschenbaum, 1986).

Relations with Others: Social Anxieties, Social Skills, and Dating

Imagined rehearsal and reinforcement are particularly appropriate for practicing the early stages of approach—making conversation and asking for dates. Use the logical imagined reinforcement of friendliness and acceptance by the other person. The natural reinforcements offered by the opposite sex are strong enough to maintain behavior once you have achieved confidence and skill.

For problematic relationships, reinforce yourself for doing what is needed to improve the relationships, and be sure to reinforce the others involved: "Hey, that was really nice. We sat and talked about our problem without anyone blowing up. I really appreciate the effort you are making."

Very often, interpersonal problems develop because one person begins to punish the other. Being punished often incites people to revenge, and a vicious circle is established. One punishment leads to the next. This, in turn, leads to more punishment, and so on until the relationship is destroyed. One way of breaking this vicious circle is to realize that you can reinforce someone else by paying attention or making some rewarding statement.

Ask yourself, "How can I reinforce desired behavior?" Your intervention plan might involve paying attention to the "good" things the other person does and reinforcing the person for them. You then reinforce yourself for reinforcing the other. In a book on how to achieve a good marriage, Knox (1971) suggests keeping records like this:

The husband records:		
Wife's desirable behavior	Wife's undesirable behavior	Husband's response to wife's behavior
The wife records:		
Husband's desirable behavior	Husband's undesirable behavior	Wife's response to husband's behavior

SOURCE: *Marriage Happiness: A Behavioral Approach to Counseling,* by D. Knox. Copyright 1971 by Research Press. Reprinted by permission.

Comparing the two records allows you to see if you are in fact trying to punish your spouse's undesired behavior instead of trying to reward his or her desirable acts. This record can also show how your spouse's behavior represents an antecedent for your behavior, and vice versa. It indicates what changes you should ask of your spouse and what changes you should try to make in yourself.

Two people working together to improve their relationship can develop specific agreements: You give up this, and I'll give up that; you do this, and I'll do that. Because certain changes in another person to whom you are close can be a strong incentive for you to change, this kind of mutual agreement is a powerful technique.

Smoking, Drinking, and Drugs

Abstinence from alcohol or drugs often brings surprising and immediate reinforcement, if you attend to it. For instance, many habitual drinkers or dopers attribute their social pleasures to the substance, whereas these pleasures (relaxation, flirtation, good humor) are actually consequences of social gatherings and a playful atmosphere. Notice that many of the pleasures are still there, even without the dope or drink.

Other advantages are also immediate—think about them. For example, giving up tobacco brings three immediate benefits: immediate clearance of smoke from your lungs, clearance of carbon monoxide from your blood, and reduced risk of sudden death (Pechacek & Danaher, 1979). Remind yourself of the immediate benefits of giving up alcohol or drugs. Better mood and feelings of pride are reinforcers you should notice even in the earliest stages of abstaining. Attend to these feelings, and use them as self-reinforcement.

Cognitive strategies are probably the most effective for abstinence. Tell yourself, "I don't need a cigarette." Remind yourself of the commitment to abstinence. These strategies, and the use of self-reinforcement by positive self-statements, are strongly associated with success in stopping smoking. Use positive statements, such as, "Think of the good example I'm going to set by stopping smoking."

Successful stoppers used these positive reinforcers; unsuccessful stoppers were more likely to have used negative or punishing self-statements, such as, "Think of how weak I'd be if I failed to stop." Use positive, rewarding self-statements (Glasgow, Klesges, Mizes, & Pechacek, 1985).

By all means involve yourself in some form of social support—family, friends, or partners. A study of married women who were stopping smoking revealed one major factor in their successful abstinence: partner support. Persuade your partner that you need to be rewarded for quitting and that you need understanding, listening, and help with developing alternate behaviors to smoking (Coppotelli & Orleans, 1985).

Studying and Time Management

Reinforcement is highly important in studying and time scheduling—much more important than unsuccessful students believe. In fact, successful students tend to develop self-reinforcement techniques on their own without a course or a book like this one (Heffernan & Richards, 1981; Perri & Richards, 1977). The use of reinforcement for studying is especially important if your study habits have not yet been well developed in high school or early college courses (Green, 1982). One of the advantages that competent students have over "disadvantaged" students is that the advantaged already reinforce themselves for studying.

But there are times of "blocking" and distraction when studying and writing will not come even for competent students—in fact, not even for professors. Programs of reinforcement have proven effective in increasing productivity even for seasoned academic writers who were temporarily "blocked" (Boice, 1982).

Often reinforcement can be obtained by a simple rearrangement. For example, use pleasant occupations (leisure or hobbies) to reinforce the more difficult ones, such as studying, so that one is directly tied to the other and reinforces it. In drawing up your time-management plan, make sure a pleasant block of time follows any particularly difficult one, and follow the rule that you must complete the difficult activity before you move to the pleasant one.

Whenever you can't arrange your activities as described above, use other reinforcers, however arbitrary—movies, candy, cash, tokens. Your basic plan should (1) be based on a firm schedule, (2) include enough pleasant activities, and (3) provide for reinforcement for following the schedule.

Studying behaviors are also more likely to improve when you have arranged for some social support. The use of mediators should be explored. Arranging study groups, with group standards, feedback, and rewards, is desirable. Publicly announcing your goals and progress is also recommended (Hayes et al., 1985).

Weight Loss and Overeating

All behavioral programs for weight loss have contingency-management features (Agras, 1987). Reinforcement is a vital element in your plan. Reinforce yourself for avoiding the situations that cue excessive consumption. Use reinforcement to strengthen all the behaviors your self-control requires, such as recording all the food you eat, resisting urges, exercising, making graphs, and avoiding temptation. Reward these *behaviors.* Do not make reward contingent on weight. Daily fluctuations in weight can be very deceiving. If you perform the correct eating and exercise behaviors, weight loss will follow.

Do not use food as a reward. As often as possible, use the natural reinforcement that your long-range self-control will bring. Consider the benefits of your diet: Do you feel better, happier, more alive? Remind yourself of the numerous rewards. One of the benefits of weight loss is lowered depression (Wing, Marcus, Epstein, & Kupfer, 1983), and better mood and feelings of pride are reinforcers that you should notice even in the earliest stages of dieting. Attend to these feelings, and use them as self-reinforcement. When dieting, look at your body in the mirror. Enjoy your improved appearance (Owusu-Bempah & Howitt, 1983).

If you are on the verge of violating your rules, say "Stop!" to yourself, breathe deeply, relax, and reward yourself with a pleasant imagined scene.

Odds are that you will continue to need other forms of reinforcement to replace the consummatory behaviors. Reinforce alternatives, and arrange for reinforcement from others. Successful weight losers received positive feedback from several external sources, such as parents and peers (Perri & Richards, 1977).

The evidence is convincing that the use of significant others as mediators will help your plan. Read the text material on pages 214–219 carefully, and include mediators in some way. Finding a group of dieters who are willing to commit themselves to good eating habits and who agree to use group rewards can provide strong and pleasant motivation (Jeffery, Gerber, Rosenthal, & Lindquist, 1983).

If you are a binge eater, attend also to this research finding: disordered eating is strongly associated with very restricted self-nurturance (Lehman & Rodin, 1989). This means that binge eaters are not nice enough to themselves in other ways; they have insufficient amounts of self-reward, relaxation, and self-praise. It is highly important that you establish a richer program of noncontingent self-reinforcement, both verbal and material. Otherwise you may continue to nurture yourself only with eating binges.

Chapter Summary

The most basic formula in self-modification is to arrange that rewards follow desired behaviors.

Discovering and Selecting Reinforcers

Your A-B-C records may reveal the reinforcers that are maintaining undesirable behavior. The simplest plan is to arrange for these same rewards to follow your new goal behavior. This is not possible with indulgent behaviors because the act consumes the reinforcer. Therefore, some other reward must be used to reinforce nonindulgence.

Intermittent reinforcement and avoidance behaviors make discovery of reinforcement difficult. Here, too, you must identify reinforcers that are available and controllable.

A wide variety of possible rewards can be used, including preferred things and preferred activities. The nature of the reward is not important so long as your plan makes the reward contingent on the desired behavior.

Using Others to Dispense Reinforcers

The use of mediators as dispensers of contingent rewards is a highly desirable feature of self-modification. Research evidence overwhelmingly supports the power of this strategy in changing behavior. The use of mediators is advisable in every case in which it can be arranged, particularly in maintaining gains. Praise by mediators is probably even more important than material reinforcement. Attention should be paid to the mediators; their cooperative behavior will also need reinforcement. Sharing reinforcers with the mediator or another partner can help provide motivation, but care should be taken to make sure your partner shares your goals.

Self-Administered Consequences

Vigorous debate surrounds the question of whether self-reward acts as a reinforcer or serves only to call attention to the behavior. Various evidence has been presented and critiqued, but the debate goes on. Virtually every psychologist agrees, however, that self-administered consequences do affect behavior.

Techniques of Self-Reinforcement

Contingent rewards should follow desired behavior as rapidly as possible. This can often be achieved by using a point system or other form of token reinforcement. Points are gained as soon as the behavior is performed and then are exchanged later for real reinforcers.

Imagined reinforcers can also be used to provide rapid rewards. In this technique, a reinforcer from your list is imagined immediately after the behavior occurs. Especially useful is imagining the long-range eventual outcome of your self-modification program.

Verbal self-reinforcement—praising yourself—following desired behavior is an effective technique that should be included in every self-change program.

Increasing the number of rewards in your life is part of the goal of self-modification. Good plans will add to the total of pleasant events in your daily schedule.

Self-Punishment and Extinction

Neither extinction nor self-punishment teaches any new behaviors. Most intervention plans that rely *solely* on self-punishment don't succeed. In some situations, self-punishment may be necessary—if, for example, no positive reinforcers are available, or if the undesired behavior is so strongly reinforcing in itself that a direct, counteracting consequence is required for not performing it. Indulgent behaviors are typical examples of this situation.

If you do decide to use punishment, you should follow these rules.

1. Remove something positive instead of adding something negative. (Always try to figure out a way to increase behavior by adding something positive.)
2. Use punishment only if it leads to more positive reinforcement.
3. Devise a plan that combines punishment with positive reinforcement.
4. You may use precommitted punishment as a deterrent strategy, but only temporarily until the desired behavior can be supported by positive consequences.

The only recommended form of "punishment" is the systematic facing of the negative long-term consequences of a problem behavior. This helps build commitment.

Reinforcement in Plans for Self-Modification

Rewards need to be integrated into plans for controlling antecedents (Chapter 5) and developing new behaviors (Chapter 6). For example, rewards can be added to *imagined rehearsal* and to *shaping*. The general point is that reinforcement should follow all new behaviors in a self-modification plan. If the natural environment does not provide it, arrange specific rewards to be delivered by yourself or your mediators.

YOUR OWN SELF-DIRECTION PROJECT: STEP SEVEN

Review the previous versions of your plan, which included elements of antecedent control and development of new behaviors, in light of what you have just learned about rearrangement of consequences. Plan to follow new behaviors with reinforcement. Be sure to include verbal self-reinforcement, as well as at least one other technique. The result may well be your final plan. Before implementing it, however, read the next chapter, which will help you combine A, B, and C elements into a comprehensive package.

8

Putting It All Together

Outline

- Combining A, B, and C Elements
- The Features of a Good Plan
- Is It Working? Evaluating Your Plan for Change
- Changing Targets
- *Tips for Typical Topics*
- *Chapter Summary*
- *Your Own Self-Direction Project: Step Eight*

Learning Objectives

Combining A, B, and C Elements

1. How are A, B, and C elements combined in a single plan?
2. Describe in detail the two-step process for dealing with consummatory behaviors.
   a. How can unwanted stimulus control by various situations be gradually eliminated?
   b. How can the two-stage process be used in projects other than those dealing with consummatory behaviors?

The Features of a Good Plan

3. What are the five features of a good plan?
   a. How are rules used in self-modification?
   b. How are goals and subgoals used?
   c. Why is it important to gather feedback?
   d. How is feedback compared with goals and subgoals?
   e. When do you make adjustments in your plan?
4. What are the major techniques in the checklist that you should use for your project?
5. How can you use brainstorming to generate more ideas on how to carry out self-change?

Is It Working? Evaluating Your Plan for Change

6. How can you use an average to see if you are making progress?
7. How can you use a percentage to see if you are progressing?
8. How can you make a graph of your personal records during your self-change project?
   a. What goes on the horizontal axis?
   b. What goes on the vertical axis?
9. How do you use your graphed data to analyze your progress?

Changing Targets

10. Do you ever change your target behavior? When?
    a. Should you have a baseline for any new target behavior?
    b. What about new, incompatible responses?

An effective plan combines antecedent, behavior, and consequence (A-B-C) elements. The goal of this chapter is to help you design such a plan and then evaluate its effectiveness. We will illustrate ways of integrating A, B, and C elements and then discuss the principles that characterize a sound plan. So far we have treated each technique and principle in isolation, but an effective plan for change integrates all these techniques and principles.

Combining A, B, and C Elements

Two Sample Projects

Two sample projects, described in some detail, will illustrate how A, B, and C elements are combined in an effective plan for self-modification.

The student. Paul wrote:

> There are several reasons why I would like to study more. I think I will develop a sense of achievement if I get all A's this semester, and it will improve my chances of getting into seminary. I will also learn discipline and build my self-esteem.

For three weeks, Paul kept a record of how much he studied. Then he began to formulate a systematic self-modification plan.

> In the first week I studied quite a bit just because I was keeping records, but by the second and third weeks my average had dropped way off, and I ended up averaging under ten hours per week. Then I began a full-blown self-modification plan.
>
> I wrote a self-contract. I specified several things to do to change: I scheduled study hours, I gradually built up the amount of time I studied at one sitting, I planned where I would study, I gave myself instructions, and I worked out rewards for studying. When problems came up, I changed my plan to cope with them.

Paul listed all these elements of the plan in his self-contract, along with three escape clauses: He would keep 4:30 to 6:30 as a time to relax, he would devote all day Sunday to church work, and he would not study more than 20 hours a week. Then Paul signed the contract and posted it in his room.

Let's analyze the different parts of Paul's plan from the point of view of antecedents, target behaviors, and consequences.

Antecedents: Paul scheduled specific hours that he would study—for example, Tuesday night, 6:30 to 8:30—and the exact places where he would do it—"my desk at home," "the college library," or "the local public library." He set certain rules: "I will study at the times designated on my schedule. I will study at least one hour before I take a break." After typing the entire set of rules, he put this contract with himself into his record-keeping notebook. Just before each study session, he gave himself instructions:

Here's another opportunity to get those A's. I must study now—I scheduled it. Sit down, look over the assignment, then concentrate on the reading and the note taking. If my attention begins to wander, take up another assignment. Read for one hour, and then reward myself.

Behaviors: Paul used shaping to gradually increase how many hours per day he scheduled for studying. First he set one and a half hours, then two, then two and a half, then increased the time by quarter hours up to three and a half hours. He started by requiring himself to study for one hour without a break, then increased this by ten-minute segments until his study periods were up to two continuous hours.

Consequences: Paul worked out a token system, earning one token for every hour of studying. Each token was worth a half hour of TV watching. Seven tokens were enough to earn his three favorite programs. If he earned 10 tokens, he earned a bonus: He would take off from studying all day Saturday. At a later stage, he raised the cost of the bonus to 15 tokens.

Problems: Paul ran into three sets of problems in trying to change his study habits.

First, I'd get a strong urge not to study, even though it was a scheduled study time. Then, while I was studying, my mind would wander. Sometimes I would think, "This is pointless. I'll never make all A's anyway." These thoughts were obviously going to keep me from reaching my goal, so I used thought substitution and told myself, "You can do this. You are an able student, and you have good self-discipline."

A second problem was that I always got hungry while I was studying, and I would take a break to eat. So I started having a snack just before my study time, and then I'd give myself reminders not to eat any more once I started studying.

Toward the end of the semester, Paul nearly reached his goal of 20 hours of studying per week, but after one particularly difficult exam he felt he needed a break, so he didn't study for two days. After that it was hard to get back to his schedule. But by this time, the end of the first term had arrived, and Paul found that the biggest reinforcer of all was a gigantic improvement in his grades. "Frankly, I was stunned. I actually made all A's! I really *can* sit down and study for two hours straight, and doing it regularly has a terrific effect on my GPA."

The putdown artist. Edgar's problem was that he denigrated his friends. "When I had a chance, I would put people down without even thinking about it." He began his self-change program by counting the number of putdowns per week and kept records for several weeks. Edgar then worked out a plan for changing and continued to make observations about his putdowns of his friends.

Antecedents: "I put down my friends as a joke. When we're horsing around, everyone is joking about something or other, and I use these putdowns as my kind of joke. *I* know I am only joking, but my friends don't like it. So I need to be careful in that kind of situation. I also asked my friends to tell me if I was putting them down. Sometimes I didn't even realize I was doing it."

Behaviors: "Each week I tried to reduce the number of putdowns I did—shaping. I also did relaxation exercises, so I could relax more in those horsing-around times. I tried modeling other people who had good interpersonal manners. I did mental practice for about three minutes each day, imagining myself saying nice things to people. I also tried to pause before saying something, so I could ask myself if what I was going to say was a putdown. Instead of putting people down, I tried to compliment them."

Note the number of different things Edgar is doing: relaxing, pausing, modeling, practicing, and substituting positive remarks for negative ones.

Consequences: "My primary reward for not putting people down was allowing myself to talk on the phone with my friends for a certain number of minutes. I worked out a table to relate the number of putdowns to how long I could talk on the phone:

Number of Putdowns	*Number of Minutes Allowed on the Phone*
20	10
17	15
15	30
10	45
5	indefinite

As the weeks went by, I changed the ratio of putdowns to time on the telephone: I had to use fewer putdowns in order to talk on the phone for the same amount of time.

After about three months, I stopped keeping records, but I still perform the mental rehearsals. Even though I still put people down sometimes, it is not to the extent it was before."

Two-Stage Process for Consummatory Behaviors

How can elements of A, B, and C be combined to cope with problems of consummatory behavior? In Chapter 5, we suggested that undesired consummatory behaviors can be reduced by a *two-stage process. In stage 1, avoid the antecedent.* For example, don't go to parties where you will be strongly tempted to smoke, or don't confront yourself with high-calorie food. Your plan should include reinforcement for this avoidance and a way of substituting other pleasant activities.

But few antecedents can be avoided permanently. Eventually you want to be able to return to parties, walk into a bakery, or go back to your morning cup of coffee without having a cigarette. *In stage 2, build new behaviors* so you can be in tempting situations but not perform the overindulging or addictive behavior.

Reinforcement is integrated into the two-stage process. In stage 1, you reward yourself for simply avoiding the tempting antecedent situation. In stage 2, you reward yourself for performing a new, desirable behavior in the presence of the tempting antecedent situation.

Larry, a man who had tried unsuccessfully several times to quit smoking, analyzed the situations in which he returned to smoking after having quit for a few days. Taking a coffee break or eating lunch with his colleagues (several of whom smoked) was the most likely time for backsliding. Smoking seemed such a pleasure under those circumstances that he didn't resist. In stage 1 of his plan, Larry avoided these antecedent situations for two weeks, explaining to his friends what he was doing and reinforcing himself for successful avoidance. He was not tempted so much on the weekends because he spent them with his wife, who didn't smoke. After he had been off cigarettes for several weeks, he entered stage 2, in which he rewarded himself specifically for not smoking with his friends at lunch. After this had worked for a week, he returned coffee breaks to his daily schedule and reinforced himself specifically for not smoking at coffee breaks. Now Larry's task was to remain vigilant for tempting antecedents and to reinforce himself for not smoking when they occurred. The morning cup of coffee, a meal, a tense period, another smoker, a party—these were the kinds of tempting antecedents he had to learn to deal with.

Rehearsal in imagination is a good technique for this kind of situation. Several times a day, Larry would imagine himself in a situation in which he was tempted to smoke—concentrating on imagining all the details, including his own strong craving for a cigarette—and he would imagine himself *not* giving in.

You may also gradually eliminate a situation's stimulus control. If there are a dozen different antecedents to smoking or overeating, try gaining control over them one at a time. This gives you a feeling of progress. The procedure is a form of shaping in which you eliminate the easier antecedents, one at a time, and then move on to the more difficult ones.

Drugs, alcohol, tobacco, and food are consumed in response to several particular antecedents—watching TV; reading; being with a person who causes tension; or feeling bored, depressed, angry, or excited. After discovering your problem antecedents, divide them into physical and emotional events. First, eliminate the stimulus control of the physical events—for example, eating while watching TV—and later eliminate the control of the emotional events—for example, drinking when depressed. For many people, physical events are easier to control than emotional ones because they are more obvious. Start with the easier situations, and gradually work up to the harder ones. This will allow you to gradually gain skills and confidence.

One of our students was overweight by more than 100 pounds. She reported:

> When I first began my project, I was unable to sit through a movie without eating popcorn. I used shaping to deal with it. First, I took snacks with me. Next, I brought only a soda. Then I chewed gum. Now

I'm quite comfortable eating nothing at all at the movies, and I don't even feel tempted by the smell of the popcorn.

This success was also an important step in skill building that allowed her to achieve normal weight.

The idea of eliminating stimulus control over unwanted behaviors is not part of "common sense." People tend *not* to examine their environment to see where it may be controlling their behaviors. You need to learn to spot those situations and to gain control over the situational antecedents that govern your unwanted behaviors. For example, you may overeat in response to the sight of food, to being in Mom's kitchen, to driving past a particular fast-food restaurant—all situational antecedents that control overeating.

The Two-Stage Process Applied to Other Problems

The two-stage process is not limited to consummatory behaviors. Many other projects can also follow a two-stage process.

Leslie and Helen worked together, and over the years their relationship deteriorated. Having to deal with each other in their jobs was extremely unpleasant. When they did talk, the inevitable result was anger and hurt feelings. The obvious solution—avoiding each other—was impossible because they had to work in the same room day after day. Leslie decided to try a two-stage intervention program. The first stage consisted of an effort to control the antecedents for both of them.

Stage 1. Leslie instituted a cooling-off period in which she didn't talk with Helen except when it was absolutely necessary. When she did talk, Leslie confined her remarks to business topics and tried to be either neutral or mildly pleasant. This was reasonably effective. After a couple of weeks, they settled down to occasional brief and relatively calm interactions. Most important, anger seemed to disappear from the picture.

This first stage of Leslie's program is an example of avoiding the controlling antecedent—in this case, talking with the other person—long enough to begin developing other, more desirable reactions. *It is very important to develop those new and more desirable behaviors.* In the case of these two women, for example, if no new behavior had been developed, the cooling-off period would have ended in failure. Eventually their work would have required them to have more substantial conversations, and they would gradually have returned to their old behavior of stimulating each other to anger.

Stage 2. Leslie then went on to a second stage, which included three elements:

1. She did not respond to annoying remarks from Helen. Thus, if Helen said, "I'm not sure you're doing a good job," Leslie would ignore her.
2. She positively reinforced Helen for pleasant remarks. Thus, if Helen said, "That seemed to work out very well," Leslie would say, "Why, thanks very much. It's kind of you to say that."
3. She praised Helen for her good work and refrained from criticizing her.

The Features of a Good Plan

There is no such thing as one perfect plan for attaining a goal. You could adopt several different plans for the same goal, any one of which might be successful. However, all good plans share certain characteristics; for example, a successful plan must be specific.

A Theoretical Overview of a Good Plan

A successful plan includes these features:

1. Rules that state the behaviors and techniques for change to use in specific situations
2. Goals and subgoals
3. Feedback on your behavior, based on your self-observations
4. A comparison of feedback with your subgoals and goals in order to measure progress
5. Adjustments in the plan as conditions change

Rules. Self-modification involves setting rules for yourself in order to reach your goals (Hayes, 1989). If some behavior is *not* a problem for you, you follow your own rules without paying much attention to them. But if you are *not* meeting a particular goal, you need to set clear, explicit rules to guide your behavior until that behavior becomes habitual. That's the whole purpose of rules—to make desired behaviors more likely (Malott, 1989).

In your plan for self-change, the rules are statements of the thoughts, behaviors, and techniques for change you will use in specific situations. Here are several examples of rules that people have included in their self-change plans:

- Every night, between 7:00 and 9:00, I will practice relaxation exercises for 20 minutes.
- I will not keep snack foods in the house.
- I will exercise for 20 minutes on Monday, Wednesday, and Friday while watching TV.

A typical plan will have more than one rule. For example:

1. Each day in my art history class, I will make at least one comment.
2. Each time I make a comment, I will make a check mark on my record card.
3. After I have accumulated five check marks, I will allow myself one glass of wine or beer in the evening.

These three separate rules describe the first shaping step for the student, the record-keeping system used, and the token system used for contingent reinforcement.

Goals and subgoals. Making goals and subgoals explicit is vital to the success of any plan (Spates & Kanfer, 1977). The writing of novels, for example, might seem dependent on the rush of inspiration and the caprice of the muse. Not so. Firm daily work goals—in terms of number of pages (or even words) written—have been used by novelists as diverse as Anthony Trollope, Arnold Bennett, Ernest Hemingway, and Irving Wallace. Each of these writers counted his output daily and compared it with his daily goal (Wallace & Pear, 1977). Each day's requirements are subgoals toward completing the final work. Even author George Sand—the "Notorious Woman," portrayed as impulsive and passionate—observed a nightly work schedule of 30 written pages no matter what her alcoholic condition, and Jack London required himself to write 1000 words a day before he visited his local saloon (Bandura, 1981).

Each subgoal has to be formulated precisely enough for you to be able to compare it with your performance and know whether or not you have achieved the subgoal. Each subgoal has its own rules. The following paragraphs give examples of rules for subgoals.

Rules for subgoal 1: "Each day I will practice the relaxation exercises (at first I'll do this 20 minutes per day), until I can relax without going through all the muscle tension-release steps."

After this subgoal is reached, a new one is substituted. The long-range goal here is relaxation in certain situations, but it is reached by carefully stating a series of subgoals and reaching them one at a time.

Rules for subgoal 2: "Each day I will spend at least 10 minutes rehearsing in my imagination applying for a job, until I can think about it with a tension rating no greater than 'mild.'"

As each step is achieved, the next step begins with new rules and new subgoals. The goal for each step is the level of performance needed to advance to the next step.

Feedback. Any effective plan must incorporate a system for gathering information about your progress. If you are learning to serve a tennis ball, you don't strike the ball and then close your eyes. You follow the path of the ball, noting its speed, twist, and whether it lands in the proper court or not. Your standard for success is "ball in the court." If your feedback tells you that it is "out," you can perform some operation to correct your behavior. Without feedback, you aren't likely to improve—and if you did, you wouldn't know it.

All goal-oriented behavior is governed by this cybernetic principle. Without some information about your performance (feedback), you cannot correct yourself, whether your goal is to be a better student, a better lover, or a better tennis player. For this reason, *your plan must include a system for collecting data.* Of course you are already doing that for baseline purposes, as outlined in Chapter 3. But you must continue to record your performance for the duration of your plan so that self-correction can occur.

Comparison of feedback with goals and subgoals. The next step in your plan is to compare feedback with your subgoal. How are you doing? The answer may be "Terrific!" The ball landed in the court; you studied 15 hours; your mate loves your lovemaking.

But sometimes things are not satisfactory, and you see that you are off your ideal standard. Then you make adjustments, and some improvement occurs. Whether these adjustments are major or minor, you won't be sure that they are the right ones—or even that they are needed—unless you record your self-observations and compare them to your goal.

This process of comparing feedback with goals and subgoals may require a short, deliberate period of taking stock. For example, a woman who has been very successful at losing weight using this book told us that she made an appointment with herself for 30 minutes to an hour each week, on weigh-in day, to review the week's eating and exercise records, judge progress, make necessary adjustments, collect her weekly reward, praise herself for successes, give herself some self-instructions, and make a weekly summary record in a journal.

Adjustments in the plan. The woman also made adjustments in her plans from week to week. As you progress, you advance to goals that require new tactics. For example, after a few weeks the woman decided that not eating a good breakfast was no longer a problem, so she stopped rewarding herself for that. However, eating too much on the weekends continued to be a problem, so she started a new token system to deal with that. Although your new plan will include different techniques, it will have the same elements that characterize all successful plans: explicit rules, precise goals, gathering of feedback, comparison of feedback to goals, and adjustments as the plan continues.

Sometimes as you progress in your plan you learn new things and have to change the focus of your plan somewhat in order to achieve your goal. One of our students told us,

> My grades were getting to be OK on multiple choice exams, but still not so good on my written papers. Then you gave that little lecture on improving our writing in which you talked about the way poor writers give too much attention to things like grammar and punctuation, and not enough to questions like, "Am I getting my ideas across?" or "Do I need to include more information," or "What can I do to make the whole presentation better?" So I changed the focus of my efforts: I reminded myself with those questions, and went back later to clean up grammar and spelling. That was much better; so were my grades.

We're not surprised it worked, incidentally, as research has shown that this kind of change particularly helps poor writers (Watkins, 1991).

Box 8-1 (on page 262) contains a checklist you can use to ensure that your self-modification plan has been designed to give you the greatest possible chance of success.

Brainstorming

Once you have reviewed procedures for each of the A, B, and C elements, you are ready to design your final plan. Before settling on a final plan, however, be creative. Use the technique of *brainstorming* (see pages 36–37). Remember that the goal of brainstorming is to generate as many ideas as possible, quickly and uncritically. The four rules for brainstorming are as follows:

1. Try for *quantity* of ideas.
2. *Don't criticize* your ideas; don't even evaluate them. You will do that later.
3. Try to think of *unusual* ideas.
4. Try to *combine* ideas to create new ones.

Jim, who had suffered from a bad case of acne in high school, had developed the habit of picking at his face. He wanted to stop this habit because it tended to inflame his sensitive skin, produced infections, and made his face look terrible. But it was an automatic habit, and he was having trouble thinking of ways to stop it. After going through the checklist in Box 8-1, Jim brainstormed solutions:

> I have to stop. Let's see. I could . . . slap my face every time I do it. No, that's dumb. [Long pause, no ideas.] Oh, yeah, I was criticizing the idea. Don't do that now. Just produce a lot of ideas, evaluate them later. OK. So, I could slap my face every time I do it. I could ask Lois to tell me to stop whenever I do it. I could ask my parents to tell me, too. I could rub my face instead of picking it. I could pull out my hair instead. Ha! I could suck my thumb, or—I could pick my nose. Ha! No criticism now! I could say to myself, "I want to stop picking my face, so I won't do it now." I could do that and rub my face instead of picking. I could remind myself that it might get red or infected. Since I do it when I'm watching TV, I could put a sign on the TV reminding me not to do it. Ditto for studying. Put a sign on my desk. I could report to Lois every day about how much I did it the previous day, and show her that I was cutting down. Ditto my parents. Every day I could cut down a little more over the day before. If I didn't, then I wouldn't get to watch TV that day; but if I did, I'd put aside some money for something—for some clothes or a record. I could force myself to do it for hours at a time until I got so sick of it I'd never do it again. I could . . .

That's how the brainstorming process works. Having written down these ideas, Jim selected the best ones, designed a tentative plan, and examined it to make sure that it was in accord with the principles he had learned.

A Sample Plan

This is the plan of a young woman who wanted to reduce her anxiety about speaking to her professors. The plan eventually worked fairly well, after several adjustments.

BOX 8-1

A Checklist for Your Plan

The primary reason people fail in self-modification attempts is that they do not use the techniques they have read about. It's not a question of stubbornness, but of not remembering all they have learned (Ley, 1986). To strengthen your memory, let's review the most important issues presented in the preceding chapters. These issues can be formulated as a series of questions. You should be able to answer yes to most of them. Read them and write *yes* or *no* for each.

Let's begin with *goal setting, commitment, and record keeping.*

____ Have you specified the goal clearly?

____ Have you made changes in the way you specified the goal as your self-understanding increased?

____ Have you taken steps to build commitment to do the work of changing?

____ Have you worked out a self-observation system you can use when the problem behavior occurs?

____ Do you keep written records?

Here's a checklist of the steps involved in controlling *antecedents.* Again, you should be able to answer yes to most of these questions.

____ If your goal is to decrease some unwanted behavior, have you taken steps to discover and eliminate the antecedents of that behavior?

____ Have you developed a plan to change thoughts that represent the antecedents of the behavior?

____ Have you examined your beliefs to see whether they are contributing to your problem behavior? Have you made plans to restructure these beliefs?

____ Have you developed a plan to cope with the physical antecedents of the behavior?

____ Have you worked out a plan to deal with the social and emotional antecedents of the behavior?

____ Have you taken steps to provide antecedents that will encourage your new, desired behavior?

____ Have you developed some thoughts you can use as antecedents of the new behavior?

____ Does your plan include specific self-instructions?

In her report, Laurel wrote:

I almost never talk with my professors. They scare me. Sometimes I have questions. At other times I would just like to talk with them. But I have spoken only to one, Prof. A., all year, and it was only a few sentences at a time. My goal is to increase talking with my professors.

I will develop my behavior gradually, on a shaping schedule. I have to start really low, because my baseline is nearly zero. This is my shaping schedule:

Step 1. Say hello to a professor.
Step 2. Talk with a professor for 15 seconds.
Step 3. Talk with a professor for 30 seconds.

____ Have you planned for physical antecedents to become cues?
____ Have you asked others to encourage you or structured your social environment to provide helpful antecedents?

Next, consider the issues involved in developing new *behaviors.* Here, too, you should be able to answer yes to most of these questions.

____ As you try to develop new behaviors, do you use some form of shaping?
____ If your goal is to decrease an unwanted behavior, are you planning to use some incompatible behavior as a substitute?
____ If your problem involves anxiety or tension, are you going to practice relaxation?
____ Have you made provisions for rehearsing any new behavior you want to develop?
____ Does your plan call for imagined rehearsal?
____ Have you made provisions for rehearsing in the real world?

Finally, here is a checklist of issues relating to *reinforcement.* Once again, you should be able to answer most of these questions positively.

____ Have you discovered through self-observation what may be reinforcing your unwanted behaviors? If so, have you developed a plan for using that same reinforcement, or an alternate reward, to strengthen a desired behavior instead?
____ Have you developed a reinforcement plan in which you are rewarded if you take appropriate steps in your plan for self-change?
____ Does your plan include a token system?
____ Does your plan include Premack-type reinforcers?
____ Does your plan include verbal self-reinforcement?
____ Does it include reminders of the reinforcement you will receive if you stick to each step of your plan?
____ Does your plan include any form of precommitted punishment?
____ Does your plan include an arrangement ensuring that you will be reinforced in the real world for any changes you make in your behavior?

Your chances of success increase if you use a variety of techniques. A solid plan involves antecedents, target behaviors, and consequences. If you have not yet worked out a plan that includes elements of all three, now is the time to do so.

Step 4. Talk for 1 minute.
Step 5. Talk for 2 minutes.

Our analysis: So far, Laurel's plan is generally satisfactory. However, she should specify how many times she will rehearse each step before moving to the next.

Collecting feedback: "My wristwatch has a sweep-second hand. If I turn the band, the watch will be on my wrist facing up. I can sort of look down to check the time without being too obvious. As soon as the conversation is over, I'll write down notes—how many seconds, the professor's name, where we were, and so forth.

"On the inside front cover of my notebook, I'll write my shaping schedule. Then I can check whether or not I have met my goals."

Techniques: "I have decided to use a combination of Premack and food reinforcers. Since I eat lunch every day at school, I'll set a rule that I won't eat lunch until I have performed whatever step is required by my schedule."

Our analysis: Selecting eating lunch as the reinforcer seems drastic, but her schedule is reasonable and develops slowly, so she probably won't need to go without food. At the same time, she gains the reinforcing effect of eating lunch.

But there are a few problems with the plan. Other techniques should be included, principally self-instructions before the conversation and self-praise after it. It would also help if Laurel would learn relaxation and then relax herself before approaching the professor. The plan sounds a bit too simple.

Results: "This plan didn't work. I could do steps 1 and 2 okay. But at step 3 I got into trouble because the professor wouldn't quit talking to me, and suddenly I was involved in a complex conversation and became quite nervous. So I worked out a second plan."

Our analysis: Good! Plans should be changed if they don't work.

Plan 2: "The reason the first plan failed was that the professor carried me too far up the schedule. Looking back, it seems inevitable that this would happen. I might have gotten up to 3 minutes, or something like that, but at some point some professor would have just continued talking to me, and I'd be in trouble. I decided to enlist the aid of one particular teacher."

Laurel continued:

> I wrote my self-change project paper early in the semester and handed it in to Prof. A., who was teaching the course. In the paper, I explained why my first plan had failed and asked for his help. I included my new schedule:
>
> Step 1. Talk with Prof. A. in the hall for 15 seconds.
> Step 2. Talk with him for 30 seconds.
> Step 3. Talk for 1 minute.
> Step 4. Talk for 90 seconds.
> Step 5. Increase 30 seconds at a time, up to 5 minutes.
>
> I was going to do each step three times before going on to the next one. There were two parts to this plan. First, I was going to do the talking in the hall. Then, after I got pretty far up the schedule, I was going to repeat the entire sequence in his office, because it was more scary to talk with him in his office than in the hall. After I got to step 4 for talking in the hall, I started step 1 for talking in the office. Even that was too hard, so I put in some new steps:
>
> Step 1a. Just stick my head in and say hello.
> Step 1b. Talk for 5 seconds in the office.
> Step 1c. Talk for 10 seconds in the office.
>
> Then I went back to the old schedule. Prof. A. agreed not to force me to talk longer than I was supposed to. Reinforcer, feedback, and comparison were all the same as before.

Our analysis: The rules are clear, though somewhat complicated. Goals are present, and feedback and record keeping seem adequate. The double shaping plan is complex but sensible. Still no self-instruction, self-praise, or relaxation in the plan.

Plan 3: "Plan 2 works better. Prof. A. and I are now talking up to 3 minutes in the hall and 2 minutes in his office. But I need to be able to generalize from Prof. A. to other professors. I have decided to use Prof. A. again. Here is my new schedule:

Step 1. Go up to Prof. A. while he is talking with another professor and say hello to both of them.
Step 2. Go up and talk to Prof. A. while he is talking with another professor. Say at least a sentence to the other one.
Step 3. Talk with the other one for 5 seconds.
Step 4. Talk with the other one for 10 seconds.
Step 5. Talk with the other one for 15 seconds.
Step 6. Talk with the other one for 30 seconds, then on up from there by 15-second jumps.

Prof. A. has agreed to cooperate. He'll know where I am in the schedule and will bail me out whenever I complete my time for that particular step. Also, some professors seem unfriendly to me and others are pretty good, so I will go up to Prof. A. only when he is talking with one of the friendly ones."

Our analysis: This is a critical step, for Laurel is building the new behavior so she can use it in a variety of situations. Also, she has realized that an unfriendly professor is a different antecedent from a friendly one, and she has decided to deal with the easier antecedent (the friendly professor).

Plan 3 was apparently successful. By semester's end, Laurel was able to talk with several friendly professors, which she considered a significant improvement.

Laurel did very well. She was wise to change plans when the first plan didn't work. Her plans were generally explicit. Her rules were clear. Her goals were divided into subgoals, and the standards for advancing were made explicit in plans 2 and 3. Her data collection was careful.

We spoke with her several months after the course ended and asked her why she hadn't included relaxation in her plan. She said she really didn't know and pointed out she could always have backed up and used it if all else had failed. "I just didn't want to wait. Besides, I was right, wasn't I? Must have been—I'm talking to you."

Once you have chosen your plan and decided on each of its elements, write it down and sign it (Kanfer, Cox, Greiner, & Karoly, 1974). This written plan becomes your contract with yourself. The contract should list your rules as well as your goals and subgoals, and it should specify how you will collect feedback. A formal contract increases your chances of success (Griffin & Watson, 1978; Seidner, 1973). Prepare it with all the seriousness of any other formal document.

Display your contract. Keep it in your notebook or on your mirror. Make it clear and explicit. When it becomes necessary to change the plan, rewrite the contract and sign the new one.

Is It Working? Evaluating Your Plan for Change

Does your plan work? This seems like a simple question, and sometimes you can answer it with a clear yes or no. The person who never smokes again, the man who has a female friend for the first time in his life, the overweight person who drops 10 pounds and keeps them off—all these self-modifiers know they are succeeding. They don't need elaborate techniques for assessing their progress. More often, though, progress is gradual rather than dramatic. Often you don't remember clearly from one week to the next exactly how you felt or how often you actually did the things you wanted to do. In fact, many people *misjudge* their progress, perhaps because they adapt to new performance levels.

People often underrate the progress they are making. Those who don't rely on their data may be tempted to stop a plan, even though it is succeeding, simply because they *believe* it is failing. The reverse, of course, can also happen, and a person may continue to follow an ineffective plan because he or she has not properly collected and examined data. *It is crucial that you continue to record your behavior throughout the operation of your plan because recording provides the evidence you need in order to know whether the plan is having the desired effect.*

There are three ways to organize your data to see if you are making progress:

- by calculating averages
- by calculating percentages
- by using a graph

Finding Averages

Sidney's goal was to reduce his anxiety about talking to women on the telephone, with the long-term goal of finding a girlfriend. He began a plan that required him to phone some female acquaintance each evening and talk to her for at least five minutes. He used several techniques to aid him in this and rated on a 5-point scale the degree of anxiety he felt during each phone call. A rating of 1 indicated he was perfectly calm, and 5 meant he was near panic; 3 meant he was "somewhat tense." For the first week, his ratings were: 2, 3, 4, 2, 3, 3, 2. For the second week, they were: 2, 3, 2, 3, 2, 2, 2. Was he making progress? How much?

To compute the average—or mean—amount of anxiety he felt each week, Sidney added the scores for that week and divided by 7 (the number of days in the week). For the first week, the total—2 + 3 + 4 + 2 + 3 + 3 + 2—was 19, which, divided by 7, equals 2.7. For the second week, the total was

16, which, divided by 7, equals 2.3. Sid could see that he was making some progress.

The formula for finding the average, or mean, of a group of scores is to add the scores and divide the resulting sum by the total number of scores. In self-directed behavior, it is generally wiser to consider weekly averages rather than daily scores. This smooths out the record and usually provides a more reliable picture than the daily fluctuations.

Finding Percentages

Tamara began dieting by carefully recording the situations in which she ate too much or ate inappropriately. She realized that she ate too fast, too often ate junk food while at work, ate too much at supper, and frequently had a late-night snack. Each of these situations called for some self-control technique, such as pausing for two minutes during a meal. But, Tamara reported, she was using the techniques on only a hit-or-miss basis. So she began to keep records of the number of times an opportunity to use a technique came up, as well as the number of times she actually used one. "That way, I could know the percentage of time I was doing what I needed to do in order to lose weight, and I could try to gradually increase the percentage of time I was coping."

During the first week, Tamara counted 28 opportunities to use some self-control technique in connection with her eating. She actually used a technique eight times. To compute the percentage of times she was using a technique when she could, she divided 8 by 28, which gave her 28.6%. Now her goal was to increase the percentage of times she used a technique when the chance arose. Over several weeks, she could see if the percentage increased.

To compute a percentage, divide the number of times an event occurred by the total number of times it could have occurred. For example, if you were assertive 3 times last week, and there were 6 times when you could have been assertive, your percentage is 3 divided by 6, or 50%.

Once you have calculated percentages, they can be examined across periods of time. Again, we recommend using weekly comparisons rather than daily. And percentages themselves can be averaged to give a picture of longer periods of time.

Making Graphs

Each day you gather your observations, and by the end of a few weeks you have so many pieces of information that interpreting them can become difficult. By putting them all together on a graph, you can see your progress or lack of it.

Marlene wants to increase her studying. For one semester, she has kept a record of how many hours she studied each week. Here is her record for the semester: 8, 9¼, 9¾, 9½, 9½, 10¼, 10¾, 10, 8, 9½, 10¼, 11, 8½, 12¼, 10¼. With that long string of numbers, it's hard to gauge progress. With a graph,

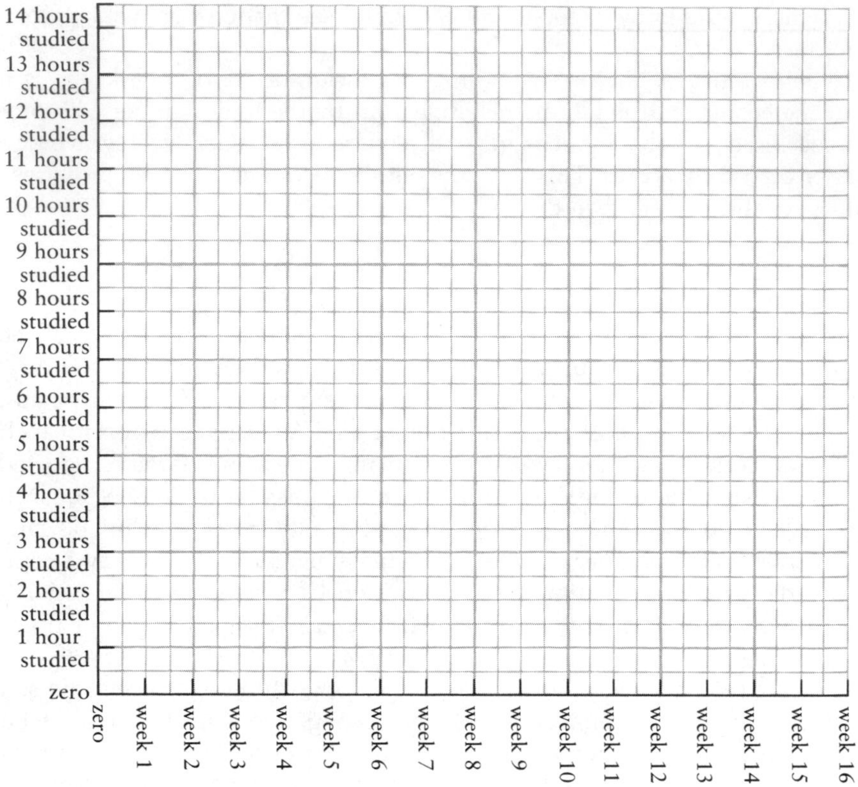

Figure 8-1 The horizontal and vertical axes of a graph

Marlene can see quite easily whether her performance has improved over the semester.

On graph paper, Marlene draws the **abscissa,** or **horizontal axis,** near the bottom of the page and divides the axis into 16 marks, one for each week of the semester. Then, beginning at the zero point on the abscissa, she draws a vertical line upward and marks off 14 equally spaced points on it, one for each hour she might have studied per week. (Her maximum goal was 14 hours.) This line is called the **ordinate,** or **vertical axis.**

Always put the passage of time—minutes, days, weeks—on the horizontal axis and the goal—the target—on the vertical axis. The point where the two axes meet should be the zero point for both axes. Figure 8-1 shows Marlene's graph.

Marlene has a record of the total number of hours she studied each week for 15 of the 16 weeks of the semester. For week 1, the total number of hours was 8. She goes up in a straight line from the "week 1" spot on the horizontal axis, until that line is opposite "8 hours studied." Where the two lines on the graph paper intersect, Marlene makes a dot. She repeats this process for each of the 15 weeks for which she has data, each time connecting the

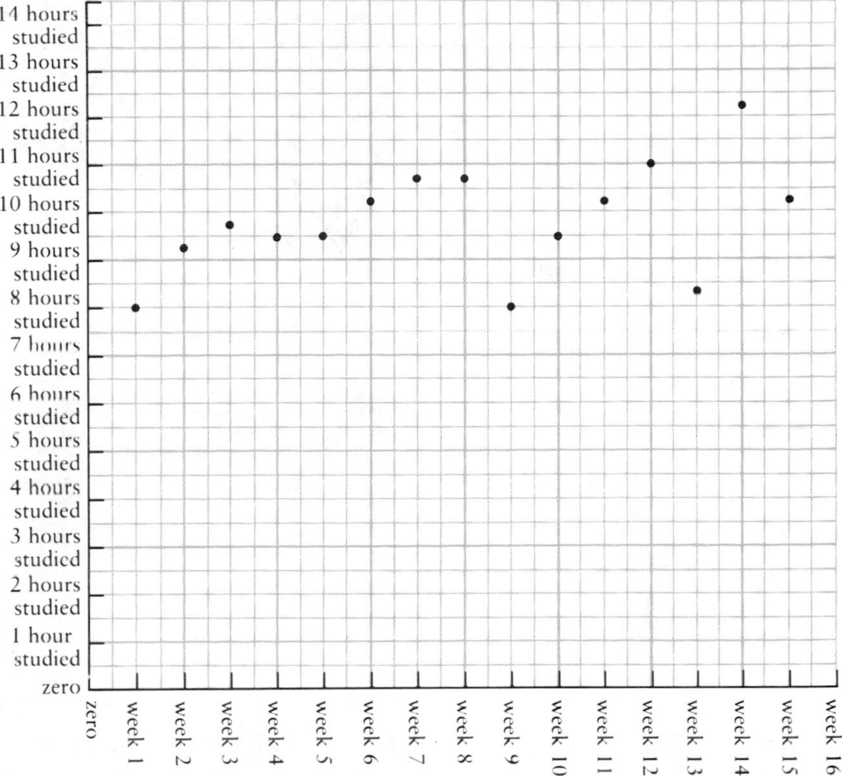

Figure 8-2 The graph with a dot placed at each point representing the total number of hours studied that week

week—for example, week 8—with the total number of hours she studied that week—for example, 10¾. Figure 8-2 shows her graph with all the dots in place.

To make her progress (or lack of it) even clearer, Marlene connects each point on the graph to the next one, moving from left to right. That gives her a finished graph, illustrated in Figure 8-3. On this graph, each point on the horizontal and vertical lines is numbered, and the whole line is labeled "weeks of the semester" or "hours studied." It is tedious to write "week 1," "week 2," "week 3," and so on, and to write "1 hour studied," "2 hours studied," "3 hours studied." The custom is to write only the numbers along each axis and to use labels underneath and at the side to describe what the numbers stand for.

Sometimes it is necessary to include all the numbers on the vertical line. Suppose you are working on losing weight, and your weekly weight varies between 148 and 135 pounds over a semester. It would be silly to start the vertical line at zero pounds and mark off 135 pounds on it before you got to one you would use in making the graph. Instead, break the line to indicate that you are not starting at zero (see Figure 8-4).

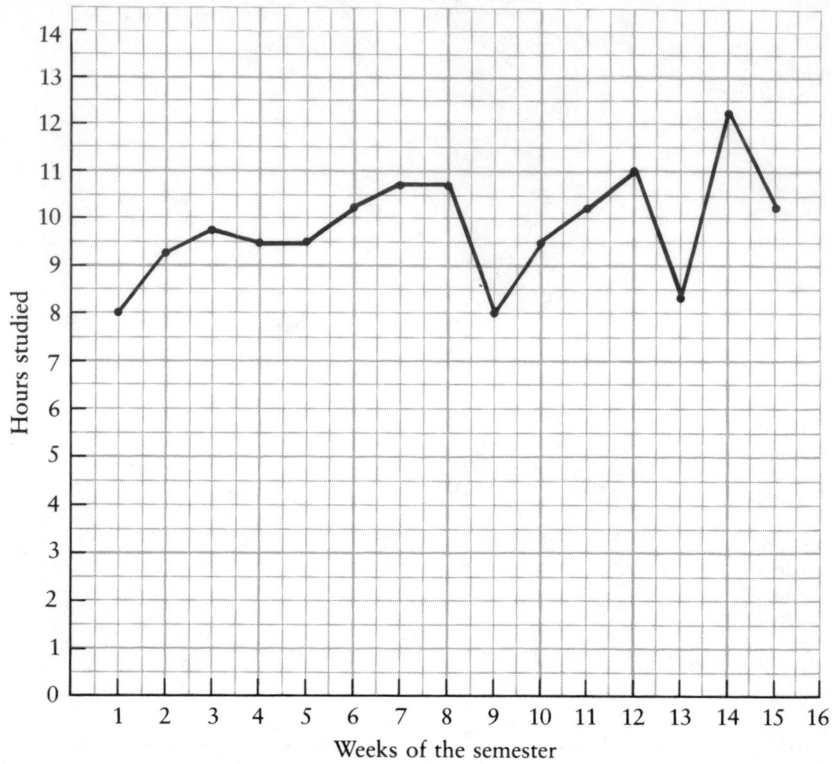

Figure 8-3 The finished graph, with dots connected to show pattern over time

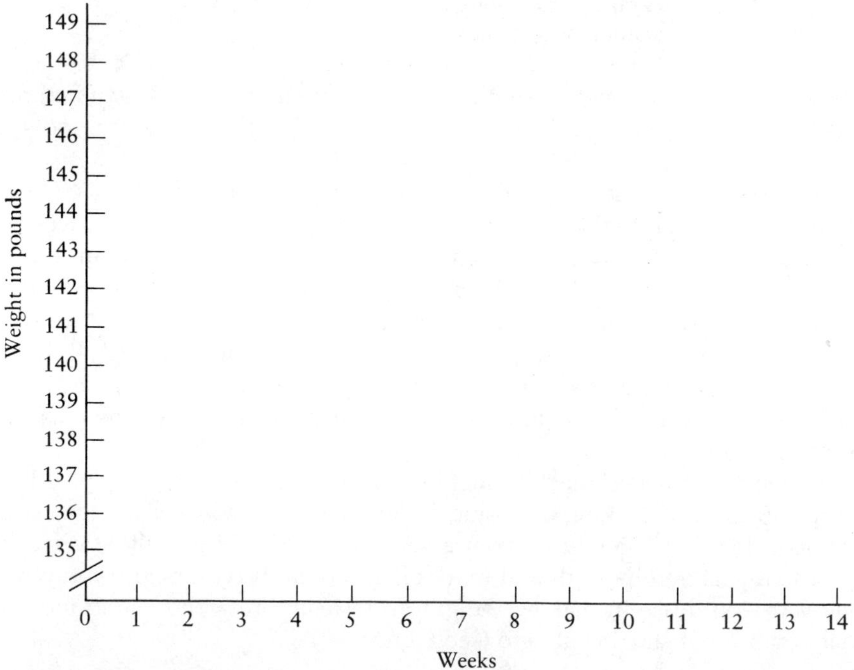

Figure 8-4 Simplified form of graph for weight

Using the Graph
By inspecting her graph, Marlene was able to see her data quite clearly. Her pattern was one of general progress, slow and steady, with minor fluctuations—except for weeks 9 and 13. She reviewed her daily logs for those weeks and found that during both she had been ill for several days. Marlene concluded that her time-management (plus reinforcement) plan was working rather well. She resolved to continue it for the following semester and raised her goal to 18 hours of studying per week.

More than one behavior can be recorded on the same graph, as is illustrated by the following student's records. Tom wanted to increase the number of comments he made in his classes. He found it difficult to speak in public because he was afraid others would think his comments were silly or trivial. This fear was particularly acute in large classes, in which he felt that whatever he wanted to say had to be good enough to justify taking the time of so many people.

Tom decided to begin by practicing in small classes and then, if that worked, to try it in larger classes. His goal was to speak at least once per day in a class. "My reinforcer was playing in my rock group. This is a very powerful reinforcer for me in two ways: I really enjoy playing guitar; and if I didn't show up for a gig, five other guys would wring my neck."

Figure 8-5 is a graph of Tom's data. Notice that in making his graph he counted only school days, so each week has only five days. He always had his notebook with him when he went to class, so it was easy for him to make a simple check on a sheet of paper every time he spoke up.

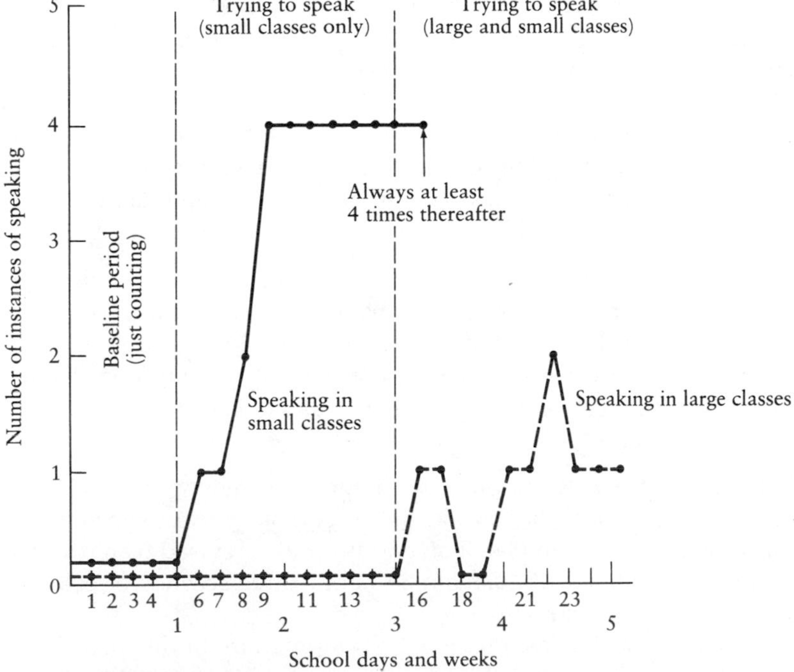

Figure 8-5 Speaking in class

Tom's graph shows a rapid improvement in his speaking behavior in small classes. Beginning on the first day of his plan, he began to speak up in class, and within four days he was engaging in what he called "constant participation." Most people progress at a slower rate, as Tom himself did when he went into the second stage of his plan—speaking in large classes. You can see from the graph that he did make some progress but that his improvements were interspersed with setbacks—days on which he didn't talk at all. This is the kind of situation in which a graph is particularly helpful, for it shows that you are making *some* progress.

Be creative with your graphs. The whole point is to give you an easy-to-read display of your problems and progress.

Changing Targets

During the course of a plan, the actual target behavior may change. For example, Ben began a plan to increase his studying, but he soon concluded that one of the reasons he didn't study enough was that he felt too stressed by events in his life. So he changed his plan and began to work to reduce the stress that accompanied his demanding schedule of activities.

Sally was very shy and withdrawn, especially in groups. She thought about her problem and concluded that if she smiled more, she would appear less withdrawn and would gain reinforcement from others. Her original goal (plan 1) was to increase smiling behavior by simply making a note on a card each time she smiled at someone she didn't know well. After she established a baseline, she worked out a plan in which she earned tokens (to be applied later to the purchase of elegant clothes) by smiling at people. She gave herself instructions to smile, and she enlisted the help of her roommates to administer the token system.

Figure 8-6 presents part of her data. Notice that at first Sally improved just because she was keeping records: her smiles increased even during the baseline period. Of course, she was quite pleased. Around day 11 or 12, she began to rethink the definition of her problem. She later wrote in her report:

> I started to realize that although I was smiling more at people, I still appeared withdrawn. This was because I was not looking at them. I was smiling but looking down at the ground. Most people feel that looking into someone's eyes is a sign of interest, so I decided that just smiling at others wasn't enough. I had to smile, *and* I had to make eye contact.

So Sally changed her definition of the target, broadening it. In plan 2, she counted not only smiling but also instances of making eye contact that lasted several seconds. She began plan 2 on day 14. In this revised plan, she earned her tokens for smiling *and* maintaining about three seconds of eye contact, and she gave herself instructions to do both.

Plan 3 represents the last phase of Sally's program. In this phase, she began shaping eye contact so that it would occur as often as smiling alone had occurred in plan 1.

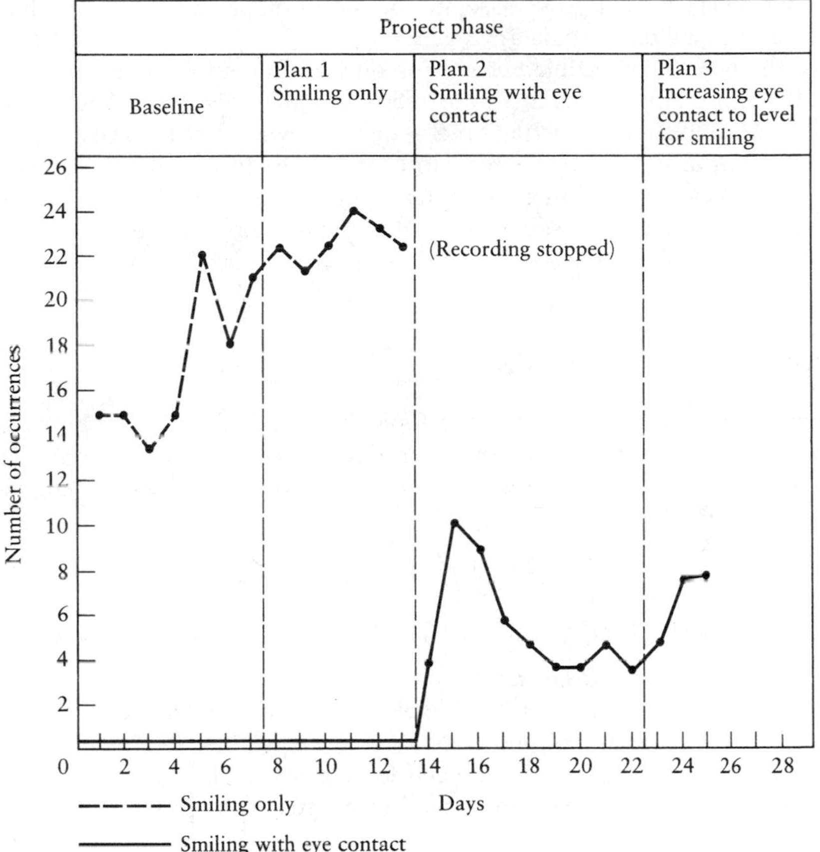

Figure 8-6 Smiling and eye contact

If the changes in target behaviors are substantial and abrupt, it's best to establish a new baseline. It is like beginning a new plan. For example, you might change your behavior from "smiling at people" to "going to public places." When Ben changed his plan from "increasing studying" to "reducing stress" he had to begin a new baseline period to learn what was setting off his stress. A major shift in the behavior to be observed calls for a new baseline.

Sometimes you will *add* something to an ongoing plan, as Sally did when she added eye contact to smiling. You can obtain a baseline by simply continuing the first target behavior for a few days and, at the same time, counting how often you perform the *new* target behavior that is to be added to the plan. For example, you might start out with "dieting" as your target and, after a few weeks, decide to add "exercising" to your plan. In that case, you would continue to reinforce changing your eating pattern for a few days while you obtain a baseline on exercising.

If your initial problem was an undesired behavior, you probably began by gathering baseline data on that behavior. Later, you may have decided to increase an incompatible response at the expense of the undesired behavior.

But you don't have a good baseline for the incompatible behavior. Should you record new baseline data?

If the new, incompatible behavior is one you intend to continue permanently—for example, deciding to increase "reading good books" as a behavior incompatible with "wasting time"—then you will want to have a separate baseline for it. If you don't intend to continue the incompatible behavior—for example, slapping your hand instead of cracking your knuckles—then it is not necessary to get a separate count of the incompatible behavior as long as you are keeping a good record of the undesired target behavior.

Tips for Typical Topics

Look up your particular goal in the Topic Index at the back of the book, and read each section of the book in which that kind of goal or problem is discussed. This will give you ideas for your plan or remind you of anything you have forgotten.

Chapter Summary

Combining A, B, and C Elements

Good plans for change must include elements of antecedent control, development of new behaviors, and control of consequences. You should expect that problems will arise, and you need to be prepared to use more than one approach. For example, you may need to approach the problem in two or more stages.

If you are addicted to overeating, smoking, or other consummatory acts, use the two-stage process. *First,* avoid the controlling antecedents, one at a time if necessary. *Second,* develop a new behavior to be performed in response to the old cue. Then, when you are once again confronted with the antecedent, you won't slip back into performing the consummatory act. Like any new behaviors, these behaviors will have to be shaped, rehearsed, and reinforced.

The Features of a Good Plan

Good plans have the following features:

1. Rules that state the techniques to use in specific situations
2. Goals and subgoals
3. Feedback about your behavior, based on your self-observations
4. A comparison of the feedback with your goals and subgoals to see if you are progressing
5. Adjustments in the plan as conditions change

Before you design your final plan, review the checklist of important elements to consider and be sure you can answer yes to most of the questions.

Be creative in designing your plan; use the brainstorming technique to generate more ideas. For additional guidance, refer to the complete sample plan provided.

Is It Working? and Changing Targets

The data you collect through your observations will lead you to certain decisions about your plan. Your record (in the form of averages, percentages, or a graph) may show such clear improvement as to warrant continuing the plan unchanged. The opposite extreme is also possible, indicating that the plan needs careful reworking. This involves rethinking each aspect of the plan for possible change: specifying a behavioral target, making observations, learning how the behavior is related to its antecedents and consequences, and making a plan for change.

YOUR OWN SELF-DIRECTION PROJECT: STEP EIGHT

1. State your goal. If it is a complex goal or one that will take a long time to achieve, state the first short-term goal. State your current level of performance. Your baseline records provide you with information to use in setting your subgoals.

2. State specific rules for each subgoal. What behaviors will you have to perform in each situation to achieve the subgoal? Examine the three preliminary plans you prepared in Chapters 5, 6, and 7, and consider various alternatives. You may select features from only one of your preliminary plans or combine elements from all of them. Consider each technique. Which ones will you use?

3. Be sure to obtain accurate self-observations and feedback all along the way and to compare your performance with your goals.

4. Fill out the checklist in Box 8-1 for the plan you are considering. Incorporate as many different techniques as you can. Write out your plan in detail, following these four steps. Sign your contract, and begin implementing it.

9

Problem Solving and Relapse Prevention

Outline

- Problem Solving
- Relapse Prevention
- *Chapter Summary*
- *Your Own Self-Direction Project: Step Nine*

Learning Objectives

Problem Solving

1. What is the "tinkering strategy" for dealing with self-change projects?
2. What are the four steps in problem solving?
   a. How can they be applied to your project?
   b. Describe the research on the value of problem solving.
3. How do failures in self-observation contribute to failure in self-modification?
4. Name the reasons people stop recording.
5. What are some reasons people might not use the techniques? What can be done to cope with each?

Relapse Prevention

6. Outline fully the relapse process.
   a. What is the difference between a lapse and a relapse?
   b. What are three common types of high-risk situation?
   c. Explain the abstinence violation effect.
7. How can you prepare for high-risk situations?
   a. How can you identify your personal high-risk situations?
   b. Describe how to have and use a relapse fantasy.
8. How can you cope with a high-risk situation?
   a. How can you use problem solving for high-risk situations?
   b. List the kinds of self-instructions you should prepare for coping with high-risk situations.
   c. How should you practice using these instructions?
9. How can you stop lapses from becoming relapses?
   a. What should you do as soon as you lapse?
   b. What kind of self-contract and reminder card should you prepare in advance?

It is realistic to expect some problems in self-modification. Anticipating problems allows you to deal with them as soon as they appear and before your newly developed behavior has disappeared. It's like keeping a fire extinguisher around. You can put out the small blazes before you need to call the fire department.

Problems can occur while you are engaged in self-modification, or they can crop up after you are finished. For example, you might move along well with your exercise project for a few weeks but then not be able to make any more progress. Or you might finish a self-change project, such as cutting back on excessive drinking, only to find to your dismay that the problem behavior has come back. In this chapter, we deal with both kinds of problems: those that come up while you are actively engaged in self-modification, and threats of relapse that occur afterwards.

Problem Solving

Tinkering with Your Plan

It often happens that your first plan is not enough by itself to change the target behavior. After you begin, you discover something that makes it more difficult to manage than you anticipated. Expect that there will be problems.

Start with the best plan you can devise. See what difficulties occur, and then tinker with the plan, making it more effective in dealing with the unexpected problems.

Rebecca wrote:

> There was this person I worked with, Jean, whom I really didn't like at all. As a Christian, I know that loving one another is an important command. But I couldn't bring myself to love Jean—not with *agape* [God's love]. She felt the same way, which made it worse.

Rebecca decided to work out a self-change plan with the goal of increasing *agape* for Jean.

Her plan seemed sound. She wrote a detailed contract that included six shaping steps for talking to Jean in a friendly way.

Step 1: Smile at Jean at least once a day at work.
Step 2: Smile and say "Hi."
Step 3: Go up and ask her, "How's everything?"
Step 4: Compliment her on something.
Step 5: Talk about upcoming events at work.
Step 6: Talk about anything else.

Rebecca gathered records carefully on a steno tablet. Her reinforcement system used candy as an immediate reward for being nice to Jean and tokens to be used to buy favorite things as longer-term reinforcers.

Results: "The first two steps worked fine, but when I asked Jean 'How's everything?' I caught her off guard, and she began talking so much that I became uncomfortable and wanted to withdraw. While I felt ready to approach her, I wasn't ready for her response. So I revised my plan."

In Rebecca's *second plan,* she dealt with a problem that she had not foreseen when she devised her first plan. She tinkered with her old plan, changing elements here and there in an effort to make the plan work better.

> I shared this new plan with one of my closest friends. He works with me and knows of my problem. I told him that I would let him know when I was planning to talk with Jean and asked him to give me about

two minutes and then call me to his office. That way I had enough time to exchange friendly greetings with Jean, without feeling uncomfortable.

The reinforcers were the same, and the record keeping continued.

Results: "The two-minute limit worked really well. If I felt like talking to Jean longer, I'd just ask my friend to please wait until I was finished. Also, I dropped the idea of complimenting Jean so deliberately. I felt this wouldn't be sincere. I decided that if she did something I felt I could honestly compliment, I would do so."

After seven weeks, Rebecca wrote:

I can honestly say that things are now fine between Jean and me. The plan really helped, but in my case all the credit goes to God, who worked in Jean's heart as well as in mine to bring us closer together.

Tinkering helped a bit, too.

Here's a second example of tinkering with a plan to make it more effective. A 55-year-old man in our class submitted this final report:

My goal: I wanted to build up to running a mile or so every other day. At the time I began, I had never run at all, so my baseline was zero.

Antecedents: What I needed was an antecedent that would get me started! I really don't think I refrained from running because I would get painfully winded or anything. It's just that there always seemed to be something else to do, so I didn't start. Going for a run requires all sorts of behaviors—putting on the shoes and shorts, stretching, then starting to run.

Intervention plan: My first plan was to require myself to run a quarter of a mile or more every day. I intended to gradually increase my running up to a mile or so. My self-contract was that I would get a dollar to spend on anything I wanted for every time I ran.

If you look at my graph [Figure 9-1], you'll see that this plan worked for the first four days, but after that I just sort of quit. I drifted for two weeks and then faced up to the fact that I wasn't running.

After several days of doing nothing, it became painfully obvious that plan 1 was not working. So I listed all the reasons why it was not working:

- I've never run a mile, and it seems like a long way to run.
- I'm afraid I might give myself a heart attack.
- I tell myself "It's too far, and it could be dangerous."
- It seems like a lot of trouble.
- I find all sorts of excuses for not going running.

I decided that I probably wouldn't have a heart attack if I ran really slowly. I made a mental note to ask my doctor about it the next time I had a checkup. I also decided that the main reason I didn't go out was that it just seemed like a long way for a duffer like me to go. I guess

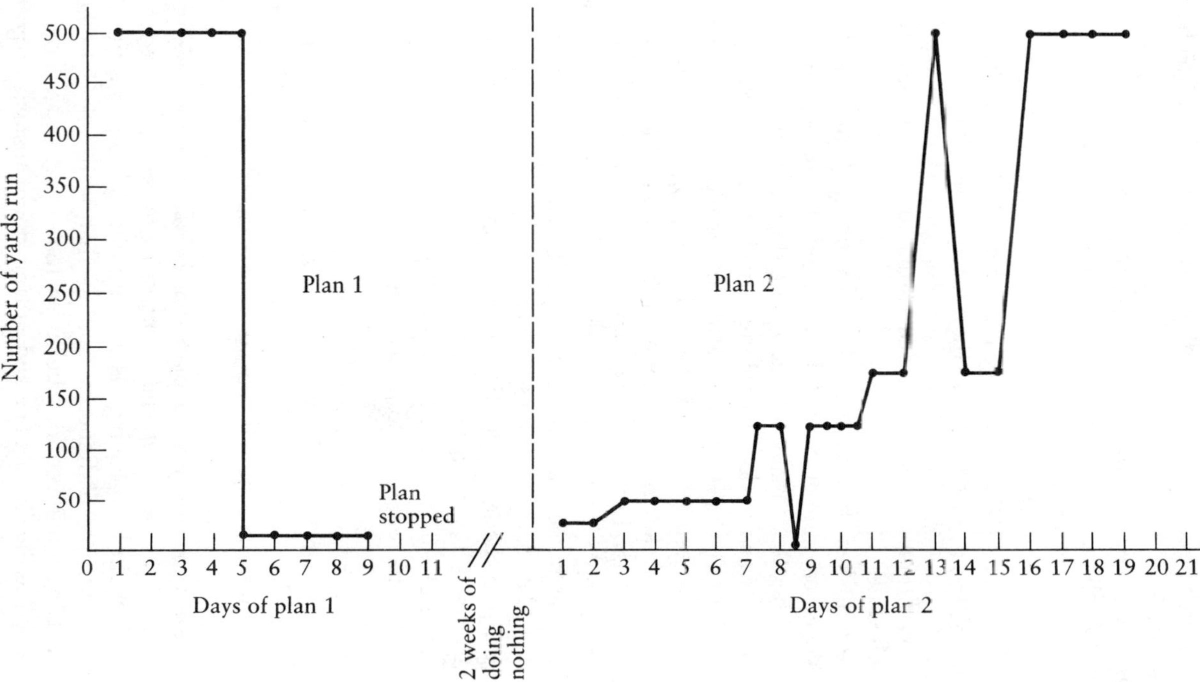

Figure 9-1 Daily running

the main reason I quit was that I was starting too high. Then I remembered the shaping rule about not starting too high. "Why should I expect to be able to start that high?" I asked myself. And I redesigned my plan as follows:

Stage 1: Put on footwear and clothes, and walk around the house (30 yards).
Stage 2: Walk around the house twice (60 yards).
Stage 3: Walk around the house four times (120 yards).
Stage 4: Walk around the house six times (180 yards).
Stage 5: Once I get to this point, I will run a quarter of a mile. When I can do that, I will try to increase to half a mile, then three-quarters of a mile, and then finally one mile.

I did several things to make sure that I stuck to this ridiculously easy shaping schedule.

First, I established the rule that I have to do my "run" before I can have a beer or eat supper. *Second,* I explained the whole thing to my wife and told her that I really wanted to build up exercising this way. I precommitted myself to do it by asking her (1) to remind me to do it, (2) to call me on it if she saw me eating or drinking a beer before I had done my exercise, and (3) to check on my progress by examining the chart I keep posted on the kitchen cupboard on which I record my daily progress. *Third,* I set aside five minutes each morning to imagine resisting the temptation to have a beer or eat when I come home. I imagine coming home and saying to myself "Wow, it's time to relax after another hard day!" I see myself getting a can of beer, and, just as I'm about to pop the top, I practice resisting this urge and saying to myself "But first, I'll go for a short run."

At the time of this writing, I am able to run a quarter of a mile regularly and hope to be able to increase it.

The right side of Figure 9-1 shows the man's progress. Notice that several things had been interfering with the man's progress: old reinforcers (having a beer as soon as he got home), thoughts (thinking he might have a heart attack), doubts (thinking a mile is too far), and shaping errors (starting too high).

When you are tinkering with a plan that is not working, ask yourself some questions: *What makes it difficult or impossible to perform the target behavior?* Is it some thought I am having? Is it something I have no control over? (Remember the example of Rebecca finding that Jean talked to her too much.) Am I getting reinforced for a behavior that makes my desired behavior difficult (such as having a beer and sitting down instead of going for run)?

Analyze the obstacles to performing your target behavior. What antecedents make it difficult to perform the target behavior, or what antecedents are lacking that would make it easier to perform? Have the correct incompatible or alternate behaviors been chosen? Are there still consequences that maintain the old, undesired behavior? Use the A-B-C system to systematically check for obstacles that prevent you from carrying out your plan.

The Technique for Solving Problems

Problem solving means thinking about the obstacles to your progress and figuring out how to overcome them. It means thinking critically about your own efforts to change (Zechmeister & Johnson, 1992). You need to be able to define the problem clearly, think of solutions, and predict the consequences of various alternatives (D'Zurilla, 1986; Kelly, Scott, Pruc, & Rychtarik, 1985). Learning to solve problems in life allows you to be more flexible and independent in coping and gives you confidence for dealing with other problems in the future (D'Zurilla & Nezu, 1989).

When you encounter a problem, follow this four-step process (D'Zurilla & Goldfried, 1971; D'Zurilla & Nezu, 1982):

1. List all the details of the problem as concretely as possible.
2. Brainstorm as many solutions as you can without at first criticizing any of them.
3. Choose one or more of the solutions.
4. Think of ways to put the solutions into operation; then check to be sure you are actually implementing them.

The following examples illustrate how each of these four steps can be used to overcome obstacles in your self-change program.

Listing the details. Kalani wrote:

> I've known for years that I overeat. Finally, I began to keep records of when I overeat—at what particular times I go off my diet. I listed these as the details of my problem. They were surprisingly regular. I often ate two or three bowls of popcorn while watching TV. I always overate after exercising on Mondays. I usually ate three of four snacks on Saturdays. So it wasn't that I overate all the time—just in specific situations. I set out to deal with those particular situations.

A woman who wanted to give up drinking coffee wrote:

> I made up a plan to stop drinking coffee, but after a few days it ground to a halt. Then I made a new plan, but it also fizzled. So I listed the details of what was happening when I went off my plan. I noticed that I'd be thinking "I need this coffee for energy." So I started a new plan to give myself some energy when I needed it, using meditation, and after that it was a lot easier to give up coffee.

Listing many alternatives. One of our colleagues who stopped smoking noted that stopping was easy, but staying off was the problem. So she made a long list of things to do when she wanted a cigarette: chew gum, eat mints, do calisthenics, walk, brush teeth, drink coffee, work with plants, cook, pay bills, make a phone call, mend clothing, iron, shop, groom, shower, take a hot bath, clean closets, drink water, fiddle with hands, smell something pleasant, and so on. When she found herself craving a cigarette, she would take out her list and try to do one or more of the things on it.

Choosing an alternative. Ruby's goal was to engage in race walking three times a week.

> After two weeks, however, I had to acknowledge that I was not keeping records because there was nothing to record. I felt I was already too busy, and the plan to race-walk three times a week was just one more thing I had to do. I needed to have some fun, so I made a list of all the things I could do for fun that would also give me some exercise. I selected ice skating, and set a goal to go skating once or twice weekly.

Putting the new plan into operation and checking to be sure it's working. Ruby continued:

> I had to force myself to make skating a priority, but I succeeded in going once a week for eight weeks. Although I often didn't want to go, I enjoyed it once I got there. I kept a record, making a check mark each week when I did go. After eight weeks, I started going twice a week. Now I have to say, I absolutely love skating!

In taking these four steps, you won't just go through the process in numerical order. Expect to go back and forth from listing details to listing possible solutions.

Larry reported that his target behavior was to stop drinking so many colas at work. He drank several cans every day. He succeeded in reducing his habit, but then he changed jobs and became a night taxi driver. Within a few weeks, he was back to drinking several cans each night to keep himself awake.

Larry listed all the relevant details of the problem:

- It keeps me high.
- There are convenient machine outlets on practically every corner.
- I tell myself that it helps me stay awake.

Then he listed possible solutions:

- Tell myself "Don't do it, Larry" whenever I approach a vending machine.
- Keep a record in the cab and a total record at home.
- Get another job.
- Substitute some less harmful drink.
- Buy the drink, then throw it in the rubbish.
- Get fully adjusted to working at night, so I don't have to use the drinks to stay awake.
- Keep track of all the money I'm spending on Cokes.™

Larry finally decided to do three things: (1) tell himself, "Don't do it"; (2) keep a record of the money he spent and the number of colas he drank each day; and (3) go to small stores where he could buy fruit juice instead of colas.

Results: "It worked very well. I haven't touched a Coke since I started this project. I have become an orange juice freak instead."

The Value of Problem Solving

Combining problem solving with self-modification techniques is a potent approach to self-change. Problem solving means thinking critically about what works and what does not in your plan for change. Richards and Perri (1978) trained students who were concerned about academic underachievement and who wanted to develop better study skills. The researchers trained *some* of these students to use simple problem-solving strategies when they ran into problems. The others did not receive such training. There was a rapid deterioration in study skills among the students who used *no* problem-solving strategies. By contrast, the students who used problem-solving techniques were able to maintain their improved study skills up to one year after completion of their training.

Ex-smokers are more likely to stay off cigarettes if they use problem-solving techniques to cope with problems they encounter (Perri, Richards, & Schultheis, 1977). College students are less likely to become depressed at upsetting life events if they are good at problem solving (Nezu, Nezu, Saraydarian, Kalmar, & Ronan, 1986.) Weight loss is greater among dieters who learn problem-solving skills (Black & Sherba, 1983). People manage the stresses in their lives better if they know the problem solving steps we've taught you here (D'Zurilla, 1990). Recent reviews of the research have shown that problem solving is helpful for a variety of problems, including various addictions, depression, stress, poor college performance, marital problems, and prevention of unwanted pregnancy (Durlak, 1983; D'Zurilla, 1986; D'Zurilla & Nezu, 1982; Nezu, 1987).

If your plan involves giving up something you enjoy—such as overeating, being lazy, drinking, smoking, or biting your nails—*expect problems.* When you falter in carrying out your first plan, notice what parts of the plan were successful and for how long. Keep the successful features in your later plans. *Notice your successes as well as your failures.*

People who focus solely on their failures are more likely to become discouraged and quit (Kirschenbaum & Tomarken, 1982). If, for example, you stop smoking for six days and then have a cigarette, don't think of it as a total failure. After all, you succeeded for six days. Can you repeat those six successful days? What went wrong on the seventh? Use problem solving to cope with that obstacle.

Whenever you get stuck in your self-modification project, review your earlier attempts. See which parts worked that you could use again. A man who had successfully completed a project to stop procrastinating reported:

> A year or so later, I started a new project—to increase social skills. It didn't work well. I knew my earlier project had been a real success, so I checked back to see what techniques I had used to stop procrastinat-

ing. In all, I had used six different techniques, and I could see that four of them could easily be modified for use in my new project. So I branched out, adding these techniques to my current plan, and now my social-skills plan is working.

Common Reasons for Failure at Self-Modification

Efforts to change are not always successful. Understanding the reasons why some people fail at self-modification can help you be on guard. What blocks success for some? What can be done to increase success? In Chapter 2 we listed some of the reasons for failure in self-change. These provide the details that you should look for in your problem solving:

- Stress
- Social pressures
- Giving up at the first mistake
- Not trying very hard
- Not believing you can change
- Ambivalence about changing

In recent years, several theorists have written about this topic (Fitzgibbon & Kirschenbaum, in press; Kirschenbaum & Tomarken, 1982; Peterson, 1983; Stuart, 1980). What follows is a distillation of their ideas and ours.

Insufficient problem solving. People who don't learn and use the problem-solving ideas in this chapter are less likely to succeed in their self-modification efforts (Fitzgibbon & Kirschenbaum, in press). That's because almost everyone encounters problems, and if you aren't prepared to deal with them, they will defeat you. Carol wrote,

> Last year I was trying to manage my time better—I was newly back in college—while coping with a divorce at the same time. A lot of the time I was just too stressed to do much about time management, until I finally realized that I should try problem solving. The next time my time management program didn't work I listed the details of the problem, and of course one of the big issues was that I often felt a lot of stress. I'd feel too stressed out to try to manage my time well. So I added daily exercise to my program as a way of coping with the stress, and my time management seemed to go better as well.

Failures in self-observation. A middle-aged woman wrote:

> After I finished your course, I continued exercising four times a week. It was the first time in my life that I'd ever been able to stick to an exercise schedule, and I kept records for several months to be sure I wouldn't quit. Then my husband and I went on a month's vacation. My daily schedule was completely different than it had been at home, and

> I quit keeping records. Perhaps that's why I stopped thinking about exercising. By the time the month was over, I had hardly exercised at all. When we returned home, I put my record sheet back up on the refrigerator door, and within two weeks I was back to my old aerobic self.

Without good self-observations, you may not hold yourself to the goals you want to achieve. It's often too easy to give in to the short-term urge instead of thinking of the more long-term goal. Continued self-observation helps deal with this problem.

Self-observations force us to think more clearly about the causes of our behavior. Kalani, the man who was trying to lose weight, wrote:

> I started a project to cut down overeating, but it wasn't getting anywhere. For more than a year, I messed around with one diet after another, but usually went off after a day or two. Then I started keeping careful records of what I ate every day. That's all—no diet, just record keeping. I was amazed. I found out I never overeat at breakfast or at a mid-morning snack. Sometimes I have a bit too much at lunch. But it's supper where I often eat twice as much as I should. And even here, it's not the same for suppers on every night. I almost never overeat on Tuesday, Wednesday, or Thursday. Friday night I go out with my family and eat too much from the buffet at our favorite restaurant. On weekends I often cook a big meal for the family and really stuff it in. Monday nights I work late, and I often eat too much when I get home. So I've learned that it is particular times of the week that stimulate my overeating.

Kalani can now start a plan for self-change that is much more specifically focused than just a vague diet. For example, he can concentrate on one particular day and meal when he overeats and learn new behaviors for that time. Then he can move on to the next day and meal, and so on, until he has the whole week's eating under control. Without such careful self-observations, he would not have known enough about his eating habits.

Keeping records even when you are not succeeding at self-change increases your chances of later success. Good self-observations bring greater understanding of the antecedents and consequences of your behavior. Without these observations, you may mislabel the antecedents and consequences or not be aware of their influence. For example, Vera complained of strong feelings of loneliness.

> I thought I was lonely because there was no one I was close to. I kept looking over the available men in my life, thinking one of them could be my boyfriend and then I'd never be lonely anymore. But none of them measured up. So I kept on being lonely. I thought the cause was a general lack of interesting men. I wasn't paying any attention to my own thoughts. When I recorded the thoughts I was having when I dealt with men, it became clear that the thoughts were very negative.

> I'd meet one of the men I knew and think, "Here goes another dull conversation. God, why are people so dull?"
>
> After keeping records on my thoughts for a few days, I could see that this was a pattern. I want to get right into important, meaningful conversations. So I have these negative thoughts when I get into situations that involve small talk. The trouble is, all social situations involve small talk. You don't just meet somebody and start right off talking about the meaning of life.
>
> So it finally dawned on me that my thoughts were creating the problem. I had to quit being so negative about chatting, because that is how you start to get to know people. That's the project I'm working on now. I think of those conversations as "openers," not "small talk."

Note where Vera's self-observation has led. Originally her complaint was loneliness. But after several days of self-observation, she realized that to some degree she was the cause of her loneliness because of her attitude toward casual social exchanges. Her new project—to be more positive in her thoughts about casual conversations—will help her in the long run to deal with her loneliness problem.

Why doesn't everyone keep good self-observation records? As we mentioned in Chapter 3, the experience of "failure" is a major reason. When you have to record a series of failures, you are likely to stop self-observation (Kirschenbaum & Tomarken, 1982). Thus, it's important to record the successes you have. Don't just record negative information about yourself—the number of missed opportunities to be assertive, for example—record your successes as well. Your successes may be small at first, but that is all the more reason to record them.

Another reason people fail to keep good records is that they are ambivalent about changing. Kalani, the overweight man, told us:

> When I was keeping records of my eating, some days I wouldn't record. After this had happened several times, I had to admit to myself that I wasn't keeping the records because I wanted to pig out. So I had to face my true feelings. Did I want to stop overeating or not? I decided I did, so I forced myself to record the reasons why I wasn't keeping a record. That worked well, and pretty soon I went back to keeping records all the time.

Not using the techniques. You might read this text, learn the ideas in it, and still not use the techniques for change in your own self-modification project. Why does this happen? The next several paragraphs contain a series of reasons that people might *not* use the techniques. Do any of these points apply to you? If so, stop to think: (1) Do I want to cope with that point? (2) How can I cope with it?

You don't believe the techniques will help you. More than 220 people who were trying to stop smoking were asked how they coped with temptations to smoke. Helpful techniques included distracting themselves, escaping from the situation, physical activity, thinking of the health consequences, delaying, and eating or drinking. They also listed two "techniques" that were of no use: self-punishment for smoking and trying simply to exert willpower to resist temptation (Shiffman, 1984).

Yet some people persist in the belief that the best way to gain self-control is through self-punishment or by simple force of willpower.

Some people believe that keeping records about one's problem is silly, or record keeping makes them uncomfortable. Yet record keeping is a keystone of self-directed behavior. A few people believe that techniques such as self-reward are self-indulgent or pointless, so they don't use them.

Are your beliefs adaptive? Do you believe that just exerting willpower is the thing to do? If so, how do you square that with Shiffman's findings that it doesn't help? Are your beliefs preventing you from testing self-modification, thus preventing you from making a judgment based on your actual experience? *Try the techniques; then evaluate them.*

You don't believe you can attain the goal you want. Your belief that you can cope with a problem affects how hard you try to overcome it, and that in turn affects your success (Bandura, 1977). The exercises in Chapter 2 for increasing self-efficacy can help establish feelings of confidence.

You may have lost confidence in your ability to change because you have been observing only your failures (Candiotte & Lichtenstein, 1981). Keeping track of your successes can increase self-confidence.

Some people take credit for their failures, but not for their successes (Dweck, 1975). "When I fail, it's my fault; when I succeed, it's luck." Monitor your thinking. Focus on your successes, and realize that *you* are responsible for the positive things that have happened so far. "When I fail, it's because I didn't try hard enough. When I succeed, it's because I *did* try hard enough."

You really don't want to change. There are times in all our lives when we are on an even keel, when nothing needs correcting. If you are sincerely satisfied with your present adjustment, work out with your instructor some way to learn the techniques without doing a self-change project. We suggest doing a project because in our experience it is the best way to learn the techniques. The purpose of this text is not to force you to change something now, but to teach you techniques for change that you can use when you need them.

If you still feel ambivalent about changing—"Do I *really* want to study more each day?"—recheck the list of advantages and disadvantages of changing that you filled out (see Chapter 2). Fill it out again. Perhaps you have changed your mind.

Sometimes we don't see the disadvantages of changing until we begin to change. A woman who had lost a lot of weight told us:

> After I began to approach normal weight, I saw some disadvantages to it that I hadn't realized before. For one thing, my friends expected me to participate in sports, but I was still as clumsy as ever. I no longer

had a ready-made excuse. I don't ever get special consideration from people anymore, like I used to when I was fat. I guess I sort of liked that special treatment.

You can't put in the time and effort required. A sincere self-modification effort does require the work of using the techniques. Try to pick a topic that is worth that work.

Sometimes a person's life is already so stressful that adding a self-change project seems too much (Peterson, 1983). One of our students who had a full-time job, was involved in divorce proceedings, and was also graduating from college said, "I know I should quit smoking, but now is just not the time to work on it." We agreed and suggested that he might work on stress reduction as his present task.

You started off with some success but then became discouraged. Dana's project was to make more friends. At first he only kept records of how often he talked with others. He showed some success almost immediately, probably because just keeping the records encouraged him to talk more. But he didn't use any other techniques. After a few days, the novelty of record keeping wore off, and he slipped back into his old, reclusive ways. He gave up his self-change project, saying that it wasn't working.

Don't expect instant success. Be prepared to use a variety of techniques, and give them a chance to work. Expect to encounter obstacles, and use problem-solving techniques to overcome them.

Other people are discouraging your use of the techniques. Others may hold beliefs such as those just described—it won't work, it's silly, you just need willpower—and may encourage you not to bother (Shelton et al., 1981). Tell them you're going to try the techniques and then decide whether or not they work.

People may also place temptation in your way: "Go ahead, have a cigarette. One won't hurt." Some people may be inconvenienced or made uncomfortable by your efforts to change and may unthinkingly sabotage your plan. They may even do it out of politeness, as when a host at a party urges food on someone who is dieting.

Sometimes other people actually punish your attempts to change. This can be true for those who are trying to be assertive. Your behavior may make people uncomfortable; a new, assertive you rocks the boat. A student told us that all her life she had done whatever her elder sister suggested. When she began to practice asserting herself, her sister complained that she was becoming "pushy." This student eventually gained her sister's cooperation by explaining her goals and the reasons for them. But this is not always possible. You may have to choose: Are your new goals worth some opposition from friends or family?

Incidentally, you should know that most people *like* appropriately assertive women more than unassertive ones and think assertive women are more competent (Levin & Gross, 1984).

Relapse Prevention

Jeb took up smoking when he was 15. When he turned 25, he decided it was time to quit. He gave himself a date: "On August 1, I will quit smoking." As the date drew near, he worried about his ability to just quit, but he wanted to try. He woke up that fateful morning, fixed his coffee, reached for a cigarette, said "No," and threw all his cigarettes, matches, and ashtrays into the garbage. During the next ten days, he did not smoke at all.

Other things were changing for Jeb during this time. He and his girlfriend were having increasing difficulties. She wanted to break up, but Jeb didn't. Finally, she told Jeb she wouldn't see him anymore. This depressed him considerably, as he had thought she was "the one." His depression lingered, made worse by the fact that his grades on his most recent tests were unexpectedly low.

That weekend, to cheer himself up, Jeb went to a local singles bar. He wasn't cheered, however. The sight of all those strangers trying to make a good impression on each other just depressed him more. It also seemed as though everyone was smoking. "God, I feel rotten," he thought. "A cigarette would sure cheer me up right now." When a man at the bar offered him a cigarette, Jeb accepted. A few minutes later, he went to the vending machine and bought a pack of his favorite brand. He ordered another drink, felt his spirits lift, and lit up.

The next day Jeb woke up, poured his coffee, and had a cigarette. A year later, he is still smoking. "I was never sure that I could quit, anyway. When I went back that night, it just proved it. I'm addicted. I can't quit."

Jeb's story contains several elements that may help you prevent a relapse—whether your problem is overeating, smoking, drinking, substance abuse, or any other kind of situation in which relapse is a distinct possibility.

First, let's define *relapse.* Jeb's first cigarette after quitting need not have signaled a relapse: it was a *lapse,* but not a relapse. It would be defined as a relapse only if you defined *any* transgression of the rule "total abstinence forever" as a relapse. Jeb made this mistake. Overeaters shouldn't overeat, gamblers shouldn't ever gamble, and smokers should quit forever—these are the final goals. But on the way to recovery, many people with these kinds of problems make slips—lots of slips. But a slip is not necessarily a fall. As the saying goes, "One swallow does not a summer make." *Expect* that you will have lapses. The trick is to keep them from becoming relapses.

When a **lapse** occurs, you perform a behavior you are trying to avoid: you smoke a few smokes, you go back to being rude to your friends. A **relapse** means going back to your full-blown pattern of unwanted behavior.

A Model of the Relapse Process

What was going on when Jeb went back to smoking? He was emotionally upset: His girlfriend had left him, and his grades were low. He went into a risky situation—a singles bar where many people were smoking. Jeb doubted his ability to quit. He believed that a cigarette would make him feel better, and in fact it seemed to do so. Jeb was unprepared when the man

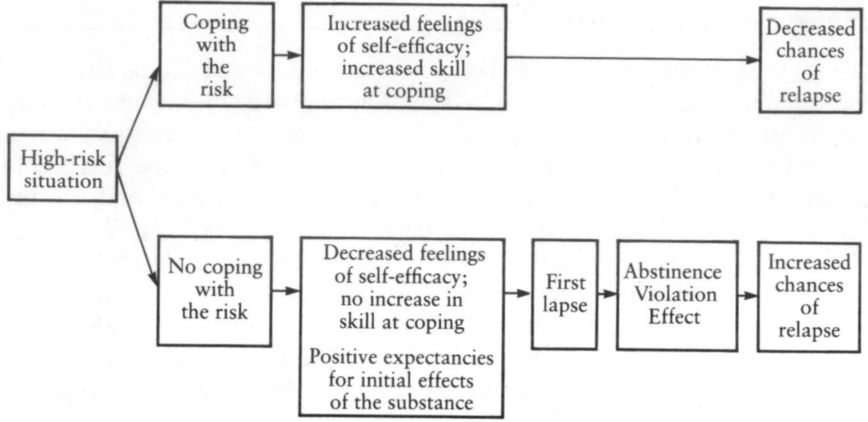

Figure 9-2 The relapse process
SOURCE: *Adapted from "Relapse Prevention: A Self-Control Program for the Treatment of Addictive Behaviors," by G. A. Marlatt, 1982. In R. B. Stuart (Ed.),* Adherence, Compliance, and Generalization in Behavioral Medicine, *(pp. 329–378) New York: Brunner/Mazel.*

offered him a cigarette, and so he accepted it. Afterwards, he felt that he had relapsed and that the relapse was due to conditions within himself—his addiction, his inability to quit, his lack of willpower. The implication was that there was no point in trying to quit again.

There are several models of the relapse process. One of the best comes from G. Alan Marlatt and his co-workers (Marlatt, 1982; Marlatt & George, 1990; Marlatt & Gordon, 1985). This model is diagrammed in Figure 9-2.

The relapse model applies *not only* to situations involving addictions, such as smoking or drinking. *It applies to any self-change project in which there is danger that you will fall back into your old, unwanted ways.* People whose problems involve gambling, exercising, studying, depression, unwanted sexual behaviors, and so on, will all benefit from learning about this model (Baer, Kivlahan, Fromme, & Marlatt, 1987; Belisle, Roskies, & Levesque, 1987; Brownell, Marlatt, Lichtenstein, & Wilson, 1986; Davis & Glaros, 1986; Gordon & Roffman, 1987; King & Frederiksen, 1984; Marques, 1987; Perri, Shapiro, Ludwig, Twentyman, & McAdoo, 1984).

For nonaddictive behaviors, such as procrastination, being rude, and so on, learning about the relapse process—and the errors in judgment you might make—can make the difference between success and failure over the long term. *For addictive behaviors, such as smoking, drinking, and taking drugs, it is absolutely essential that you use the ideas in this section so as to be successful in your efforts to change* (Glasgow & Lichtenstein, 1987).

We can use Jeb's experience to follow through the model. Jeb was in a high-risk situation when he became depressed, went to the singles bar, and was offered a cigarette. A high-risk situation is one that presents a greater than usual temptation to lapse into the unwanted behavior. What makes a situation high-risk depends to some degree on your individual learning history. Your Aunt Jenny's rhubarb pie may be an irresistible temptation to you, but not to everyone. There are, however, common patterns to high-risk situations, which Jeb's case illustrates.

Jeb's high-risk situations were these: He was upset and depressed. His girlfriend had left him. He felt as though everyone else in the bar was smoking. And, finally, someone offered him a cigarette. He was in a negative emotional state, and he felt social pressure to smoke.

At this point, Jeb might have coped with the risk. He could have noted that he was very upset, realized that a lapse was likely, and done something about it. That would take him through the top part of the model, where coping in the face of a high-risk situation leads to increased self-efficacy—and, we would add, to increased skill through practice of the coping behavior. This, in turn, lessens the chance of a relapse.

Unfortunately for Jeb, his behavior followed the bottom part of the model. He did not recognize that he was in a high-risk situation and did nothing to cope with it. He expected that he cigarette would be good, and he was *not* confident that he could stay off cigarettes. He used his old way of coping with depression—smoking—and had his first lapse. This combination of factors—not coping effectively with a high-risk situation, the belief that the indulgent behavior will make one feel better, and the belief that one probably can't give up the stuff anyway—greatly increases the chances of an initial lapse turning into a relapse (Marlatt & Gordon, 1985).

Jeb could have got up the next morning and gone right back to nonsmoking. But Jeb experienced what is called the **abstinence violation effect.** In this situation, the person is committed to *total abstinence:* The gambler takes the pledge never to gamble again; the smoker takes the pledge never to have another cigarette. When these people do backslide, they feel guilty, blame themselves for the lapse, and feel there is nothing they can do about it (Curry, Marlatt, & Gordon, 1987).

Once he had smoked in the bar, Jeb felt that his behavior demonstrated what he had always believed—that he could *not* quit smoking. He saw it as a personal failing. He ignored the transient nature of the situation that had caused his behavior—his low mood, being in the bar, being offered a cigarette—and focused instead on his own personal characteristics. Ignoring the effects of the situation in causing our behavior is a common pattern in human thinking (Nisbett & Ross, 1980). In Jeb's case, it led to real problems. Jeb's bad feelings about smoking, piled on top of his depression, made him feel worse, and he turned to his old way of feeling better—smoking—to lighten his mood. Later he told himself that the lapse was due to his personal failings and that there was no point in trying to quit again. Thus, the initial lapse became a full-blown relapse.

What can you do to lessen the chances that this will happen to you?

1. Recognize your own high-risk situations.
2. Cope with them when you meet them.
3. Prevent any lapse that occurs from becoming a relapse.

Recognizing High-Risk Situations

Actually, high-risk situations for behaviors like smoking, compulsive gambling, drug use, drinking, or overeating are fairly predictable (Marlatt &

George, 1990; Velicer, Diclemente, Rossi, & Prochaska, 1990). The following are typical high-risk situations:

- Being upset—experiencing negative emotions at home or at work
- Being in an interpersonal conflict, such as not getting along with a loved one
- Social settings in which other people encourage you to engage in the behavior you want to stop

It is extremely important to learn to recognize and cope with these tempting situations. People who do *something* to cope with high-risk situations are more likely to be successful than people who just trust to luck (Grilo, Shiffman, & Wing, 1989; Shiffman, 1982). And the more competently you cope with high-risk situations, the better your chances are of avoiding relapse (Davis & Glaros, 1986). Different kinds of situations call for different kinds of coping. You need to learn new ways to relax, and to recognize when you're feeling social pressure to engage in your old, unwanted behavior (Lichtenstein, Weiss, et al., 1986).

One situation in which people don't cope is when they temporarily lose interest in their goals, particularly health goals (Velicer, Lichtenstein, DiClemente, Rossir, & Prochaska, 1990). One sign that you are doing this, and thus are risking relapse, is that you stop exercising (Garvey, Heinold, & Rosner, 1989).

Being emotionally upset—depressed, angry, frustrated, bored, or anxious—is a major high-risk situation for everyone. In the past, you may have used your unwanted behavior—smoking, drinking, overeating, watching TV, or whatever—as a way of lightening your mood. Thus, you have been reinforced for the very behavior that is now unwanted. A father said to us,

> I've tried three times in the past two weeks to stop smoking. Each time, an argument with my teenage son got me back to smoking. He's in a rebellious period, and his actions upset me a lot. I take a walk to cool off—and invariably end up down at the corner store buying a pack of cigarettes.

Your personal high-risk situations can be learned through self-observation. This is why *it is critically important to continue to keep records even if your plan for self-modification is failing.* After the father made accurate self-observations, he was in a position to do something effective: He gave himself instructions not to react so strongly to what his son did, and he practiced relaxation when he got upset. He also went for longer walks and didn't let himself pass the store on the way.

Another risky situation involves *social pressure* from others to engage in your unwanted behavior. You want to quit overeating, but your Aunt Jenny bakes her special rhubarb pie and brings it over to your house. Her feelings will be hurt if you don't eat some. Or your old drinking buddy encourages you to drop your attempts to stop drinking. He doesn't want to lose *his* drinking buddy. Your friends offer you the foods they know you like because they want to be hospitable and friendly.

Social situations are particularly risky if the other people are doing the very thing you are trying to stop doing. It's much harder to stop smoking, for example, if you socialize a lot with people who smoke (Mermelstein, Cohen, Lichtenstein, Baer, & Kamarck, 1986). If you want to exercise every day at 5:00 P.M., don't spend that time with people who hate exercise. If you want to increase your studying in the evening, don't schedule that time to be with people who goof off every evening.

Beyond the three risky situations already described, a generally risky situation occurs when you have been drinking. *Alcohol makes us less self-aware* (Hull, 1987). Any time you have been watching yourself carefully to be sure you don't backslide, the risk is greater when you are drinking because you are paying less attention to yourself. Therefore, you are more likely to smoke, overeat, be rude, or whatever else it is that you're trying to stop. One of our students said to us, "I've stopped having discussions—arguments, really—with my husband when I've been drinking. I know I fall back on my old, mean ways of talking to him then."

Your self-observations may show you the situations that are high-risk for you—being in a singles bar, social situations, being at a dinner party, or your own thoughts. Use the four broad risk factors already discussed—negative emotions, interpersonal conflict, social pressures, and drinking—to help you find the specific situations that are high-risk for you.

Keep records of your thoughts when you are upset and have a lapse. "I'm upset. I'd feel better if I ate." "A cigarette would sure relax me now." "A few tokes and I'd feel better." "I need to lighten up. Have a little drink." "I've been under a lot of stress. I owe myself a drink." If you believe that nice things will happen as a result of lapsing, you'll probably tell yourself, "Go ahead, it would feel good." Through self-statements, you are tempting yourself.

Another technique for discovering your own personal high-risk situations is to have a relapse fantasy (Marlatt & Parks, 1982). Sit down, close your eyes, and pretend you are relapsing. What kinds of situations would it take to get you back to your old behavior? Imagine the scene as clearly as you can so you will know the details of the situation. Here are samples of relapse fantasies our students have told us about. A student who wanted to be more assertive: "I eat at a restaurant. When the bill comes, it seems too high. I start to call the waiter over, but he gives me a superior sneer, and I end up not saying anything." A student who wanted to get up early and go jogging: "The alarm clock goes off, but I'm sleepy because I got to bed late the night before. I groan and think to myself, 'Sleep is more important.' Then I turn off the alarm and go back to sleep." A student who wanted to increase her study time: "I've planned to study all Thursday evening, but when I check the TV listings I see there is a fantastic special on, so I watch that instead."

Do not dwell on this relapse fantasy or repeat it unnecessarily. That would constitute imagined rehearsal!

It's even possible that you may deliberately, but unthinkingly, place yourself in a high-risk situation (Daley, 1991; George & Marlatt, 1986). You may make some apparently irrelevant decision—to stop at the shopping center on the way home (where that fantastic bakery is) or to get a newspaper (where they sell cigarettes)—and then find yourself in a situation that leads to lapse.

Chain-of-events analysis (see Chapter 5) will help here. What starts you off on the chain of behaviors that leads to a highly tempting situation? Are you making some apparently unimportant decisions, such as to go home one way instead of another, that later put you in a high-risk situation?

The first step in preventing relapse, then, is to know your own high-risk situations.

Coping with High-Risk Situations

The second step is to develop skills to cope with high-risk situations. By learning such skills, you can increase your chances of dealing successfully with high-risk situations when they arise (Chaney, O'Leary, & Marlatt, 1978; Hall, Rugg, Tunstall, & Jones, 1984).

The easiest way to cope with high-risk situations is to avoid them. In Chapter 5, we discussed the idea of deliberately staying away from situations in which you have performed the problem behavior in the past. This is particularly important if you are trying to get rid of some addiction, such as smoking, drinking, or drugs. When you have been used to satisfying your addiction in certain situations—always drinking with the same friends in the same place, for example—your addictive reaction is actually conditioned to that situation (Leavitt, 1982). This means that mere exposure to the situation leads to physical withdrawal symptoms now that you are trying to stop the addictive behavior. If you go back to the place where you used to indulge, you're going to experience the pain of withdrawal again and be tempted to reduce it by lapsing into the old, unwanted behavior. If you stay away, you'll not only feel better but be less likely to lapse.

This means that smokers should stay away from the old situations in which they used to enjoy smoking—the after-work TGIFs, for example. Drinkers should stay away from bars, and drug users should avoid the places where and people with whom they used to indulge.

Some kinds of situations can be avoided forever. "I've just passed a rule. My husband and I never have discussions about problems we've been having when either of us has had anything to drink." But some kinds of risky situations cannot always be avoided. When you can't avoid them, *use problem-solving skills to deal with high-risk situations* (Marlatt & Gordon, 1985):

1. List the details of the problem.
2. Think of as many solutions to the problem as you can.
3. Select solutions to use.
4. Check to be sure you are actually implementing the solutions.

Sherwin had given up excessive drinking but was still tempted now and then.

> I listed the details of situations in which I drank. One was when I wanted to relax. Another was when I was with a bunch of people. Sometimes I had liquor in the house that was left there after a party. I worked out alternative ways of dealing with those situations. To get

> myself to relax, I tried meditating and exercising. I made lists of self-instructions to use when I was with other people. I decided to pour out all liquor that was left after a party.

Listing the details of situations in which you are tempted to lapse will suggest specific problems. Instead of thinking, "I drink too much" or "I eat too much," substitute, "I drink (or eat) when I am really upset and alcohol (or food) is present." Then your problem is more specific, and you can focus your attack on the problem more closely on the real issues. You might decide that you need to spend less time being upset, for example, and set out to solve some of the problems that often upset you. If you give in to social pressure, then rehearse not giving in. If you overindulge to reduce stress, then you need to develop other ways of reducing stress. If you overindulge to celebrate, work on other ways of celebrating.

Some people who overindulge in a substance or activity—drinking, smoking, overeating, or gambling—do so because they feel they aren't getting enough out of life (Marlatt,1982; Marlatt & George, 1990). The "shoulds" in their daily routines outweigh the "wants." People who are trying but failing to increase their exercise often feel the same way: "It's the end of a very hard day, and now I'm supposed to drag my body around the park?" Listing the details of a problem may reveal this kind of thinking. "Hell, go ahead and have a drink. You've done nothing but work all week, and life is short!" Or "Give yourself a break; don't jog today." If this kind of thinking pops up in your list of details of the problem, then direct your attack toward getting a few more "wants" gratified.

Besides general problem solving, you may want to practice specific skills. *As soon as you realize you are in a high-risk situation, give yourself instructions on how to deal with it.* First say to yourself, "Danger! This is risky. I could have a lapse here." Then tell yourself specific things to do. These can be instructions on behaviors you want to perform: (1) leave the situation, (2) be assertive in turning down the tempting substance, and (3) relax.

Tell yourself not to perform the old, unwanted behavior, and review what specific things you should do to avoid performing it. Sherwin wrote:

> One Friday after work, the whole office decided to go out for a beer. I wanted to go, to be with them and have some fun, but I knew it was risky. I told myself, "Be careful. This is a high-risk situation. Order ginger ale. If someone says 'Come on, have a beer,' I will say 'No, thanks, I prefer ginger ale.'"

He was warning himself, and also telling himself what to do and how to cope with social pressure to lapse.

Recognize that you may want to give in to the temptation, and give yourself instructions to cope with the rationalizations you make. Sherwin says to himself, "When I get there, I may say to myself, 'I'll just have one beer.' But I won't have one, I'll have several, and I really don't want to do that. So don't have the first one."

Remind yourself of the advantages of changing your old, unwanted behavior. Sherwin thinks,

I'm tempted to drink now, but I really want to stop drinking because it will make me feel better and be healthier, make me look better, be better for my work, and improve my social life. The advantages outweigh the disadvantages, so I won't drink.

Self-instructions can also help you cope with the feeling of wanting to indulge right now. Distract yourself, or switch from hot to cool thoughts about the object of your desire. Instead of thinking, "Man, a beer would sure taste good now," Sherwin switches to thinking, "The beer looks like a urine specimen." It's important not to continue having hot thoughts about the tempting substance, for you are more likely to give in and lapse if you have those thoughts (Mischel, 1981).

To minimize "hot" thinking, try taking a detached view of your craving for a tempting substance (George & Marlatt, 1986). Instead of thinking, "Oh, I really gotta have a beer right now," Sherwin tells himself, "I am experiencing an urge to drink now." Or he could say, "I feel it coming from a distance, trying to build up, but it's not too awful. If I wait just a couple of minutes, it will pass. I'm going to surf right through this urge." It is true that these cravings do pass fairly quickly. Remind yourself of this.

Don't focus on how strong the urge feels; instead, distract yourself from it. "I am experiencing an urge to drink (or smoke, or eat, or whatever) now, but the feeling will pass in a minute. Meanwhile, I should distract myself. Let's see: I can focus on this man sitting next to me, find out about him."

It's also important to remind yourself of the times you have coped with this kind of situation in the past. Perhaps the most important aspect of resisting an urge is your belief that you *can* resist (Abrams, 1987). "Here's that urge again. Well, I've surfed it out before. I can do several things to get myself through this period. Let's see . . ."

To sum up, there are several kinds of self-instructions and other coping skills that you should prepare in advance so that you will have them available when you meet with a high-risk situation:

1. Warn yourself. ("Danger!")
2. Give yourself instructions on what behaviors to perform: relax, be mildly assertive, leave, or whatever.
3. Remind yourself of rationalizations you may make, and remind yourself you don't want to indulge.
4. Remind yourself of the advantages of changing.
5. Cope with feelings of wanting to indulge: distract yourself, or switch from hot to cool thoughts about the substance.
6. Take a detached view of any craving you feel, remind yourself that it will pass, and tell yourself what to do until it does pass.
7. Remind yourself of any successes you've had in the past coping with urges.

Practice these skills in your imagination before you get into high-risk situations. Return to the relapse fantasies that you used to predict your high-risk situations. Now replay those situations, imagining yourself using the coping skills. Use the principles for imagined rehearsal discussed in Chapter 6.

Remember that you have spent a lifetime developing your problem behavior, and now you are trying to learn a new habit. Mistakes are inevitable. But *don't give up.* One of our students wrote:

> I was sitting around the dinner table with the whole family, and we were talking after the meal, a situation in which I usually keep on eating. I was giving myself instructions not to eat. That worked for nearly an hour, but we all just kept sitting there, talking on and on, and after an hour I was suddenly eating again. At first I was really discouraged. But later I realized: Yes, the self-instructions do work. For the first time in my life I sat at a table full of food and didn't eat for nearly an hour!

Techniques such as self-instructions have to be developed, like any good habit, with practice, and in the process you're going to make some mistakes—particularly if you stay in some tempting situation, as this student did. But they will work if you keep on using them. Recall that the people who are successful at quitting smoking, for example, are the ones who try the longest. Keep using these techniques. And notice your successes, not just your failures. ("All right! I went a whole hour sitting at a table full of food without eating anything!")

Putting on the Brakes: Stopping Lapses from Becoming Relapses

Suppose you make a mistake and lapse. You smoke, you drink, you overeat, you gamble, or whatever. What now? A plan for coping with lapses—for putting on the brakes before you totally relapse—is essential. After a night of lapses, Jeb got up the next morning and went right back to smoking as though he'd never stopped. One of his mistakes was having no plan to cope with lapses. A study compared people who lapsed but eventually stopped smoking with those who lapsed and stayed relapsed. Of the eventual successes, 100% said they had some plan for coping following a lapse. Only half of those who failed had any plan (Candiotte & Lichtenstein, 1981). A lapse does not mean total failure and incompetence. We learn from mistakes, and being prepared to recover from them is sound planning.

The first step in your plan for coping with lapses is to make self-observations. Reinstate counting your cigarettes, keep a structured diary of the situations that lead to smoking, or both. Often when people lapse, they become upset by the lapse and stop self-observation. But it is important to continue self-monitoring. If you have not been self-monitoring lately, reinstate it. If you do so, you are much more likely to reinstate a complete plan for self-modification.

The second step is to make a self-contract for what you will do if you lapse. What should you put into your contract? Make plans to get back into a self-modification program. If you have not been using a full plan—for example, you are no longer counting, you aren't self-reinforcing, you aren't thinking about antecedents, and so on—you should go back to a full plan:

antecedent control for wanted behavior, shaping, reinforcement, imaginary rehearsal, relaxation, and so on. Write a self-contract: "I promise myself that if I lapse, I will immediately begin counting my lapses. I will continue to count as long as I am lapsing. Also, I will reinstate a full self-modification project to cope with my problem behavior." Sign this, and keep it in your wallet.

Third, make a reminder card to carry with you. Here is the reminder card used in a study with smokers who wanted to quit:

> A slip is not all that unusual. It does not mean that you have failed or that you have lost control over your behavior. You will probably feel guilty about what you have done, and will blame yourself for having slipped. This feeling is to be expected; it is part of what we call the Abstinence Violation Effect. There is no reason why you have to give in to this feeling and continue to smoke. The feeling will pass in time. Look upon the slip as a learning experience. What were the elements of the high-risk situation which led to the slip? What coping response could you have used to get around the situation? Remember the old saying: One swallow doesn't make a summer. Well, one slip doesn't make a relapse, either. Just because you slipped once does not mean that you are a failure, that you have no willpower, or that you are a hopeless addict. Look upon the slip as a single, independent event, something which can be avoided in the future with an alternative coping response. (Marlatt, 1982, pp. 359–360)

As the reminder card points out, you must be wary of the *abstinence violation effect.* If you believe that total abstinence is necessary for you to have personal control over the problem behavior, then you will consider any violation of abstinence a loss of control (Marlatt, 1982). But total abstinence is not likely at first. You may have spent years practicing the behavior you now want to stop, and it's overly optimistic to expect that the first time you quit, you will quit forever. Expect slips, but don't let them snowball. If you are disgusted with yourself, think you don't have any willpower, and can't control this behavior, remember: That's just the usual abstinence violation effect.

Your persistence following a lapse can profoundly affect your long-term success. If you think, "Well, that lapse was due to the particular circumstances I was in," rather than, "I lapsed because I just don't have enough willpower," then you are more likely to persist in your efforts to change (Kernis, Zuckerman, Cohen, & Spadafora, 1982). Blame the situation (including your own lack of preparedness in not anticipating the situation) instead of your personality. If you find you've fallen back into being rude to your friends, for example, don't conclude that you have a basically rude personality and are unchangeable. Instead, realize that particular circumstances—too much stress or alcohol, for example—have led to this particular lapse and that you can reinstate your plan for changing. Then activate your plans to keep the lapse from becoming a relapse. Put on the brakes.

Lapses and problems are part of the learning process. You will never attain perfection. Instead, your goal is steady improvement—more and more consistent behavior.

Chapter Summary

Problem Solving

When your plan for change proves inadequate, tinker with it. Start off with your best plan, and observe what interferes with it. Then revise the plan, taking into consideration the sources of interference. Analyze your mistakes, and learn from them.

Using formal problem solving increases your chances of success, particularly if you run into difficulties. The four steps in problem solving are as follows:

1. List the concrete details of the problem.
2. Try to think of as many solutions as possible.
3. Choose one or more solutions to implement.
4. Check to be sure you are carrying out the solution.

Common reasons for failure at self-modification are lack of problem solving, inadequate self-observation, and failure to use the techniques. Problem solving has to be used when the inevitable problems in attempts at self-change arise. Self-observation is essential to understanding the antecedents and consequences of your behavior and to measuring your progress. Encourage self-observation and self-confidence by recording positive as well as negative information. Failure to use the techniques may reflect a lack of confidence in the techniques or in yourself, discouragement by others or yourself, a lack of personal commitment, or your own ambivalence about changing. Learning to recognize these problems will help you cope with them appropriately.

Relapse Prevention

High-risk situations, if successfully managed, can lead to increased feelings of self-efficacy and an increase in one's skill level, which in turn leads to decreased chances of a relapse. Alternately, encountering a high-risk situation can lead to *no* coping with the risk, which leads to decreased feelings of self-efficacy and no increase in skill level. These, in turn, lead to the first lapse and the *abstinence violation effect,* which leads to increased chances of relapse.

Common high-risk situations are those involving negative emotional states, interpersonal conflict, social pressures, and alcohol. Through self-observation and relapse fantasies, you can learn about your own personal high-risk situations.

To lessen the chances of relapse:

1. Prepare for high-risk situations.
2. Develop skills for coping during high-risk situations.
3. Develop plans to keep lapses from becoming relapses.

YOUR OWN SELF-DIRECTION PROJECT: STEP NINE

Solving Problems

Be prepared to tinker with your self-change plan. What makes performing the target behavior difficult? How can the plan be made more effective?

Practice problem solving. Use the four steps to solve problems in your project.

Here is a checklist of the most common reasons for failure. Check any that apply to you, and take steps to cope with the issue. Reread the appropriate section of the chapter, think how it applies to your project, and then act on the implications.

___ Not using problem solving when problems in self-change come up.

Failures in self-observation:

___ lack of records
___ noticing failures only

Misuse of techniques:

___ infrequent or no reinforcement
___ use of punishment
___ attempts to suppress a behavior instead of developing another in its place
___ use of too few techniques

Not using the techniques:

___ too much stress in your life
___ your belief that the techniques won't help
___ low self-efficacy
___ ambivalence about changing
___ lack of time to do a self-change project
___ discouragement from others
___ giving up at the first failure

Preventing Relapse

Keep records of your lapses. Look for negative emotional states, interpersonal conflict, or social pressures as causes of lapses, and look for events specific to your behavior. Have a relapse fantasy to see what might cause a lapse. Find out what your personal high-risk situations are.

Use problem-solving techniques to cope with high-risk situations. Do this work now, before you are involved in the situation. List the details of your personal high-risk situations, think of as many solutions as you can, select solutions to use, and be sure you are using the solutions.

Take time now to prepare the self-statements you will use when you meet with a high-risk situation:

1. Use a warning statement.
2. Prepare self-instructions on what behaviors to perform.
3. Remind yourself of any rationalizations you may make.
4. Make a list of the advantages of not giving in to the urge to lapse.
5. Make plans on how to distract yourself and how to switch from hot to cool thoughts.
6. Practice taking a detached view.

Make a written list of these self-instructions, and read it when you find yourself in a high risk situation.

Once you have made up the self-instructions, use imaginary rehearsal to practice them. Set aside periods in which you imagine suddenly being in a high-risk situation. Give yourself a warning, tell yourself what behaviors to perform, and give yourself the self-instructions. Imagine yourself being reinforced by feelings of pride and self-efficacy.

Make out a relapse-prevention contract now. This will include plans, first, to resume self-observation immediately after any lapse, and second, to resume a full self-change project. Sign this contract and keep it with you. Also make a reminder card to carry with you.

Take all these steps now, *before* you run into a high-risk situation. If you meet one unprepared, you are more likely to lapse—and relapse.

10

Termination and Beyond

Outline

- Formal Termination: Planning to Maintain Gains
- Beyond the Ending
- *Chapter Summary*
- *Your Own Self-Direction Project: Step Ten*

Learning Objectives

Formal Termination: Planning to Maintain Gains

1. What are the issues of maintenance and transfer of a newly learned behavior?
2. How can you evolve natural reinforcements for a new behavior?
3. Explain how to use thinning.
4. How should you deal with lack of reinforcement from others?
5. How can you obtain social support for new behaviors?
6. How confident are you that you can maintain the new behaviors? How is this confidence measured?
7. How do you program for transfer to new settings?
8. How important is practice in developing new behaviors? What does it mean to say, "Practice *of* perfect–not practice *makes* perfect"?

Beyond the Ending

9. Do people ever carry out lifelong self-modification projects? When might this be necessary?
10. When should you seek professional help?
11. What happens in psychotherapy?
12. How should you choose a therapist?
13. How can you increase the chances that you will use self-change techniques when they are needed in the future?

Some self-modification plans die a natural and almost unnoticed death because their useful life spans have ended. The goal is reached, and it is no longer necessary to use self-reinforcement, shaping, or self-instructions. The new, desirable behavior has become a habit. The old, undesirable behavior no longer seems a problem. This can happen when you reach the goal you originally set for yourself—"I wanted to quit biting my nails, and I have"—or when you reach a goal you weren't even aware of at the beginning—"I learned that I had to smile at people and not interrupt them but listen carefully, and when I had learned that, my new behaviors just started happening." When a depression has lifted or loneliness ended, the plan for change receives less attention and is finally ignored.

Formal self-change plans are a temporary expedient, a device to use when you are trapped in a problem that requires particular planning to solve. When self-modification planning becomes no longer necessary, you have really succeeded in achieving an adjustment whereby you (and your environment) are supporting a pattern that you endorse.

Often people slack off in their efforts to change after they have made some progress toward their goal, even though they haven't reached it. Kalani, who started out to lose 40 pounds, found that after losing 20 he was no longer sticking to his self-change plan.

> I think what happened was that I felt better and looked better. But I still enjoy overeating, and I'm not really sure I want to give it up entirely. It's a pleasure, and what is life for? Maybe I'll stay 20 pounds overweight. It's not so bad.

This reflects a change in Kalani's goals.

If you find that your plan has petered out before you reached your original goal, list the advantages and disadvantages of changing (see Chapter 2), this time starting from your new level. You may find that you are now content. Or perhaps the list will show you that you still want to change. The danger here is drifting—halfway to some original goal, pleased with your progress, but disappointed because you haven't gone all the way to your goal. The listing will help you clarify your values so that you can be either completely pleased with your progress or prepared to redouble your efforts to change.

There is a real risk that Kalani (or any other dieter) will regain the 20 pounds he lost. Suppose he wants to be sure this doesn't happen? It's not unusual for people to revert to their old, unwanted behaviors. People who lose weight have to remain vigilant so their old, weight-adding behaviors don't come back. If they aren't vigilant, they will stop coping, and lo, they're overweight again (Westover & Lanyon, 1990). Smokers, too, sometimes show a pattern of vigilant coping early in their antismoking campaign, but then relax their guard—and stop coping—after a few successes. Then they relapse and are smoking again (Shiffman & Jarvik, 1987). You can guard against this danger by **formal termination,** in which you take deliberate steps to keep the problem from arising.

Formal Termination: Planning to Maintain Gains

When you develop new behaviors to reach your goal, remember that they are *new* behaviors. Not being well practiced, they can be lost, and the old, unwanted habits may reappear. At this point, you have two goals (Marholin & Touchette, 1979): (1) *to maintain gains,* and (2) *to make sure that any newly learned behavior transfers to new situations.*

Suppose you have increased your studying to a new, satisfying level, but after a few months you notice it is dropping back toward the old level. That is a **maintenance** problem. Or suppose you have developed good study habits for certain courses but still don't seem to be studying well for the other courses. That is a **transfer** problem. Either way, you are not performing the desired behavior at the level you want.

You can do several things to be sure you maintain your gains and to help them transfer to new situations. If you work out a plan for maintenance and transfer, you are much more likely to keep your new gains (Perri et al., 1988; Whisman, 1990).

Evolving Natural Reinforcements

In the early stages of termination, it's a good idea to remind yourself of the rewards that bolster your behavior. A woman who lost many pounds was delighted to discover that other people found her more attractive. She had many more dates. When she stopped the formal reinforcement, she posted a reminder on the refrigerator door: "Dieting keeps the telephone ringing!"

But you also want rewards from the rest of the world. Suppose you have successfully increased your study time and improved your study habits after a lifetime of being a poor student. Now you should *plan natural situations that will reinforce your new competence without punishing you for skills you still lack* (Stokes & Osnes, 1989). Where will your studying be reinforced? If you take an advanced course that has several prerequisites—courses that you did poorly in earlier—you place yourself at a disadvantage. Choose instead courses in which you are making a fresh start. Then you will be much more likely to be reinforced for the new, good study habits that you have learned.

Elizabeth, who had learned through her self-change project to talk comfortably with men, wrote: "I'm still careful in striking up conversations. I look for guys who seem easy to get to know and stay away from the stuck-up ones." She is very sensibly putting herself into situations where she can reasonably expect to be rewarded.

Jack felt awkward in small peer groups, alternating between strained silence and sarcastic remarks. When he was assigned to a six-person team project in one of his courses, he decided to take the opportunity of being a member of the team to change his behavior. Jack reinforced the friendly and task-related statements he made to other group members, using as a reinforcement the amount of time he allowed himself to spend surfing each week. Jack improved his performance and his comfort, but because he was still not satisfied with his level of improvement when the course was over, he looked for another situation in which to practice. From among several possibilities, he chose to attend evening meetings of a writers' club. This was a good choice because he was interested in writing and had much to say on the subject. Further, lapses into his more aggressive behavior wouldn't be punished too severely because criticism of other members' work was part of the club's function. In short, this group was one into which he could bring his newly acquired abilities and from which he could expect enjoyment and relative lack of punishment. The situation reinforced and increased the kind of participation he valued.

When your new target behavior has become well established through your self-intervention plan, search for opportunities to practice it in which other people will reinforce you for that behavior:

1. *Remind yourself of the rewards you get for your new behavior.*
2. *List the situations in which you can perform the behavior and be reinforced for it.*

Thinning: Building Resistance to Extinction

In your self-modification plan, you probably are reinforced every time you perform some desired behavior. That's the way you produce the fastest change. But out in the world, reinforcement isn't so predictable. Once you start thinking about transferring to naturally occurring reinforcers, you should take steps to ensure that your newly gained behaviors are not lost because of extinction. This is necessary because a behavior that has been reinforced *continuously* is most likely to be extinguished when reinforcements do not continue to occur.

Don't stop self-modification abruptly. *The best way to ensure that extinction does not occur is to use an intermittent reinforcement schedule.*

Odette had been working to be more assertive in certain situations—such as when other people made unreasonable requests. Every time she performed an act of assertion, she gave herself one token. Later she used these tokens to select from a menu of favorite foods. After several weeks, she felt she was now being assertive when it was called for.

At this point, instead of stopping her reinforcement system, she started preparing for the fact that the world out there couldn't be counted on to reinforce her behavior. She prepared by **thinning** her reinforcement schedule—moving to an intermittent schedule of reinforcement. She began to thin in the simplest way—by not getting a token every time. At first she cut down so that she got tokens only 75% of the time. She then reduced further, to one every other time (50%) and later to only 25%. She did this over several days, slowly, to guard against extinction of her newly learned behavior.

In thinning, continue to count the frequency of the target behavior. It may decline. Some drop from your upper goal might be acceptable, but you'll want to know if there has been a drop, and if so, how much. If the frequency drops too low, go back to full, 100% reinforcement.

Dealing with Lack of Reinforcement from Others

Rick took a short course in how to increase open communication in marriage. He carried out a self-change project toward this goal. But his wife, Roberta, was irritated by Rick's efforts to change their mode of communication. Obviously, she was not going to reinforce his new behavior. Rick then started a plan in which he would invite Roberta to cooperate and try to persuade her to discuss why she was opposed to his attempts to improve their communication. He praised her for her participation in this kind of discussion and reminded himself to be patient and not to expect her to change too quickly. He realized that in the long run he might be reinforced for his changes—when Roberta, too, had changed—but meanwhile, he continued to reinforce himself and to keep records of his new behavior. He did so because he felt that the new behavior would drop away from lack of reinforcement if he did not.

When you change yourself, you may affect others, and they may not reinforce your new behavior. Though not actively punishing you, they may continue to act in ways that don't reward your new efforts (Lichtenstein, Glasgow, & Abrams, 1986). In these situations, you must notice your own gains and benefits and remind yourself of your goals. See that you are being reinforced for your new acts even though others may be slow in reinforcing you.

Are You Confident You Can Maintain the New Behaviors?

One of our pessimistic students said, "You know, I've been using all these techniques you teach, and I have been successful in changing. But I bet when I finish this course—which is really like a crutch—I'll flop right back to my old behaviors."

"Yeah, you're right," we agreed.

"What?" he said, surprised, "I thought you said these techniques work."

"They do. But it's you who have done the work, not the course. You're giving it all the credit. As long as you think that, you don't really think you personally have control over the behavior. So you probably won't try to control it, and you won't."

You have to understand that the new behavior is under your personal control if you are to have a good chance of maintaining it (Katz & Vinciguerra, 1982). As your behavior changes, you should deliberately notice that it is coming more and more under your own control. If you do so, you increase the chances that you will maintain the behavior (Sonne & Janoff, 1982). For example, if ex-smokers think their quitting was due to something other than their own self-control, they are less able to stay away from cigarettes (Harackiewicz, Sansone, Blair, Epstein, & Manderlink, 1987).

In fact, you are better equipped than you've ever been before, for research has shown that taking a course like this increases your strength to resist relapse. You have developed skills that really do give you greater self-control (Glasgow & Lichtenstein, 1987; Hall, Rugg, Tunstall, & Jones, 1984).

Before you stop your formal self-modification plan, rate your ability to maintain the new behavior without the plan.

My estimation of my ability to control my behaviors without my self-modification plan is:

1	2	3	4	5
No chance at all				Total certainty

If your rating is low—below 4—then it's not yet time to stop formal self-modification (see Baer, Holt, & Lichtenstein, 1986).

Your ability to maintain the new behavior without your plan need not be an all-or-nothing issue. You may need to continue part of the plan, and the part you are most likely to need to continue is self-observation (Hall, 1980). If you are not yet sure about stopping, give yourself a trial period while continuing careful self-observation.

Remember, too, that your ability to control your new behavior will vary from one situation to another. You may be confident that you can go home to your early-evening studying on most days, but can you keep to that schedule when you've been feeling stressed and have had two beers? Self-efficacy varies, depending on the situation.

Here is a list of different situations a smoker might have to cope with:

1. Poor performance on an exam
2. Stood up by a date; feeling disappointed
3. Fight with spouse, boy/girlfriend; angry and upset
4. Feeling relaxed at the end of an evening
5. Finished dinner in a restaurant with friends; coffee served; others light up
6. Out with friends who are smoking; don't want others to know of participation in a smoking program
7. Difficult day at school or work
8. In a bad mood; thinking about failures in life
9. Watching TV
10. Studying
11. Reading a novel or magazine
12. Attending a sports or entertainment event
13. On the phone
14. Drinking coffee or nonalcoholic beverages
15. After a meal
16. Talking or socializing
17. Playing cards*

If your goal is nonsmoking in all situations, rate your ability to control yourself in each of the preceding situations, and note the dangerous ones for which you should continue conscious self-modification. You might have to be sure to use self-instructions or keep records in these situations.

Whatever your target problem, list the situations in which you will be tempted to relapse. *Rate your confidence in each situation.* If you know the situations in which you feel least confident that you can get along without deliberate self-modification, you can use self-control techniques just in those situations. Finally, prepare yourself for difficult circumstances. Box 10-1 contains instructions for stress-proofing yourself.

Programming for Transfer to New Situations

When a behavior is first developing into a habit, it is tied to particular situations. When new situations occur, the behavior may not transfer to them. For example, a man who had learned to control his depression during the fall was surprised to see his mood collapse with the arrival of the holidays—and the loss of pleasant, school-related activities. A woman who exercised

*SOURCE: "The Smoking Self-Efficacy Questionnaire (SSEQ): Preliminary Scale Development and Validation" by G. Colletti, J. A. Supnick, and T. J. Payne, 1985, *Behavioral Assessment, 7,* pp. 249–260. Copyright 1985, Pergamon Press, Ltd. Reprinted by permission.

BOX 10-1

Stress-Proofing Yourself

In a book on managing anxiety, Helen Kennerley (1990) gives excellent advice about long-term coping with anxiety. It applies to depression, smoking, overeating, and drug use as well. In fact, it is sound advice for anyone who has just changed some important part of his or her behavior, thoughts, or feelings. Read this and think carefully about how these ideas apply to you:

There are ways in which you can make life easier for yourself in the long term.

1. When you get anxious, don't run away. Instead, welcome the opportunity to practice and improve your skills of control;
   breathe slowly;
   relax;
   distract yourself;
   control your thoughts.
2. Practice relaxing every day, especially before a difficult situation. Be prepared.
3. Don't let stress build up. If something is worrying you, seek advice. Find out where to go for support.
4. Look forward and not back. Don't dwell on past difficulties, but plan to make the future better.
5. Avoid getting over-tired. Make sure you have a break from work and don't take on too much.
6. Do as many pleasurable things as possible.
7. Remember to recognize your achievements and praise yourself. Don't downgrade yourself.
8. Don't avoid what you fear. If you do find something is becoming difficult for you to face up to, approach the situation in small, safe steps.

Remember: You will have set-backs, and these are only to be expected. They are a normal part of progress and should not be allowed to interfere with your practice. From *Managing Anxiety*, by Helen Kennerley. Copyright 1990 by Oxford University Press, Inc. Reprinted by permission.

regularly in one town found to her chagrin that when she moved away, she stopped jogging. To avoid losing a new behavior through lack of transfer to new situations, *program for transfer.*

A group of clients who had "shy bladder" problems—inability to urinate in public restrooms when anyone was around—were taught to relax in public restrooms, with the result that the time required for them to urinate decreased markedly. Half these clients were also trained to practice using different restrooms, under varying conditions. This gave them experience in transferring the newly learned ability to relax. The other half received no such treatment. Then all were tested under severe conditions, using a crowded public restroom at a sports event. The clients who had been trained to transfer their relaxation were able to relax and use the facilities, but the clients who had not been trained for transfer were unable to relax in the press of a crowded arena restroom (Shelton, 1981b). The behavior they had learned under one condition did not transfer to the new condition *because they had not practiced transfer.*

You should test for transfer before stopping your self-change plan. Melanie, whose study habits in algebra and French had improved following self-modification, also wanted to improve her studying in other subjects. Before stopping her plan, she tested to see whether she could perform at the same level in the new subjects.

Principles of Transfer

Several researchers have studied and written about transfer over the years, and in what follows we have distilled their ideas and added some of our own to present several principles of transfer (Belmont, Butterfield, & Ferretti, 1982; Farr, 1987; Horner, Dunlap, & Koegel, 1988; Kendall, 1989; Stockert, 1989; Stokes & Osnes, 1989). You should think about how each of these applies to your case, and take steps to deal with the issues each raises.

1. *Transfer will occur only if you try for it.* Your new behavior probably will *not* transfer to many new situations if you don't make a conscious effort to make it transfer. You have to do the work in this chapter, or you may lose the benefits of all the work you've done so far.

2. *Transfer effects can be very specific to situations.* Unless you are a professional behavior analyst, it is difficult to predict the exact situations to which some newly learned behavior will transfer. The prudent thing to do is *not* to expect automatic transfer, but to deliberately build it in.

3. *Obstacles to transfer often occur.* So often, in fact, that you should expect them. When the obstacles arise, use your problem-solving skills to think of solutions.

Carlo wrote:

> I had lost about ten pounds: then a whole series of dinners-out came along, and I sort of drifted off my weight loss program. I wasn't gaining, but I wasn't losing either. I realized I had been successful in the past because I hadn't had to cope with eating out very often. So, I had to go back to the drawing board and figure out how to cope with eating out.

He used problem solving, began self-observation again, and worked out a new plan.

4. *To transfer your new skills, you need to practice.* Look for opportunities to practice your newly learned acts. Remind yourself often to practice them. When in new situations, give yourself instructions to practice. "Whoa! I've never had to be assertive in this kind of situation. Better remember what to do. Now, remember . . .."

At some point, a behavior will "take hold." It becomes easy to do, automatic, a habit. This take-hold point is the result of a complicated system of schedules of reinforcements and antecedents, but it is also related to the number of times the behavior is practiced. John Shelton (1979) writes: "Regardless of the particular methods chosen to promote transfer, practice is crucial. Recall that individuals lose 50% of what they learn during the day following the learning trial. . . . Practice is the one way to overcome this" (p. 238). The more available a response is to a person, the more likely the transfer is, and the availability of the response is directly affected by practice (Goldstein, Lopez, & Greenleaf, 1979).

Think about learning to drive. When you begin, you have to concentrate fully on every aspect of your driving behavior. You dare not take your mind off it for a second. But after several years of driving experience, you can drive long distances without this concentrated attention.

The need for practice implies that *you should not terminate your program as soon as you reach your goal.* Many years ago Mandler (1954) trained people at a task until they could perform it without error 0, 10, 30, 50, or 100 times. The more practice her subjects had, the more easily they transferred their training to new situations. Plan to "overlearn" by practicing beyond your first success. Goldstein and his colleagues write: "The guiding rule should not be practice *makes* perfect (implying simply practice until one gets it right, and then move on), but practice *of* perfect (implying numerous overlearning trials of correct responses *after* the initial success)" (Goldstein, Lopez, & Greenleaf, 1979, p. 14).

How many overlearning trials should you use? The more, the better. A trial at thinning reinforcement will tell you whether you have adequately overlearned. Continue to keep records. If the target behavior drops alarmingly as soon as you begin to thin the reinforcement, you know you haven't practiced enough. A second kind of test is to try the target behavior in a new situation. If difficulties arise, go back to practicing with a formal self-change plan. In general, *the target behavior is more likely to remain strong and transfer to other situations if you have had a lot of practice and if you have practiced in a number of different situations* (Goldstein, Lopez, & Greenleaf, 1979).

Beyond the Ending

Long-Term Projects

Some goals can be achieved only through a long-term effort. If you have been a heavy smoker, for example, you may have to maintain vigilance for years to stay off cigarettes and to reactivate self-change plans if you slip back into smoking.

There are several reasons you can expect old habits such as smoking, overeating, or nonexercising to reappear. You may deceive yourself a bit and say, "Now that I have this under control, I can do it just a little bit." So you try smoking just at parties or overeating just on special occasions. But because such acts have been heavily developed as habits in the past, they return easily. You may soon find yourself smoking or overeating in many situations.

The rule for all these problems is the same: expect the habit to return, and reinstate a plan for changing as soon as it does. Follow the steps for relapse prevention. Learn from your mistakes. Suppose you quit smoking but after three months say to yourself, "Well, I can smoke just a couple at this party." Two weeks later, you're back to a pack a day. *Learn from that.* The next time you quit, be prepared to deal with parties. It would be a mistake to conclude that you have no willpower. Instead, conclude that you must attend carefully to the particular situations that tempt you.

Once you have learned techniques for self-change, you can continue to be a personal scientist. Continue informally to observe your behavior, it antecedents, and its consequences. Occasionally you may decide that some new goal needs a systematic self-direction plan. Whenever you have a goal that you are not reaching, use formal self-modification to help you achieve it. Whenever you lapse into an old, unwanted behavior, use relapse prevention and systematic self-modification to change again.

Seeking Professional Help

At least three conditions limit the usefulness of a self-modification project:

1. Your personal goals may not be clear enough to permit the choice of goal behaviors.
2. The technical problems of designing a plan may be greater than the skills that can be acquired by reading this book.
3. The natural environment itself may be too chaotic or unyielding to allow a plan to succeed.

Under any of these circumstances, professional advice may be helpful.

What do professionals do? Although they may take different approaches, they all employ one general strategy: they help establish situations that encourage the development of new behaviors and emotions.

The principles governing professional help are the same as those by which self-change operates. Helping professionals don't force behaviors and experiences on people against their will. Unless the client's self-guiding, self-directing functions are engaged in the process, behavioral and emotional changes simply do not occur during psychological treatment. Counselors and psychotherapists point out that their help is effective only when the client is motivated to change.

Thus, even if you choose professional help, you will still find yourself engaged in building personal self-direction skills. Professionals don't solve the problems. They help *you* solve them. They do this by helping you create an environment that fosters your own efforts to change.

Psychological helpers use a variety of techniques to create these new environmental supports. Some procedures have been developed into schools of treatment, and dispute exists among practitioners over preferred methods. Ideally, different methods should be selected for different clients with different problems.

Ralph Nader's group has published a booklet on being a consumer of professional help (Adams & Orgel, 1975). It emphasizes several points: Shop around for someone with whom you think you can work. Use the initial interview with a therapist to make your decision. Should you stick with this person? You need to feel confident and comfortable with your counselor and free to talk about your problems, but whether or not you like the person is not especially important. Do some comparison shopping. Search for a good price. More expensive doesn't mean better help.

Many groups suggest that therapist and client have a written contract specifying the goals and techniques of the process. The contract should spell out goals, costs and time involved. For example, you may feel you want someone with whom you can discuss your uncertainty about career goals or your fears about your upcoming marriage. Make clear to the prospective therapist that these are your goals. If you and the therapist don't come to an understanding about this vital point, you may end up spending a lot of time dealing with things that the therapist thinks are important but in which you have little interest. The contract should be flexible, allowing you to change goals during the course of therapy.

Those who suggest a contract emphasize that it strengthens your commitment to change. The contract system is far from typical among counselors and therapists, but its principles are highly desirable. Its goals can also be achieved by verbal agreement.

Self-Modification as a Lifelong Practice

As you terminate your self-change project, what lies ahead? Blue skies and cloudless days, with no problems to darken the horizon? We wish you well, but we predict that sooner or later something in your life will benefit from another systematic application of self-change techniques.

You have learned these techniques by using them on one personal problem, and you have been tested on them. Will you think to use them two years from now, when a new problem comes into your life? You can increase the chances that you will continue to use the techniques if you make a plan *now* for another self-change project (Barone, 1982).

You should practice the techniques in more than one kind of project. If you practice record keeping or positive self-instructions in several different projects, you will be more likely to keep records and to self-instruct when you need these techniques in the future.

Anticipating problems and thinking of ways to use self-change techniques in dealing with them can also increase your chances of remembering the techniques when the time comes. For example:

> I know I spend my money unwisely. So far it hasn't made much difference, but it's just a matter of time until I am on my own, and then it's

going to matter a lot. When that happens, I could keep records, set rules, and state those rules as self-instructions.

Or: "Everybody says the job interviews for graduates are very difficult and competitive. Well, I could practice relaxation beforehand." Stop now and think about problems you are likely to encounter in the next couple of years. How will you cope with them?

For all of us, self-direction is a daily habit. As you worked on your project, you had to proceed step by step to achieve the kind of performance you wanted. But in many areas of your life, self-regulation is already something you do without the formal statements of a self-modification plan. You begin to feel a bit blue, so you tell yourself "Cheer up!" You notice the good things in your life, and you schedule some fun activities. Without thinking about it, you have been doing the things we recommend for someone who is depressed. You use self-instructions, and you notice and schedule rewards. Or when you realize that you are growing uncomfortably tense in some situation, you can tell yourself "Relax," release tension from your muscles, and begin to cope.

In sum, you always use self-management to deal with life's problems. When you run into problems that require relatively formal self-direction, remember the techniques you have learned.

Chapter Summary

Formal Termination: Planning to Maintain Gains

Your newly developed behaviors will require special attention if they are to be *maintained* over time and *transferred* to additional situations. You can strengthen maintenance and transfer by planning for natural reinforcements to occur—that is, by seeking out situations in which the new behavior will be valued or successful. Simultaneously, you can increase resistance to extinction by thinning self-administered reinforcement to an intermittent schedule. Find social support for new, desirable behaviors, and honestly rate your ability to control the new behaviors without a formal self-modification plan.

The following are some important principles of transfer of new learning:

- Transfer will occur only if you try for it.
- Transfer effects can be very specific to situations.
- Obstacles to transfer often occur.
- To be able to transfer your new skills, you need to practice them often and in many situations.

Program yourself for transfer of new behaviors to new, unexpected situations by practicing the behavior in a variety of situations, practicing the behavior well past the first point of learning it, continuing to keep records of your behavior, and using problem-solving techniques.

Beyond the Ending

Even after formal termination of your plan, your life conditions may change in ways that cause your new habits to lapse. This is not unusual, and it can be countered by the quick application of relapse prevention. Learn from those conditions that bring about lapses.

You may need professional help in changing if your goals are confused, if the technical problems of designing a plan are too great for you, or if your natural environment is too chaotic or unyielding to support your change efforts.

Professionals can help you change, but they cannot change for you. Select a professional carefully. Shop around. Inquire carefully about the techniques and goals the professional offers. Make sure there is clear agreement over the goals, techniques, and costs.

Self-direction is a lifelong practice. Use the techniques you have learned in a variety of situations. Have them ready when needed.

YOUR OWN SELF-DIRECTION PROJECT: STEP TEN

As you consider termination, follow these procedures:

1. Make a list of opportunities for practicing your newly learned behavior. Rate these opportunities in terms of how likely you are to be naturally reinforced for the new behavior.
2. If you suspect that your new behavior will not be naturally reinforced, continue to reinforce yourself or arrange for reinforcement from others.
3. Program for resistance to extinction by thinning your self-reinforcement.
4. Find social support for the new behavior.
5. Rate your ability to control the new behavior without a self-modification plan.
6. Program and test for transfer. Practice the behavior in a variety of situations. Continue to keep records.
7. Practice using the problem-solving steps to deal with new difficulties.
8. Practice the new behavior until you perform it perfectly, then continue to practice doing it perfectly. The more you practice after you have reached your goal level, the more likely it is that your behavior will persist.
9. For long-term projects, be ready to reinstate a plan as soon as an unwanted behavior begins to reappear.

Bibliography

Aaronson, N. K., Ershoff, D. H., & Danaher, B. G. (1985). Smoking cessation in pregnancy: A self-help approach. *Addictive Behaviors, 10,* 103–108.

Abrams, D. B. (1987, November). *Roles of psychological stress, smoking cues, and coping in smoking relapse prevention.* Paper presented at the annual meeting of the Association for the Advancement of Behavior Therapy, Boston.

Adams, J. A. (1987). Historical review and appraisal of research on the learning, retention, and transfer of human motor skills. *Psychological Bulletin, 101,* 41–74.

Adams, S., & Orgel, M. (1975). *Through the mental health maze.* Washington, DC: Health Research Group.

Agran, M., & Martin, J. E. (1987). Applying a technology of self-control in community environments for individuals who are mentally retarded. In M. Hersen, R. M. Eisler, & P. M. Miller (Eds.), *Progress in behavior modification* (Vol. 21, pp. 108–151), Newbury Park, CA: Sage.

Agras, W. S. (1987). *Eating disorders: Management of obesity, bulimia, and anorexia nervosa.* New York: Pergamon Press.

Ainslee, G. (1975). Specious reward: A behavioral theory of impulsiveness and impulse control. *Psychological Bulletin, 82,* 463–496.

Ainslee, G. (1987). Self-reported tactics of impulse control. *International Journal of the Addictions, 22,* 167–179.

Ajzen, I., & Fishbein, M. (1980). *Understanding attitudes and predicting social behavior.* Englewood Cliffs, NJ: Prentice-Hall.

Altmaier, E., Ross, S., Leary, M., & Thornbookrough, M. (1982). Matching stress inoculations treatment components to clients' anxiety mode. *Journal of Counseling Psychology, 29,* 331–334.

American College of Sports Medicine. (1983). Position stand on proper and improper weight loss programs. *Medicine and Science in Sports and Exercise, 15,* ix–xiii.

Annon, J. S. (1975). *The behavioral treatment of sexual problems: Vol. 2. Intensive therapy.* Honolulu, HI: Enabling Systems.

Appley, M. H., & Trumbull, R. (Eds.). (1986). *Dynamics of stress: Physiological, psychological, and social perspectives.* New York: Plenum.

Arnkoff, D. B., & Glass, C. R. (1982). Clinical cognitive constructs: Examination, evaluation, and elaboration. In P. C. Kendall (Ed.), *Advances in cognitive-behavioral research and therapy* (Vol. 1, pp. 1–34). New York: Academic Press.

Arrick, C. M., Voss, J., & Rimm, D. C. (1981). The relative efficacy of thought-stopping and covert assertion. *Behaviour Research and Therapy, 19,* 17–24.

Ascher, L. M. (1973). An experimental analog study of covert positive reinforcement. In R. D. Rubin, J. P. Brady, & J. D. Henderson (Eds.), *Advances in behavior therapy* (Vol. 4, pp. 127–138). New York: Academic Press.

Axelrod, S., & Apsche, J. (Eds.). (1983). *The effects of punishment on human behavior.* New York: Academic Press.

Azrin, N. H., Hake, D. F., Holz, W. C., & Hutchinson, R. R. (1965). Motivational aspects of escape from punishment. *Journal of the Experimental Analysis of Behavior, 8,* 31–44.

Azrin, N. H., & Nunn, R. G. (1973). Habit reversal: A method of eliminating nervous habits and tics. *Behaviour Research and Therapy, 11,* 619–628.

Azrin, N. H., Nunn, R. G., & Frantz-Renshaw, S. E. (1982). Habit reversal vs. negative practice treatment of self-destructive oral habits (biting, chewing, or licking of the lips, cheeks, tongue, or palate). *Journal of Behavior Therapy and Experimental Psychiatry, 13,* 49–54.

Azrin, N. H., & Peterson, A. L. (1990). Treatment of Tourette syndrome by habit reversal: A waiting-list control group comparison. *Behavior Therapy, 21,* 305–319.

Baer, J. S., Holt, C. S., & Lichtenstein, E. (1986). Self-efficacy and smoking reexamined: Construct validity and clinical utility. *Journal of Consulting and Clinical Psychology, 54,* 846–852.

Baer, J. S., Kivlahan, D. R., Fromme, K., & Marlatt, G. A. (1987, November). *Relapse prevention with college student high-risk drinkers.* Paper presented at the annual meeting of the Association for the Advancement of Behavior Therapy, Boston.

Bajtelsmit, J. W., & Gershman, L. (1976). Covert positive reinforcement: Efficacy and conceptualization. *Journal of Behavior Therapy and Experimental Psychiatry, 7,* 207–212.

Bandura, A. (1971). Vicarious and self-reinforcement processes. In R. Glaser (Ed.), *The nature of reinforcement* (pp. 228–278). New York: Academic Press.

Bandura, A. (1977). Self-efficacy: Toward a unifying theory of behavioral change. *Psychological Review, 84,* 191–215.

Bandura, A. (1981). In search of pure unidirectional determinants. *Behavior Therapy, 12,* 30–40.

Bandura, A. (1986). *Social foundations of thought and action: A social-cognitive theory.* Englewood Cliffs, NJ: Prentice-Hall.

Bandura, A. (1989). Human agency in social cognitive theory. *American Psychologist, 44,* 1175–1184.

Bandura, A. (1991). Human agency: The rhetoric and the reality. *American Psychologist, 46,* 157–162.

Bandura, A., Jeffrey, R. W., & Gajdos, E. (1975). Generalizing change through participant modeling with self-directed mastery. *Behaviour Research and Therapy, 13,* 141–152.

Bandura, A., & Mahoney, M. J. (1974). Maintenance and transfer of self-reinforcement functions. *Behaviour Research and Therapy, 12,* 89–97.

Bandura, A., Reese, L., & Adams, N. E. (1982). Microanalysis of action and fear arousal as a function of differential levels of perceived self-efficacy. *Journal of Personality and Social Psychology, 43,* 5–21.

Bandura, A., Taylor, C. B., Williams, S. L., Mefford, I. N., & Barchas, J. D. (1985). Catecholamine secretion as a function of perceived coping self-efficacy. *Journal of Consulting and Clinical Psychology, 53,* 406–414.

Bandura, A., & Wood, R. (1989). Effect of perceived controllability and performance standards on self-regulation of complex decision making. *Journal of Personality and Social Psychology, 56,* 805–814.

Barlow, D. (1988). *Anxiety and its disorders: The nature and treatment of anxiety and panic.* New York: Guilford Press.

Barone, D. F. (1982). Instigating additional self-modification projects after a personal adjustment course. *Teaching of Psychology, 9,* 111.

Barrera, M., & Glasgow, R. (1976). Design and evaluation of a personalized instruction course in behavioral self-control. *Teaching of Psychology, 3,* 81–83.

Barrera, M., & Rosen, G. M. (1977). Detrimental effects of a self-reward contracting program on subjects' involvement in a self-administered desensitization. *Journal of Consulting and Clinical Psychology, 45,* 1180–1181.

Barrios, B. A., & Shigetomi, C. C. (1979). Coping skills training for the management of anxiety: A critical review. *Behavior Therapy, 10,* 491–522.

Barrios, B. A., & Shigetomi, C. C. (1980). Coping skills training: Potential for prevention of fears and anxieties. *Behavior Therapy, 11,* 431–439.

Barrios, F. X. (1985). A comparison of global and specific estimates of self-control. *Cognitive Therapy and Research, 9,* 455–469.

Baumeister, R. F., & Scher, S. J. (1988). Self-defeating behavior patterns among normal individuals: Review and analysis of common self-destructive tendencies. *Psychological Bulletin, 104,* 3–22.

Beck, A. T., & Emery, G. (1985). *Anxiety and phobias: A cognitive perspective.* New York: Basic Books.

Beck, A. T., Rush, A. G., Shaw, B. F., & Emery, G. (1979). *Cognitive therapy of depression.* New York: Guilford Press.

Beck, F. M., Kaul, T. J., & Russell, R. K. (1978). Treatment of dental anxiety by cue-controlled relaxation. *Journal of Counseling Psychology, 25,* 591–594.

Becker, M. H., & Green, L. W. (1975). A family approach to compliance with medical treatment. *International Journal of Health Education, 18,* 175–182.

Belisle, M., Roskies, E., & Levesque, J. M. (1987). Improving adherence to physical activity. *Health Psychology, 6,* 159–172.

Bellack, A. S., Rozensky, R., & Schwartz, J. (1974). A comparison of two forms of self-monitoring in a behavioral weight reduction program. *Behavior Therapy, 5,* 523–530.

Belmont, J. M., Butterfield, E. C., & Ferretti, R. P. (1982). To secure transfer of training instruct self-management skills. In D. K. Detterman & R. J. Sternberg (Eds.), *How and how much can intelligence be increased?* Norwood, NJ: ABLEX.

Berecz, J. M. (1984). Superiority of a low-contrast smoking cessation method. *Addictive Behaviors, 9,* 273–278.

Bergin, A. E. (1969). A self-regulation technique for impulse control disorders. *Psychotherapy: Theory, Research, and Practice, 6,* 113–118.

Berk, L. E. (1986). Relationship of elementary school children's private speech to behavioral accompaniment to task, attention, and task performance. *Developmental Psychology, 22,* 671–680.

Bernard, H. S., & Efran, J. S. (1972). Eliminating versus reducing smoking using pocket tokens. *Behaviour Research and Therapy, 10,* 399–401.

Bernier, M., & Avard, J. (1986). Self-efficacy, outcome, and attrition in a weight-reduction program. *Cognitive Therapy and Research, 10,* 319–338.

Bernstein, D. A., & Borkovec, T. D. (1973). *Progressive relaxation training: A manual for the helping professions.* Champaign, IL: Research Press.

Betz, N. E., & Hackett, G. (1986). Applications of self-efficacy theory to understanding career choice behavior. *Journal of Social and Clinical Psychology, 4,* 279–289.

Biglan, A., & Campbell, D. R. (1981). Depression. In J. L. Shelton, R. L. Levy, and contributors, *Behavioral assignments and treatment compliance: A handbook of clinical strategies* (pp. 111–146). Champaign, IL: Research Press.

Black, D. R., & Sherba, D. S. (1983). Contracting to problem solve versus contracting to practice behavioral weight loss skills. *Behavior Therapy, 14,* 100–109.

Blackwell, B. (1979). Treatment adherence: A contemporary overview. *Psychosomatics, 20,* 27–35.

Blanchard, E. B. (1970). Relative contributions of modeling, informational influences, and physical contact in extinction of phobic behavior. *Journal of Abnormal Psychology, 76,* 55–61.

Blanchard, E. B., Andrasik, F., Guarnieri, P., Neff, D. F., & Rodichok, L. D. (1987). Two-, three-, and four-year follow-up on the self-regulatory treatment of chronic headache. *Journal of Consulting and Clinical Psychology, 55,* 257–259.

Blanchard, E. B., & Draper, D. O. (1973). Treatment of a rodent phobia by covert reinforcement: A single subject experiment. *Behavior Therapy, 4,* 559–564.

Blanchard, E. B., Nicholson, N. L., Taylor, A. E., Steffek, B. C., Radnitz, C. L., & Appelbaum, K. A. (1991). The role of regular home practice in the relaxation treatment of tension headache. *Journal of Consulting and Clinical Psychology, 59,* 467–470.

Blanchard, E. E., Schwarz, S. P., Neff, D. F., & Gerardi, M. A. (1988). Prediction of outcome from the self-regulatory treatment of irritable bowel syndrome. *Behaviour Research and Therapy, 26,* 187–190.

Bloomquist, M., Heshmat-Farzaneh-Kia, Swanson, K., & Braswell, L. (1987, November). *Effects of a comprehensive school-based cognitive-behavioral intervention for non-self-controlled children.* Paper presented at the annual meeting of the Association for the Advancement of Behavior Therapy, Boston.

Boice, R. (1982). Increasing the writing productivity of "blocked" academicians. *Behaviour Research and Therapy, 20,* 197–207.

Bootzin, R. R., & Nicassio, P. M. (1979). Behavioral treatments for insomnia. In M. Hersen, R. Eisler, & P. Miller (Eds.), *Progress in behavioral modification* (Vol. 6, pp. 1–45). New York: Academic Press.

Borkovec, T. D., Wilkinson, L., Folensbee, R., & Lerman, C. (1983). Stimulus control applications to the treatment of worry. *Behaviour Research and Therapy, 21,* 247–251.

Bornstein, P. H., Hamilton, S. B., & Bornstein, M. T. (1985). Self-monitoring procedures. In A. R. Ciminero, K. S. Calhoun, & H. E. Adams (Eds.), *Handbook of behavioral assessment* (2nd ed., pp. 176–222). New York: Wiley.

Boudreau, L. (1972). Transcendental meditation and yoga as reciprocal inhibitors. *Journal of Behavior Therapy and Experimental Psychiatry, 3,* 97–98.

Brehm, S. S. (1976). *The application of social psychology to clinical practice.* New York: Wiley.

Brehm, S. S., & Smith, T. W. (1982). The application of social psychology to clinical practice: A range of possibilities. In G. Weary & H. L. Mirels (Eds.), *Integrations of clinical and social psychology* (pp. 9–24). New York: Oxford University Press.

Brigham, T. A. (1982). Self-management: A radical behavioral perspective. In P. Karoly & F. H. Kanfer (Eds.), *Self-management and behavior change: From theory to practice* (pp. 32–59). New York: Pergamon Press.

Brigham, T. A. (1989). *Self-management for adolescents.* New York: Guilford Press.

Brigham, T. A., Hopper, C., Hill, B., deArmas, A., & Newsom, P. (1985). A self-management program for disruptive adolescents in the school: A clinical replication analysis. *Behavior Therapy, 16,* 99–115.

Brigham, T. A., Moseley, S. A., Sneed, S., & Fisher, M. (in press). Excel: An intensive and structured program of advising and academic support to assist minority freshmen to succeed at a large state university.

Britt, E., & Singh, N. H. (1985). Reduction of rapid eating by normal adults. *Behavior Modification, 9,* 116–125.

Broder, D. M., & Shapiro, E. S. (1985). Applications of self-management to individuals with severe handicaps: A review. *Journal of the Association for Persons with Severe Handicaps, 10,* 200–208.

Brown, G. (1978). Self-administered desensitization of a cemetery phobia using sexual arousal to inhibit anxiety. *Journal of Behavior Therapy and Experimental Psychiatry, 9,* 73–74.

Brown, H. K. (1987). *Self-directed eating.* Manuscript, University of Hawaii, Honolulu, HI.

Brown, J. D. (1991). Staying fit and staying well: Physical fitness as a moderator of life stress. *Journal of Personality and Social Psychology, 60,* 555–561.

Brown, S. A., Stetson, B. A., & Beatty, P. A. (1989). Cognitive and behavioral features of adolescent coping in high-risk drinking situations. *Addictive Behaviors, 14,* 43–52.

Brownell, K. D., & Foreyt, J. P. (Eds.). (1986). *Handbook of eating disorders.* New York: Basic Books.

Brownell, K. D., Heckerman, C. L., Westlake, R. J., Hayes, S. C., & Monti, P. M. (1978). The effect of couples training and partner cooperativeness in the behavioral treatment of obesity. *Behaviour Research and Therapy, 16,* 323–333.

Brownell, K. D., Marlatt, G. A., Lichtenstein, E., & Wilson, G. T. (1986). Understanding and preventing relapse. *American Psychologist, 41,* 765–782.

Brownlee, A. (1978). The family and health care: Explorations in cross-cultural settings. *Social Work in Health Care, 4,* 179–198.

Burnette, M. M., Koehn, K. A., Kenyon-Jump, R., Hutton, K., & Stark, C. (1991). Control of genital herpes recurrences using progressive muscle relaxation. *Behavior Therapy, 22,* 237–247.

Buss, A. H. (1980). *Self-consciousness and social anxiety.* San Francisco: W. H. Freeman.

Campbell, D. R., Bender, C., Bennett, N., & Donnelly, J. (1981). Obesity. In J. L. Shelton, R. L. Levy, & contributors, *Behavioral assignments and treatment compliance: A handbook of clinical strategies* (pp. 187–221). Champaign, IL: Research Press.

Candiotte, M. M., & Lichtenstein, E. (1981). Self-efficacy and relapse in smoking cessation programs. *Journal of Consulting and Clinical Psychology, 49,* 648–658.

Cantor, N., Mischel, W., & Schwartz, J. (1982). Social knowledge: Structure, content, use, and abuse. In A. H. Hastorf & A. M. Isen (Eds.), *Cognitive social psychology* (pp. 33–72). New York: Elsevier/North Holland.

Cappe, R. F., & Alden, L. E. (1986). A comparison of treatment strategies for clients functionally impaired by extreme shyness and social avoidance. *Journal of Consulting and Clinical Psychology, 54,* 796–801.

Carey, M. P., Snel, D. L., Carey, K. B., & Richards, C. S. (1989). Self-initiated smoking cessation: A review of the empirical literature from a stress and coping perspective. *Cognitive Therapy and Research, 13,* 323–341.

Carlson, C. R., Collins, F. L., Nitz, A. J., Sturgis, E. T., & Rogers, J. L. (1990). Muscle stretching as an alternative relaxation training procedure. *Journal of Behaviour Therapy and Experimental Psychiatry, 21,* 29–38.

Carver, C. S., & Ganellen, R. J. (1983). Depression and components of self-punitiveness: High standards, self-criticism, and overgeneralization. *Journal of Abnormal Psychology, 92,* 330–337.

Carver, C. S., & Scheier, M. F. (1982). Control theory: A useful conceptual framework for personality—social, clinical, and health psychology. *Psychological Bulletin, 92,* 111–135.

Carver, C. S., & Scheier, M. F. (1986). Analyzing shyness: A specific application of broader self-regulatory principles. In W. H. Jones, J. M. Cheek, & S. R. Briggs (Eds.), *Shyness: Perspectives on research and treatment* (pp. 173–185). New York: Plenum.

Carver, C. S., & Scheier, M. F. (1990). Principles of self-regulation: Action and emotion. In E. T. Higgins & R. M. Sorrentino (Eds.), *Handbook of motivation and cognition: Foundations of social behavior* (Vol. 2, pp. 3–52). New York: Guilford Press.

Castro, F. (1987, August). *Concurrent changes on non-targeted health behaviors in a 28-day behavior change trial.* Paper presented at the meeting of the American Psychological Association, New York.

Castro, L., dePérez, G. C., de Albanchez, D. B., & de León, E. P. (1983). Feedback properties of "self-reinforcement": Further evidence. *Behavior Therapy, 14,* 672–681.

Castro. L., & Rachlin, H. (1980). Self-reward, self-monitoring, and self-punishment as feedback in weight control. *Behavior Therapy, 11,* 38–48.

Catania, A. C. (1975). The myth of self-reinforcement. *Behaviorism, 3,* 192–199.

Catania, A. C., Matthews, B. A., and Shimoff, E. H. (1990). Properties of rule-governed behavior and their implications. In D. E. Blackman & H. Lejune (Eds.), *Behavior analysis in theory and practice: Contributions and controversies* (pp. 215–230). Hillsdale, NJ: Erlbaum.

Cautela, J. R. (1966). A behavior therapy treatment of pervasive anxiety. *Behaviour Research and Therapy, 4,* 99–109.

Cautela, J. R. (1972). The treatment of overeating by covert conditioning. *Psychotherapy: Theory, Research, and Practice, 9,* 211–216.

Cautela, J. R. (1973). Covert processes and behavior modification. *Journal of Nervous and Mental Disease, 157,* 27–36.

Cautela, J. R. (1983). The self-control triad: Description and clinical applications. *Behavior Modification, 7,* 299–315.

Cautela, J. R., & Kearney, A. J. (1986). *The covert conditioning handbook.* New York: Springer.

Cautela, J. R., & Samdperil, L. (1989). Imagaletics: The application of covert conditioning to athletic performance. *Applied Sport Psychology, 1,* 82–97.

Cerone, D. (1989). Effects of envisioning future activities on self-efficacy judgments and motivations: An availability heuristic interpretation. *Cognitive Therapy and Research, 13,* 247–261.

Cervone, D., Jiwani, N., & Wood, R. (1991). Goal setting and the differential influence of self-regulatory processes on complex decision-making performance. *Journal of Personality and Social Psychology, 61,* 257–266.

Chaney, E. F., O'Leary, M. R., & Marlatt, G. A. (1978). Skill training with alcoholics. *Journal of Consulting and Clinical Psychology, 46,* 1092–1104.

Ciminero, A. R. (1974). *The effects of self-monitoring cigarettes as a function of the motivation to quit smoking.* Paper presented at the meeting of the Southeastern Psychological Association, Hollywood, FL.

Clark, D. M., Ball, S., and Paper, D. (1991). An experimental investigation of thought suppression. *Behaviour Research and Therapy, 29,* 253–257.

Clements, C. B., & Beidleman, W. B. (1981). Undergraduate self-management projects: A technique for teaching behavioral principles. *Academic Psychology Bulletin, 3,* 451–461.

Coates, T. J., & Thoresen, C. E. (1977). *How to sleep better.* Englewood Cliffs, NJ: Prentice-Hall.

Cohen, S., Lichtenstein, E., Prochaska, J. O., Rossi, J. S., Gritz, E. R., Carr, C. R., Orleans, C. T., Schoenbach, V. J., Biener, L., Abrams, D., DiClemente, C., Curry, S., Marlatt, G. A., Cummings, K. M., Emont, S. L., Giovino, G., & Osspi-Klein, D. (1989). Debunking myths about self-quitting: Evidence from ten prospective studies of persons who attempt to quit smoking by themselves. *American Psychologist, 44,* 1355–1365.

Cohen, R., De James, P., Nocera, B., & Ramberger, M. (1980). Application of a simple self-instruction procedure on adults' exercise and studying: Two case reports. *Psychological Reports, 46,* 443–451.

Cohen, S., & Lichtenstein, E. (1990). Partner behaviors that support quitting smoking. *Journal of Consulting and Clinical Psychology, 58,* 304–309.

Colletti, G., Supnick, J. A., & Payne, T. J. (1985). The Smoking Self-Efficacy Questionnaire (SSEQ): Preliminary scale development and validation. *Behavioral Assessment, 7,* 249–260.

Collins, K. W., Dansereau, D. F., Garland, J. C., Holley, C. D., & McDonald, B. A. (1981). Control of concentration during academic tasks. *Journal of Educational Psychology, 73,* 122–128.

Cooper, J., & Axsom, D. (1982). Effort justification in psychotherapy. In G. Weary & H. L. Mirels (Eds.), *Integrations of clinical and social psychology* (pp. 214–230). New York: Oxford University Press.

Cappotelli, H. C., & Orleans, C. T. (1985). Partner support and other determinants of smoking cessation maintenance among women. *Journal of Consulting and Clinical Psychology, 53,* 455–460.

Craighead, L. W., & Blum, M. D. (1989). Supervised exercise in behavioral treatment for moderate obesity. *Behavior Therapy, 20,* 49–59.

Cummings, C., Gordon, J. R., & Marlatt, G. A. (1980). Relapse: Prevention and prediction. In W. R. Miller (Ed.), *The addictive behaviors* (pp. 291–321). Oxford: Pergamon Press.

Curry, S. G., & Marlatt, A. (1987). Building self-confidence, self-efficacy and self-control. In W. M. Cox (Ed.), *Treatment and prevention of alcohol problems* (pp. 117–137). New York: Academic Press.

Curry, S. G., Marlatt, G. A., & Gordon, J. R. (1987). Abstinence violation effect: Validation of an attributional construct with smoking cessation. *Journal of Consulting and Clinical Psychology, 55,* 145–149.

Curtis, R. (1991). Toward an integrative theory of psychological change in individuals and organizations: A cognitive-affective regulation model. In R. C. Curtis & G. Stricken (Eds.), *How people change* (pp. 191–210). New York: Plenum.

Daley, D. C. (1991). *Kicking addictive habits once and for all.* Lexington, MA: Heath.

Daly, M. J., & Burton, R. L. (1983). Self-esteem and irrational beliefs: An exploratory investigation with implications for counseling. *Journal of Counseling Psychology, 30,* 361–366.

Davidson, A., Denney, D. R., & Elliott, C. H. (1980). Suppression and substitution in the treatment of nailbiting. *Behaviour Research and Therapy, 18,* 1–9.

Davis, J. R., & Glaros, A. G. (1986). Relapse prevention and smoking cessation. *Addictive Behaviors, 11,* 105–114.

deBortali-Tregerthan, G. (1984). *Self-change and attribution-change training: Implications for primary prevention.* Unpublished doctoral dissertation, University of Hawaii, Honolulu, HI.

Deffenbacher, J. L. (1981). Anxiety. In J. L. Shelton, R. L. Levy, & contributors, *Behavioral assignments and treatment compliance: A handbook of clinical strategies* (pp. 93–109). Champaign, IL: Research Press.

Deffenbacher, J. L. (1988). Cognitive-relaxation and social skills treatments of anger: A year later. *Journal of Counseling Psychology, 35,* 234–236.

Deffenbacher, J. L. (in press). Anger reduction: Issues, assessment, and intervention strategies. In A. W. Siegman & T. W. Smith (Eds.), *Anger, hostility, and the heart.* Hillsdale, NJ: Erlbaum.

Deffenbacher, J. L., & Craun, A. M. (1985). Anxiety management training with stressed student gynecology patients: A collaborative approach. *Journal of College Student Personnel, 26,* 513–517.

Deffenbacher, J. L., & Hahnloser, R. M. (1981). Cognitive and relaxation coping skills in stress inoculation. *Cognitive Therapy and Research, 5,* 211–215.

Deffenbacher, J. L., McNamara, K., Stark, R. S., & Sabadell, P. M. (1990). A combination of cognitive, relaxation, and behavioral coping skills in the reduction of general anger. *Journal of College Student Development, 31,* 351–358.

Deffenbacher, J. L., & Michaels, A. C. (1981). Anxiety management training and self-control desensitization—fifteen months later. *Journal of Counseling Psychology, 28,* 459–462.

Deffenbacher, J. L., & Shepard, J. M. (1989). Evaluating a seminar on stress management. *Teaching of Psychology, 16,* 79–81.

Deffenbacher, J. L., & Suinn, R. M. (1982). The self-control of anxiety. In P. Karoly & F. H. Kanfer (Eds.), *Self-management and behavior change: From theory to practice* (pp. 393–442). New York: Pergamon Press.

Delmonte, M. M. (1985). Meditation and anxiety reduction: A literature review. *Clinical Psychology Review, 5,* 91–102.

Denney, D. R. (1980). Self-control approaches to the treatment of test anxiety. In I. G. Sarason (Ed.), *Test anxiety: Theory, research, and applications* (pp. 209–243). Hillsdale, NJ: Erlbaum.

de Silva, P. (1985). Early Buddhist and modern behavioral strategies for the control of unwanted intrusive cognitions. *The Psychological Record, 35,* 437–443.

DiCara, L. (1970, January). Learning in the autonomic nervous system. *Scientific American,* pp. 30–39.

Dickson-Parnell, B. E., & Zeichner, A. (1985). Effects of a short-term exercise program on caloric consumption. *Health Psychology, 4,* 437–448.

Dodd, D. K. (1986). Teaching behavioral self-change: A course model. *Teaching of Psychology, 13,* 82–85.

Doerfler, L. A., & Richards, C. S. (1981). Self-initiated attempts to cope with depression. *Cognitive Therapy and Research, 5,* 367–371.

Doerfler, L. A., & Richards, C. S. (1983). College women coping with depression. *Behavioral Research Therapy, 21,* 221–224.

Doyne, E. J., Ossip-Klein, D. J., Bowman, E. D., Osborn, K. M., McDougall-Wilson, I. B., & Neimeyer, R. A. (1987). Running versus weight lifting in the treatment of depression. *Journal of Consulting and Clinical Psychology, 55,* 748–754.

Dubbert, P. M., Martin, J. E., & Epstein, L. H. (1986). Exercise. In K. A. Holroyd & T. L. Creer (Eds.), *Self-management of chronic disease* (pp. 127–162). New York: Academic Press.

Dubbert, P. M., Martin, J. E., Raczynski, J., & Smith, P. O. (1982, March). *The effects of cognitive-behavioral strategies in the maintenance of exercise.* Paper presented at the third annual meeting of the Society of Behavioral Medicine, Chicago.

Dubren, R. (1977). Self reinforcement by recorded telephone messages to maintain nonsmoking behavior. *Journal of Consulting and Clinical Psychology, 45,* 358–360.

Durlak, J. A. (1983). Social problem-solving as a primary prevention strategy. In R. D. Felner, L. A. Jason, J. N. Moritsugu, & S. S. Farber (Eds.), *Preventive psychology: Theory, research, and practice* (pp. 31–48). New York: Pergamon Press.

Dush, D. M., Hirt, M. L., & Schroeder, H. (1983). Self-statement modification with adults: A meta-analysis. *Psychological Bulletin, 94,* 408–422.

Dweck, C. S. (1975). The role of expectations and attributions in the alleviation of learned helplessness. *Journal of Personality and Social Psychology, 31,* 674–685.

D'Zurilla, T. J. (1986). *Problem-solving therapy: A social competence approach to clinical intervention.* New York: Springer.

D'Zurilla, T. J. (1990). Problem solving training for effective stress management and prevention. *Journal of Cognitive Psychotherapy, 4,* 327–354.

D'Zurilla, T. J., & Goldfried, M. R. (1971). Problem solving and behavior modification. *Journal of Abnormal Psychology, 78,* 107–126.

D'Zurilla, T. J., & Nezu, A. (1982). Social problem solving in adults. In P. C. Kendall (Ed.), *Advances in cognitive-behavioral research and therapy* (Vol. 1, pp. 201–274). New York: Academic Press.

D'Zurilla, T. J., & Nezu, A. M. (1989). Clinical stress management. In A. M. Nezu & C. M. Nezu (Eds.), *Clinical decision making in behavior therapy: A problem solving perspective* (pp. 371–400). Champaign, IL: Research Press.

Egan, G. (1977). *You and me: The skills of communicating and relating to others.* Pacific Grove, CA: Brooks/Cole.

Eifert, G. H., Craill, L., Carey, E., & O'Conner, C. (1988). Affect modification through evaluative conditioning with music. *Behaviour Research and Therapy, 26,* 321–330.

Eisenberger, R., & Adornetto, M. (1986). Generalized self-control of delay and effort. *Journal of Personality and Social Psychology, 51,* 1020–1031.

Eiser, J. R., van der Pligt, J., Raw, M., & Sutton, S. R. (1985). Trying to stop smoking: Effects of perceived addiction, attributions for failure, and expectancy of success. *Journal of Behavioral Medicine, 8,* 321–341.

Elliott, L. S., & Dweck, C. S. (1988). Goals: An approach to motivation and achievement. *Journal of Personality and Social Psychology, 54,* 5–12.

Ellis, A. (1979). The theory of rational-emotive therapy. In A. Ellis & J. M. Whiteley (Eds.), *Theoretical and empirical foundations of rational-emotive therapy* (pp. 33–60). Pacific Grove, CA: Brooks/Cole.

Ellis, A., & Dryden, W. (1987). *The practice of rational-emotive therapy.* New York: Springer.

Emmelkamp, P. M. G. (1990). Anxiety and fear. In A. S. Bellack, M. Hersen, & A. E. Kazdin (Eds.), *International handbook of behavior modification and therapy* (pp. 283–306). New York: Plenum.

Epstein, L. H., & Hersen, M. (1974). A multiple baseline analysis of coverant control. *Journal of Behavior Therapy and Experimental Psychiatry, 5,* 7–12.

Epstein, L. H., Miller, P. M., & Webster, J. S. (1976). The effects of reinforcing concurrent behavior on self-monitoring. *Behavior Therapy, 7,* 89–95.

Epstein, L. H., & Peterson, G. L. (1973a). The control of undesired behavior by self-imposed contingencies. *Behavior Therapy, 4,* 91–95.

Epstein, L. H., & Peterson, G. L. (1973b). Differential conditioning using covert stimuli. *Behavior Therapy, 4,* 96–99.

Epstein, L. H., Webster, J. S., & Miller, P. M. (1975). Accuracy and controlling effects of self-monitoring as a function of concurrent responding and reinforcement. *Behavior Therapy, 6,* 654–666.

Epstein, R. (1984). An effect of immediate reinforcement and delayed punishment, with possible implications for self-control. *Journal of Behavior Therapy and Experimental Psychiatry, 15,* 291–298.

Erber, R. & Tesser, A. (1991). *The mood-absorbing qualities of work: Task effort and the self-regulation of moods.* Unpublished manuscript, Department of Psychology, University of Virginia, Charlottesville, VA.

Ernst, F. A. (1973). Self-recording and counterconditioning of a self-mutilative compulsion. *Behavior Therapy, 4,* 144–146.

Fanning, P. (1990). *Lifetime weight control.* Oakland, CA: New Harbinger.

Fantuzzo, J. W., Rohrbeck, C. A., & Azar, S. T. (1987). A component analysis of behavioral self-management interventions with elementary school children. *Child and Family Behavior Therapy, 9,* 33–43.

Farber, B. (1987). *Making people talk.* New York: Morrow.

Farmer, R., & Nelson-Gray, R. (1990). The accuracy of counting versus estimating event frequencies in behavioral assessment: The effects of behavior frequency, number of behaviors monitored, and time delay. *Behavioral Assessment, 12,* 425–442.

Farr, M. J. (1987). *The long-term retention of knowledge and skills: A cognitive and instructional perspective.* New York: Springer-Verlag.

Ferguson, J. M. (1975). *Learning to eat.* Palo Alto, CA: Bell.

Ferretti, A., & Hollandsworth, J. G. (1987, November). *Effects of exercise on young and old adults applying different program strategies.* Paper presented at the meeting of the Association for the Advancement of Behavior Therapy, Boston.

Ferster, C. B., Nurnberger, J. I., & Levitt, E. G. (1962). The control of eating. *Journal of Mathetics, 1,* 87–109.

Finney, J. W., Rapoff, M. A., Hall, C. L., & Christophersen, E. R. (1983). Replication and social validation of habit reversal treatment for tics. *Behavior Therapy, 14,* 116–126.

Fischer, K. W. (1980). A theory of cognitive development: The control and construction of hierarchies of skills. *Psychological Review, 87,* 477–531.

Fisher, E. B., Jr., Levenkron, J. C., Lowe, M. R., Loro, A. D., & Green, L. (1982). Self-initiated self-control in risk reduction. In R. B. Stuart (Ed.), *Adherence, compliance, and generalization in behavioral medicine* (pp. 169–191). New York: Brunner/Mazel.

Fisher, E. B., Jr., Lowe, M. R., Levenkron, J. C., & Newman, A. (1982). Reinforcement and structural support of maintained risk reduction. In R. B. Stuart (Ed.), *Adherence, compliance, and generalization in behavioral medicine* (pp. 145–168). New York: Brunner/Mazel.

Fitzgibbon, M. L., & Kirschenbaum, D. S. (in press). Who succeeds in losing weight? In J. D. Fisher, J. Chinsky, Y. Klan, & A. Nadler (Eds.), *Initiating self-change: Social psychological and clinical perspectives.* New York: Springer-Verlag.

Fixen, D. L., Phillips, E. L., & Wolf, M. M. (1972). Achievement place: The reliability of self-reporting and peer-reporting and their effects on behavior. *Journal of Applied Behavior Analysis, 5,* 19–30.

Flanagan, C. M. (1990). *People and change.* Hillsdale, NJ: Erlbaum.

Flannery, R. F., Jr. (1972). A laboratory analogue of two covert reinforcement procedures. *Journal of Behavior Therapy and Experimental Psychiatry, 3,* 171–177.

Flaxman, J. (1978). Quitting smoking now or later: Gradual, abrupt, immediate, and delayed quitting. *Behavior Therapy, 9,* 260–270.

Fo, W. (1975). *Behavioral self-control: Training students in the self-improvement of studying.* Unpublished doctoral dissertation, University of Hawaii, Honolulu, HI.

Ford, E. E. (1989). Fostering self-control: Comments of a counselor. In W. Hershberger (Ed.), *Volitional action. Conation and control* (pp. 469–479). Amsterdam: North Holland.
Forsterling, F. (1985). Attributional retraining: A review. *Psychological Bulletin, 98,* 495–512.
Frankel, A. J. (1975). Beyond the simple functional analysis—The chain: A conceptual framework for assessment with a case study example. *Behavior Therapy, 6,* 254–260.
Freeman, A., & Zaken-Greenburg, F. (1989). Cognitive family therapy. In C. Figley (Ed.), *Psychological stress.* New York: Brunner/Mazel.
Fuchs, C. Z., & Rehm, L. P. (1977). A self-control behavior therapy program for depression. *Journal of Consulting and Clinical Psychology, 45,* 206–215.
Gambrill, E., & Richey, C. (1985). *Taking charge of your social life.* Belmont, CA: Wadsworth.
Garvey, A. J., Heinold, J. W., & Rosner, B. (1989). Self-help approaches to smoking cessation: A report from the normative age study. *Addictive Behaviors, 14,* 23–33.
Gauthier, J., & Pellerin, D. (1982). Management of compulsive shoplifting through covert sensitization. *Journal of Behavior Therapy and Experimental Psychiatry, 13,* 73–75.
Gauthier, J., Pellerin, D., & Renaud, P. (1983). The enhancement of self-esteem: A comparison of two cognitive strategies. *Cognitive Therapy and Research, 7,* 389–398.
George, W. H., & Marlatt, G. A. (1986). Problem drinking. In K. A. Holroyd & T. L. Creer (Eds.), *Self-management of chronic disease* (pp. 59–98). New York: Academic Press.
Gershman, L., & Stedman, J. M. (1971). Oriental defense exercises as reciprocal inhibitors of anxiety. *Journal of Behavior Therapy and Experimental Psychiatry, 2,* 117–119.
Ghosh, A., & Marks, I. M. (1987). Self-treatment of agoraphobia by exposure. *Behavior Therapy, 18,* 3–16.
Gilchrist, L. D., Schinke, S. P., Bobo, J. K., & Snow, W. H. (1986). Self-control skills for preventing smoking. *Addictive Behaviors, 11,* 169–174.
Glasgow, R. E., Klesges, R. C., Mizes, J. S., & Pechacek, T. F. (1985). Quitting smoking: Strategies used and variables associated with success in a stop-smoking contest. *Journal of Consulting and Clinical Psychology, 53,* 905–912.
Glasgow, R. E., & Lichtenstein, E. (1987). Long-term effects of behavioral smoking cessation interventions. *Behavior Therapy, 18,* 297–324.
Glynn, S. M., & Ruderman, A. J. (1986). The development and validation of an eating self-efficacy scale. *Cognitive Therapy and Research, 10,* 403–420.
Goldfried, M. R. (1971). Systematic desensitization as training in self-control. *Journal of Consulting and Clinical Psychology, 37,* 228–234.
Goldfried, M. R. (1977). The use of relaxation and cognitive relabelling as coping skills. In R. B. Stuart (Ed.), *Behavioral self-management: Strategies, techniques, and outcomes* (pp. 82–116). New York: Brunner/Mazel.
Goldfried, M. R. (1979). Anxiety reduction through cognitive-behavioral intervention. In P. C. Kendall & S. D. Hollon (Eds.), *Cognitive-behavioral interventions: Theory, research, and procedures* (pp. 117–152). New York: Academic Press.
Goldfried, M. R. (1986). Self-control skills for the treatment of anxiety disorders. In B. F. Shaw, Z. V. Segal, T. M. Valis, & F. E. Cashman (Eds.), *Anxiety disorders* (pp. 165–178). New York: Plenum.
Goldfried, M. R. (1988). Application of rational restructuring to anxiety disorders. *The Counseling Psychologist, 16,* 50–68.
Goldfried, M. R., & Goldfried, A. P. (1977). Importance of hierarchy content in the self-control of anxiety. *Journal of Consulting and Clinical Psychology, 45,* 124–131.
Goldfried, M. R., Padawer, W., & Robins, C. (1984). Social anxiety and the semantic structure of heterosexual interactions. *Journal of Abnormal Psychology, 93,* 87–97.
Goldfried, M. R., & Robins, C. (1982). On the facilitation of self-efficacy. *Cognitive Therapy and Research, 6,* 361–380.
Goldfried, M. R., & Trier, C. S. (1974). Effectiveness of relaxation as an active coping skill. *Journal of Abnormal Psychology, 83,* 348–355.
Goldiamond, I. (1965). Self-control procedures in personal behavior problems. *Psychological Reports, 17,* 851–868.
Goldstein, A. P., & Kanfer, F. H. (Eds.). (1979). *Maximizing treatment gains: Transfer enhancement in psychotherapy.* New York: Academic Press.
Goldstein, A. P., Lopez, M., & Greenleaf, D. O. (1979). Introduction. In A. P. Goldstein & F. H. Kanfer (Eds.), *Maximizing treatment gains: Transfer enhancement in psychotherapy* (pp. 1–22). New York: Academic Press.
Goldstein, A. P., Sprafkin, R. P., & Gershaw, N. J. (1979). *I know what's wrong, but I don't know what to do about it.* Englewood Cliffs, NJ: Prentice-Hall.

Goldstein-Fodor, I., & Epstein, R. C. (1983). Assertiveness training for women: Where are we failing? In E. B. Foa & P. M. G. Emmelkamp (Eds.), *Failures in behavior therapy* (pp. 137–158). New York: Wiley.

Goodall, T. A., & Halford, W. K. (1991). Self-management of diabetes mellitus: A critical review. *Health Psychology, 10,* 1–8.

Gordon, J. R., & Marlatt, G. A. (1981). Addictive behaviors. In J. L. Shelton, R. L. Levy, & contributors. *Behavioral assignments and treatment compliance: A handbook of clinical strategies* (pp. 167–186). Champaign, IL: Research Press.

Gordon, J. R., & Roffman, R. (1987, November). *Relapse prevention training as an AIDS reduction procedure.* Paper presented at the annual meeting of the Association for the Advancement of Behavior Therapy, Boston.

Gormally, J., Black, S., Daston, S., & Rardin, D. (1982). The assessment of binge eating severity among obese persons. *Addictive Behaviors, 7,* 47–55.

Gottfriedson, G. D. (1990, August). *Applications and research using Holland's theory of careers: Where we would like to be and suggestions for getting there.* Paper delivered at the annual meeting of the American Psychological Association, Boston.

Gottman, J., Notarius, C., Gonso, J., & Markman, H. (1976). *A couple's guide to communication.* Champaign, IL: Research Press.

Graziano, A. M. (1975). Futurants, coverants, and operants. *Behavior Therapy, 6,* 421–422.

Green, L. (1982). Minority students' self-control of procrastination. *Journal of Counseling Psychology, 29,* 636–644.

Greist, J. H., Marks, I. M., Berlin, F., Gournay, K., & Noshirvani, H. (1980). Avoidance versus confrontation of fear. *Behavior Therapy, 11,* 1–14.

Griffin, D. E., & Watson, D. L. (1978). A written, personal commitment from the student encourages better course work. *Teaching of Psychology, 5,* 155.

Grilo, C. M., Shiffman, S., & Wing, R. R. (1989). Relapse crises and coping among dieters. *Journal of Consulting and Clinical Psychology, 57,* 488–495.

Gritz, E. R. (1978). Women and smoking: A realistic appraisal. In J. Schwartz (Ed.), *Program in smoking cessation: International Conference on Smoking Cessation* (pp. 119–141). New York: American Cancer Society.

Gross, A. M., & Drabman, R. S. (1982). Teaching self-recording, self-evaluation, and self-reward to nonclinic children and adolescents. In P. Karoly & F. H. Kanfer (Eds.), *Self-management and behavior change: From theory to practice* (pp. 285–315). New York: Pergamon Press.

Hall, S. M. (1980). Self-management and therapeutic maintenance: Theory and research. In P. Karoly & J. Steffen (Eds.), *Improving the long term effects of psychotherapy* (pp. 263–300). New York: Gardner Press.

Hall, S. M., Rugg, D., Tunstall, C., & Jones, R. T. (1984). Preventing relapse to cigarette smoking by behavioral skill training. *Journal of Consulting and Clinical Psychology, 52,* 372–382.

Hamilton, S. B. (1980). Instructionally based training in self-control: Behavior-specific and generalized outcomes resulting from student-implemented self-modification projects. *Teaching of Psychology, 7,* 140–145.

Hamilton, S. B., & Waldman, D. A. (1983). Self-modification of depression via cognitive-behavioral intervention strategies: A time series analysis. *Cognitive Theory and Research, 7,* 99–106.

Harackiewicz, J. M., Sansone, C., Blair, L. W., Epstein, J. A., & Manderlink, G. (1987). Attributional processes in behavior change and maintenance: Smoking cessation and continued abstinence. *Journal of Consulting and Clinical Psychology, 55,* 372–378.

Harris, C. S., & McReynolds, W. T. (1977). Semantic cues and response contingencies in self-instructional control. *Journal of Behavior Therapy and Experimental Psychiatry, 8,* 15–17.

Harris, G. M., & Johnson, S. B. (1980). Comparison of individualized covert modeling, self-control desensitization, and study-skills training for alleviation of test anxiety. *Journal of Consulting and Clinical Psychology, 48,* 186–194.

Harris, G. M., & Johnson, S. B. (1983). Coping imagery and relaxation instructions in a covert modeling treatment for test anxiety. *Behavior Therapy, 14,* 144–157.

Hawkins, R. C., & Clement, P. (1980). Development and construct validation of a self-report measure of binge eating tendencies. *Addictive Behaviors, 5,* 219–226.

Hayes, S. C. (Ed.). (1989). *Rule-governed behavior: Cognition, contingencies, and instructional control.* New York: Plenum.

Hayes, S. C., & Nelson, R. O. (1986). Assessing the effects of therapeutic interventions. In R. O. Nelson & S. C. Hayes (Eds.), *Conceptual foundations of behavioral assessment* (pp. 430–460). New York: Guilford Press.

Hayes, S. C., Rosenfarb, I., Wulfert, E., Munt, E. D., Korn, Z., & Zettle, R. D. (1985). Self-reinforcement effects: An artifact of social standard setting? *Journal of Applied Behavior Analysis, 18,* 201–214.

Hays, V., & Waddell, K. (1976). A self-reinforcing procedure for thought stopping. *Behavior Therapy, 7,* 559.

Hazaleus, S. L., & Deffenbacher, J. L. (1986). Relaxation and cognitive treatments of anger. *Journal of Consulting and Clinical Psychology, 54,* 222–226.

Heatherington, L., & Kirsch, I. (1984). The generality of negative self-reinforcement effects: Implications for the use of extrinsic rewards. *Cognitive Therapy and Research, 8,* 67–76.

Heatherton, T. F., & Baumeister, R. F. (1991). Binge eating as escape from self-awareness. *Psychological Bulletin, 110,* 86–108.

Heffernan, T., & Richards, C. S. (1981). Self-control of study behavior: Identification and evaluation of natural methods. *Journal of Counseling Psychology, 28,* 361–364.

Heiby, E. M. (1981). Depression and frequency of self-reinforcement. *Behavior Therapy, 12,* 549–555.

Heiby, E. M. (1982). A self-reinforcement questionnaire. *Behaviour Research and Therapy, 20,* 397–401.

Heiby, E. M. (1983a). Depression as a function of the interaction of self- and environmentally controlled reinforcement. *Behavior Therapy, 14,* 430–433.

Heiby, E. M. (1983b). Toward the prediction of mood change. *Behavior Therapy, 14,* 110–115.

Heiby, E. M. (1986). Social versus self-control skills deficits in four cases of depression. *Behavior Therapy, 17,* 158–169.

Heiby, E. M. (1987, August). *Toward the unification of the psychology of depression: Contributions from a paradigmatic behavioral theory.* Paper presented at the meeting of the American Psychological Association, New York.

Heiby, E. M., Ozaki, M., & Campos, P. E. (1984). The effects of training in self-reinforcement and reward: Implications for depression. *Behavior Therapy, 15,* 544–549.

Heins, E. D., Lloyd, J. W., & Hallahan, D. P. (1986). Cued and noncued self-recording of attention to task. *Behavior Modification, 10,* 235–254.

Heinzelmann, F., & Bagley, R. W. (1970). Response to physical activity programs and their effects on health behavior. *Public Health Reports, 85,* 905–911.

Herren, C. M. (1989). A self-monitoring technique for increasing productivity in multiple media. *Journal of Behavior Therapy and Experimental Psychiatry, 20,* 69–72.

Herrnstein, R. J. (1990). Rational choice theory: Necessary but not sufficient. *American Psychologist, 45,* 356–367.

Hiebert, B., & Fox, E. E. (1981). Reactive effects of self-monitoring anxiety. *Journal of Counseling Psychology, 28,* 187–193.

Higgins, R. L., Frisch, M. B., & Smith, D. (1983). A comparison of role-played and natural responses to identical circumstances. *Behavior Therapy, 14,* 158–169.

Holden, A. E., O'Brien, G. T., Barlow, D. H., Stetson, D., & Infantino, A. (1983). Self-help manual for agoraphobia: A preliminary report of effectiveness. *Behavior Therapy, 14,* 545–556.

Hollon, S. D., & Beck, A. T. (1979). Cognitive therapy of depression. In P. C. Kendall & S. D. Hollon (Eds.), *Cognitive-behavioral interventions: Theory, research, and procedures* (pp. 153–203). New York: Academic Press.

Holman, J., & Baer, D. M. (1979). Facilitating generalization of on-task behavior through self-monitoring of academic tasks. *Journal of Autism and Developmental Disorders, 9,* 429–446.

Holroyd, K. A., & Creer, T. L. (Eds.). (1986). *Self-management of chronic disease.* New York: Academic Press.

Horan, J. J., Baker, S. B., Hoffman, A. M., & Shute, R. E. (1975). Weight loss through variations in the coverant control paradigm. *Journal of Consulting and Clinical Psychology, 43,* 68–72.

Horan, J. J., & Johnson, R. G. (1971). Coverant conditioning through a self-management application of the Premack principle: Its effect on weight reduction. *Journal of Behavior Therapy and Experimental Psychiatry, 2,* 243–249.

Horn, D. (1972). Determinants of change. In R. G. Richardson (Ed.), *The second world conference on smoking and health* (pp. 58–74). London: Pitman Medical.

Horner, R. H., Dunlap, G., & Koegel, R. L. (1988). *Generalization and maintenance: Life-style changes in applied settings.* Baltimore, MD: Brooks.

Hull, J. (1987). Self-awareness model. In H. Blaine & K. Leonard (Eds.), *Psychological theories of drinking and alcoholism* (pp. 272–301). New York: Guilford Press.

Hunt, W. A., & Matarazzo, J. D. (1973). Three years later: Recent developments in the experimental modification of smoking behavior. *Journal of Abnormal Psychology, 81,* 107–114.

Israel, A. C., & Saccone, A. J. (1979). Follow-up of effects of choice of mediator and target of reinforcement on weight loss. *Behavior Therapy, 10,* 260–265.

Jacobson, E. (1938). *Progressive relaxation* (2nd ed.). Chicago: University of Chicago Press.

Janis, I. L. (Ed.). (1982). *Counseling on personal decisions: Theory and research on short-term helping relationships.* New Haven, CT: Yale University Press.

Jeffery, R. W., French, S. A., & Schmid, T. L. (1990). Attributions for dietary failures: Problems reported by participants in the hypertension prevention trial. *Health Psychology, 9,* 315–329.

Jeffery, R. W., Gerber, W. M., Rosenthal, B. S., & Lindquist, R. A. (1983). Monetary contracts in weight control: Effectiveness of group and individual contracts of varying size. *Journal of Consulting and Clinical Psychology, 51,* 242–248.

Jeffery, R. W., Hellerstedt, W. L., & Schmid, T. L. (1990). Correspondence programs for smoking cessation and weight control: A comparison of two strategies in the Minnesota Heart Health Program. *Health Psychology, 9,* 585–598.

Jeffery, R. W., & Wing, R. R. (1983). Recidivism and self-cure of smoking and obesity: Data from population studies. *American Psychologist, 38,* 852.

Johnsgard, K. W. (1989). *The exercise prescription for depression and anxiety.* New York: Plenum.

Johnson, D. J., & Rusbult, C. E. (1989). Resisting temptation: Devaluation of alternative partners as a means of maintaining commitment in close relationships. *Journal of Personality and Social Psychology, 57,* 967–980.

Johnson, M. (1985). The origin of memories. In P. C. Kendall (Ed.), *Advances in cognitive-behavioral research and therapy* (Vol. 4, pp. 1–27). New York: Academic Press.

Johnson, W. G. (1971). Some applications of Homme's coverant control therapy: Two case reports. *Behavior Therapy, 2,* 240–248.

Johnston-O'Connor, E. J., & Kirschenbaum, D. S. (1986). Something succeeds like success: Positive self-monitoring for unskilled golfers. *Cognitive Therapy and Research, 10,* 123–136.

Kamarck, T. W., & Lichtenstein, E. (1987, November). *Program adherence and coping strategies as predictors of success in a smoking treatment program.* Paper presented at the annual meeting of the Association for the Advancement of Behavior Therapy, Boston.

Kanfer, F. H. (1970). Self-regulation: Research, issues, and speculations. In C. Neuringer & J. L. Michael (Eds.), *Behavior modification in clinical psychology* (pp. 178–220). New York: Appleton-Century-Crofts.

Kanfer, F. H. (1975). Self-management methods. In F. H. Kanfer & A. P. Goldstein (Eds.), *Helping people change: A textbook of methods* (pp. 334–389). New York: Pergamon Press.

Kanfer, F. H. (1977). The many faces of self-control, or behavior modification changes its focus. In R. B. Stuart (Ed.), *Behavioral self-management: Strategies, techniques, and outcomes* (pp. 1–48). New York: Brunner/Mazel.

Kanfer, F. H. (1984). Self-management in clinical and social interventions. In R. P. McGlynn, J. E. Maddux, C. D. Stoltenberg, & J. H. Harvey (Eds.), *Social perception in clinical and counseling psychology* (pp. 141–163). Lubbock, TX: Texas Tech University Press.

Kanfer, F. H., Cox, L. E., Greiner, J. M., & Karoly, P. (1974). Contracts, demand characteristics, and self-control. *Journal of Personality and Social Psychology, 30,* 605–619.

Kanfer, F. H., & Hagerman, S. (1987). A model of self-regulation. In F. Halish & J. Kuhl (Eds.), *Motivation, intention, and volition* (pp. 293–307). Berlin: Springer-Verlag.

Kanfer, F. H., & Karoly, P. (1972). Self-control: A behavioristic excursion into the lion's den. *Behavior Therapy, 3,* 398–416.

Kanfer, F. H., & Schefft, B. K. (1987). Self-management therapy in clinical practice. In J. S. Jacobson (Ed.), *Psychotherapists in clinical practice: Cognitive and behavioral perspectives* (pp. 10–77). New York: Guilford Press.

Kanfer, F. H., & Stevenson, M. K. (1985). The effects of self-regulation on concurrent cognitive processing. *Cognitive Therapy and Research, 9,* 667–684.

Kanter, N. J., & Goldfried, M. R. (1979). Relative effectiveness of rational restructuring and self-control desensitization in the reduction of interpersonal anxiety. *Behavior Therapy, 10,* 472–490.

Karoly, P. (1991). Self-management in health-care and illness prevention. In C. R. Snyder & D. R. Forsyth (Eds.), *Handbook of social and clinical psychology* (pp. 579–606). New York: Pergamon Press.

Karoly, P., & Bay, R. C. (1990). Diabetes self-care goals and their relation to children's metabolic control. *Journal of Pediatric Psychology, 15,* 83–95.

Karoly, P., & Kanfer, F. H. (Eds.). (1982). *Self-management and behavior change: From theory to practice.* New York: Pergamon Press.

Katz, R. C., & Vinciguerra, P. (1982). On the neglected art of "thinning" reinforcers. *Behavior Therapist, 5,* 21–22.

Kau, M. L., & Fischer, J. (1974). Self-modification of exercise behavior. *Journal of Behavior Therapy and Experimental Psychiatry, 5,* 213–214.

Kazdin, A. E. (1973). The effect of response cost and aversive stimulation in suppressing punished and non-punished speech disfluencies. *Behavior Therapy, 4,* 73–82.

Kazdin, A. E. (1974a). Effects of covert modeling and model reinforcement on assertive behavior. *Journal of Abnormal Psychology, 83,* 240–252.

Kazdin, A. E. (1974b). Self-monitoring and behavior change. In M. J. Mahoney & C. E. Thoresen (Eds.), *Self-control: Power to the person* (pp. 218–246). Pacific Grove, CA: Brooks/Cole.

Kazdin, A. E. (1982). The separate and combined effects of covert and overt rehearsal in developing assertive behavior. *Behaviour Research and Therapy, 20,* 17–25.

Kazdin, A. E. (1984). Covert modeling. In P. C. Kendall (Ed.), *Advances in cognitive-behavioral research and therapy* (Vol. 3, pp. 103–129). New York: Academic Press.

Kelley, H. H. (1983). Love and commitment. In H. H. Kelley, E. Berscheid, A. Christensen, J. H. Harvey, T. L. Huston, G. Levinger, E. McClintock, L. A. Peplau, & D. R. Peterson (Eds.), *Close relationships* (pp. 265–314). New York: W. H. Freeman.

Kelly, M. L., Scott, W. O. M., Prue, D. M., & Rychtarik, R. G. (1985). A component analysis of problem solving training. *Cognitive Therapy and Research, 9,* 429–441.

Kendall, P. C. (1989). The generalization and maintenance of behavior change: Comments, considerations, and the "no-cure" criticism. *Behavior Therapy, 20,* 357–364.

Kendall, P. C., & Ingram, R. (1987). The future for cognitive assessment of anxiety: Let's get specific. In L. Michelson & L. M. Ascher (Eds.), *Anxiety and stress disorders* (pp. 89–104). New York: Guilford Press.

Kendall, P. C., Stark, K. D., & Adam, T. (1990). Cognitive deficit or cognitive distortion in childhood depression. *Journal of Abnormal Child Psychology, 18,* 255–270.

Kennerley, H. (1990). *Managing anxiety.* Oxford: Oxford University Press.

Kernis, M. H., Zuckerman, M., Cohen, A., & Spadafora, S. (1982). Persistence following failure: The interactive role of self-awareness and the attributional basis for negative expectancies. *Journal of Personality and Social Psychology, 43,* 1184–1191.

King, A. C., & Frederiksen, L. W. (1984). Low-cost strategies for increasing exercise behavior. *Behavior Modification, 8,* 3–21.

Kirk, J. (1989). Cognitive-behavioural assessment. In K. Hawton, P. M. Salkovakis, J. Kirk, & D. M. Clark (Eds.), *Cognitive behaviour therapy for psychiatric problems: A practical guide* (pp. 13–51). Oxford: Oxford University Press.

Kirschenbaum, D. S. (1984). Self-regulation and sport psychology: Nurturing an emerging symbiosis. *Journal of Sport Psychology, 6,* 159–183.

Kirschenbaum, D. S. (1985). Proximity and specificity of planning: A position paper. *Cognitive Therapy and Research, 9,* 489–506.

Kirschenbaum, D. S. (1987). Self-regulatory failure: A review with clinical implications. *Clinical Psychology Review, 7,* 77–104.

Kirschenbaum, D. S., & Flanery, R. C. (1984). Toward a psychology of behavioral contracting. *Clinical Psychology Review, 4,* 597–618.

Kirschenbaum, D. S., Humphrey, L. L., & Malett, S. D. (1981). Specificity of planning in adult self-control: An applied investigation. *Journal of Personality and Social Psychology, 40,* 941–950.

Kirschenbaum, D. S., & Perri, M. G. (1982). Improving academic competence in adults: A review of recent research. *Journal of Counseling Psychology, 29,* 76–94.

Kirschenbaum, D. S., & Tomarken, A. J. (1982). On facing the generalization problem: The study of self-regulatory failure. In P. C. Kendall (Ed.), *Advances in cognitive-behavioral research and therapy* (Vol. 1, pp. 119–200). New York: Academic Press.

Knapp, T., & Shodahl, S. (1974). Ben Franklin as a behavior modifier: A note. *Behavior Therapy, 5,* 656–660.

Knowlton, G. E., & Harris, W. (1987, November). *A comparison of two treatment components of an anxiety management program to improve the freethrow performance on a women's collegiate basketball team.* Paper presented at the annual meeting of the Association for the Advancement of Behavior Therapy, Boston.

Knox, D. (1971). *Marriage happiness: A behavioral approach to counseling.* Champaign, IL: Research Press.

Kornblith, S. J., Rehm, L. P., O'Hara, M. W., & Lamparski, D. M. (1983). The contribution of self-reinforcement training and behavioral assignments to the efficacy of self control therapy for depression. *Cognitive Therapy and Research, 7,* 499–528.

Krop, H., Calhoon, B., & Verrier, R. (1971). Modification of the "self-concept" of emotionally disturbed children by covert reinforcement. *Behavior Therapy, 2,* 201–204.

Krop, H., Perez, F., & Beaudoin, C. (1973). Modification of "self-concept" of psychiatric patients by covert reinforcement. In R. D. Rubin, J. P. Brady, & J. D. Henderson (Eds.), *Advances in behavior therapy* (Vol. 4, pp. 139–144). New York: Academic Press.

Kuhl, J., & Beckmann, J. (Eds.). (1985). *Action control: From cognition to behavior.* Berlin: Springer-Verlag.

Kuiper, N. A., & Olinger, L. J. (1986). Dysfunctional attitudes and a self-worth contingency model of depression. In P. C. Kendall (Ed.), *Advances in cognitive-behavioral research and therapy* (Vol. 5, pp. 115–142). New York: Academic Press.

Lacks, P., Bertelson, A. D., Gans, L., & Kunkel, J. (1983). The effectiveness of three behavioral treatments for different degrees of sleep onset insomnia. *Behavior Therapy, 14,* 593–605.

Lakein, A. (1973). *How to get control of your time and your life.* New York: New American Library.

Lascelles, M. A., Cunningham, S. J., McGrath, P., & Sullivan, M. J. L. (1989). Teaching coping strategies to adolescents with migraine. *Journal of Pain and Symptom Management, 4,* 135–145.

Lawson, D. M., & Rhodes, E. C. (1981, November). *Behavioral self-control and maintenance of aerobic exercise: A retrospective study of self-initiated attempts to improve physical fitness.* Paper presented at the meeting of the Association for the Advancement of Behavior Therapy, Toronto.

Layden, M. A. (1982). Attributional style therapy. In C. Antaki & C. Brewin (Eds.), *Attributions and psychological change* (pp. 63–82). London: Academic Press.

Lazarus, A. (1971). *Behavior therapy and beyond.* New York: McGraw-Hill.

Leary, M. R., & Atherton, S. C. (1986). Self-efficacy, social anxiety, and inhibition in interpersonal encounters. *Journal of Social and Clinical Psychology, 4,* 256–267.

Leavitt, F. (1982). *Drugs and behavior* (2nd ed.). New York: Wiley.

LeBow, M. D. (1981). *Weight control: The behavioral strategies.* New York: Wiley.

LeBow, M. D. (1989). *Adult obesity therapy.* New York: Pergamon Press.

Lee, C. (1983). Self-efficacy and behaviour as predictors of subsequent behaviour in an assertiveness training program. *Behaviour Research and Therapy, 21,* 225–232.

Lees, L. A., & Dygdon, J. A. (1988). The initiation and maintenance of exercise behavior: A learning theory conceptualization. *Clinical Psychology Review, 8,* 345–353.

Lehman, A. K., & Rodin, J. (1989). Styles of self-nurturance and disordered eating. *Journal of Consulting and Clinical Psychology, 57,* 117–122.

Leon, G. R. (1979). Cognitive-behavior therapy for eating disturbances. In P. C. Kendall & S. D. Hollon (Eds.), *Cognitive-behavioral interventions: Theory, research, and procedures* (pp. 357–388). New York: Academic Press.

Lepper, M. R., & Greene, D. (1975). Turning play into work: Effects of adult surveillance and extrinsic rewards on children's intrinsic motivation. *Journal of Personality and Social Psychology, 31,* 479–486.

Lerner, J. V., Baker, N., & Lerner, R. M. (1985). A person-context goodness of fit model of adjustment. In P. C. Kendall (Ed.), *Advances in cognitive-behavioral research and therapy* (Vol. 4, pp. 111–136). New York: Academic Press.

Levendusky, P., & Pankratz, L. (1975). Self-control techniques as an alternative to pain medication. *Journal of Abnormal Psychology, 84,* 165–168.

Levin, R. B., & Gross, A. M. (1984). Reactions to assertive versus nonassertive behavior: Females in commendatory and refusal situations. *Behavior Modification, 8,* 581–592.

Leviton, L. C. (1979). Observer's reactions to assertive behavior. *Dissertation Abstracts International, 39,* (11-B), 5652.

Lewinsohn, P. M., Biglan, A., & Zeiss, A. M. (1976). Behavioral treatment of depression. In P. O. Davidson (Ed.), *The behavioral management of anxiety, depression, and pain* (pp. 91–146). New York: Brunner/Mazel.

Lewinsohn, P. M., Sullivan, J. M., & Grosscup, S. J. (1980). Changing reinforcing events: An approach to the treatment of depression. *Psychotherapy: Theory, Research, and Practice, 17,* 322–334.

Lewis, L. E., Biglan, A., & Steinbock, E. (1978). Self-administered relaxation: Training and money deposits in the treatment of recurrent anxiety. *Journal of Consulting and Clinical Psychology, 46,* 1274–1283.

Ley, P. (1986). Cognitive variables and noncompliance. *The Journal of Compliance in Health Care, 1,* 171–188.

Lichtenstein, E., Glasgow, R. E., & Abrams, D. B. (1986). Social support in smoking cessation: In search of effective interventions. *Behavior Therapy, 17,* 607–619.

Lichtenstein, E., Weiss, S. M., Hitchcock, J. L., Leveton, L. B., O'Connell, K. A., & Prochaska, J. O. (1986). Task force 3: Patterns of smoking relapse. *Health Psychology, 5* (Supplement), 29–40.

Linehan, M. M. (1979). Structural cognitive-behavioral treatment of assertion problems. In P. C. Kendall & S. D. Hollon (Eds.), *Cognitive-behavioral interventions: Theory, research, and procedures* (pp. 205–240). New York: Academic Press.

Lipton, D. N., & Nelson, R. O. (1980). The contribution of initiation behaviors to dating frequency. *Behavior Therapy, 11,* 59–67.

Locke, E. A., & Latham, G. P. (1990). Work motivation and satisfaction: Light at the end of the tunnel. *Psychological Science, 1,* 240–246.

Long, B. C., & Haney, C. J. (1988). Coping strategies for working women: Aerobic exercise and relaxation interventions. *Behavior Therapy, 19,* 75–83.

Loper, A. B., & Murphy, D. M. (1985). Cognitive self-regulatory training for underachieving children. In D. L. Forrest-Pressley, G. E. MacKinnon, & T. G. Weller (Eds.), *Metacognition, cognition, and human performance* (pp. 223–265). New York: Academic Press.

Lucic, K. S., Steffen, J. J., Harrigan, J. A., & Stuebing, R. C. (1991). Progressive relaxation training: Muscle contraction before relaxation? *Behavior Therapy, 22,* 249–256.

Luria, A. (1961). *The role of speech in the regulation of normal and abnormal behaviors.* New York: Liveright.

Lutzker, S. Z., & Lutzker, J. R. (1974, April). *A two-dimensional marital contract: Weight loss and household responsibility performance.* Paper presented at the meeting of the Western Psychological Association, San Francisco.

Lydon, J. E., & Zanna, M. P. (1990). Commitment in the face of adversity: A value-affirmation approach. *Journal of Personality and Social Psychology, 58,* 1040–1047.

Mace, F. C., & Kratochwill, T. R. (1985). Theories of reactivity in self-monitoring. *Behavior Modification, 9,* 323–343.

MacPhillamy, D. J., & Lewinsohn, P. M. (1982). The Pleasant Events Schedule: Studies on reliability, validity, and scale intercorrelation. *Journal of Consulting and Clinical Psychology, 50,* 363–380.

Maher, C. A. (Ed.). (1985). *Professional self-management: Techniques for special services providers.* Baltimore, MD: Brooks.

Mahoney, M. J. (1974). *Cognition and behavior modification.* Cambridge, MA: Ballinger.

Mahoney, M. J. (1977). On the continuing resistance to thoughtful therapy. *Behavior Therapy, 8,* 673–677.

Mahoney, M. J., & Bandura, A. (1972). Self-reinforcement in pigeons. *Learning and Motivation, 3,* 293–303.

Mahoney, M. J., Bandura, A., Dirks, S. J., & Wright, C. L. (1974). Relative preference for external and self-controlled reinforcement in monkeys. *Behaviour Research and Therapy, 12,* 157–163.

Mahoney, M. J., & Moura, N. G. M., & Wade, T. C. (1973). Relative efficacy of self-reward, self-punishment, and self-monitoring techniques for weight loss. *Journal of Consulting and Clinical Psychology, 40,* 404–407.

Maletzky, B. M. (1974). Behavior recording as treatment: A brief note. *Behavior Therapy, 5,* 107–111.

Malott, R. W. (1989). The achievement of evasive goals: Control by rules describing contingencies that are not direct acting. In S. C. Hayes (Ed.), *Rule-governed behavior.* New York: Plenum.

Mandler, G. (1954). Transfer of training as a function of degree of response overlearning. *Journal of Experimental Psychology, 47,* 411–417.

Marholin, D., & Touchette, P. E. (1979). The role of stimulus control and response consequences. In A. P. Goldstein & F. H. Kanfer (Eds.), *Maximizing treatment gains: Transfer enhancement in psychotherapy* (pp. 303–351). New York: Academic Press.

Marlatt, G. A. (1982). Relapse prevention: A self-control program for the treatment of addictive behaviors. In R. B. Stuart (Ed.), *Adherence, compliance, and generalization in behavioral medicine* (pp. 329–378). New York: Brunner/Mazel.

Marlatt, G. A., & George, W. H. (1990). Relapse prevention and the maintenance of optimal health. In S. Schumaker, E. Schron, & J. K. Ockene (Eds.), *The handbook of health behavior change* (pp. 44–63). New York: Springer.

Marlatt, G. A., & Gordon, J. R. (1980). Determinants of relapse: Implications for the maintenance of behavior change. In P. O. Davidson & S. M. Davidson (Eds.), *Behavioral medicine: Changing health lifestyles* (pp. 410–452). New York: Brunner/Mazel.

Marlatt, G. A., & Gordon, J. R. (1985). *Relapse prevention: Maintenance strategies for addictive behavior change.* New York: Guilford Press.

Marlatt, G. A., & Marques, J. K. (1977). Meditation, self-control, and alcohol use. In R. B. Stuart (Ed.), *Behavioral self-management: Strategies, techniques, and outcomes* (pp. 117–153). New York: Brunner/Mazel.

Marlatt, G. A., & Parks, G. A. (1982). Self-management of addictive disorders. In P. Karoly & F. H. Kanfer (Eds.), *Self-management and behavior change: From theory to practice* (pp. 443–488). New York: Pergamon Press.

Marques, J. K. (1987, November). *An experimental relapse program for sex offenders.* Paper presented at the annual meeting of the Association for the Advancement of Behavior Therapy, Boston.

Marshall, W. L., Boutilier, J., & Minnes, P. (1974). The modification of phobic behavior by covert reinforcement. *Behavior Therapy, 5,* 469–480.

Martin, J. E., Dubbert, P. M., Katell, A. D., Thompson, J. K., Raczynski, J. R., Lake, M., Smith, P. O., Webster, J. S., Sikora, T., & Cohen, R. E. (1984). Behavioral control of exercise in sedentary adults: studies one through six. *Journal of Consulting and Clinical Psychology, 52,* 795–811.

Martinsen, E. W. (1990). Benefits of exercise for the treatment of depression. *Sports Medicine, 9,* 380–389.

Martzke, J. S., Andersen, B. L., & Cacioppo, J. T. (1987). Cognitive assessment of anxiety disorders. In L. Michelson & L. M. Ascher (Eds.), *Anxiety and stress disorders* (pp. 62–88). New York: Guilford Press.

Masters, J. C., Burrish, T. C., Hollon, S. D., & Rimm, D. C. (1987). *Behavior therapy: Techniques and empirical findings* (3rd ed.). New York: Harcourt Brace Jovanovich.

Masterson, J. F., & Vaux, A. C. (1982). The use of a token economy to regulate household behaviours. *Behavioural Psychotherapy, 10,* 65–78.

Matson, J. L. (1977). Social reinforcement by the spouse in weight control: A case study. *Journal of Behavior Therapy and Experimental Psychiatry, 8,* 327–328.

Mayer, J. (1968). *Overweight.* Englewood Cliffs, NJ: Prentice-Hall.

Mayer, R. E. (1988, August). *Teaching for thinking: Research on the teachability of thinking skills.* G. Stanley Hall lecture presented at the annual meeting of the American Psychological Association, Atlanta, GA.

Mayo, L. L., & Norton, G. R. (1980). The use of problem solving to reduce examination and interpersonal anxiety. *Journal of Behavior Therapy and Experimental Psychiatry, 11,* 287–289.

McCann, I. L., & Holmes, D. S. (1984). Influence of aerobic exercise on depression. *Journal of Personality and Social Psychology, 46,* 1142–1147.

McFall, R. M., & Dodge, K. A. (1982). Self-management and interpersonal skills learning. In P. Karoly & F. H. Kanfer (Eds.), *Self-management and behavior change: From theory to practice* (pp. 353–392). New York: Pergamon Press.

McGlynn, F. D., Kinjo, K., & Doherty, G. (1978). Effects of cue-controlled relaxation, a placebo treatment, and no treatment on changes in self-reported anxiety among college students. *Journal of Clinical Psychology, 34,* 707–714.

McKeachie, W. J. (1978). *Teaching tips: A guidebook for the beginning college teacher* (7th ed.). Lexington, MA: Heath.

McKnight, D. L., Nelson, R. O., Hayes, S. C., & Jarrett, R. B. (1984). Importance of treating individually assessed response classes in the amelioration of depression. *Behavior Therapy, 15,* 315–335.

McReynolds, W. T., Green, L., & Fisher, E. B. (1983). Self-control as choice management with reference to the behavioral treatment of obesity. *Health Psychology, 2,* 261–276.

Meichenbaum, D. H. (1977). *Cognitive behavior modification: An integrative approach.* New York: Plenum.

Meichenbaum, D. (1985). *Stress inoculation training.* New York: Pergamon Press.

Meichenbaum, D., & Turk, D. C. (1987). *Facilitating treatment adherence: A practitioner's guidebook.* New York: Plenum.

Menges, R. J., & Dobroski, B. J. (1977). Behavioral self-modification in instructional settings: A review. *Teaching of Psychology, 4,* 168–174.

Mermelstein, R., Cohen, S., Lichtenstein, E., Baer, J., & Kamarck, T. (1986). Social support and smoking cessation and maintenance. *Journal of Consulting and Clinical Psychology, 54,* 447–453.

Mermelstein, R., Lichtenstein, E., & McIntyre, K. (1983). Partner support and relapse in smoking-cessation programs. *Journal of Consulting and Clinical Psychology, 51*, 465–466.

Miller, G. A., Galanter, E., & Pribram, K. H. (1960). *Plans and the structure of behavior.* New York: Holt, Rinehart & Winston.

Miller, N. E. (1969, January). Learning of visceral and glandular responses. *Science,* pp. 434–445.

Miller, R. K., & Bornstein, P. H. (1977). Thirty-minute relaxation: A comparison of some methods. *Journal of Behavior Therapy and Experimental Psychiatry, 8*, 291–294.

Mischel, W. (1981). Metacognition and the rules of delay. In J. H. Flavell & L. Ross (Eds.), *Social cognitive development: Frontiers and possible futures* (pp. 240–271). Cambridge: Cambridge University Press.

Mitchell, C., & Stuart, R. (1984). Effect of self-efficacy on dropout from obesity treatment. *Journal of Consulting and Clinical Psychology, 52*, 1100–1101.

Mizes, J. S., Morgan, G. D., & Buder, J. (1987, November). *Global versus specific cognitive measures and their relationship to assertion deficits.* Paper presented at the annual meeting of the Association for the Advancement of Behavior Therapy, Boston.

Moon, J. R., & Eisler, R. M. (1983). Anger control: An experimental comparison of three behavioral treatments. *Behavior Therapy, 14*, 493–505.

Morawetz, D. (1989). Behavioral self-help treatment for insomnia: A controlled evaluation. *Behavior Therapy, 20*, 365–379.

Morgan, W. G., & Bass, B. A. (1973). Self-control through self-mediated rewards. In R. D. Rubin, J. P. Brady, & J. D. Henderson (Eds.), *Advances in behavior therapy* (Vol. 4, pp. 117–126). New York: Academic Press.

Morris, E. K. (1991, August). *Cogniphilia and cogniphobia in behavior modification.* Address presented at the Division 25 meeting of the American Psychological Association, San Francisco.

Moss, M. K., & Arend, R. A. (1977). Self-directed contact desensitization. *Journal of Consulting and Clinical Psychology, 45*, 730–738.

Murphy, T. J., Pagano, R. R., & Marlatt, G. A. (1986). Lifestyle modification with heavy alcohol drinkers: Effects of aerobic exercise and meditation. *Addictive Behaviors, 11*, 175–186.

Nakano, K. (1990). Operant self-control procedure in modifying Type A behavior. *Journal of Behavior Therapy and Experimental Psychiatry, 21*, 249–255.

Neimeyer, R. A., & Feixas, G. (1990). The role of homework and skill acquisition in the outcome of group cognitive therapy for depression. *Behavior Therapy, 21*, 281–292.

Nelson, R. O. (1977). Methodological issues in assessment via self-monitoring. In J. D. Cone & R. P. Hawkins (Eds.), *Behavioral assessment: New directions in clinical psychology* (pp. 217–240). New York: Brunner/Mazel.

Nelson, R. O., Hayes, S. C., Spong, R. T., Jarrett, R. B., & McKnight, D. L. (1983). Self-reinforcement: Appealing misnomer or effective mechanism? *Behaviour Research and Therapy, 21*, 557–566.

Newman, A., & Bloom, R. (1981a). Self-control of smoking—I. Effects of experience with imposed, increasing, decreasing, and random delays. *Behaviour Research and Therapy, 19*, 187–192.

Newman, A., & Bloom, R. (1981b). Self-control of smoking—II. Effects of cue salience and source of delay imposition on the effectiveness of training under increasing delay. *Behaviour Research and Therapy, 19*, 193–200.

Nezu, A. M. (1987). Social problem solving and depression: A literature review and proposal of a pluralistic model. *Clinical Psychology Review, 7*, 121–144.

Nezu, A. M., & D'Zurilla, T. J. (1981). Effects of problem definition and formulation on the generation of alternatives in the social problem-solving process. *Cognitive Therapy and Research, 5*, 265–271.

Nezu, A. M., & D'Zurilla, T. J. (1989). Social problem solving and negative affective states. In P. C. Kendall & D. Watson (Eds.), *Anxiety and depression: Distinctive and overlapping features.* New York: Academic Press.

Nezu, A. M., Nezu, C. M., Saraydarian, L., Kalmar, K., & Ronan, G. F. (1986). Social problem solving as a moderating variable between negative life stress and depressive symptoms. *Cognitive Therapy and Research, 10*, 489–498.

Nicki, R. M., Remington, R. E., & MacDonald, G. A. (1984). Self-efficacy, nicotine-fading/self-monitoring, and cigarette-smoking behaviour. *Behaviour Research and Therapy, 22*, 477–485.

Nisbett, R. E., & Ross, L. (1980). *Human inference: Strategies and shortcomings of social judgment.* Englewood Cliffs, NJ: Prentice-Hall.

Noel, R. (1980). The effect of visuo-motor behavior rehearsal on tennis performance. *Journal of Sport Psychology, 2,* 221–226.
Nolan, J. D. (1968). Self-control procedures in the modification of smoking behavior. *Journal of Consulting and Clinical Psychology, 32,* 92–93.
O'Banion, D., Armstrong, B. K., & Ellis, J. (1980). Conquered urge as a means of self-control. *Addictive Behaviors, 5,* 101–106.
O'Connor, K. P., & Stravynski, A. (1982). Evaluation of a smoking typology by use of a specific behavioural substitution method of self-control. *Behaviour Research and Therapy, 20,* 279–288.
Okwumabua, T. M., Meyers, A. W., Schleser, R., & Cooke, C. J. (1983). Cognitive strategies and running performance: An exploratory study. *Cognitive Therapy and Research, 7,* 363–370.
O'Leary, A. (1985). Self-efficacy and health. *Behaviour Research and Therapy, 23,* 437–451.
Ollendick, T. H., & King, N. J. (1991). Origins of childhood fears: An evaluation of Rachman's theory of fear acquisition. *Behaviour Research and Therapy, 29,* 117–123.
O'Neill, H. K., Sandgren, A. K., McCaul, K. D., & Glasgow, R. E. (1987). Self-control strategies and maintenance of a dental hygiene regimen. *The Journal of Compliance in Health Care, 2,* 85–89.
Orme, C. M., & Binik, Y. M. (1987). Recidivism and self-cure of obesity: A test of Schachter's hypothesis in diabetic patients. *Health Psychology, 6,* 467–475.
Ost, L.-G. (1987). Applied relaxation: Description of a coping technique and review of controlled studies. *Behaviour Research and Therapy, 25,* 397–409.
Owusu-Bempah, J., & Howitt, D. L. (1983). Self-modeling and weight control. *British Journal of Medical Psychology, 56,* 157–165.
Paquin, M. J. R. (1982). Daily monitoring to eliminate a compulsion. In H. L. Millman, J. T. Huber, & D. R. Diggins (Eds.), *Therapies for adults: Depressive, anxiety, and personality disorders* (pp. 266–268). San Francisco: Jossey-Bass.
Passman, R. (1977). The reduction of procrastinative behaviors in a college student despite the "contingency fulfillment problem": The use of external control in self-management techniques. *Behavior Therapy, 8,* 95–96.
Patterson, C. J., & Mischel, W. (1975). Plans to resist distraction. *Developmental Psychology, 11,* 369–378.
Paul, G. L. (1966). *Insight vs. desensitization in psychotherapy.* Stanford, CA: Stanford University Press.
Pawlicki, R., & Galotti, N. (1978). A tic-like behavior case study emanating from a self-directed behavior modification course. *Behavior Therapy, 9,* 671–672.
Payne, P. A., & Woudenberg, R. A. (1978). Helping others and helping yourself: An evaluation of two training modules in a college course. *Teaching of Psychology, 5,* 131–134.
Pearce, J. W., LeBow, M. D., & Orchard, J. (1981). Role of spouse involvement in the behavioral treatment of overweight women. *Journal of Consulting and Clinical Psychology, 49,* 236–244.
Pechacek, T. F., & Danaher, B. G. (1979). How and why people quit smoking: A cognitive-behavioral analysis. In P. C. Kendall & S. D. Hollon (Eds.), *Cognitive-behavioral interventions: Theory, research, and procedures* (pp. 389–422). New York: Academic Press.
Perkins, D., & Perkins, F. (1976). *Nail biting and cuticle biting.* Dallas, TX: Self-Control Press.
Perri, M. G., McAdoo, W. G., McAllister, D. A., Lauer, J. B., & Yancy, D. Z. (1986). Enhancing the efficacy of behavior therapy for obesity: Effects of aerobic exercise and a multicomponent maintenance program. *Journal of Consulting and Clinical Psychology, 54,* 670–675.
Perri, M. G., McAllister, D. A., Gange, J. J., Jordan, R. C., McAdoo, W. G., & Nezu, A. M. (1988). Effects of four maintenance programs on the long-term management of obesity. *Journal of Consulting and Clinical Psychology, 56,* 529–534.
Perri, M. G., & Richards, C. S. (1977). An investigation of naturally occurring episodes of self-controlled behaviors. *Journal of Counseling Psychology, 24,* 178–183.
Perri, M. G., Richards, C. S., & Schultheis, K. (1977). Behavioral self-control and smoking reduction: A study of self-initiated attempts to reduce smoking. *Behavior Therapy, 8,* 360–365.
Perri, M. G., Shapiro, R. M., Ludwig, W. W., Twentyman, C. T., & McAdoo, W. G. (1984). Maintenance strategies for the treatment of obesity: An evaluation of relapse prevention training and posttreatment contact by mail and telephone. *Journal of Consulting and Clinical Psychology, 52,* 404–413.
Peterson, L. (1983). Failure in self-control. In E. B. Foa & P. M. G. Emmelkamp (Eds.), *Failures in behavior therapy* (pp. 172–196). New York: Wiley.

Posobiec, K., & Renfrew, J. W. (1988). Successful self-management of severe bulimia: A case study. *Journal of Behavior Therapy and Experimental Psychiatry, 19,* 63–68.

Prochaska, J. O. (1983). Self-changers versus therapy changers versus Schachter. *American Psychologist, 38,* 853–854.

Prochaska, J. O., DiClemente, C. O., Velicer, W. F., Ginpil, S., & Norcross, N. C. (1985). Predicting change in smoking status for self-changers. *Addictive Behaviors, 10,* 395–406.

Propst, L. R. (1980). The comparative efficacy of religious and nonreligious imagery for the treatment of mild depression in religious individuals. *Cognitive Therapy and Research, 4,* 167–178.

Rachlin, H. (1974). Self control. *Behaviorism, 2,* 94–107.

Rachman, S. (1977). The conditioning theory of fear acquisition: A critical examination. *Behaviour Research and Therapy, 15,* 375–387.

Radnitz, C. L., Appelbaum, K. A., Blanchard, E. B., Elliott, L., & Andrasik, F. (1988). The effect of self-regulatory treatment on pain behavior in chronic headache. *Behaviour Research and Therapy, 26,* 253–260.

Rakos, R. F., & Grodek, M. V. (1984). An empirical evaluation of a behavioral self-management course in a college setting. *Teaching of Psychology, 11,* 157–162.

Rehm, L. P. (1982). Self-management in depression. In P. Karoly & F. H. Kanfer (Eds.), *Self-management and behavior change: From theory to practice* (pp. 522–567). New York: Pergamon Press.

Rehm, L. P. (1988). Self-management and cognitive processes in depression. In L. B. Alloy (Ed.), *Cognitive processes in depression* (pp. 143–176). New York: Guilford Press.

Rehm, L. P., Kaslow, N. J., & Rabin, A. S. (1987). Cognitive and behavioral targets in a self-control therapy program for depression. *Journal of Consulting and Clinical Psychology, 55,* 60–67.

Rehm, L. P., & Marston, A. R. (1968). Reduction of social anxiety through modification of self-reinforcement: An instigation therapy technique. *Journal of Consulting and Clinical Psychology, 32,* 565–574.

Reich, J. W., & Zautra, A. (1981). Life events and personal causation: Some relationships with satisfaction and distress. *Journal of Personality and Social Psychology, 41,* 1002–1012.

Rescoria, R. A. (1988). Pavlovian conditioning: It's not what you think it is. *American Psychologist, 43,* 151–160.

Richards, C. S. (1976). Improving study behaviors through self-control techniques. In J. D. Krumboltz & C. E. Thoresen (Eds.), *Counseling methods* (pp. 462–467). New York: Holt, Rinehart & Winston.

Richards, C. S. (1985). Work and study problems. In M. Hersen & A. S. Bellack (Eds.), *Handbook of clinical behavior therapy with adults* (pp. 557–571). New York: Plenum.

Richards, C. S., & Perri, M. G. (1978). Do self-control treatments last? An evaluation of behavioral problem solving and faded counselor contact as treatment maintenance strategies. *Journal of Counseling Psychology, 25,* 376–383.

Rickard-Figueroa, K., & Zeichner, A. (1985). Assessment of smoking urge and its concomitants under an environmental smoking cue manipulation. *Addictive Behaviors, 10,* 249–256.

Rimm, D. C., & Masters, J. C. (1979). *Behavior therapy: Techniques and empirical findings.* New York: Academic Press.

Robinson, F. P. (1970). *Effective study* (4th ed.). New York: Harper & Row.

Rodin, J., Schooler, C., & Schaie, K. W. (1990). *Self-directedness: Cause and effects throughout the life course.* Hillsdale, NJ: Erlbaum.

Rogoff, B. (1982). Integrating context and cognitive development. In M. E. Lamb & A. L. Brown (Eds.), *Advances in developmental psychology* (Vol. 2, pp. 125–170). Hillsdale, NJ: Erlbaum.

Rogoff, B., & Lave, J. (Eds.). (1984). *Everyday cognition: Its development in social contexts.* Cambridge, MA: Harvard University Press.

Rosen, G. M. (1990, August). *Self-help or hype? Comments on psychology's failure to advance self-care.* Paper presented at the annual convention of the American Psychological Association, San Francisco.

Rosen, L. W. (1981). Self-control program in the treatment of obesity. *Journal of Behavior Therapy and Experimental Psychiatry, 12,* 163–166.

Rosenbaum, M. (1983). Learned resourcefulness as a behavioral repertoire for the self-regulation of internal events: Issues and speculations. In M. Rosenbaum, C. M. Franks, & Y. Jaffe (Eds.), *Perspectives on behavior therapy in the eighties* (pp. 54–73). New York: Springer.

Rosenbaum, M. (1988). A model for research on self-regulation: Reducing the schism between behaviorism and general psychology. In I. M. Evans (Ed.), *Paradigmatic behavior therapy: Critical perspectives on applied social behaviorism.* New York: Springer.

Rosenbaum, M., & Rolnick, A. (1983). Self-control behaviors and coping with seasickness. *Cognitive Therapy and Research, 7,* 93–98.

Ross, M., & Conway, M. (1986). Remembering one's own past: The construction of personal histories. In R. M. Sorrentino & E. T. Higgins (Eds.), *Handbook of motivation and cognition* (pp. 122–144). New York: Guilford Press.

Rozensky, R. H. (1974). The effect of timing of self-monitoring behavior on reducing cigarette consumption. *Journal of Behavior Therapy and Experimental Psychiatry, 5,* 301–303.

Rush, A. J. (Ed.). (1982). *Short-term psychotherapies for depression.* New York: Guilford Press.

Russell, R. K., & Lent, R. W. (1982). Cue-controlled relaxation and systematic desensitization versus nonspecific factors in treating test anxiety. *Journal of Counseling Psychology, 29,* 100–103.

Russell, R. K., Miller, D. E., & June, L. N. (1975). A comparison between group systematic desensitization and cue-controlled relaxation in the treatment of test anxiety. *Behavior Therapy, 6,* 172–177.

Russell, R. K., & Sipich, J. F. (1974). Treatment of test anxiety by cue-controlled relaxation. *Behavior Therapy, 5,* 673–676.

Russell, R. K., Wise, F., & Stratoudakis, J. P. (1976). Treatment of test anxiety by cue-controlled relaxation and systematic desensitization. *Journal of Counseling Psychology, 3,* 563–566.

Russo, D. C. (1990). A requiem for the passing of the three-term contingency. *Behavior Therapy, 21,* 153–165.

Saccone, A. J., & Israel, A. C. (1978). Effects of experimenter versus significant other-controlled reinforcement and choice of target behavior on weight loss. *Behavior Therapy, 9,* 271–278.

Sandifer, B. A., & Buchanan, W. L. (1983). Relationship between adherence and weight loss in a behavioral weight reduction program. *Behavior Therapy, 14,* 682–688.

Sarason, I. G. (Ed.). (1980). *Test anxiety: Theory, research, and applications.* Hillsdale, NJ: Erlbaum.

Sato, R. A. (1986). *Increasing exercise adherence among Honolulu Marathon Clinic participants.* Unpublished master's thesis, University of Hawaii, Honolulu, HI.

Schachter, S. (1982). Recidivism and self-cure of smoking and obesity. *American Psychologist, 37,* 436–444.

Schafer, W. (1992). *Stress management for wellness* (2nd ed.). Fort Worth, TX: Harcourt Brace Jovanovich.

Schlunk, D. H. (1986). Vicarious influences on self-efficacy for cognitive skill learning. *Journal of Social and Clinical Psychology, 4,* 316–327.

Schuele, J. G., & Wiesenfeld, A. R. (1983). Autonomic response to self-critical thought. *Cognitive Therapy and Research, 7,* 189–194.

Schwartz, R. M. (1986). The internal dialogue: On the asymmetry between positive and negative coping thoughts. *Cognitive Therapy and Research, 10,* 591–605.

Schwartz, R. M., & Garamoni, G. L. (1986). A structural mode of positive and negative states of mind: Asymmetry in the internal dialogue. In P. C. Kendall (Ed.), *Advances in cognitive-behavioral research and therapy* (Vol. 5, pp. 1–62). New York: Academic Press.

Schwartz, S. H., & Inbar-Saban, N. (1988). Value self-confrontation as a method to aid in weight loss. *Journal of Personality and Social Psychology, 54,* 396–404.

Seidner, M. L. (1973). *Behavior change contract: Prior information about study habits treatment and statements of intention as related to initial effort in treatment.* Unpublished doctoral dissertation, University of Cincinnati.

Selby, V. C., DiLorenzo, T. M., & Steinkamp, C. A. (1987, November). *An examination of the behaviors and characteristics distinguishing exercisers, non-exercisers, and drop-outs.* Paper presented at the annual meeting of the Association for the Advancement of Behavior Therapy, Boston.

Seligman, M. P. (1990). *Learned optimism.* New York: Knopf.

Sewitch, T. S., & Kirsch, I. (1984). The cognitive content of anxiety: Naturalistic evidence for the predominance of threat-related thoughts. *Cognitive Therapy and Research, 8,* 49–58.

Shapiro, D. H., & Walsh, R. (Eds.). (1980). *The science of meditation: Theory, research, and experience.* Hawthorne, NY: Aldine.

Shelton, J. L. (1979). Instigation therapy: Using therapeutic homework to promote treatment gains. In A. P. Goldstein & F. H. Kanfer (Eds.), *Maximizing treatment gains: Transfer enhancement in psychotherapy* (pp. 225–245). New York: Academic Press.

Shelton, J. L. (1981a). Nonassertion. In J. L. Shelton, R. L. Levy, & contributors, *Behavioral assignments and treatment compliance: A handbook of clinical strategies* (pp. 305–330). Champaign, IL: Research Press.

Shelton, J. L. (1981b). The use of behavioral assignments in clinical practice. In J. L. Shelton, R. L. Levy, and contributors, *Behavioral assignments and treatment compliance: A handbook of clinical strategies* (pp. 1–19). Champaign, IL: Research Press.

Shelton, J. L., Levy, R. L., and contributors (1981). *Behavioral assignments and treatment compliance: A handbook of clinical strategies.* Champaign, IL: Research Press.

Sherman, A. R. (1972). Real-life exposure as a primary therapeutic factor in the desensitization treatment for fear. *Journal of Abnormal Psychology, 79,* 19–28.

Sherman, A. R. (1975). Two-year follow-up of training in relaxation as a behavioral self-management skill. *Behavior Therapy, 6,* 419–420.

Sherman, A. R., & Plummer, I. L. (1973). Training in relaxation as a behavioral self-management skill: An exploratory investigation. *Behavior Therapy, 4,* 543–550.

Sherman, A. R., Turner, R., Levine, M., & Walk, J. (1975, December). *A behavioral self-management program for increasing or decreasing habit responses.* Paper presented at the meeting of the Association for the Advancement of Behavior Therapy, San Francisco.

Shiffman, S. (1982). Relapse following smoking cessation: A situational analysis. *Journal of Consulting and Clinical Psychology, 50,* 71–86.

Shiffman, S. (1984). Coping with temptations to smoke. *Journal of Consulting and Clinical Psychology, 52,* 261–267.

Shiffman, S., & Jarvik, M. E. (1987). Situational determinants of coping in smoking relapse crises. *Journal of Applied Social Psychology, 17,* 3–15.

Shiffman, S., Shumaker, S., Abrams, D., Cohen, S., Garvey, A., Grunberg, N., & Swan, G. (1986). Task force 2: Models of smoking relapse. *Health Psychology, 5* (Supplement), 13–27.

Simons, A. D., McGowan, C. R., Epstein, L. H., Kupfer, D. J., & Robertson, R. J. (1985). Exercise as a treatment for depression: An update. *Clinical Psychology Review, 5,* 553–568.

Skinner, B. F. (1953). *Science and human behavior.* New York: Macmillan.

Smith, J. C. (1985). *Relaxation dynamics: Nine world approaches to self-relaxation.* Champaign, IL: Research Press.

Smith, R. J., Arnkoff, D. B., & Wright, T. L. (1987, November). *Test anxiety and academic competence: A comparison of alternative models.* Paper presented at the annual meeting of the Association for the Advancement of Behavior Therapy, Boston.

Snyder, A. L., & Deffenbacher, J. L. (1977). Comparison of relaxation as self-control and systematic desensitization in the treatment of test anxiety. *Journal of Consulting and Clinical Psychology, 45,* 1202–1203.

Snyder, C. R., Harris, C., Anderson, J. R., Holleran, S. A., Irving, L. M., Sigmon, S. T., Yoshinobu, L., Gibb, J., Langelle, C., & Harney, P. (1991). The will and the ways: Development and validation of an individual differences measure of hope. *Journal of Personality and Social Psychology, 60,* 570–585.

Sohn, D., & Lamal, P. A. (1982). Self-reinforcement: Its reinforcing capability and its clinical utility. *Psychological Record, 32,* 179–203.

Sonne, J. L., & Janoff, D. S. (1982). Attributions and the maintenance of behavior change. In C. Antaki & C. Brewin (Eds.), *Attributions and psychological change* (pp. 83–96). New York: Academic Press.

Sowers, J., Verdi, M., Bourbeau, P., & Sheehan, M. (1985). Teaching job independence and flexibility to mentally retarded students through the use of a self-control package. *Journal of Applied Behavior Analysis, 18,* 81–85.

Spates, C. R., & Kanfer, F. H. (1977). Self-monitoring, self-evaluation, and self-reinforcement in children's learning: A test of a multi-stage self-regulation model. *Behavior Therapy, 8,* 9–16.

Speidel, G. E., & Tharp, R. T. (1980). What does self-reinforcement reinforce: An empirical analysis of the contingencies in self-determined reinforcement. *Child Behavior Therapy, 2,* 1–22.

Spinelli, P. R., & Packard, T. (1975, February). *Behavioral self-control delivery systems.* Paper presented at the National Conference on Behavioral Self-Control, Salt Lake City, UT.

Spurr, J., & Stevens, V. J. (1980). Increasing study time and controlling student guilt: A case study in self-management. *Behavior Therapist, 3,* 17–18.

Staats, A. W. (1968). *Learning, language, and cognition.* New York: Holt, Rinehart & Winston.

Stalonas, P. M., & Kirschenbaum, D. S. (1985). Behavioral treatments for obesity: Eating habits revisited. *Behavior Therapy, 16,* 1–14.

Stanley, M. A., & Maddux, J. E. (1986). Self-efficacy theory: Potential contributions to understanding cognitions in depression. *Journal of Social and Clinical Psychology, 4,* 268–278.

Stark, K. D., Reynolds, W. M., & Kaslow, N. J. (1987). A comparison of the relative efficacy of self-control therapy and a behavioral problem-solving therapy for depression in children. *Journal of Abnormal Child Psychology, 15,* 91–113.

Steenman, H. F. (1986). *Cognitive coping and chronic pain.* Unpublished doctoral dissertation, University of Hawaii, Honolulu, HI.

Stevenson, D. W., & Delprato, D. J. (1983). Multiple component self-control program for menopausal hot flashes. *Journal of Behavior Therapy and Experimental Psychiatry, 14,* 137–140.

Stevenson, H. C., & Fantuzzo, J. W. (1986). The generality and social validity of a competency-based self-control training intervention for underachieving students. *Journal of Applied Behavior Analysis, 19,* 269–276.

Stock, J., & Cervone, D. (1990). Proximal goal-setting and self-regulatory processes. *Cognitive Therapy and Research, 14,* 483–498.

Stockert, N. A. (1989). *Using attitude change techniques to enlighten.* Unpublished master's thesis, University of Hawaii–Manoa, Honolulu, HI.

Stockton, W. (1987, November 16). Just how far, and how fast, for fitness? *New York Times,* p. Y33.

Stokes, T. F., & Baer, D. M. (1977). An implicit technology of generalization. *Journal of Applied Behavior Analysis, 10,* 349–368.

Stokes, T. F., & Osnes, P. G. (1989). An operant pursuit of generalization. *Behavior Therapy, 20,* 337–355.

Stuart, R. B. (1967). Behavioral control of overeating. *Behaviour Research and Therapy, 5,* 357–365.

Stuart, R. B. (1977). Self-help group approach to self-management. In R. B. Stuart (Ed.), *Behavioral self-management: Strategies, techniques, and outcomes* (pp. 278–305). New York: Brunner/Mazel.

Stuart, R. B. (1980). Weight loss and beyond: Are they taking it off and keeping it off? In P. O. Davidson & S. M. Davidson (Eds.), *Behavioral medicine: Changing health lifestyles* (pp. 151–194). New York: Brunner/Mazel.

Stuart, R. B., & Davis, B. (1972). *Slim chance in a fat world: Behavioral control of obesity.* Champaign, IL: Research Press.

Stunkard, A. J. (1958). The management of obesity. *New York State Journal of Medicine, 58,* 79–87.

Sudnow, D. (1978). *Ways of the hand: The organization of improvised conduct.* Cambridge, MA: Harvard University Press.

Suinn, R. M. (1976, July). Body thinking: Psychology for Olympic champs. *Psychology Today,* pp. 38–40.

Suinn, R. M. (1977). *Manual for anxiety management training (AMT).* Fort Collins, CO: Rocky Mountain Behavioral Science Institute.

Suinn, R. M. (1983). Imagery and sports. In A. A. Sheikh (Ed.), *Imagery: Current theory, research, and application* (pp. 507–534). New York: Wiley.

Suinn, R. M. (1985). The 1984 Olympics and sport psychology. *Sport Psychology Today, 1,* 321–329.

Suinn, R. M. (1987). Psychological approaches to performance enhancement. In M. Asken & J. May (Eds.), *Sports psychology: The psychological health of the athlete* (pp. 41–57). New York: Spectrum.

Suinn, R. M. (1989). Behavioral intervention for stress management in sports. In D. Hackfort & C. Spielberger (Eds.), *Anxiety in sports: An international perspective.* New York: Hemisphere.

Suinn, R. M. (1990). *Anxiety management training: A behavior therapy.* New York: Plenum.

Tec, L. (1980). *Targets: How to set goals for yourself and reach them.* New York: Harper & Row.

Temoshok, L. (1990). On attempting to articulate the biopsychosocial model: Psychological-physiological homeostasis. In H. Friedman (Ed.), *Personality and disease* (pp. 203–225). New York: Wiley.

Tharp, R. G., & Gallimore, R. (1988). *Rousing minds to life.* New York: Cambridge University Press.

Tharp, R. G., Gallimore, R., & Calkins, R. P. (1984). On the relationship between self-control and control by others. *Avances en Psicología Clínica Latinoamericana, 3,* 45–58.

Tharp, R. G., Jordan, C., Speidel, G. E., Au, K. H., Klein, T. W., Calkins, R. P., Sloat, K. C. M., & Gallimore, R. (1984). Product and process in applied developmental research: Education and the children of a minority. In M. E. Lamb, A. L. Brown, & B. Rogoff (Eds.), *Advances in developmental psychology* (Vol. 3, pp. 91–144). Hillsdale, NJ: Erlbaum.

Tharp, R. G., Watson, D. L., & Kaya, J. (1974). Self-modification of depression. *Journal of Consulting and Clinical Psychology, 42,* 624. (Extended Report, University of Hawaii)

Tharp, R. G., & Wetzel, R. J. (1969). *Behavior modification in the natural environment.* New York: Academic Press.

Thase, M. E., & Moss, M. K. (1976). The relative efficacy of covert modeling procedures and guided participant modeling on the reduction of avoidance behavior. *Journal of Behavior Therapy and Experimental Psychiatry, 7,* 7–12.

Thorpe, G. L., Amatu, H. I., Blakey, R. S., & Burns, L. E. (1976). Contributions of overt instructional rehearsal and "specific insight" to the effectiveness of self-instructional training: A preliminary study. *Behavior Therapy, 7,* 504–511.

Throll, D. A. (1981). Transcendental meditation and progressive relaxation: Their psychological effects. *Journal of Clinical Psychology, 37,* 776–781.

Tinling, D. C. (1972). Cognitive and behavioral aspects of aversive therapy. In R. D. Rubin, H. Fensterheim, J. D. Henderson, & L. P. Ullmann (Eds.), *Advances in behavior therapy* (pp. 73–80). New York: Academic Press.

Tobin, D. L., Holroyd, K. A., Baker, A., Reynolds, R. V. C., & Holm, J. (1988). Development and clinical trial of a minimal contact, cognitive-behavioral treatment for tension headache. *Cognitive Therapy and Research, 12,* 325–339.

Todd, F. J. (1972). Coverant control of self-evaluative responses in the treatment of depression: A new use for an old principle. *Behavior Therapy, 3,* 91–94.

Turk, D. M., Holzman, A. D., & Kerns, R. D. (1986). Chronic pain. In K. A. Holroyd & T. L. Creer (Eds.), *Self-management of chronic disease* (pp. 441–472). New York: Academic Press.

Turner, R. M. (1986). Behavioral self-control procedures for disorders of initiating and maintaining sleep. *Clinical Psychology Review, 6,* 27–38.

Turner, S. M., Holzman, A., & Jacob, R. G. (1983). Treatment of compulsive looking by imaginal thought-stopping. *Behavior Modification, 7,* 576–582.

Twentyman, C., Boland, T., & McFall, R. M. (1981). Heterosocial avoidance in college males: Four studies. *Behavior Modification, 5,* 523–552.

Upper, D. (1974). Unsuccessful self-treatment of a case of "writer's block." *Journal of Applied Behavior Analysis, 7,* 497.

Velicer, W. F., DiClemente, C. C., Rossi, J. S., & Prochaska, J. O. (1990). Relapse situations and self-efficacy: An integrative model. *Addictive Behaviors, 15,* 271–283.

von Schlumperger, B. (1985). Formation and maintenance of an exercise habit: An exploratory study of a self-management approach. *Dissertation Abstracts International, 47,* 776B.

Vygotsky, L. S. (1965). *Thought and language* (E. Hantmann & G. Vokar, Eds. and Trans.). Cambridge, MA: MIT Press.

Vygotsky, L. S. (1978). *Mind and society.* Cambridge, MA: Harvard University Press.

Wallace, I., & Pear, J. J. (1977). Self-control techniques of famous novelists. *Journal of Applied Behavior Analysis, 10,* 515–525.

Watkins, L. (1991). *The critical standards used by college students in evaluating narrative and argumentative essays.* Unpublished master's thesis, University of Hawaii–Manoa, Honolulu, HI.

Watson, D. L. (1992). *Psychology.* Pacific Grove, CA: Brooks/Cole.

Watson, D. L., Tharp, R. G., & Krisberg, J. (1972). Case study of self-modification: Suppression of inflammatory scratching while awake and asleep. *Journal of Behavior Therapy and Experimental Psychiatry, 3,* 213–215.

Watson, J. B., & Rayner, R. (1920). Conditioned emotional reactions. *Journal of Experimental Psychology, 3,* 1–14.

Wegner, D. M., & Guiliano, T. (1983). On sending artifact in search of artifact: Reply to McDonald, Harris, & Maher. *Journal of Personality and Social Psychology, 44,* 290–293.

Wegner, D. M., & Schneider, D. J. (1989). Mental control: The war of the ghosts in the machine. In J. S. Uleman & J. A. Bargh (Eds.), *Unintended thought* (pp. 287–305). New York: Guilford Press.

Wegner, D. M., Shortt, J. W., Blake, A. W., & Page, M. S. (1990). The suppression of exciting thoughts. *Journal of Personality and Social Psychology, 58,* 409–418.

Weisz, G., & Bucher, B. (1980). Involving husbands in treatment of obesity—effects on weight loss, depression, and marital satisfaction. *Behavior Therapy, 11,* 643–650.

Wenzlaff, R. M., Wegner, D. M., and Roper, D. W. (1988). Depression and mental control: The resurgence of unwanted negative thoughts. *Journal of Personality and Social Psychology, 55,* 882–892.

Wertsch, J. V. (Ed.). (1985). *Vygotsky and the social formation of mind.* Cambridge, MA: Harvard University Press.

Westover, S. A., & Lanyon, R. I. (1990). The maintenance of weight loss after behavioral treatment. *Behavior Modification, 14,* 123–137.

Whisman, M. A. (1990). The efficacy of booster maintenance sessions in behavior therapy: Review and methodological critique. *Clinical Psychology Review, 10,* 155–170.

Wiener, N. (1948). *Cybernetics: Control and communication in the animal and the machine.* Cambridge, MA: MIT Press.

Wine, J. D. (1980). Cognitive-attentional theory of test anxiety. In I. G. Sarason (Ed.), *Test anxiety: Theory, research, and applications* (pp. 349–385). Hillsdale, NJ: Erlbaum.

Wing, R. R., Epstein, L. H., Nowalk, M. P., & Scott, N. (1988). Self-regulation in the treatment of Type II diabetes. *Behavior Therapy, 19,* 11–23.

Wing, R. R., Marcus, M. D., Epstein, L. H., & Kupfer, D. (1983). Mood and weight loss in a behavioral treatment program. *Journal of Consulting and Clinical Psychology, 51,* 153–155.

Wisocki, P. A. (1973). A covert reinforcement program for the treatment of test anxiety: Brief report. *Behavior Therapy, 4,* 264–266.

Wolpe, J. (1958). *Psychotherapy by reciprocal inhibition.* Stanford, CA: Stanford University Press.

Wolpe, J. (1981). The dichotomy between classical conditioned and cognitively learned anxiety. *Journal of Behavior Therapy and Experimental Psychiatry, 12,* 35–42.

Wood, Y. R., Hardin, M., & Wong, E. (1984, January). *Social network influences on smoking cessation.* Paper presented at the meeting of the Western Psychological Association, Los Angeles.

Woolfolk, R. L., Lehrer, P. M., McCann, B. S., & Rooney, A. J. (1982). Effects of progressive relaxation and meditation in cognitive and somatic manifestations of daily stress. *Behaviour Research and Therapy, 20,* 461–467.

Worthington, E. L. (1979). Behavioral self-control and the contract problem. *Teaching of Psychology, 6,* 91–94.

Wurtele, S. K. (1986). Self-efficacy and athletic performance: A review. *Journal of Social and Clinical Psychology, 4,* 290–301.

Youdin, R., & Hemmes, N. S. (1978). The urge to overeat: The initial link. *Journal of Behavior Therapy and Experimental Psychiatry, 9,* 339–342.

Zechmeister, E. B., & Johnson, J. E. (1992). *Critical thinking: A functional approach.* Pacific Grove, CA: Brooks/Cole.

Zemore, R. (1975). Systematic desensitization as a method of teaching a general anxiety-reducing skill. *Journal of Consulting and Clinical Psychology, 43,* 157–161.

Zettle, R. D., & Hayes, S. C. (1982). Rule-governed behavior: A potential theoretical framework for cognitive-behavioral therapy. In P. C. Kendall (Ed.), *Advances in cognitive-behavioral research and therapy* (Vol. 1, pp. 73–118). New York: Academic Press.

Zimmerman, J. (1975). If it's what's inside that counts, why not count it? 1. Self-recording of feelings and treatment by "self-implosion." *Psychological Record, 25,* 3–16.

Zimmerman, R. S., Warheit, G. J., Ulbrich, P. M., & Auth, J. B. (1990). The relationship between alcohol use and attempts and success at smoking cessation. *Addictive Behaviors, 15,* 197–207.

Zitter, R. E., & Fremouw, W. J. (1978). Individual versus partner consequation for weight loss. *Behavior Therapy, 9,* 808–813.

Name Index

Aaronson, N. K, 24
Abrams, D. B., 298, 310
Adam, T., 155
Adams, J. A., 9
Adams, N. E., 40
Adams, S., 316
Adornetto, M., 10
Agran, M., 24
Agras, S. W., 159, 203, 248
Ainslee, G., 7, 154, 221
Ajzen, I., 44
Alden, L. E., 201
Altmaier, E., 155
Amatu, H. I., 136
American College of Sports Medicine, 204
Andraski, F., 24
Annon, J. S., 140
Applebaum, K. A., 24
Apsche, J., 115
Armstrong, B. K., 99
Arnkoff, D. B., 136, 198
Ascher, L. M., 227
Auth, J. B., 158
Axelrod, S., 115
Axsom, D., 53
Azar, S. T., 23
Azrin, N. H., 115, 167, 168

Baer, D. M., 88, 214
Baer, J., 295
Baer, J. S., 292, 310
Bagley, R. W., 217
Bajtelsmit, J. W., 230
Baker, A., 24
Baker, N., 3
Baker, S. B., 227
Ball, S., 150
Bandura, A., 43, 44, 105, 106, 107, 125, 190, 220, 221, 223, 259, 289
Barlow, D. H., 23, 154, 192, 198
Barone, D. F., 316
Barrera, M., 20, 22, 241
Barrios, B. A., 10, 175
Barrios, F. X., 10
Bass, B. A., 221
Baumeister, R. F., 58, 160, 203
Bay, R. C., 24
Beatty, P. A., 140, 201
Beaudoin, C., 231
Beck, A. T., 154, 156, 169
Beck, F. M., 180
Becker, M. H., 214
Beidleman, W. B., 22
Belisle, M., 292
Bellack, A. S., 89
Belmont, J. M., 313
Bender, C., 100
Bennett, A., 259
Bennett, N., 100
Berecz, J. M., 158
Bergin, A. E., 140
Berk, L. E., 110
Berlin, F., 186
Bernard, H. S., 202
Bernstrein, D. A., 175
Bertelson, A. D., 139
Biglan, A., 97, 169, 175
Binik, Y. M., 19
Black, D. R., 285
Black, S., 191
Blackwell, B., 214
Blair, L. W., 310
Blake, A. W., 150
Blakey, R. S., 136
Blanchard, E. B., 24, 180, 190, 227
Bloom, R., 141
Bloomquist, M., 25
Blum, M. D., 203
Bobo, J. K., 24
Boice, R., 247
Boland, J., 98
Bootzin, R. R., 139
Borkovec, T. D., 139, 176
Bornstein, M. T., 88
Bornstein, P. H., 88, 175
Boudreau, L., 173
Bourbeau, P., 25
Boutilier, J., 227
Braswell, L., 25
Brigham, T. A., 20, 24, 151, 222
Britt, E., 74
Broder, D. M., 24
Brown, G., 172
Brown, H. K., 81, 192, 285
Brown, J. D., 197, 201
Brown, S. A., 140
Brownell, K. D., 38, 214, 216, 292
Brownlee, A., 214
Buchanan, W. L., 141
Bucher, B., 214, 216
Buder, J., 96
Burnette, M. M., 179
Burns, L. E., 136
Burrish, T. C., 137

Burton, R. L., 136
Butterfield, E. C., 313

Calhoon, B., 227, 231
Calkins, R. P., 108, 109
Campbell, D. R., 97, 100
Campos, P. E., 220
Candiotte, M. M., 289
Cantor, N., 139
Cappe, R. F., 201
Carey, E., 172
Carey, K. B., 158
Carey, M. P., 158
Carlson, C. R., 175
Carver, C. S., 97, 105, 106, 156, 157
Castro, F., 22
Castro, L., 222, 223
Catania, A. C., 110, 220, 221
Cautela, J. R., 150, 178, 184, 188, 227, 230, 239
Cervone, D., 56, 185
Chaney, E. F., 296
Christophersen, E. R., 167
Ciminero, A. R., 88
Clark, D. M., 150
Clement, P., 191
Clements, C. B., 22
Coates, T. J., 51
Cohen, A., 300
Cohen, R., 149
Cohen, S., 19, 202, 216, 219, 295
Collins, F. L., 175
Collins, K. W., 182
Conway, M., 65
Cooke, C. J., 166
Cooper, J., 53
Coppotelli, H. C., 214, 216, 247
Cox, L. E., 265
Craill, L., 172
Craighead, L. W., 203
Craun, A. M., 197
Cummings, C., 140
Cunningham, S. J., 84
Curry, S. G., 48, 50, 243

Daley, D. C., 295
Daly, M. J., 136
Danaher, B. G., 24, 202, 246
Dansereau, D. F., 182
Daston, S., 191
Davidson, A., 165, 167
Davis, B., 38, 92, 159
Davis, J. R., 292, 294
de Albanchez, D. B., 223
deBortali-Tregerthan, G., 22
Deffenbacher, J. L., 20, 147, 177, 179, 182, 190, 197, 198
De James, P., 147
de Leon, E. P., 223
Delmonte, M. M., 174
Delprato, D. J., 24
Denney, D. R., 165, 180
de Perez, G. C., 223
de Silva, P., 147, 166, 167, 237
DiCara, L., 122
Dickson-Parnell, B. E., 203
DiClemente, C. C., 294
DiLorenzo, T. M., 200
Dirks, S. J., 220
Dobroski, B. J., 22
Dodd, D., 22
Dodge, K. A., 10
Doerfler, L. A., 147, 151, 155
Doherty, G., 180
Donnelly, J., 100
Doyne, E. J., 199
Drabman, R. S., 88
Draper, D. O., 227
Dryden, W., 136
Dubbert, P. M., 166, 200
Dunlap, G., 310
Durlak, J. A., 285
Dush, D. M., 146
Dygdon, J. A., 244
D'Zurilla, T. J., 32, 36, 283, 290, 285

Efran, J. S., 202
Egan, G., 200
Eifert, G. H., 172, 182
Eisenberger, R., 10
Eisler, R. M., 155
Elliot, L., 24, 56
Elliott, C. H., 165
Ellis, A., 136
Ellis, J., 89
Emery, G., 154, 169
Emmelkamp, P. M. G., 190
Epstein, J. A., 310
Epstein, L. H., 24, 81, 199, 200, 227, 231, 248
Epstein, R., 56
Erber, R., 199
Ernst, F. A., 180, 181
Ershoff, D. H., 24
Evans, I., 175

Fanning, P., 48
Fantuzzo, J. W., 23
Farber, B., 201
Farmer, R., 95
Farr, M. J., 313
Feixas, G., 23
Ferguson, J. M., 75
Ferretti, A., 200
Ferretti, R. P., 313
Ferster, C. B., 140
Finney, J. W., 167
Fischer, J., 20, 229
Fischer, K. W., 7
Fishbein, M., 44
Fisher, E. B., Jr., 5, 217
Fitzgibbon, M. L., 160, 286
Fixen, D. L., 88
Flanagan, C. M., 48
Flannery, R. F., Jr., 11, 48, 190
Flaxman, J., 202

Fo, W., 152
Folensbee, R., 139
Ford, E. E., 44
Foreyt, J. P., 38
Forsterling, F., 43
Fox, E. E., 96
Frankel, A. J., 143, 144
Franklin, B., 76–77
Frantz-Renshaw, S. E., 167
Frederiksen, L. W., 292
Freeman, A., 156
Fremouw, W. J., 218
Freud, S., 8, 24
Frisch, M. B., 198
Fromme, K., 292
Fuchs, C. Z., 156, 199, 244

Gajdos, E., 190
Galanter, E., 105
Gallimore, R., 107, 108, 109
Galotti, N., 20
Gambrill, E., 98
Gandhi, M., 7, 51
Ganellen, R. J., 97, 156
Gans, L., 139
Garamoni, G. L., 137
Garland, J. C., 182
Garvey, A. J., 294
Gauthier, J., 97, 237
George, W. H., 158, 292, 294, 295, 297, 298
Gerardi, M. A., 24
Gerber, W. M., 217, 248
Gershaw, N. J., 195
Gershman, L., 172, 187, 230
Gilchrist, L. D., 24
Glaros, A. G., 292, 294
Glasgow, R. E., 20, 22, 23, 247, 292, 310
Glass, C. R., 136
Glynn, S. M., 47, 135
Goldfried, A. P., 179, 186
Goldfried, M. R., 9, 44, 98, 122, 136, 147, 155, 170, 188, 189, 283, 175, 179, 186
Goldiamond, I., 139
Goldstein, A. P., 190, 195, 314
Gonso, J., 201
Goodall, T. A., 41
Gordon, J. R., 42, 98, 140, 292, 293, 296
Gormally, J., 191
Gottman, J., 201
Gournay, K., 186
Graziano, A. M., 53
Green, L., 7, 241, 247
Green, L. W., 214
Greene, D., 241
Greenleaf, D. O., 314
Greiner, J. M., 265
Greist, J. H., 186
Griffin, D. E., 59, 265
Grilo, C. M., 294
Gritz, E. R., 216
Grodek, M. V., 22
Gross, A. M., 88, 290
Grosscup, S. J., 244

Hagerman, S., 125
Hahnloser, R. M., 182, 198
Hake, D. F., 115
Halford, W. K., 41
Hall, C. L., 167
Hall, S. M., 214, 296, 310
Hallahan, D. P., 92
Hamilton, S. B., 20, 21, 88
Haney, C. J., 197
Harackiewicz, J. M., 310
Hardin, M., 216
Harris, G. M., 185, 189, 198
Harris, W., 198
Hawkins, R. C., 191
Hayes, S. C., 91, 97, 106, 110, 125, 214, 221, 247
Heatherington, L., 241
Heatherton, J. F., 160, 203
Heckerman, C. L., 214
Heffernan, T., 138, 221, 247
Heiby, E. M., 97, 220, 230, 231
Heinold, J. W., 294
Heins, E. D., 92
Heinzelmann, F., 217
Helleretedt, W. L., 216
Hemingway, E., 259
Hemmes, N. S., 159, 237
Herren, C. M., 19
Hersen, M., 231
Heshmat-Farzaneh-Kia, 25
Hiebert, B., 96
Higgins, R. L., 198
Hirt, M. L., 146
Hoffman, M. L., 227
Holden, A. E., 23
Hollandsworth, J. G., 200
Holley, C. D., 182
Hollon, S. D., 137, 156
Holm, J., 24
Holman, J., 88
Holmes, D. S., 199
Holt, C. S., 310
Holyroyd, K. A., 24
Holz, W. C., 115
Holzman, A. D., 24, 150
Homer, 7
Horan, J. J., 213, 227
Horn, D., 19
Horner, R. H., 313
Howitt, D. L., 248
Hull, J., 295
Humphrey, L. L., 158
Hunt, W. A., 153
Hutchinson, R. R., 115
Hutton, K., 179

Inbar-Saban, H., 58
Infantino, A., 23
Ingram, R., 137
Israel, A. C., 214

Jacob, R. G., 150
Jacobson, E., 175
Janis, I. L., 48
Janoff, D. S., 310
Jarrett, R. B., 97, 221
Jarvik, M. E., 307
Jawani, N., 56
Jeffery, R. W., 19, 190, 216, 217, 248
Johnsgard, J. W., 172, 197
Johnson, D. J., 140
Johnson, J. E., 6, 283
Johnson, M., 65
Johnson, R. G., 213
Johnson, S. B., 185, 189, 198
Johnson, W. G., 213
Johnston-O'Connor, E. J., 75, 245
Jones, R. T., 296
Jordan, C., 108
June, L. N., 180

Kalmar, K., 285
Kamarck, T. W., 22,, 99, 295
Kanfer, F. H., 25, 26, 59, 105, 106, 108, 110, 125, 171, 190, 220, 221, 259
Kanter, N. J., 147
Karoly, P., 24, 108, 110, 125, 265
Kaslow, N. J., 24, 199
Katz, R. C., 310
Kau, M. L., 20, 229
Kaul, T. J., 180
Kaya, J., 20, 78, 143, 171, 233
Kazdin, A. E., 169, 188, 189, 198, 199, 235, 239
Kearney, A. J., 188
Kelley, H. H., 53
Kelly, M. L., 283
Kendall, P. C., 137, 155, 313
Kennerley, H., 312
Kenyon-Jump, R., 179
Kernis, M. H., 300
Kerns, R. D., 24
King, A. C., 292
King, N. J., 123
Kinjo, K., 180
Kirk, J., 78
Kirsch, I., 154, 241
Kirschenbaum, D. S., 4, 11, 41, 43, 56, 75, 84, 158, 160, 203, 245, 285, 286, 288
Kivlahan, D. R., 292
Kleiges, R. C., 247
Knowlton, G. E., 198
Knox, D., 246
Koegel, R. L., 313
Koehn, K. A., 179
Kornblith, S. J., 244
Kratochwill, T. R., 88
Krisberg, J., 20, 90
Krop, H., 227, 231
Kuhl, J., 125
Kunkel, J., 139
Kupfer, D., 248
Kupfer, D. J., 199

Lacks, P., 139
Lakein, A., 159
Lamal, P. A., 221
Lamparski, D. M., 244
Lanyon, R. I., 307
Lascelles, N. A., 84
Latham, G. P., 55
Lauer, J. B., 203
Lave, J., 108
Layden, M. A., 75, 97
Lazarus, A., 53
Leary, M., 155
Leavitt, F., 296
LeBow, M. D., 38
Lees, L. A., 244
Lehman, A. K., 231, 248
Lehrer, P. M., 174
Lent, R. W., 180
Leon, G. R., 159
Lepper, M. R., 237
Lerman, C., 139
Lerner, J. V., 3
Lerner, R. M., 3
Levendusky, P., 180
Levenkron, J. C., 7, 217
Levesque, J-M., 292
Levin, R. B., 290
Levine, M., 20
Leviton, L. C., 243
Levitt, E. G., 140
Levy, R. L., 53, 214
Lewinsohn, P. M., 169, 231, 244
Lewis, L. E., 175
Lichtenstein, E., 22, 99, 216, 219, 289, 292, 294, 295, 310
Lindquist, R. A., 217
Linehan, M. M., 155
Lipton, D. N., 201
Lloyd, J. W., 92
Locke, E. A., 55
London, J., 259
Long, B. C., 197
Loper, A. B., 24
Lopez, M., 314
Loro, A. D., 7
Lowe, M. R., 7, 217
Lucic, K. S., 175
Ludwig, W. W., 292
Luria, A., 109, 110
Lutzker, J. R., 236
Lydon, J. E., 58

MacDonald, G. A., 152
Mace, F. C., 88
MacPhillamy, D. J., 231
Maher, C. A., 20
Mahoney, M. J., 19, 76, 220
Malett, S. D., 158
Maletzky, B. M., 88
Mallot, R. W., 56
Manderlink, G., 310
Marcus, M. D., 248

Marholin, D., 307
Markman, H., 201
Marks, I. M., 186
Marlatt, G. A., 42, 48, 50, 99, 138, 140, 158, 172, 173, 184, 202, 231, 292, 293, 295, 296, 297, 298, 300
Marques, J. K., 173, 292
Marshall, W. L., 227
Marston, A. R., 19
Martin, J. E., 24, 156, 166, 200
Martinsen, E. W., 199
Masters, J. C., 137, 155
Masterson, J. F., 226
Matarazzo, J. D., 153
Matson, J. L., 215
Matthews, B. A., 110
Mayo, L. L., 32
McAdoo, W. G., 203, 292
McAllister, D. A., 203, 308
McCann, B. S., 184
McCann, I. L., 199
McCaul, K. D., 23
McDonald, B. A., 182
McFall, R. M., 10, 98
McGlynn, F. D., 180
McGowan, C. R., 199
McGrath, P., 84
McIntrye, K., 216
McKeachie, W. J., 4
McKnight, D. L., 97, 221
McNamara, K., 147
Meichenbaum, D. H., 53, 54, 96, 110, 146, 230
Menges, R. J., 22
Mermelstein, R., 216, 295
Meyers, A. W., 166
Michaels, A. C., 179
Miller, D. E., 175
Miller, G. A., 105
Miller, N. E., 122
Miller, P. M., 81
Miller, R. K., 180
Minnes, P., 227
Mischel, W., 10, 53, 139, 140
Mizes, J. S., 96, 247
Monti, P. M., 214
Moon, J. R., 155
Morawetz, D., 24
Morgan, G. D., 96
Morgan, W. G., 221
Morris, E. K., 125
Moss, M. K., 190
Moura, N. G. M., 19
Murphy, D. M., 24
Murphy, T. J., 202

Nader, R., 316
Neff, D. F., 24
Neimeyer, R. A., 23
Nelson, R. O., 91, 95, 97, 201, 221
Nelson-Gray, R., 95
Newman, A., 129, 201
Nezu, A., 32, 36, 283, 285
Nezu, C. M., 285
Nicassio, P. M., 139
Nicki, R. M., 152, 158
Nisbett, R. E., 65, 293
Nitz, A. J., 175
Nocera, B., 147
Noel, R., 187
Nolan, J. D., 139
Norton, G. R., 32
Noshirvani, H., 186
Notarius, C., 201
Nowalk, M. P., 24
Nunn, R. G., 167, 168
Nurnberger, J. I., 140

O'Banion, D., 99
O'Brien, G. T., 23
O'Conner, C., 172
O'Connor, K. P., 99
Odysseus, 7
O'Hara, M. W., 244
Okwumabua, T. M., 166
O'Leary, M. R., 296
Ollendick, T. H., 123
O'Neill, H. K., 23
Orchard, J., 216
Orgel, M., 316
Orleans, C. T., 214, 216, 247
Orme, C. M., 19
Osnes, P. G., 217, 308, 313
Ost, L.-G., 179
Owusu-Bempah, J., 248
Ozaki, M., 220

Packard, T., 213
Padawer, W., 98
Pagano, R. R., 202
Page, M. S., 150
Pankratz, L., 180
Paper, D., 150
Paquin, M. J. R., 89
Parker, D., 46
Parks, G. A., 138, 158, 172, 184, 202, 231
Passman, R., 55
Patterson, C. J., 51–53
Paul, G. L., 177, 184
Pawlicki, R., 20
Payne, P. A., 22
Pear, J. J., 259
Pearce, J. W., 216
Pechacek, T. F., 202, 246, 247
Pellerin, D., 97, 237
Perez, F., 231
Perkins, D., 20
Perkins, F., 20
Perri, M. G., 4, 22, 203, 221, 247, 248, 285, 292, 308
Peterson, A. L., 167
Peterson, G. L., 227
Peterson, L., 48, 217, 218, 290
Phillips, E. L., 88
Plummer, I. L., 179

Premack, D., 212
Pribram, K. H., 105
Prochaska, J. O., 19, 294
Propst, L. R., 185
Prue, D. M., 283

Rabin, A. S., 199
Rachlin, H., 7, 220, 221, 222, 223, 236, 237
Rachman, S., 123
Raczynski, J. R., 166
Radmitz, C. L., 24
Rakos, R. F., 22, 58
Ramberger, M., 147
Rapoff, M. A., 167
Rardin, D., 191
Raw, M., 38
Rayner, R., 121
Reese, L., 44
Rehm, L. P., 19, 75, 97, 145, 155, 156, 169, 199, 230, 244
Reich, J. W., 231
Remington, R. E., 152
Renaud, P., 97
Rescorda, R. A., 125
Reynolds, W. M., 24
Reynolds, R. V. C., 24
Richards, C. S., 19, 22, 74, 137, 147, 151, 155, 158, 221, 247, 248, 285
Richey, C., 98
Rickard-Figueroa, K., 158
Rimm, D. C., 137, 155
Robertson, R. J., 199
Robins, C., 44, 98
Robinson, F. P., 4, 202
Rodin, J., 9, 231, 248
Roffman, R., 292
Rogers, J. L., 175
Rogoff, B., 108
Ronan, G. F., 285
Rooney, A. J., 174
Rohrbeck, C. A., 23
Roper, D. W., 156
Rosen, G. M., 20, 237, 241
Rosen, L. W., 159
Rosenbaum, M., 10, 11
Rosenfarb, I., 247
Rosenthal, B. S., 217
Roskie, E., 292
Rosner, B., 294
Ross, L., 65, 293
Ross, M., 65
Ross, S., 155
Rossi, J. S., 294
Rozensky, R. H., 89
Rubin, S., 52
Ruderman, A. J., 47. 135
Rugg, D., 296
Rusbult, C. E., 140
Rush, A. G., 169, 199
Russell, R. K., 180
Rychtarik, R. G., 283

Sabadell, P. M., 147
Saccone, A. J., 214
Samdperil, L, 184, 188, 227, 230
Sand, G., 259
Sandgren, A. K., 23
Sandifer, B. A., 141
Sansone, C., 310
Sarason, I. G., 171
Saraydarian, L., 285
Schachter, S., 19
Schafer, W., 10, 41
Schaie, K. W., 9
Schefft, B. K., 26
Scheier, M. F., 105, 106, 157
Schinke, S. P., 24
Schleser, R., 166
Schlunk, D. H., 38
Schneider, D. J., 150, 166
Schmid, T. L., 216
Schooler, C., 9
Schroeder, H., 146
Schuele, J. G., 122
Schultheis, K., 221
Scher, S. J., 58
Schwartz, J., 139
Schwartz, R. M., 137
Schwartz, S. H., 58
Schwartz, S. P., 24
Scott, N., 24
Scott, W. O. M., 283
Seidner, M. L., 59, 265
Selby, V. C., 200
Seligman, M. P., 185
Sewitch, T. S., 154
Shakespeare, W., 6
Shapiro, D. H., 173
Shapiro, E. S., 24
Shapiro, R. M., 292
Shaw, B. F., 169
Sheehan, M., 25
Shelton, J. L., 53, 198, 199, 214, 230, 243, 313, 314
Shepard, J., 20
Sherba, D. S., 285
Sherman, A. R., 20, 179, 190
Shiffman, S., 51, 138, 158, 202, 234, 289, 294, 307
Shigetomi, C. C., 10, 175
Shimoff, E. H., 110
Shortt, J. W., 150
Shute, R. E., 227
Simons, A. D., 199
Singh, N. E., 74
Sipich, J. F., 180
Skinner, B. F., 125, 222
Smith, D., 198
Smith, J. C., 174, 175
Smith, P. O., 166
Smith, R. J., 198
Snel, D. L., 158
Snow, W. H., 24
Snyder, A. L., 175
Sohn, D., 221
Sonne, J. L., 310
Sowers, J., 25
Spadafora, S., 300
Spates, C. R., 259

Spinelli, P. R., 213
Spinoza, 44
Sprafkin, R. P., 195
Sprong, R. T., 221
Spurr, J., 139
Staats, A. W., 122
Stalonas, P. M., Jr., 203
Stark, C., 179
Stark, K. D., 24, 155
Stark, R. S., 147
Stedman, J. M., 172, 189
Steenman, H., 154
Steffan, J. J., 175
Steinbock, E., 175
Steinkamp, C. A., 200
Stetson, B. A., 140, 201
Stetson, D., 23
Steubing, R. C., 175
Stevens, V. J., 139
Stevenson, D. W., 24
Stevenson, H. C., 25
Stevenson, M. K., 105
Stockert, N. A., 313
Stockton, W., 200
Stokes, T. F., 214, 217, 308, 313
Stratoudakis, J. P., 180
Stravynski, A., 99
Stuart, R. B., 38, 55, 92, 153, 159
Stunkard, A. J., 65
Sturgis, E. T., 175
Sudnow, D., 146
Suinn, R. M., 139, 156, 179, 182, 183, 184, 187, 190, 200
Sullivan, J. M., 244
Sullivan, M. J. L., 84
Swanson, K., 25

Tec, L., 34
Tesser, A., 199
Tharp, R. G., 20, 78, 90, 107, 108, 109, 143, 171, 214, 233
Thase, M. E., 190
Thoresen, C. E., 51
Thornbookrough, M., 155
Thorpe, G. L., 136
Throll, D. A., 173, 174
Tinling, D. C., 165
Tobin, D. L., 24
Todd, F. J., 213
Tomarken, A. J., 75, 285, 288
Touchette, P. E., 307
Trier, C. S., 175
Trollope, A., 259
Tunstall, C., 296
Turk, D. M., 24, 53, 54
Turner, R., 20
Turner, R. M., 24, 139, 180
Turner, S. M., 150
Twain, M., 197
Twentyman, C., 98, 292

Ulbrich, P. M., 158
Upper, D., 23

Vaux, A. C., 226
Velicer, W. F., 294
Verdi, M., 25
Verrier, R., 227, 231
Vinciguerra, P., 310
von Schlumperger, B., 24
Vygotsky, L. S., 108, 109, 110

Wade, T. C., 19
Waldman, D. A., 20, 21
Walk, J., 20
Wallace, I., 259
Walsh, R., 173
Warheit, G. J., 158
Watson, D. L., 20, 58, 78, 90, 143, 171, 233, 265
Watson, J. B., 121
Webster, J. S., 81
Wegner, D. M., 150, 156, 166
Weiss, S. M., 294
Weisz, G., 214, 216
Wenzlaff, R. M., 156
Wertsch, J., 108
Westlake, R. J., 214
Westover, S. A., 307
Wetzel, R. J., 214
Whisman, M. A., 308
Wiener, N., 105
Wiesenfeld, A. R., 122
Wilkinson, L., 139
Wilson, G. T., 292
Wine, J. T., 96
Wing, R. R., 19, 24, 248, 294
Wise, F., 180
Wisocki, P. A., 184, 227, 230
Wolf, M. M., 88
Wolpe, J., 122, 150
Wong, E., 216
Wood, R., 43, 56
Wood, Y. R., 216, 217
Woolfolk, R. L., 174
Worthington, E. L., 235
Woudenberg, R. A., 22
Wright, C. L., 220
Wright, T. L., 198

Yancey, D. Z., 203
Youdin, R., 159, 237

Zaken-Greenburg, F., 156
Zanna, M. P., 58
Zautra, A., 231
Zeckmeister, E. B., 6, 283
Zeichner, A., 158, 203
Zeiss, A. M., 169
Zemore, R., 179
Zettle, R. D., 106
Zimmerman, J., 134
Zimmerman, R. S., 158
Zitter, R. E., 218
Zuckerman, M., 300

Subject Index

A-B-C analysis, 14, 25, 65–72, 82–85, 95, 96, 100, 133, 252–257, 274 (*see also* Antecedents; Behaviors-in-situations; Consequences; Recording of behavior)
Abscissa, 268
Abstinence violation effect, 42, 293, 300
Activator, 106
Addiction and addictive behaviors, 292–293, 297 (*see also* Consummatory behaviors)
Adjustment:
  and the behavioral model, 14
  definition of, 3–4
  and learning, 12–14, 116, 118
  and the medical model, 7–8
  as a skill, 9–12
  and values, 3
  and willpower, 6–7
Alcohol, effects of, 295
Alcoholics Anonymous, 55
Alcoholism, *see* Topic Index: Smoking, drinking, and drug use
Analzying data, 266–272
Antecedents, 116–119, 121–122, 127, 131–161, 262 (*see also* A-B-C analysis; Chain of events; High-risk situations)
  arranging new, 119, 145–154, 161
  and avoidance behavior, 118
  avoidance of, 51, 137–138, 238, 255–257, 296
  behavior of others as, 133–134, 138, 151, 157
  beliefs as, *see* Beliefs; Self-statements
  and extinction, 118
  identification of, 133–137, 160, 293–295
  modifying old, 134–137, 160–161
  narrowing, 139
  new stimulus control, 150–152, 161
  and operant behaviors, 117–118
  problems in analysis, 134–135, 255–257
  and reinforcement, 117–118, 238
  reperceiving, 139–140
  self-instructions as, 135, 145–150
  thoughts as, 147–150
Approximations, *see* Shaping
Astrology, 6
Attention, concentrating, 170–171
Attributions and attribution theory, 125, 310–311
Assertion, *see* Topic Index
Automatic behavior, 108, 107, 116, 121–122, 146, 241
Averages, 266–277
Avoidance behavior and avoidance learning 51, 113, 118, 169–170, 210–211
Avoiding situations, *see* Antecedents, avoidance of

Baseline data, 93–95, 210
  of incompatible behaviors, 273–274
  length of, 94–95
  on new categories, 273–274
  omitted, 95, 274
  reactivity of, 94, 95
  reliability of, 94–95
  use in shaping, 191–196
Behaviors-in-situations, 11, 31–32, 60–61, 654, 311, 313
  tactics for specifying, 31–36, 60–61
Beliefs (*see also* Self-statements), 135–137
  identification of, 135–137
  influence of, on success, 43–44, 44–46, 124, 298
  maladaptive, 136–137, 155–156, 172
Brainstorming, 36, 37, 261
Buddhism, 150, 166, 167, 237

Chain of events:
  analysis of, 35, 134, 158
  case study of, 144
  changing, 140–144, 146
  emotional components, 122, 293
  pauses in, 141–142
  recording and reactivity in, 142
  scrambling, 141
  unlinking, 142–143
Cheating, 240
Checklist for formulating a plan, 262–263
Coaching (coaxing), self-instructions as, 145, 155, 157, 197
Cognitions (*see also* Distractions):
  cool, 10, 53, 139–140, 298
  effects, 124–125
  hot, 10, 53, 139–140, 298
Commitment (*see also* Precommitment):
  building, 51–59, 61, 62, 228, 262
  public, 53
Comparator(s), 105–106
Conditioned stimuli, 120–122, 127, 296
Conditioning, *see* Respondent behavior
Consequences, 13, 110–116, 126–127 (*see also* A-B-C analysis; Reinforcement and reinforcers)
Consummatory behaviors, 137–138, 201, 209, 255–257
Contingency:
  definition of, 112–113
  in intervention, 209, 212

noncontingent positive events, 230–231
Contracts, 58, 59, 155, 265, 299, 316
Control theory, 106
Covert techniques, *see* Modeling, imagined; Punishment, imagined; Rehearsal, imagined; Reinforcement, imagined
Critical thinking, 6
Cues, 117, 133, 150 (*see also* Antecedents)
Cybernetics, 105–107, 155, 221, 259

Depression, *see* Topic Index
Desensitization, 185
Diary, structured, *see* Recording of behavior
Discouragement, avoiding, 75–77, 190, 290
Discriminative stimuli, 117 (*see also* Antecedents)
Distractions and distracting behavior, 10, 51–52, 156–157, 166, 298–299
Drinking, *see* Topic Index: Smoking, drinking, and drug use
Drug abuse, *see* Topic Index: Smoking, drinking, and drug use

Emotions (*see also* Recording of feelings; Respondent behavior):
  conditioning of, 121–122, 123, 128
Escape behavior, 113, 242
Escape clauses, 54–55
Exercise, *see* Topic Index: Exercise and athletics
Extinction, 115–116, 118, 234, 250
  and avoidance behavior, 118
  building resistance to, 309, 317
  definition of, 115
  and intermittent reinforcement, 115–116
  vs. punishment, 115–116
  resistance to, 115–116

Fantasies, 150, 170, 227
Fears (*see also* Topic Index):
Feedback, 221–222, 223, 259–260
Frequency counts, 17, 72–75, 111, 309

Generalization, *see* Transfer of training
Goals:
  changing, 38–39, 272–274
  choosing, 26, 37, 262
  evolution of, 38–39
  and feedback, 259–260
  nonbehavioral, 37–38
  planning for, 55–56, 57, 259
  reinforcing value of, 220–221
  reminding oneself of, 55, 221
  and rules, 259
  shared, 218, 246
  specifying, 31–40, 62, 259
  subgoals, 55, 259
  when unclear, 35–36, 315
Graphs, 93, 267–274

Habit reversal, 167–168
Help from others (*see also* Mediators; Models for behavior; Professional help; Reminders, from others):
  in being reminded of one's goals, 153
  as confederates, 153, 218–219, 248
  in cueing, 153
  in dispensing punishment, 236–238
  in dispensing reinforcement, 153, 214–219, 228–229, 247, 249
  in recording, 89, 216
  reinforcement of, 218, 246
  in relaxation, 194–195
  in shaping, 194–195, 196
Higher-order conditioning, 121, 127
High-risk situations, 184, 293–299

Imagined modeling, *see* Modeling, imagined
Imagined punishment, *see* Punishment, imagined
Imagined rehearsal, *see* Rehearsal, imagined
Imitative learning, *see* Modeling
Incompatible behaviors:
  for anxiety, 169–183
  definition of, 167
  recording of, 169
  substituting for undesirable behaviors, 31–35, 90, 167–169, 204–205
Indulgent behaviors, *see* Consummatory behaviors; Topic Index: Smoking, drinking, and drug use
Intermittent reinforcement, *see* Reinforcement and reinforcers, intermittent

Karate, 190
Kung fu, 171–172

Language:
  and conditioning, 122
  development, 108–110
  regulation of behavior, 108–110
  and self-control, 99–100
  and thinking, 109
Lapse(s), *see* Relapse
Learned resourcefulness, 108
Long-term projects, 314–315

Maintenance of new behaviors, 307–314, 317
Maladjustment, *see* Adjustment
Mantra, 174
Mediators, 215–219, 235–236, 248 (*see also* Help from others)
  case study, 215
Medical model, 8
Meditation, 173–174
Memory, accuracy of, 65
Modeling, 13, 35–36, 122–124, 128, 187–188
  imagined, 188–189
Models for behavior, *see* Modeling

Narrowing stimulus control, *see* Antecedents
Negative practice, 89–90, 167
Neurotic behavior, 118

Observational learning, *see* Modeling
Obsessions, 150

Olympic games, 184
Operant behavior, 111, 117, 222
Ordinate, 267
Overeating, *see* Topic Index: Weight loss and overeating
Overjustification hypothesis, 241
Overlearning, 314

Pauses, building in, 141–142
Percentages, 267
Personality traits, 30–31, 42
Phobias, *see* Topic Index: Anxiety and stress; Fears, specific
Plateaus, 196, 206
Pleasant activities or events, increasing, 156, 199, 233, 244
Point systems, *see* Reinforcement and reinforcers, token
Positive events, noncontingent, 231–232
Practice, *see* Negative practice; Overlearning; Rehearsal
Praise, self-, 230–231
Precommitment, 152–154, 188, 236–237
Premack principle, 212–213, 228–229, 264
Problem solving, 32, 36, 261, 279–290, 301–303 (*see also* Brainstorming)
Professional help, 24, 315–316, 318
Psychoanalysis, 8
Psychotherapy, *see* Professional help
Punishment (*see also* Avoidance behavior; Escape behavior; Self-punishment):
  definition of, 114–115, 127
  effects of, 115, 234–238, 290
  imagined (covert), 237
  of models, 123
  and negative reinforcement, 114
  by others, 290, 309
  of others, 245, 257–258
  reasons not to use, 234–235
  resistance to effects of, 234
  as temporary solution, 237–238
  types of, 114

Rating scales, 78–81, 96, 266–267, 310
Rational restructuring, 172–173
Reactivity, 87–89
Recording of behavior (*see also* Baseline data):
  antecedents, 65–72, 134
  consequences, 65–72
  counting, 72–75
  devices, 85–86
  duration, 74, 100–101
  emotions, 65–70, 78–81, 101
  failure in, 286–288
  during failure of plan, 266, 287–288, 294, 295
  feelings, 65–70, 78–81
  frequencies, 72–75, 100–101, 227
  during intervention, 259–260, 266
  during lapses, 294
  others' behavior, 246
  positive events, 75–77, 285–286
  prerecording to minimize a behavior, 89, 142
  problems in recording, 89–92, 101, 286–288
  reliability of, 94–95
  relaxation, 183
  reward of, 91, 101
  rules for, 87, 101
  in specifying the problem, 33, 254–260, 286–288
  storage of, 86–87
  structured diary, *see* Structured diary
  of successes, 76–77
  during thinning, 309
  thoughts, 66–70
Reflexes, 119
Regulation theory, 105–107, 123–124, 125, 221
Rehearsal, 183, 198, 205
  imagined (covert), 183–187, 205, 239–240, 256, 298
Reinforcement and reinforcers, 112–114, 210, 263, 309
  activity, 211–212
  and antecedent control, 238
  cataloging, 210–214
  contingent, 210, 212
  continuous, 116, 309
  covert, *see* Reinforcement and reinforcers, imagined
  definition of, 112
  discovering, 209–214, 249
  of a group, 217, 225
  imagined (covert), 227–234, 249
  and imagined rehearsal, 239–240
  intermittent, 115–116, 210, 309 (*see also* Thinning of reinforcements)
  intrinsic, 227, 241, 308–309
  logical, 227
  loss of, 230–231
  of models, 123
  mutual, 246
  natural, 227, 240, 308–309
  negative, 112, 126–127
  noncontingent, 230–231
  of other's behavior, 218, 246, 257, 309–310
  positive, 112, 126–127, 211–214
  potency of, 214
  Premack reinforcers, *see* Premack principle
  problems in, 309–310
  prompt, 222–224
  selecting, 209–214
  self-, *see* Self-reinforcement
  sharing, 218, 225–226
  timing of, 222–224
  token, 224–227, 228–229, 309
  verbal, 112, 230–231, 243, 249
  withdrawal of, *see* Extinction
Relapse, (*see also* High-risk situations)
  coping with lapses, 293–301
  definition, 291
  fantasy, 295
  model of the process, 291–293
  prevention, 184, 291–301, 315

Relaxation, 174–183, 205
  as coping response, 174–176, 179, 189
  in different situations, 178–179
  with imagined rehearsal, 185–187, 239–240
  as incompatible response, 179–182
  integrative breathing method, 175
  meditation method, 173–174
  practicing, 178–179, 186, 197–198
  progressive method, 174
  recording, 183
  and self-instructions, 182
  tension-release method, 175–178
Reliability, *see* Recording of behavior, reliability of
Reminders:
  from others, 55, 90, 92, 153
  self-, 53, 54, 91, 92, 153, 237, 298, 309
  self-instructions as, 147
Respondent behavior, 119–122
  conditioning of, 119–122, 127, 297
  definition of, 120
  and emotions, 120–122
  and language, 122
Rewards, *see* Reinforcement and reinforcers; also Consequences
Rules and rule-governed behavior, 110

Sabotage:
  by others, 290
  self-, 40–45, 60, 288–290
Self-change, *see* Self-directed behavior; Self-modification
Self-control, 10–11, 150, 196, 220–221
Self-control triad, 230
Self-directed behavior (*see also* Self-modification; Self-regulation):
  overview, 9–12, 316–317
  in psychotherapy, 315–316
  skills in, 3–5, 9–12, 25
Self-efficacy, 151, 152, 158, 187, 191
  beliefs, 43–46, 60, 289, 310–311
  scale, 47, 310–311
Self-instructions:
  as antecedents, 109–110, 135
  case study, 148–149
  development of, 107–110
  eliminating negative, 145
  initiating positive, 146–147
  and relapse prevention, 297, 298, 303
  and relaxation, 185
Self-modification, 11–13, 17, 24–25 (*see also* Self-directed behavior)
  common reasons for failure, 40–44, 191, 286–290
  criteria for good projects, 27, 258–266, 274
  lifelong practice, 314–315, 316–317
  limits, 315, 317
  research evidence on effectiveness, 19–20, 20–22, 24–25, 59
  steps in, 14–15, 25
  unsuccessful cases, 22–23
  use of techniques, 16, 23, 258–261, 288
Self-observation, 16, 32–33, 21–211, 223, 227, 259–260, 262, 286–288 (*see also* Baseline data; Recording of behavior)
Self-punishment, 18, 222, 223,234–238, 250
Self-regulation, 105–110, 123–124, 126, 220 (*see also* Cybernetics; Regulation theory)
  and control by others, 107–110, 126
  by language, 108–110, 118, 124, 126
Self-reinforcement, 220–234, 249
  effects of, 221–222
  learning, 220–221
  objections to, 241–242
Self-statements (*see also* Self-instructions):
  beliefs as, 135–137, 147
  emotional effects, 122
  identification of, 135–137
  interpretations as, 137
  reinforcement of, 201
  stopping, *see* Thought stopping
  substituting of new, 147, 156, 169, 172–173, 199, 231, 247
Sensor(s), 105
Sexual arousal, as incompatible behavior, 170–172
Shaping, 190–197, 205–206, 240
  antecedents, 256
  case studies, 192–193, 194, 261–265, 279–280
  definition of, 190
  problems in, 195–196, 240
  and reinforcement, 240
  and relaxation, 194–195
  rules for, 191–192
  and subgoals, 55, 191–193
  and willpower, 196
Shyness, *see* Topic Index: Relations with others: Social Anxieties, social skills, and dating
Situation, effects of, 6–7, 13, 293–299 (*see also* A-B-C analysis; Antecedents)
Skill, 9–12
Smoking, *see* Topic Index: Smoking, drinking, and drug use
Social anxiety, *see* Topic Index: Relations with others: Social anxieties, social skills, and dating
Social learning theory, 106
SOLER, 200–201
Standard(s) (*see also* Goals Shaping):
  in cybernetic theory, 106–107
  in shaping, 190
Stimulus control, 118–119, 150–152, 256–257 (*see also* Antecedents)
Stimulus generalization, 152 (*see also* Transfer of training)
Stress, *see* Topics Index: Anxieties and stress
Structured diary, 65–72, 100
Subvocal speech, 109–110, 135
Successive approximations, 39 (*see also* Shaping)
Symbolic reinforcers, *see* Reinforcement and reinforcers, token
Symptoms, 8

Target behaviors, 14, 59–60, 65, 68

Task/skill mismatch, 10–12
Temptation, 56, 294–299 (*see also* High risk situations)
  coping with, 51–54, 256, 294
  preparing for, 51–55
  resistance to, 6, 7, 10, 41, 139–140
Termination, formal, 307–314,317
Test anxiety, *see* Topic Index: Anxieties and stress
Thermostat, 105–106
Thinking and behavior, 124–125
Thinning of reinforcements, 309–314
Thoughts, substitution of, 137, 147–150, 156, 170, 204–205, 232 (*see also* Antecedents; Self-statements; Cognition)
Thought stopping, 150, 230, 248
Tinkering, 279–283
Tokens, *see* Reinforcements and reinforcers, token
Transfer of training, 189–190, 307–308, 313–314, 317
Two-stage process, 255–257

Values:
  and adjustment, 3
  and individual goals, 307
  and reactivity, 88
  and termination, 307
Verbal self-control, *see* Language; Self-instructions

Weight loss, *see* Topic Index: Weight loss and overeating
Weight Watchers, 55
Willpower, 6–7, 196, 206, 300

Topic Index

The topics listed in this index include but are not restricted to those covered in the "Tips" sections of the book.

Anger, 20, 137, 141, 182, 188
Anxiety and stress, 20, 41, 169–183, 312 (*see also* Fears)
  "Tips" sections, 96, 154–155, 197–198
Assertion, 31–32, 32–33, 34–35, 45, 67–68, 189, 239–240, 290, 309
  "Tips" sections, 96–97, 155, 198–199, 243–244
Athletics, *see* Exercise and athletics
Bulimia, 19
Classroom behavior, 20, 74, 77, 180–181
Creativity, 19
Dating, *see* Relations with others, dating and the other sex
Dental hygiene, 22–23
Depression and low self-esteem, 20, 21, 34, 38–39, 71, 72, 74, 75, 76, 78–79, 81, 143, 147, 169, 231
  "Tips" sections, 97, 155–156, 199, 244
Dieting, *see* Exercise and athletics; Weight loss and overeating
Exercise and athletics, 20, 22, 24, 40, 43, 49, 53, 139, 151, 184, 187, 188, 199, 203, 211, 222–223, 228–229, 280–282, 284, 286–287
  "Tips" sections, 97–98, 156–157, 200, 244–245
Fears, specific (*see also* Anxiety and stress):
  of birds, 194–195, 240
  of cats, 190
  of cemeteries, 172
  of closed places, 172
  of flying, 189, 190
  of professors, 261–265
  of school, 192–193
  of sex, 169
  of snakes, 44
  of speaking in public or class, 80, 152, 187, 271–272
  of tests and exams, 32, 170, 179–180, 185–186, 190, 198
Friends, *see* Relations with others, friends
Gossiping, 15–17
Headache, 24, 84
Honest thoughts and statements, 232–233
Housekeeping, 88, 95, 225–226, 236
Insomnia, 24, 139, 179
Lifestyle changes, 22, 232–234 (*see also* Exercise and athletics; Weight loss and overeating)
Loneliness, 13, 91
Masturbation, 138, 238
Menopausal hot flashes, 24
Money management, 74, 85, 154, 241, 316–317
Other sex, *see* Relations with others, dating
Overeating, *see* Weight loss and overeating
Pain, chronic, 24, 179
Parents and children, *see* Relations with others, parents and children
Posture, 188
Practicing music, 72–73, 87, 146
Procrastination, 34, 42, 57
Relations with others: Social anxieties, social skills, and dating, 12, 15–17, 19, 68, 82–83, 85, 94, 134–136, 145, 146, 150, 173, 195
  couples, 55–56, 88, 115–116, 133, 140, 295
  co-workers, 20, 85, 91, 111, 167, 257, 279–280
  dating and the other sex, 13–14, 34, 90–91, 115–116, 134, 145, 166, 195, 239, 266–267, 287–288
  friends, 36, 39, 80, 113, 137, 225
  parents and children, 32, 39, 66–67, 74, 75, 89, 142, 144, 165–166, 173, 216–217
  social anxieties (shyness), 19, 34, 117–118, 171, 272–273
  social skills, 45, 254–255, 286–287, 307–308
  "Tips" section, 98–99, 157, 200–201, 245–246
Self-injurious habits, 17–18, 20, 167–168
  eyelash plucking, 168
  face picking, 261
  hair pulling, 20
  knuckle cracking, 90, 167
  mouth biting, 180–181
  nail biting, 17–18, 20, 66, 167, 168
  scratching, 20, 74, 90, 167
  teeth grinding, 20
Shy bladder, 312–313
Shyness, *see* Relations with others, social anxieties
Smoking, drinking, and drug use, 19, 137, 138, 141, 151–152, 184, 231, 256, 292, 295, 296, 297
  drinking, 47, 50, 55, 89, 92, 134, 141, 296–297
  drug use (hard drugs, marijuana, caffeine) 19, 238, 283, 284–285
  smoking, 18, 19, 24, 25, 41, 42, 46, 52, 54, 93, 94, 153, 202, 216, 236–237, 255–256, 283–284, 288–289, 290–293, 294, 300, 311
  "Tips" sections, 99, 157–158, 201–202, 246–247
Speaking in class, (*see* Fears, of speaking in public)
Stress, *see* Anxiety and stress
Studying and time management, 3–4, 19, 33, 45, 46, 48, 49, 73–74, 76, 77, 85, 138, 139, 148–

149, 151, 191, 210, 212, 253–254, 260, 267–271, 286, 307–308
"Tips" sections, 99–100, 158–159, 202–203, 247
Sulking, 139
Swearing, 224
Test anxiety, *see* Fears, of tests and exams
Tics, 167–168
Urination, excessive, 142–143
Vocabulary, increasing, 73
Weight loss and overeating, 19, 31, 35, 41, 42, 46, 47, 48, 58, 65, 70–71, 71–72, 73, 74, 77, 85, 89, 118, 137, 138, 143, 145, 190–191, 214, 215–217, 223, 226–227, 227–228, 236, 237, 239, 256–257, 260, 267, 269, 283, 287, 288, 289–290, 297, 299, 307, 313 (*see also* Exercise and athletics)
"Tips" sections, 100, 159–160, 203–204, 248
Writing, creative and professional, 35, 74, 86–87, 151, 195, 259–260, 288

TO THE OWNER OF THIS BOOK:

We enjoyed writing *Self-Directed Behavior*, 6th edition, and it is our hope that you have enjoyed reading it. We'd like to know about your experiences with the book; only through your comments and the comments of others can we assess the impact of this book and make it a better book for readers in the future.

School: ____

Instructor's name: ______________________________________

1. What did you like *most* about the book? ____________________

____

____

____

2. What did you like *least* about the book? ____________________

____

____

____

3. How useful were the *step-by-step self-direction project* and the *Tips for Typical Topics* at the end of the chapters?__________________________________

____

____

4. What class did you use this book for?_________________________

____

5. In the space below or in a separate letter, please tell us what it was like for you to read this book and how you used it; please give your suggestions for revisions and any other comments you'd like to make about the book.

Optional:

Your name: ______________________________ Date: ______________________

May Brooks/Cole quote you, either in promotion for *Self-Directed Behavior* or in future publishing ventures?

Yes: ________ No: ________

Sincerely,

David L. Watson
Roland G. Tharp

FOLD HERE

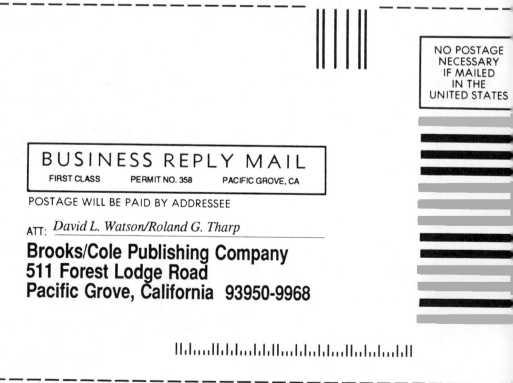

NO POSTAGE NECESSARY IF MAILED IN THE UNITED STATES

BUSINESS REPLY MAIL
FIRST CLASS PERMIT NO. 358 PACIFIC GROVE, CA

POSTAGE WILL BE PAID BY ADDRESSEE

ATT: *David L. Watson/Roland G. Tharp*

Brooks/Cole Publishing Company
511 Forest Lodge Road
Pacific Grove, California 93950-9968

FOLD HERE